# ROCK 100

## DAVID DALTON AND LENNY KAYE

GROSSET & DUNLAP   PUBLISHERS
A Filmways Company
NEW YORK

## ACKNOWLEDGMENTS

ROCK 100 would have been a much lesser volume without the editorial guidance of Penny Zug, whose diplomacy and angelic encouragement never faltered throughout the two years this book took shape; Alan Betrock, who kept our facts straight and our photos well-researched; and the advice, assistance, and inspiration of Margaret Wolf, Wendy Werris, Steve Dossick, Richard and Lisa Robinson, Lillian Roxon, Danny Fields, Pat Fisher, Helen Roberts, Ellen Hochberg, Susann Dalton, Richard Meltzer, Steven Holden, Bill Millar, Charlie Gillett, Phil Groia, *Record Exchanger*, *Bim Bam Boom*, Joel Whitburn's *Record Research*, the editors of *Cavalier* magazine, M. Shepatin, Patti Lee and the boys (Ivan, Jay Dee, DNV), Nick Tosches, Jonathan Cott, SKF J66, and rock and rollers everywhere.

DD/LK

The publishers gratefully acknowledge the cooperation of the publicity departments of the following record companies and talent agencies: Decca Records, p. 8; Cadence Records, p. 25; Monument Records, p. 30; MGM Records, p. 36; Shaw Artists Corporation, pp. 39, 40, 45, 140, 230; Associated Booking Corporation, p. 41 left; Ember Records, p. 41 right; Gee Records, p. 49; General Artists Corporation, p. 53; William Morris Agency, Inc., pp. 75, 154; RCA Victor, p. 76; Philips/VJ Records, p. 77; Beatles USA Ltd., pp. 91, 94; Official Beatles Fan Club, p. 92 lower, p. 93; Strawberry Fields Archives, 310 Franklin St. #117, Boston, Mass. 02110, pp. 91–94; MCA Records, pp. 108 top, 274; PTA, p. 109; Epic Records, pp. 119, 120, 149; York-Pala Records, p. 159; Atlantic Records, p. 162 right; Elektra Records, p. 165; Verve/Folkways Records, p. 178; Colgems Records, p. 187; Bizarre Records, p. 191 top; A & M Records, p. 194; Warner Brothers Records, p. 208; Universal Attractions, Inc., p. 220; King Records, p. 221; Curtom Records, p. 228; Shelter Records, p. 238; Paragon Agency, p. 239; Capricorn Records, p. 240; Capitol Records, pp. 260, 261.

*Cover Photo by Michael Holt/Image Bank*

*Book design by Helen Roberts*

Published simultaneously in Canada
Library of Congress catalog card number: 74–27945
ISBN: 0–448–12228–6 (hardcover edition)
         0–448–12240–5 (paperback edition)

*First printing*
*Printed in the United States of America*

# Contents

# Introduction

Taking formal shape in the mid-1950s as a purely American phenomenon, and bursting worldwide in the 1960s to become a dominating cultural mode encompassing more styles and genres than it excludes, rock has literally, in the words of Phil Spector, become "tomorrow's sound — today." *Rock 100* celebrates the first two (and some) decades of a lusty, life-or-death music. It is a blurred oblong of history as aware of its own inner contradictions as of its similarly healthy disregard for them.

Our approach has been to treat the chronology of rock through its major figures, providing a collective biography focusing on those performers who located the symbolic and vinyl sites where the real and imaginary feed on each other to create the star. These are the archetypes of rock, a legendary cast of originals, visionaries, revolutionaries and evolutionaries who fused their music and personality to a mythic level, and formed the hall of fame, which we present here.

In writing these portraits we have endeavored to present the essence of each artist, using biographical details, musical history, an attempt to locate specific musical influences, early recording information, label data, relevant names and places, etc., without burdening the reader with statistics and exhaustive discographies. We have looked at geographical, social, and personal inputs to suggest the elements of their style and contribution, as well as to illuminate the power brokers behind the scenes — producers, managers, promoters and soothsayers. Documentary material and the artist's own words evoke the personal texture of each. The terms "rock" and "rock & roll" have been used interchangeably (with a slight nod to "rock & roll" to identify music of the 1950s), and we have included artists from a number of disparate fields — country, blues, middle-of-the-road, folk, R&B, soul, and other equally ill-defined categories — in so far as they affected and altered the genealogy of rock.

Our criterion for selection was not necessarily how many records these artists sold, or even how long they remained in the public eye, but rather the basis of their stature in relation to their audiences, musical contemporaries, and probable descendants. Our tribute to them is the Top 100, that free-wheeling marketplace which provides the physical representation of commerce and art for pop music, the all-crucial charts by which success is gauged and measured. Often, it might be remembered, these cherished numerals are as important for what they leave out as for what they stamp "with a bullet."

This book is meant to be read loud. Turn it up.

David Dalton
Lenny Kaye

# 1
# The King

## ELVIS PRESLEY

"THAT'S FINE, MAN," CHORTLES SAM
Phillips over the studio intercom at 760 Union
Avenue, Memphis. "Hell, that's different. That's
a pop song now."

The date is July 5, 1954. Inside the small
enclosure, Scotty Moore and Bill Black rest their
instruments to listen to the playback. As
supporting musicians, they had been working
for weeks with a young singer named Elvis Aron
Presley, trying to mold his raw talent into a
commercially acceptable form, concentrating
mostly on country-based ballad material. But
Phillips had a broader idea, convinced that if he
could find a white singer with "the Negro sound
and the Negro feel," he could unite the various
strains of music hovering about the South into
one irresistible package.

Elvis Presley had wandered into this simple
philosophy shortly after his graduation from
L. C. Humes High School in June of 1953. Born
in Tupelo, Mississippi, on January 8, 1935, he
survived his twin brother Jesse who had died
at birth. The family was classically poor, and
following the trail of industrial expansion after
World War II, the Presleys loaded their
belongings into an old Pontiac and moved to
Memphis. To supplement their income, Elvis
worked sporadically mowing lawns and as an
usher, and entertained himself by playing a
guitar given him on his eleventh birthday.

It was an ordinary adolescence. His taste for
loud clothes — pink and black seemed to be his
favorite color combination — and a tendency to
wear his hair long and greasy with prominent
sideburns did not signify undue rebellion; in
fact, he regularly attended church and played on
the Humes football team. He was shy about
performing, but did on occasion bring his guitar
to school to play for homeroom picnics and
variety shows. The class yearbook's will and
prophecy noted: "Donald Williams, Raymond
McCraig and Elvis Presley leave hoping there
will be someone to take their places as 'teacher's
pets'????" His majors were shop, history and
English, and he enjoyed ROTC training.

It was while working as a delivery truck
driver for Crown Electric company, studying at
night to become an electrician, that he made a
fateful stop at the Memphis Recording Service to
take advantage of their demo facilities. Marion
Keisker, office manager of Sun Records, treated
him as just another customer ("When he first

## Elvis Presley

came in, I wondered if he wanted a handout. We get a lot of drifters here along Union Avenue.'') accepting his four dollars, instructing him to sing after the recording light flashed on.

She was taken with Elvis' voice, however, and made an extra tape of the two songs Presley performed on that day. Elvis gave her his name and address, and misspelling "Pressley," Marion added the small notation, "Good ballad singer. Hold." She dutifully passed the information on to Sam Phillips, who, vaguely interested, filed it for future reference. In January of 1954, Elvis returned to Sun to make another dub, met Phillips personally and reminded him of his availability. This time, Sam paid more attention. Even untrained, the boy had a distinctive feel for music. "I suppose it was all the gospel singing Elvis had done that gave me a hint of that special thing."

Under Marion's urgings, Elvis was put in the hands of Scotty Moore and Bill Black to "develop a style." Early results were not promising, but the trio persevered. "I'd run across a ballad written by a prisoner in the

Tennessee State pen and I wanted a crooner," Sam recalled later. "Elvis toyed around with it. I decided he needed a couple of good rhythm men back of him so I called in Scotty and Bill and still nothing happened. Then I got the notion of trying some of the old 'Big Boy' Crudup material. Although it seemed incomprehensible to have a white man do those songs, I just got a notion and I called Elvis."

The song was "That's All Right (Mama)," a blues written and recorded by Crudup for RCA-Victor's Bluebird label in 1947. "Elvis lived ten, fifteen blocks away, but before I had hung up the phone he came panting in the door. He was so excited he had run all the way. We all worked it over, and there was a feel to the session — a pleading quality to Elvis' voice — Crudup's 'That's All Right' was just right for him. When we cut, things happened. I said right then, 'That's it.' I knew we had a hit.'' For the flip side, they similarly modernized a country favorite, Bill Monroe's "Blue Moon of Kentucky."

But they were all dressed with no place to

Elvis and Bill Haley, 1958

*(United Press International)*

go. "We were up a gum stump, so to speak. The white disc jockeys wouldn't touch what they regarded as a Negro's music, and the Negro deejays didn't want anything to do with a record made by a white man. It wasn't a western, and it wasn't a pop tune. There wasn't any ready-made place for it."

The only available outlet, in fact, was Dewey Phillips' (no relation) *Red, Hot and Blue* show on WHBQ in Memphis. Phillips agreed to play the record one Saturday night in July, and a nervous Elvis avoided the family radio to watch *High Noon* in a local theatre. Carefully noting that the singer was an alumnus of Humes (thus alerting his listeners that Elvis was white), Dewey debuted "That's All Right." At 9:30 that night, Dewey called the Presleys. "Mrs. Presley," he said, "you just get that cotton-pickin' son of yours over here to the station. I played that record of his and the phones haven't stopped ringing since. I want him on the air." In a haze of excitement, Elvis went down to the station for his first live interview.

Even Sam Phillips was amazed at the reaction. "Elvis went from high school boy to hit entertainer so fast it was hard for any of us to realize the change had come."

That they hadn't yet assimilated the revolutionary nature of their newest star was made apparent in one of Elvis' first professional appearances, in Memphis's Overton Park on August 10, 1954. "That's All Right" was selling well locally, and Sam talked promoter Bob Neal into adding Elvis to a show featuring established country artists like Slim Whitman, Carl Smith, Minnie Pearl and Webb Pierce. Perhaps slightly unnerved by the presence of so much talent, Elvis performed two of his favorite country songs in the afternoon show, "Old Shep" (with which he'd placed second in a state fair talent contest while still living in Mississippi) and "That's When Your Heartaches Begin." The response was polite, but Dewey felt only unfavorable comparison could come from doing traditional country songs in a country setting. Accordingly, they programmed "Good Rockin' Tonight" and "That's All Right" for the evening's entertainment.

*(Collection Greg Shaw)*

"I came out on stage and I was scared stiff," Elvis recalled later. "I was doing a fast type tune, one of my first records, and everybody was hollering and screaming and everything. I came off stage and my manager told me everyone was hollering because I was wiggling. So I went back out for an encore and did it a little more and the more I did it the more they screamed."

The accepted pop style of attraction had been formulated around the figure of Frank Sinatra, a dreamy-eyed romantic swooner meant for moonlit drives and cheek-to-cheek dancing. Presley's grinding hips and lascivious motions put a heated end to all that. He was greeted with a predictable chill at the *Grand Ole Opry*, finding a more appreciative radio home on the *Louisiana Hayride* out of Shreveport. Scotty and Bill accompanied him on a long series of one-nighters. By January of 1955, he was being managed by Bob Neal, "Good Rockin' Tonight" had become his second record for Sun, and he was tabbed eighth on *Billboard*'s Most Promising poll of "hillbilly" and country western stars.

He had also come to the attention of Colonel Tom Parker, an impresario whose medicine show style had taken him from the carnival circuit of the late 1930s to the personal management of Eddy Arnold and Hank Snow. Parker's forte was as a promoter, and he used his considerable business acumen to market his performers outside their musical base, spinning off products and endorsements, keeping them on a constant string of personal appearances with a keen eye for potential publicity. As Elvis' fame and notoriety spread, Parker began helping Neal book him throughout the South and Southwest, often placing him on package shows with Snow. When "Baby, Let's Play House," Presley's fourth record, snuck onto the national country charts in mid-1955, major labels were attentively bidding for his services, and Parker began to formally assume control.

Elvis, dazzled by his sudden success (cars and girls, in that order), appeared willing, and the Colonel worked steadfastly on the Presley parents and Sam Phillips himself. Phillips had several other performers waiting in the wings, notably Carl Perkins, and as the dollar signs built in magnitude he swayed with the tide. In the winter of 1955, Parker closed a deal with RCA-Victor for $35,000, with an extra bonus of $5,000 to Elvis for signing, an unheard-of total in those days. For RCA the risk was greater than might be suspected, but with Parker's tenacious zeal trumpeting his arrival, Elvis' impact was at once explosive and dizzying, not only as an entertainer but as an immoderate symbol of fifties' youth.

As Presley had merged divergent types of music with Sam Phillips' support, so he would sweep across continents with Parker as his mentor, and would become one of the most important performers of his time. It was a grand scale only the Colonel could foresee, and in his wheelings and dealings he aimed for nothing less.

Presley's first official record for RCA, "Heartbreak Hotel," was released in the same week of January 28, 1956, that he made his debut bow on Tommy and Jimmy Dorsey's nationally televised *Stage Show*. Using his guitar more as afterthought than instrument, Elvis embellished every phrase of the song with abrupt, snapping body movements, flaunting his confidence before the camera and into millions of homes. "Heartbreak Hotel" entered the charts by February's end. In itself it wasn't much different from the Sun sound — minimal instrumentation over an echoed and turbulent vocal — but a year and a half of prominence had varnished the naive qualities of Presley's voice, and his delivery was now shaded by the knowledge of its effect. Teenagers had begun screaming again.

Lines were drawn, if a bit hazily. Youth had found a spokesman and had ascribed to him the usual restless fears and frustrations. Primitive, ostensibly moody, Elvis was a carefully molded character, removed from the psychological turmoil of a Marlon Brando or a James Dean by the pressurized release of his singing, the primal scream permanently seized in the open mouth of his first album cover.

But as Elvis became a household word, he was damned as immoral in many quarters, an instrument of the devil for corrupting adolescents not old enough to know better. Elvis the Pelvis. He couldn't carry a tune from here to the train station. He sang "jungle music." He mumbled. He sneered too much for his own good.

Except for a short collapse from exhaustion in March, and a mistimed April opening in Las Vegas, Elvis remained relatively calm in the face of this hysteria. Parker had him on a grueling schedule of television (Steve Allen, Milton Berle) and personal appearances, and with each new week greater security precautions were required to protect him from the ardor of his fans. After one typical performance, his limousine was dismantled piece-by-piece by a horde of ravenous admirers. In September of 1956, the double success of "Hound Dog"/"Don't Be Cruel" prompted RCA to take the unprecedented step of releasing seven Presley singles concurrently, along with the ballad theme from his forthcoming movie, *Love Me Tender*. Ed Sullivan paid him $50,000 for three

# 5

## Elvis Presley

*Toast of the Town* segments. On September 9, to a record audience of 54 million people, Mr. Broadway felt obliged to edit Presley's frontal assault by showing him only from the waist up during the performance of "Hound Dog." In his stage show today, Elvis still makes light of the occurrence, stooping down during "Hound Dog," slashing at his mid-section to ask, "Does this look familiar?"

When he wasn't on stage, which was seldom, Elvis set the image of a southern gentleman, unfailingly considerate and polite. He bought his parents a house with his first money, and allowed the Colonel to do his talking to the press. The picture that emerged may have proved disappointing in terms of · sensationalism, but was essentially true to Presley's own personality. Despite his inflammatory image and his fleet of Cadillacs, the country boy essence showed no signs of tarnish. His public romantic involvements were brief, favoring "well-scrubbed" girls who "do not use off-color words, drink or smoke"; and though he was linked at one time to nearly every starlet in America (Natalie Wood was perhaps the strongest possibility), specific sexuality was underplayed in favor of a more universal appeal. Parker didn't want sentiment for Elvis to lose heart for even an instant; there were all those teddy bears left to be sold.

Elvis' records continued to dominate the charts throughout the mid-fifties, and he could draw from the best songwriters simply because he could literally guarantee a hit. Usually, both sides of his current release ascended the charts, as was the case with "All Shook Up"/"That's When Your Heartaches Begin," "Let Me Be Your Teddy Bear"/"Loving You," "Don't"/"I Beg Of You" and on, surprisingly, until the early sixties. He bore the brunt of much stereotyped criticism (contrary to popular belief, he had a rich and extraordinarily malleable voice) and to a lesser extent, the same was true of his budding film career. His movies increasingly became personal vehicles, but Elvis was an engaging and eager actor, and *Lovin' You, Jailhouse Rock* and *King Creole* at least placed him in suitably seedy surroundings, a realistic far cry from his later glossy epics.

Presley was drafted in early 1958, after a postponement to allow him to complete *King Creole*, and the Colonel proved able to turn even this liability into an asset. "Operation Elvis," as it was known, was covered by a battalion of photographers and journalists, each eager to prove that, yes, Elvis was just another recruit in

(© 1976 Bob Gruen)

the military, from his first GI haircut to his eventual station with the 3rd Armored Division in Germany, driving a jeep. RCA doled out the precious Elvis material they had left in their vaults (spicing up several of his albums with old Sun standards), and as the Colonel was supervising publicity releases, his name hardly had a chance to be out of the public eye. There was, simply, no one to replace him.

The Colonel promised that upon his discharge, Elvis would resume where he'd left off, but such was not to be totally the case. His first television appearance, following a tumultuous return, was with Frank Sinatra, which placed Elvis in a show business league he had once threatened to destroy. The dismay of his fans aside, Parker was looking toward Hollywood. Elvis would make two live showings at benefits in 1961, and though it wasn't announced to the public, they would be his last until he returned to the stage in 1969. The movies beckoned, three films a year contracted by Parker for one million dollars apiece.

Routine settled over the Presley empire. With the constant attendance of the Memphis Mafia, an on-payroll entourage of his oldest chums and cronies, Elvis relaxed in Graceland glory. He never quite became a sophisticated actor, but his screen roles were varied and enjoyable — in *Kid Galahad*, *Roustabout*, *Girl Happy*, among others. Often, the film's locale took precedence over matters of plot, showcasing Elvis in Hawaii (*Blue Hawaii*; *Paradise, Hawaiian Style*), Las Vegas (*Viva*), Acapulco (*Fun In*). The new order was crested when Elvis married Priscilla Beaulieu on the morning of May 1, 1967 (they were later divorced). For those who had once seen him as a threat to the republic, Elvis had become a tamed pussycat, the embodiment of virtue and family taste.

Both Elvis and the Colonel were aware that Presley's gargantuan popularity was beginning to slip; his current image could hardly be expected to draw any newer fans. Accordingly, after much discussion, it was announced that Elvis would star in a Christmas television special of his own in December 1968. For those expecting him to be another lamb in the manger, surprises were in store. Dressed in black leather, informally fooling around, reminiscing about his career, he once again became, with effective distance, a rocker. His film roles were growing meatier (*Charro* was his first nonmusical), and his records took on a new relevance; "In The Ghetto" told a stark tale of social consciousness that would have been decreed out-of-bounds only a few short months earlier.

The live Elvis came home at the International Hotel in Las Vegas later in 1969. He would never shake a feeling of ambivalence about his work, the pre-Army style of "Burning Love" placed against the maddening filler of most of his albums. Still, with Parker as flamboyant as ever, Elvis has remained "back," touring America liberally, filling every arena where he cares to make a stand. The new Presley touches on his older hits for the sake of tradition, but he saves his concentration for the slower songs, the ones in which he can fully cushion a ready string section, the Sweet Inspirations/J. D. Sumner and the Stamps chorus to one side, all working off the lushness of his own peculiarly beautiful voice.

He hits his stride on "You've Lost That Lovin' Feelin'," touching height with "Bridge Over Troubled Water." From there, the only place he can possibly go is "The Battle Hymn of the Republic" (part of Mickey Newbury's "American Trilogy"), the kind of show-stopper reserved for a state hero and/or national monument.

After that, he sets about to deliberately cool things down. First a melancholy "Funny How Time Slips Away," with Elvis walking around the stage, singing to different parts of the hall; a forthright "I Can't Stop Loving You," which continues the message portion of the farewell; finally, into probably his most lovely song, "Can't Help Falling In Love." And then, when it's over, he takes his cape, spreads it across his shoulders, and with arms outstretched, kneels to the audience, head bowed in grateful salute. They are his, he theirs. This is the supreme moment. For royalty, there can be no others.

# 2
# The Originators

## BILL HALEY

ALTHOUGH IT WAS SOMEWHAT OF A FALSE start, rock & roll officially began with Bill Haley and The Comets' 1955 hit "Rock Around The Clock." Originally released the previous year, it had flopped. In 1954 what was to become rock & roll was almost exclusively black music, inaccessible to the white audience whose taste would ultimately define rock & roll. It was what would now be called rhythm and blues and was then classified as "race records," which only got played on black stations and were not distributed in white areas. Ironically it was not through record stores or deejays that rock & roll made its first breakthrough, but in the movies.

A year after its release, "Rock Around The Clock" was used as the theme song for *Blackboard Jungle*, a movie about latent juvenile delinquency in an interracial public school in the Bronx. The song itself is totally innocuous, but in the context of the film it got fused into an

# 8

**Bill Haley**

expression of teenage rebellion, eventually becoming the largest-selling rock record of all time, some 22 million copies, and reaching its chart peak in 1965!

Haley thought of it as a novelty song, high-spirited party music, and today it seems

*(Collection Peter Kanze)*

more evocative of a boozy New Year's party than a teenage war chant. Bill Haley vehemently denied that his music caused juvenile delinquency, and followed up "Rock Around The Clock" with a bowdlerized version of blues shouter Joe Turner's "Shake, Rattle and Roll." As Bill said, "we don't want to offend anybody."

Before he was ten Bill was strumming on a pasteboard guitar, and when the family moved

from Michigan to Booth Corner, Pennsylvania, he made his first public performance while working at the Auction Mart. Because Bill was shy about performing in public, his boss had secretly rigged a microphone in his office with a PA system outside, so that (unbeknownst to him) he was heard all over town. After three of these "chamber" concerts, he was persuaded to play at the Auction Mart for one dollar a night on weekends. Two years later at fifteen he joined a traveling medicine show. In Hartford, Connecticut, he teamed up with a group called the Down Homers, then played Dixieland, western and semi-pop material with The Saddlemen, before stumbling onto rock & roll. His version of rock & roll, in fact, was an offshoot of Dixieland, with a beat listeners could clap along with and dance to.

Bill Haley and The Comets had a minor chart hit with "Crazy Man Crazy" in 1953, a year before the record breaking "Rock Around The Clock." His first recording was "Rocket 88" in 1951 with The Saddlemen, on the Essex label. Perhaps inspired by their space-age single or taking a rare opportunity to make a pun on Halley's discovery, later that year they changed their name to The Comets.

They had a number of hits (most of them written and produced by Haley) following "Shake, Rattle and Roll" — "Razzle Dazzle," "See You Later Alligator" — but by 1957, their place on the charts had started to slip. They never again even approached the success of "Rock Around The Clock."

Bill Haley has always been a bit embarrassed by the *thing* he let loose upon the world like some pubescent plague, and there is something appropriately absurd about this mild-mannered, paunchy, baby-faced man in his madras jacket opening the flood gates of rock. A more unlikely father of rock with all its bizarre progeny could hardly be imagined, and yet year after year, regular as clockwork he turns up at rock revivals , his spitcurl glued in place, the bass player still rolling on his back, the sax player bobbing like a plastic duck, to remind us of the accidental, and innocent, beginnings, still cosmic as a comic, and comic as a Comet.

# CHUCK BERRY

CHUCK BERRY IS AT THE CORE OF ROCK &
roll, and it was his first hit, "Maybelline," that
really got rock rolling. From the honking guitar
in the opening, "Maybelline" is the ideal fusion
of fast car, guitar, girl and beat that made it the
synthesis of just about everything that obsessed
the teen mind.

The songs which followed "Maybelline" are
now landmarks in rock history: "Brown-Eyed
Handsome Man," "Roll Over Beethoven"
— even "Too Much Monkey Business" with its
overt criticism of the American way of
life — but it wasn't until his fifth song, "School
Days," a year and a half after "Maybelline" that
Chuck Berry scored his second hit. Here he
stumbled upon the teen dream, a rich vein of
fantasy, which he would stake out forever with
his perfect flashback details, like snapshots in a
wallet. He captured the texture of adolesence

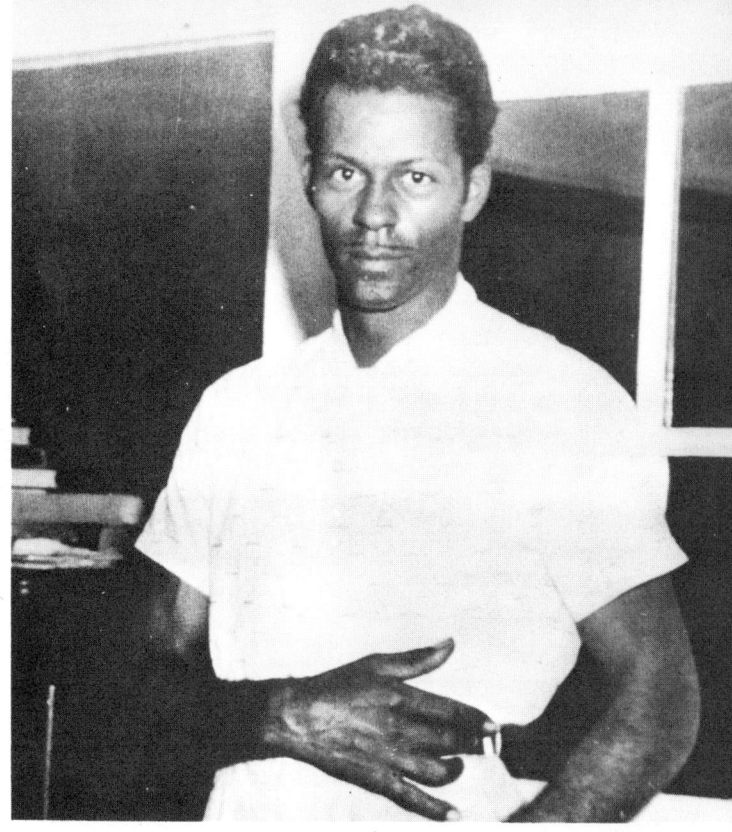

JKP082901-8/29/59-MERIDIAN,Miss.-Negro Rock'n'Roll Star Char les
(Chuck)Berry awaits questioning in jail here 8/28 on charges he
tried to date a Mississippi white girl while filling a one-night
stand at a high school dance. Released on bond, he was escorted
out of town by police.          UPI TELEPHOTO          ff
          *(United Press International)*

*(Globe Photos)*

and evoked a world of hops, juke boxes, hot rods, canteen lunches and bop-crazed bobby-soxers as if he had never left it.

Berry was thirty at the time "School Days" came out, and his uncanny ability to re-create these teen tableaus can perhaps be traced back to his own schooldays — "Maybelline" was the name of a cow from his third grade reader at Simmons Grade School in St. Louis, and it was his high school music teacher, Miss Julia Davis, whom he credits as the most important influence on his life. With encouragement from her, he made his singing debut at his own Senior Prom with a version of "Confessin' the Blues."

You could hardly tell the Chuck Berry story more succinctly and lyrically than in his own fictionalized histories, "Johnny B. Goode" and "Bye Bye Johnny," both "country boy becomes star" stories. The facts of his life are really less evocative: born in 1927 in California, he grew up in St. Louis, where his father was a carpenter. He sang along with his mother, a soprano, in the choir at the Antioch Baptist Church. After high school he enrolled in Gibbs Beauty School and eventually graduated with a degree in cosmetology.

The blues, as Chuck Berry has often said, was "his music," the music he and his friend Johnny Johnson (whose eccentric piano can be heard on Berry's early records) loved to play on weekends at St. Louis nighteries like Huff Gardens and The Cosmopolitan Club. Chuck admired the cool jazz style of guitarist Charlie Christian, and idolized a bewildering variety of singers from Nat King Cole and Sinatra to blues shouters like Howlin' Wolf and Muddy Waters. It was Muddy Waters who encouraged Chuck to come to Chicago in the summer of 1955 and sent him along to the small label, Chess Records, for whom he recorded.

The Chess brothers, Leonard and Phil, had in the past mainly recorded the giants of Chicago blues like Muddy Waters, Howlin' Wolf and John Lee Hooker, whose songs sold steadily but not spectacularly to southern and ghetto markets. But they had gotten a hint that there was a monster audience out there waiting to devour a new kind of platter. They began

*(Collection Andrea Dalton)*

John Lennon jams with his idol, Chuck Berry

breaking into white record areas with two soft R & B groups, the Flamingos and the Moonglows, both subsequently covered by white artists Pat Boone and the McGuire Sisters. Suddenly distributors who had formerly rejected what Chess was dishing out as "race records" began to put the discs in their racks.

Leonard and Phil Chess had no reason to believe that Chuck Berry was anything more than another blues singer, but they asked him to send them a tape of his material. Back in St. Louis, Chuck put down half a dozen songs on a home tape recorder. Among these was a blues called "Wee Wee Hours" and a novelty song, "Maybelline."

Phil and Leonard Chess liked "Wee Wee Hours," but with a shrewd intuition, they thought they heard in "Maybelline" that *new thing.* When they got Chuck up to Chicago to cut it, they took the precaution of inviting two deejays to sit in on the session. The two, Alan Freed and Russ Frato, allegedly helped refashion the lyrics for white ears. Naturally, with such a personal involvement in the waxing, they were not about to let "Maybelline" just fade away, but played it until Chuck's record started to overtake "Doggie in the Window," "Que Sera Sera" and "Tennessee Waltz" on its way up the charts. *Billboard* awarded him its triple crown (most requested on radio, most played on juke boxes and most popular single). More important, it was a hit not only in R & B and pop charts, but even made it into C & W country.

One of the reasons given for the speed with which this R & B song caught on with white audiences was that it "passed" on radio stations as a country song. The tune was, in fact, similar to a country song, "Ida May." Berry's clear delivery, flat whine, narrative lyrics and alternating chunky chords on the verses with lead country-type licks on the breaks, gave it the cool sound that was to become the formula for most early sixties English guitar styles. All Chuck's subsequent songs carried this identifying ba-doo-doo-dah, ba-dooh-dah riff (borrowed from Carl Hogan), which made his sound recognizable.

If Chuck Berry taught us the basics of Rock, the massive reaction of his youthful audience to "Maybelline" was a lesson to him about what shape the teen beat was to take. Blues like "Wee Wee Hours" which languished on the flip side of his first hit was *his* music, a sound that Johnny Johnson loved to play, the subtle sophisticated jazz-tinged sound of T-Bone Walker and Charlie Christian. For Chuck and Johnny "Maybelline" had been a humorous spacer in their jazz/blues sets, but for their new audience it was a reality.

It is amazing that, having hit upon the teen turf formula in his "School Days" vignettes, Chuck Berry did not trade in his inventiveness for mere repetition and exploitation. Perhaps it was because Berry was such a superb craftsman, customizing all his songs like his V-8 Ford, that he kept the magic in the music. His songs are so styled, almost "coifed," that they stand like images of frozen time. It took another generation to realize just *how* ingenious his songs were, with their clever word coinings and sly stories told with cool, comic delivery, like his "Nadine."

In 1959 he was arrested in Mississippi allegedly for the crime of trying to date a white high school girl; four years later, the melody from his best-known hit, "Sweet Little Sixteen," was used to co-author the Beach Boys' first national hit, "Surfin U.S.A." A year later everybody was doing his songs, and in 1964 he even had a string of English hits with reissues and unreleased material, but his subsequent career was somewhat checked by the double bind of being elevated to rock legend by the English groups while being fossilized as a golden oldie. It was with a group of English musicians that he got his first certified million seller in 1970 with the embarrassingly regressive wee-wee song, "My Dingaling."

What English groups and revivalists like Creedence Clearwater Revival appreciated most in him — the personal style of his crisp guitar and the greatest primitive poetry in all rock — was what actually limited him in the fifties. Aside from "Maybelline" and "School Days" he had only four other hits: "Sweet Little Sixteen," "Memphis," "Rock and Roll Music" and "Johnny B. Goode."

Although he had no imitators in the fifties, Chuck Berry is the matrix of rock & roll, the creator of its grammar and source to which a coming generation of rock musicians would turn. What also appealed to his inheritors was an *attitude*, intensely involved, and yet removed, which moves through his songs "like a cool breeze."

The "I" in Chuck Berry's songs is the eye of the camera (he actually considered becoming a professional photographer while at cosmetology school) which accounts for both a clarity and a distance between him and his subjects and gives his images their incredible focus. It was these images of American adolescence that gave Berry an affinity with the English rock groups, who only knew America from records and movies anyway, and allowed them to use his snapshots as the basis for their *Blow-up* vision of America.

# LITTLE RICHARD

IT HARDLY SEEMS POSSIBLE, BUT LITTLE Richard's stage act was even more preposterous than the records themselves. "Long Tall Sally" was originally called "The Thang" and it is what Richard calls his "thang," that participation and induced frenzy of his performances and early records, which makes his sound more than just a category of gospel blues or New Orleans boogie zipped out at a dizzying rate.

On stage Little Richard, with his "wings held high" launches into one of his many set monomanialogues that introduce, punctuate and even interrupt his songs: "Look anywhere . . . I am the only thing left. The beauty's on duty. I *am* the beautiful Little Richard from way down in Macon, Georgia. You know Otis Redding is from there, and James Brown is from there too but I was the best lookin' one, prettiest thing in the kitchen, so I was the first to leave. I want you to know I am the Bronze Liberace! If you hear a funny tone in my voice that's the Angeltown sound . . . Now all the womenfolk say 'woooh' an' let all the men say 'uhnnn!' Shut up, shut up, I rather do it myself!"

The Naked Ego speaks! Apparently totally derailed, and yet blissfully cocooned in his dizzying self-inflation, Little Richard reappeared in the late sixties after eight years of exile like some Sleeping Beauty kissed back to life by a new generation of rockers. He has been the inspiration for three generations of flamboyant performers, from Otis Redding and James Brown through Mick Jagger and Jimi Hendrix to the glitter rock of the seventies.

Little Richard is not simply the freaky supershowman of rock, but the perpetrator of what is perhaps the most daring act in all of rock & roll. He was the first to abscond with gospel music, take that "angeltown sound" out of the chapel and use it for blatantly commercial purposes. He is the first rock and roll singer to make the sanctified sound into a hit record, and it was a sense of guilt about his sacrilegious act that drove the King of Rock and Soul into exile.

While on a tour of Australia in 1959, he saw Sputnik streaking across the heavens, took it to be a sign from God that unless he gave up his sinful ways he would be condemned to hellfire, threw away his rings and his gold lamé suits and disappeared from rock until the mid-sixties when he became a minister at Oakwood College in Huntsville, Alabama.

Little Richard's recording career began in 1951 when he cut a number of Roy Brown's infectious dance songs for RCA, and a batch of blues for other companies, but it was in 1955 that he almost accidentally came up with his dada masterpiece, "Tutti Frutti." The original version was a stream of abusive insults aimed at his boss in the diner at the Greyhound bus terminal in Macon, Georgia. When Art Rupe and Bumps Blackwell (Richard's future collaborator) from Specialty Records heard its insane refrain, "A-wop-bop-a-loo-a-wop-bam-boom" during a break while cutting some standards like "Baby," "Kansas City" and "I'm Just A Lonely Guy," they dropped the ballads, brought in a songwriter, Dorothy La Bostrie, to clean up the lyrics, got it in three takes and put it out.

It sold half a million copies, and a true crazy was unleashed on the world. The contagious, induced explosion of "Tutti Frutti" was no fluke. Apparently Richard, whose given name was Penniman, had been this way as long as anyone could remember. His father, unable to deal with this natural lunatic, had thrown him out of the house when he was thirteen. "That man has just gone clean crazy," Richard recalls him saying as he walked off into the blue. Subsequently he was adopted by a white couple, the Johnsons, who owned a night spot called the Tick Tock Club. It was there Richard got his first taste of "the wild music" when Lloyd Price came to town. On the theory that anything anyone else could do, he could do more outrageously, Richard made a tape, sent it to Lloyd Price's label (Specialty) in L. A. and set off for New Orleans. It was there at the funky Tijuana Club that Bumps and Art Rupe first heard him playing with the Tempo Toppers.

# 13
## Little Richard

(Collection Greg Shaw)

away with his percussive vocal at dizzying speed (comically running out of breath on "Jenny, Jenny, Jenny"). His "attack" on a song gives the impression that *emotion itself*, shaking, wriggling, "making the liver quiver, the bladder splatter, the knees freeze" is forcing its own way through the words in its most elemental form. Most of his lyrics sound like they were just made up on the spot, strings of non sequiturs lurching along, with Richard knocking them out as they pop into his head only to slug them again as they come up a little for air.

Even in the seventies, when flagrant exhibitionism and machomysticism seemed to have reached the outer limits, few performers could match Little Richard's part jive hustler, part sanctified preacher pose for its sheer exuberance. In the dour climate of the Eisenhower fifties, as the self-styled king of rock & roll, he was paraded regally on stage with an entourage of costumed Beefeaters bearing a flag with his picture on it. His "guards" unrolled a red carpet as he stepped down from his throne. A typical stage antic involved "His Majesty" frothing at the mouth and clawing his way up the proscenium curtain mid-song only to fall back apparently injured or paralyzed onto the stage. Halfway down the aisle he would miraculously recover, and leap right off the stretcher back into the song directly on the beat.

Most of Little Richard's songs are basically the same song done in minutely different ways ("True Fine Mama" is virtually "Good Golly Miss Molly" in a higher register) and almost all have either no story line or totally contradict themselves. But this was their beauty. Who could have wanted anything better than more of the same? Little Richard's principle in dealing with a song seems to be: take a riff and just keep pushing it over the edge until it turns into something else out of pure exhaustion. It was the chaotic, overwhelming inarticulateness of Little Richard that made him all the more attractive to his audience on the principle that less meaning equals more expression. His delivery paralleled the surging emotions and unspeakable fantasies of the hordes of teenagers who devoured his records.

They signed him on the spot.

Scat — the effect jazz singers get with nonsense syllables to imitate the sound of an instrument — is an old technique, but the rat-tat-tat of "Tutti Frutti" sounded like no known instrument unless it was a jack hammer. He followed it up with a string of hits — "Long Tall Sally," "Rip It Up," "Good Golly Miss Molly," "Ready Teddy," "Jenny, Jenny, Jenny," "Lucille" — all with the same eruptive sound, notes slippin' and slidin' out of control in whoops and squeals, breathless hammering

# FATS DOMINO

FATS DOMINO IS A TIME CAPSULE OF ROCK & roll's infancy, its playful endearing "cuddly" child, a curiosity of early rock & roll. He was neither a sex symbol like Elvis, nor an outrageous performer with a bag of antics like Little Richard—he hardly budges his huge frame, except to twinkle his eye and flash an ingenuous smile as he swivels on his piano bench to sing one of his classic hits.

The name itself suggests a pudgy piano keyboard, and that's where you can find the Fat Man almost any night of the year at whatever nitery he's booked into, decked out in one of his three hundred snazzy suits, gobs of diamond rings encrusting his chubby fingers. He's in perennial good humor, relaxed and bubbly as he pumps out his jaunty beat as relentlessly as a steam roller.

Yet so infectious was the boogie woogie flu let loose by this tubby tinkler in the fifties that he almost got rock & roll banned for good in San Jose (the California legislature seriously considered it) after a riot broke out following one of his concerts.

His simple, catchy, danceable tunes are all perennials (some like "La La" have a total of a dozen different words) and flow on as predictably as the Mississippi. "His vocal style has been compared with the style of Joe DiMaggio" say the liner notes on an early Imperial album, and Fats' appeal has always been universal, like DiMaggio's or Babe Ruth's, a beloved institution, one of the few rock originals who remain equally popular with rockers, and the patrons of tacky lounges, or the fleshy-flashy Flamingo in Las Vegas. Although he no longer makes records, only a tinge of nostalgia surrounds his classics like "Blue Monday," "Blueberry Hill" and "I'm Walking."

He spoke French before he spoke English and his thick cajun accent was not only endearing ("I'm gwoin hoh-em") but its distinctive flavor preserved him from the insipid cover versions inflicted on most other rock and blues artists. Of course, some foolishly attempted it anyway, like Pat Boone's unforgiveable cover of Fats' first hit, "The Fat Man," and Bobby Darin's pointless version of "Margie." Only Ricky Nelson got away with it when he did "I'm Walkin'."

Fats is an embodiment of New Orleans contained in one mass: that sultry seaport with its diverse racial background of Spanish, French, West Indian and freed Delta slaves, its 38 blocks of pungent brothels and dives, its streets teeming with gamblers, pimps, hustlers and musical oddities like Professor Longhair. Cajun blues, boogie piano, calypso and jazz all incubated here. Fats' modified jump blues and the black soul of today's New Orleans derives from jazz hot bands. Its distinctive "second line," an extra syncopated rhythm, comes from the bass drum of nineteenth-century funeral parades, the exuberance of Mardi Gras Festivals. Fats almost physically seems to incorporate all this richness of influence and tradition, and as he bumps the grand piano off the stage for his finale, "The Saints Go Marchin' In," he is a holiday and a parade in himself.

His phenomenal chart successes (over 65 million records) in both rock & roll and R & B opened the gates of the city of New Orleans to an unending stream of musicians from Lloyd Price through Lee Dorsey, Merle Haggart, Huey Piano Smith, down to Dr. John and the Meters. Fats' "funk" (indigenous New Orleans slang) is the sound of a city, the exhalation of a small big town. As Earl Finn puts it, "New Orleans bands have adjusted themselves to a certain mental tune."

After World War II, when the great age of jazz gave way to jump blues combos which used heavy drums, bass, guitar, piano and emphasized vocals and tenor saxophone, Fats developed a bouncing boogie beat on uptempo, tunes like "I'm Walkin' "; it had a classic R & B walking/talking rhyme scheme and a swirling shuffle that blurred the beat on the slow, sad songs. In jump blues a whole band was now playing what a boogie piano player would maintain with his left hand alone.

In collaboration with his producer David

# 16

## Fats Domino

Bartholomew (an ex-Duke Ellington horn player) he developed his laid-back style of singing with a big beat which set him apart from the typical New Orleans bands of the late forties and made him a national celebrity.

On his classic records, Fats' songs have a plaintive almost pathetic tone, although his tunes (almost all written by himself and his producer Dave Bartholomew) are often lyrically bitter and reproachful. The effect of such tunes as "Ain't That A Shame," "Blueberry Hill," "I'm Gonna Be A Wheel Someday (And Then I Won't Want You)" is almost self-parody, neutralized by his confident, unflagging piano and Herb Hardesty's exuberant tenor sax ("He's the one who do all the solos," says Fats). All his songs exude an irrepressible effervescence, and why shouldn't they? He's been happily married to Rosemary, his childhood sweetheart, since he was seventeen, and lives in their rock & roll dreamhouse with seven children whose names all begin with A ("That's cause my name is Antoine!" he says).

Fats was born Antoine Domino into a family of nine on May 10, 1929. His father was a nightclub violinist and his uncle, Harrison Verette (who had learned banjo with Kid Ory's dixieland band), taught the five-year-old Domino the names of the keyboard notes, writing the names in black on the white keys and taping names onto the black keys. When Dave Bartholomew heard the teenage Fats playing in a local bar, he got him a job playing nightly at the Hideaway Club. Fats continued to work days in a factory, until a pile of mattresses fell on him and crushed his hands. The doctor at first thought his hands would have to be amputated, but two years later Fats was back playing at the Hideaway. Lew Chudd, a producer for Imperial Records in Los Angeles, heard him there and signed him on the spot.

He recorded his first hit, "The Fat Man" (a celebration sung in a high tenor voice with whoops and scats and a rolling boogie beat), when he was twenty years old, already a star in his home town. His second single, "Every Night About This Time," was an even bigger hit on the R & B charts, but it was five years and 25 singles later, when "Ain't That A Shame" got onto the national charts, and Fats Domino's career in rock & roll began. Both "Ain't That A Shame" and its follow-up "Blueberry Hill" were oldies dating back to the twenties, but by this time, Dave Bartholomew and Fats had smoothed out the rough qualities of earlier vocals and had mastered their own distinctive sound. Fats' voice on these hits was deeper and more plaintive. The R & B quality of the early sessions had given way to a pronounced back beat with an irresistible momentum that was to become classic rock & roll. For four years, the hits kept rolling out: "It's You I Love," "The Big Beat," "I'm in Love Again," "I'm Walkin'," "I Want To Walk You Home," "Whole Lotta Lovin'" with Fats doing his naughty "smacking" sound effect.

Fats and Dave Bartholomew stuck pretty much to the classic Domino formula until the early sixties, when strings and often pointless choruses muddied up the essence of Fats' sound, his simplicity. Nostalgia, the disease of the comeback, seemed to be creeping in as early as 1960; appropriately enough, his last song to make it on the singles chart was "Stop The Clock/Did You Ever See A Dream Walking" in 1962.

In 1968 Warner Brothers put out one of the best comeback albums ever recorded, *Fats Is Back*, produced by Richard Perry. But the single from the album, "Lady Madonna," a Beatles tribute to the Fat Man himself done with Domino gusto, slid out of the charts.

Some "oldies" artists have grown tired and mechanical after years of repeating their hits, but Fats still plays his classics night after night with the same relish, because for him it's as if time has stopped. Fats doesn't think of his songs as oldies, he just keeps singing them as if he were still in New Orleans, "way back when."

# CARL PERKINS

"I WAS PLAYING AT A PLACE CALLED THE Roadside Inn," Carl Perkins recalls about the night he wrote his hillbilly masterpiece, "Blue Suede Shoes." "It was a gutbucket barroom; the tough boys went there and we had a good lively crowd. One night I heard this boy tell the girl he was dancing with 'Watch out, don't step on mah suedes' and I looked down at his feet, and he had on this pair of blue suede shoes. It kinda stuck to me. I thought, well anybody that proud of a pair of shoes to caution a good-lookin' girl to stay off 'em, you know you'd have to be out of your mind!"

Carl himself is a mild-mannered country boy, but there was something about those blue suede shoes that seemed to fit the teen toe to a tee. They just wouldn't let him sleep, and early next morning, starting out with the words from a children's game, "Well, it's one for the money, two for the show . . . ," he began scribbling the lyrics on an old brown paper potato sack, the only piece of paper he had around the house.

The next day, Carl called Sam Phillips, the owner of Sun Records for whom he'd recorded his first two singles ("Turn Around" in 1953 and "Let The Juke Box Keep On Playing," the following year), to tell him about those blue suedes. As Carl remembers, Phillips asked him "Is it anything like 'O Dem Golden Slippers'?" and I said, "Nossir, this is a rock song!" Teenagers, country fans and blacks alike must have had the same emphatic reaction because "Blue Suede Shoes" not only made it to number five on *Billboard's* national charts, it broke through to become an R & B hit as well as making it to the top of the country charts all at the same time. It was recorded in one take on December 17, 1955, and unleashed on the national ear New Year's Day, 1956.

"Blue Suede Shoes" became the first million selling record in the hillbilly style. It was an irresistible fusion of country music and rhythm and blues combined with an expression of teenage arrogance. Teen culture was already making itself visible through the movies, notably *Rebel Without A Cause*, released only

three months earlier. But aside from Alan Freed's Moondog Rock 'n' Roll Parties few had *seen* what a real live rock & roll star looked like. It was still just a beat.

Of all people, it was "Mr. Nice Guy," Perry Como, who was the first to book a rock & roll act on his show. On March 22, 1956, Carl, in a pair of custom made iridescent blue suede shoes,

*(Collection Greg Shaw)*

# 18

## Carl Perkins

was on his way to the Perry Como Show with his two brothers and the band when their car crashed into a bridge, thus preventing "The Boy With The Blue Suede Shoes," as he was then billed, from making the breakthrough for rock & roll on nation wide TV. Carl and his seriously injured brother, J. B., watched from their hospital beds as Elvis grabbed the spot on the Saturday night Jackie Gleason Show.

Elvis had a hit with "Blue Suede Shoes," too, but he hadn't borrowed his *style* from Carl, just the song. Country boys had been working at the same blend for some time. You can hear the beginnings of rockabilly on Hank Williams's faster songs, and Elvis had already put a rock beat behind Bill Monroe's ballad "Blue Moon Over Kentucky" on his first recording. Carl had even made up a rocking version of "Home On The Range" at the age of twelve.

Carl, born April 9, 1932, came from a poor white farming family in Lake County, Tennessee, and it was in the cotton fields around his home that he first heard black workers "make that rhythm thing with their mouths, ba-*dum*, ba-*dum*, ba-*dum*, 'cause they couldn't take instruments out in the fields." He learned guitar from an old black man, Uncle John, and his dad made him his first one out of a cigar box and baling wire.

Carl grew up directly across the Mississippi River from Johnny Cash over in Arkansas, although they did not know each other as kids, and he can easily remember the flood in Cash's country hit "Five Feet High And Rising." For eight years, Carl and The Tennessee Three opened The Johnny Cash Spectacular with his uptempo rockers like "Matchbox" — the first song Dylan recorded for a small Minnesota label. Carl Perkins was possibly The Beatles' favorite songwriter, and when they invited him to sit in on the session where they recorded "Matchbox" as well as "Honey Don't" and "Everybody's Trying To Be My Baby," he gave George Harrison a few tips on those country licks.

At the Memphis studios of Sun records in 1955, Carl, Cash, Jerry Lee Lewis and Elvis, all in their prime, put together two hours of what is probably the most valuable unreleased tape of all time — The Million Dollar Quartet, as it is referred to, harmonized together on country gospel, Fats Domino tunes and just plain rocking out. Of the four artists, only Elvis has completely managed to move out of the country field.

Carl escaped the grinding poverty he vividly evoked in "I'm Tired" with his tasty guitar riffs and colorful, humorous country tales; "Movie Magg," written when he was twelve, tells about taking a girl to the "movie show" on horseback and quaking as he takes her home to find her daddy waiting for him with a shotgun.

"In the part of the country I'm from, music was way *out*," Carl says about what kept him going through the years of playing Arkansas and West Tennessee schoolhouses and "gutbuckets," barely earning enough to make the payments on the car. "Poverty's what caused a good deal of songs to be written, and a country boy had to really put his heart into it, to tell his story and make it real and beautiful." This is the essence of Carl Perkins and his music, which is full of down home details and country flavorings; "drinking liquor from an old fruit jar," "dixie fried" joints or Carl sending his love to his wife Valda via the moon from his motel window while on the road.

He's suffered a lot of disappointments and grief — J. B.'s death after the crash, the more recent death of his other brother, Clayton, his twice-thwarted career (he was about to make a comeback in 1965 when a hunting accident prevented him from following through) — but he salts them down with his own resigned philosophy. As Carl says, "Life, I don't think for any of us, was meant to be a smooth thing. So if you took all the rough spots in livin' — if I had been raised a rich boy, and never had known what it was like to be hungry and cold and want things, and have to order from Sears and Roebuck, and wait, and it'd be too little and you'd send it back and wait again, you know . . . these were the things that I called knocks in life. They're the things that make you appreciate it when it does smooth out." Or, as he put it melodically to writer Michael Lydon, "If it weren't for the rocks in its bed the stream would have no song."

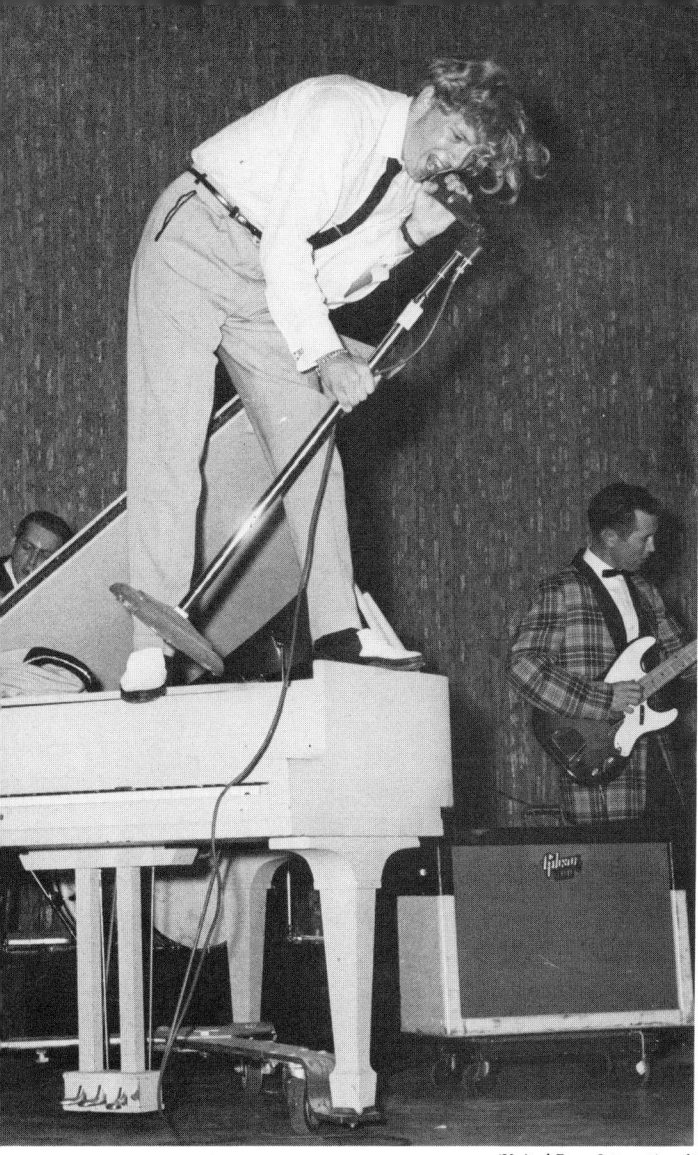

# JERRY LEE LEWIS

IN FEBRUARY OF 1956 JERRY LEE AND HIS dad Elmo sold thirty-three dozen eggs, said goodbye to mother Mamie working in the truck garden in back of their five-room shack and started off on the three-hundred mile trip from Ferriday, Louisiana, to Memphis. They were going to see Mr. Sam Phillips, who had sent a number of good old country boys (Elvis, Johnny Cash, Carl Perkins) on their way with gold-plated platters. Phillips was *the* man in rockabilly music, and of the multitudes of hillbillies, mountain boys, flatland pickers and cajun fiddlers that knocked on his door after the rockabilly revolution, Jerry Lee Lewis was the most talented and the wildest ("Ah came out jumpin' ").

Jerry Lee's musical career began when he learned to play "Silent Night" at the age of eight on the old Stark upright his father bought by mortgaging the house. But before he was into his teens, Jerry was absorbing considerably more funky sounds, sneaking in by the back door of local black R & B clubs like Haney's Big House and Junior's, to hear blues masters Ray Charles, B. B. King and Piano Red. At twelve, he was knocking them out at the local Ford dealership with "Wine Spoo Dee O Dee," and soon after began playing Natchez dives like the Hilltop and Blue Cat Club. His basic style was equally influenced by Dal Wood and Piano Red.

When Jerry Lee and Elmo pulled up in front of Sun Records' Memphis studio ("a lil' ol' shack

## Jerry Lee Lewis

with a stack of Caddies in the back"), Mr. Phillips was not available. By threatening to camp out on the doorstep, they were eventually let in. Sam Phillips, who'd heard just about every preposterous claim known to man, listened to Jerry Lee and his Pumping Piano and was impressed, but two problems remained. The songs were *too* countrified, even at Jerry Lee's frantic pace, and a bigger problem was the piano. Except for black New Orleans boogie-woogie piano players like Fats Domino and Little Richard, all the rock & roll singers who had made it were guitar players. "They had the freedom to move on

Jerry Lee Lewis with 13-year-old Myra Lewis

*(United Press International)*

stage where they could project their material," says Phillips. "Now, how in the hell were we going to take a piano and put action into it? But Jerry found a way!" Jerry Lee once climaxed an Alan Freed show that he was not allowed to close by pouring lighter fluid on the keyboard and setting fire to it, saying, "Ah'd like to see any s.o.b. follow *that!*" as he stalked offstage.

Initially he was signed only as a piano player, but when Phillips heard him wailing "My Blue Heaven" during a Carl Perkins take, he decided to cut him. While cutting "My Blue Heaven," Jerry Lee took a break by singing "Crazy Arms," a Ray Price hit. That did it. "Crazy Arms" went out and was a hit instantly. But Jerry Lee still had the real monsters tucked up his sleeve. When he lit into "Whole Lotta Shakin' Goin' On" during a take of his cartoon classic "It'll Be Me," the first frantic, frenzied full-tilt Jerry Lee lunacy was sprung on the world. At first it got nowhere; not surprisingly country deejays found it obscene. Jerry Lee has always had a way of insinuating sexuality into the most innocent lyric, but this one — with its seductive "All you gotta do, honey, is kinda stand in one spot, just wiggle it around a little bit," which he flagrantly underlined on stage by salaciously twirling his pinky—was just not for the ears of little babes. It wasn't until he got away with it on live television, on the Steve Allen Show, that it started getting played. Five months later, shaking his outrageous blond mane, eyes looking like a man insane or possibly just electrocuted, he crashed the top of the charts with "Great Balls Of Fire."

His next hit, "High School Confidential" (he opened the movie of the same name insanely thrashing about on the platform of a truck), was so fast it was vertiginous — "Honey get your dancin' shoes, before the juke box blows a fuse." But as suddenly as he had appeared, like some UFO zooming from outer space, he was eclipsed by his own outrageousness.

He'd always maintained he "jus' was a hillbillah boyah an' ah play hillbillah speeded up," but it was just those old hillbilly ways that finally got him into deep water across the Atlantic. He'd somehow forgotten to divorce his two "exes," Dorothy and Jane, when he married

# 21
## Jerry Lee Lewis

his thirteen-year-old second cousin, Myra Gail, in 1958 and, while not such an uncommon thing in the South, it was just the juicy stuff the British press needed to jazz up a dull week. Jerry Lee was never one to run for cover. When he stepped off the plane in London with his "little queenie," the reporters quaintly asked, "Who is this, Mr. Lewis?" When Jerry Lee told them plain as could be that this "child" was his bride, the tabloids and Sunday pictorials had a field day with "this satanic cradle robber," turning Myra Gail into his nine-year-old cousin (one even described her as his sister). He was drummed out of England, and when he got back to the States, even his old friend Sam Phillips, whom he'd once described as "crazy as a fox squirrel," wouldn't stand behind him on this one. He cut a couple of albums of other people's hits after that and had a near chart success with "What I'd Say," but for all intents and purposes, Jerry Lee was finished. So at twenty-three, having sold some 25,000,000 records, it was all over for the most calculated madman in rock & roll, and by 1959, with Chuck Berry in jail, and Little Richard a penitent evangelist, it looked like it was all over for rock & roll too.

His wild antics and hyperventilated vocals, so outrageous in the fifties, became fashionable in the sixties and seventies. John Lennon calls "Whole Lotta Shakin' Goin' On" the best rock song ever written and revived a number of Jerry Lee's classics on his *Roots* album. His sexually drenched vocals and defiant attitude influenced the Rolling Stones, especially in songs like "Down The Line." Flattered as he was by all this adulation, Jerry Lee was not about to become a victim of paralytic nostalgitis, refused to participate in R & R revivals and miraculously brought about the Second Coming of Jerry Lee Lewis.

In early 1958 he turned to his country roots and became a truly innovative country singer, thumbing his nose at the smooth slick "Nashville Sound," and went back to a traditional honky tonk sound. Using his urgent southern drawl, smooth piano style and bluesy fiddle backup, he cut an album appropriately entitled *Another Time Another Place*.

The hit was "What Made Milwaukee Famous (Has Made A Loser Out Of Me)" and began a string of country hits for him with double-barreled, double-entendre titles, cynically comic and pathetically vengeful open letters to ex-lovers, ex-wives: "She Even Woke Me Up To Say Goodbye," "She Still Comes Around (To Love What's Left Of Me)," "When He Walks On You (Like You Have Walked On Me)," "How's My Ex Treating You Now."

Like his stage act, they are an incredible *put on* put-on for real. This is the core of the "Killer's" (as he is affectionately called) personality, a shark-like, insolently beautiful double take that infects his music.

It is an essential part of the man himself, who enjoys tearin' up a joint now and then and occasionally abandons all carnal, worldly and liquid pleasures for the Assembly Church of God. The Memphis Mauler can be mean and lean and full of spleen (appropriately, he played the part of Iago in a rock version of Othello), a southern charmer, religious penitent, purveyor of grotesque porno puns like "Meatman," a ladies' man and a one-man wrecking team. But it's just this unpredictability that creates the excitement in his performance on record and in person, a sense of dangerous irruptibility, a lethal alternating current of threat and charm.

Jerry Lee relishes his mimicked madness on stage — kicking in the teeth of his "rockin' 88's," or jumping on top of the piano — but he is completely under control.

As "possessed" as he appears on stage, he is very much more calculated than his main influence, Little Richard, and his attitude, for a man who appears to be suffering from delirium tremens, is aloof, almost sneering, as if parodying the material. It is Jerry Lee's "put-on" of R & B — sometimes approaching black face — that actually constitutes his basic honesty. He does not pretend to be anything other than what he is, a white southerner singing black music, but he hardly underestimates himself either. Assessing his impact on popular music with characteristic arrogance, he lists *the* four great stylists of all time, Al Jolson, Jimmie Rogers, Hank Williams and, of course, Jerry Lee himself.

## 22
**Bo Diddley**

(Checker Records)

# BO DIDDLEY

BO DIDDLEY HAS ALWAYS TRAVELED WITH A weird cast of characters: Jerome Green, rattling mean maracas on Bo's early songs and trading insults with him on the outrageous "Say Man"; the Duchess, his half-sister, in her sexy silver lamé toreador pants; her comic counterparts Cookie and Sleepy King. Even Bo Diddley's bizarre line of guitars, which he customizes himself and with which he occasionally carries on conversations, have their own geometric personalities. But most of his Bo-dacious caricatures are pure Diddley daydreams out of a dada Disneyland as idiosyncratic as that cartoon self-portrait, "Bo Diddley," which climbed to the top of the charts in late 1955. With its crude, direct energy it had one of the most compulsive and unusual rhythms in all of rock & roll.

Bo Diddley is rock & roll's funky Uncle Remus, whose stories, part nursery rhyme and part street jive, tell of reactions to his shifting environment, laid down with a relentless bump-and-grind shuffle. "That's how I got me my name, Bo Diddley," he confesses, "from messin' 'round."

He was named Ellas McDaniel, but his musical history consists of an extended catalogue of impersonations, beginning with Bo Diddley, then maturing into "Diddley Daddy" and other improbable projections of that fantastic original: Bo Diddley as Gunslinger, Roadrunner, Gladiator, Puffesor of rock & roll and voodoo chile. Bo Diddley becomes anything he chooses as if changing his shape were just a matter of shifting his infectious version of 4/4 time to suit his new creation.

If many of Bo's songs are in the novelty vein, there are also some sinister suggestions lurking behind his comic camouflages. The assertive congas, menacing maracas and thick bass line are always there to remind you that he may be "messin' 'round," but he's no fool. If you can't hear his message, as he tells you on "You Can't Judge A Book By The Cover," you've got your radio turned down too low. Bo *knows* who he is under all the disguises, and if you can't tell, he spells it out for you on the flip side of his first single, "I'm A Man — Spell It M-A-N."

Although Bo was never placated with a pair of "coonskin-alligator hide" booties like the baby in "Hush Your Mouth," and has no such cousin as

*(Don Paulsen)*

Bo Diddley and his sister, the Duchess, at the Apollo Theatre

# 24

## Bo Diddley

"Little John The Conqueroo," his background is Creole and he likes to spice his songs with potent bayou potions. "Hot sauces are where my music comes from; that sound you hear is my blood beating." His sinister, sexually loaded rhythm pulses almost lethally through his ferocious voodoo love song, "Who Do You Love?" The rasping delivery against the vrooming bass, stinging guitar and menacing maracas gives the lyrics a chilling ceremonial quality:

> I got 47 miles of barbwire,
> I use a cobra snake as a necktie
> I got a brand new house on the roadside,
> Made of rattlesnake hide,
> I got a brand new chimney made on top,
> Made out of human skulls,
> Now, c'mon, take a little walk with me, Arlene,
> An' tell me, who do you love. . . .
> Got a tombstone hand and a graveyard mind,
> Just 22 and I don't mind dying,
> Who do you love,
> Yeah,
> Who do you love?*

Bo's real mother was Cajun (McDaniel is the name of his adopted family) and he was born on the Mississippi Delta, but he grew up with the pieties of the Ebenezer Baptist Church in Chicago, where his family moved when he was five. He studied classical violin with a Professor O. W. Fredericks for seven years, but got his real musical education on the street corner of Langley Avenue where he began playing for dimes and quarters at the age of thirteen. By the time he was twenty, he'd formed the Langley Avenue Jive Cats with his friend Jerome, and they began playing smokey dives like the 708 Club on Chicago's Southside. It was here, panhandling on the streets of Chicago, that Bo and Jerome developed their incredible "the dozens" raps, hilarious, outrageous exchanges of good-humored insults that formed the basis of Bo Diddley's second hit "Say Man."

By 1955 Bo and Jerome had developed their revved-up syncopated boogie and smoldering suspenseful style to the point

where they began knocking on record companies doors. The Chess brothers, who owned a small company with the slogan "Built on a Sound Foundation," had both Muddy Waters and Howlin' Wolf on their roster, as well as Chuck Berry, and were the only record company willing to listen. They recognized Bo's infectious beat as rock & roll and his "basic bottom" beat became in fact one of the most imitated in all of rock, but as he says resignedly, "you can't copyright a beat." Bo and Chuck soon became the superstars of Chess and their subsidiary Checker, and although Bo did not have as many hits, his records sold steadily into the early sixties, popular as dance sounds at high school proms and hops. Bo did not get rich from his hits but there were visible rewards, not the least of which were the new Cadillacs he kept getting every year.

Rediscovery of Bo by the English groups like the Stones and the Animals proved a mixed blessing. While he merged as a rock folk hero and toured a lot, he became unwillingly fossilized in the rock & roll Hall of Fame, although unlike many of the original stars of rock & roll, his style was not really dated, only his legend. His 1971 release, *Black Gladiator*, with Bo suited Ben Hur-like in leather and studs, showed he was still contemporary and capable of more transformations.

It was on his funky back beat, and inventive spacy sound effect guitar lines, in fact, that artists like Jimi Hendrix had learned how to expand their music into a personal, futuristic style. Like many of the white superblues guitarists of the sixties, he looks on his guitar as part gun, part souped-up hot rod and part sexual extension of himself — "this joker'll do everything but ball," he says of his most recent custom job.

Resigned to being an "immortal" in the rock cosmos, he lives in New Mexico on a ranch spilling over with concoctions salvaged from the junk yards he likes to root around in. He loves to zoom supersonically across the flat straight desert roads, and for his next incarnation or maybe just his next album, he plans to run for sheriff.

---

*"Who Do You Love" by Ellas McDaniels. Copyright © 1956 Arc Music Corp. All rights reserved. Used by permission.

# 3
# Flying Saucers Rock & Roll

## THE EVERLY BROTHERS

TIRED OF BEING BOOKED AS RELICS OF ROCK & roll, the Everly Brothers on Friday the 13th, 1973, gave their last performance. After playing at a kind of cowboy Disneyland outside of Los Angeles, Phil smashed his guitar and walked offstage and Don, somewhat inebriated, finished the set alone. It was an unexpected conclusion to the career of two of the most influential singers in rock & roll. Don and Phil, after all, had always appeared so professional, with their swirling pompadours like customized Brylcream fins above their wholesome country faces.

They'd been professionals for close to 20 years, starting with Don's own radio show at the age of seven, "The Little Donnie Show" out of Shenandoah, Iowa. For fifteen minutes every morning he sang songs like "Put My Little Shoes Away," and both Don and Phil worked with their parents on hundreds of radio stations from coast to coast. During the summers when farmers got up too early to tune in, the Everly family would work county fairs and harvest festivals.

The Everlys were living in Knoxville, Tennessee, when Don and Phil hit their teens and their parents gave up the radio shows. The two

(Collection Peter Kanze)

*(Collection Peter Kanze/Edward S. Brinker)*

The Everly Brothers meet Dick Clark

brothers headed for nearby Nashville to try to peddle their tunes. Don's first effort was a tearjerker called "Thou Shalt Not Steal." The king of guitar pickers Chet Atkins was an old family friend who later supervised their sessions and introduced them to Archie Bleyer of Cadence Records. They had cut a record for Columbia which went nowhere, "Let The Sun Keep Shining" / "Keep A Lovin' Me," but at their first session for Cadence they recorded a hit — "Bye, Bye Love." It slowly scaled the charts in the summer of 1957 and though it didn't reach the top, it stayed on the charts for an incredible six months. Four months later they got a number one

# 27

## The Everly Brothers

record — "Wake Up, Little Susie"—with its saucy, insouciant lyric, and for the next two years they had a continuous stream of hits: "This Little Girl Of Mine," "Devoted To You," "Problems," "Claudette," "Cathy's Clown," "Bird Dog," "Let It Be Me," "Take A Message To Mary," and "When Will I Be Loved."

Most of these hits were written by the songwriting team of Felice and Boudleaux Bryant, giving their sound the same kind of consistency as if they had written the songs themselves. Their style was so recognizable and so popular that many of their songs went up the charts with astounding speed. "All I Have To Do Is Dream" took only four weeks to get to the top and hung around for well over 32 weeks until it was gobbled up by Sheb Wooley's "Purple People Eater" in August of 1958. The Everlys' next howling success was "Bird Dog," their fourth million seller.

The Everly Brothers, sighing, softly crying voices seemed to drift over the surface of their songs, putting the listener into a subliminal space. As a fan magazine put it, "The Everlys put you on Cloud 9 with their naturally blended no-strain, sweet-pain vocals." It was a Teen Dream space of soft-padded whispers as close as a pillow to the dewy cheek of a pubescent lover separated from the love object by parents and resigned to a life of fantasizing. "All I Have To Do Is Dream" was a typical Everly evocation with its nervous lilting voices, soft whine, precise, piercing harmonies and reflective phrasing of words broken up into chunks, all backed up by a tasty acoustic country twanging on the guitar and a beat that kept it well within the domain of rock & roll.

The Everly Brothers were fed on pure American grain, the high, lonesome mountain harmonies of Kentucky. They dug into this background on *Songs Our Daddy Taught Us* which came out in the early sixties and in *Roots*, their beautiful country album, released in 1968, that interspersed clips from the original Everly radio shows with more recent material.

They grew up listening to the picking and strumming of family standards and spirituals. The brothers literally inherited their vocal blend, their practically identical inflections sounding almost like Les Paul and Mary Ford double-tracking. The two-part harmony they brought to rock depends on precise pitch — the two most important notes in a chord are picked out and carefully overlayed on each other. Their personal heritage reflected the white musical heritage of America, connecting them back to the early settlers of Kentucky and Virginia who brought their ancient ballads with them from England and Ireland and refined them to a thin airy purity in their mountain fastness.

The Everly Brothers' mellow harmonies evolved from family sing-alongs. Harmony was the blending of the members of a family into one voice. This act of vocal blending suggested a collective spirit and in a new setting was to become the main ingredient of the new music of the sixties and a new culture. The Beatles and later the Byrds were to use it to create a fusion between themselves and the audience. Part of the Everlys' huge success and immense staying power of their hits from 1957 to 1962 was that they appealed to a wide audience, which included not only teenagers and standard country and western listeners, but Moms and Dads who also liked their "easy listening" sound.

Considering the number of groups indebted to them, the fate of the Everly Brothers still seems particularly cruel. When the Beatles struck in 1964, Don and Phil were scarcely older than the wave of singers who inherited their style, and yet, along with the older names of early rock & roll, they were compulsorily retired to the rock Hall of Fame. On their 1971 album, *Stories We Could Tell*, Don expressed the frustration of being locked in history, underlining the outer limits of self-parody that a legend can lend itself to in the lyrics of "I'm Tired Of Singing My Song In Las Vegas."

Almost every rock harmonizing group owes its vocal style to the Everly Brothers: The Beatles (John and Paul once called themselves the Foreverly Brothers); the Byrds; The Mamas & the Papas; Simon & Garfunkel; the Hollies; Crosby, Stills, Nash & Young; not to mention the gang of C&W revival groups who sprang up in the wake of Bob Dylan's *Nashville Skyline* album. Only a couple of months before their final split Dylan had written a song for them, "Wanted Man," because, as he said, "We owe everything to these guys — they started it all."

# BUDDY HOLLY

*We're sure that all you kats and kits out in rock 'n'
roll land enjoy holidays, but we're also positive
that there's a special one that you must dig the
most. It's called a Holly-day. What's that you say?
You've never heard of it! Well, let us clue you in.
There's a certain young man by the name of Buddy
Holly — he's the lead singer of a rock 'n' roll group
called The Crickets — who's had a couple of
records cut on his own. Now, whenever you hear
Bud's tone, it makes you feel like reachin' for a
phone and declarin' a "Holly-day"!\**

*Hit Parader 1958*

   Twelve years and five months after his death
in 1959, July 3rd was declared "Buddy Holly
Memorial Day" in his hometown of Lubbock,
Texas. Holly, The Big Bopper (who had just made
it big with "Chantilly Lace") and Ritchie Valens
("Donna") died during a snowstorm when their
chartered four-seat Bonanza plane crashed on
landing. According to newspaper accounts, Holly
had decided to make a fast hop between dates so
they could get their shirts laundered.

   Buddy Holly's sudden death at the early age
of twenty-one, after a brief but meteoric rise to
stardom, led to cults similiar to those attached to

\*Reprinted by permission of Hit Parader magazine.

the late James Dean. Holly's producer Norman
Petty dug up some homemade tapes Holly had
made in high school and released them backed by
a group called the Firebirds. The ghostly effect of
the dozens of posthumous reissues on the Coral
label which kept appearing after his death did
little to dispel the beliefs of his more fanatical
followers that he was alive but hiding somewhere
in New Mexico, and it was easy enough for the
cultists to find hidden "messages" in songs like
"That'll Be The Day (That I Die)."

   Born Charles Hardin Holly in September,
1936, in the musically fertile region of west Texas,
he entered a talent contest when he was five and
by the time he was thirteen he and a friend Bob
Montgomery, formed a duo and cut a record
called "Western Pop." After a brief but
unsuccessful stab in Nashville as a studio
musician on some Everly Brothers records, he
took some homemade tapes to Norman Petty at his
studios in Clovis, New Mexico, and that's when
his career really began.

   Holly and his back-up group, The Crickets,
put out some records in a C & W vein, like "Modern
Don Juan," which did not catch on. It was only when
Petty began recording Holly as a solo artist and The
Crickets as a group with Holly as lead singer that
they suddenly began having double million sellers,
with Holly's "Words Of Love" and "Peggy Sue" (on
Coral) and with The Crickets' "That'll Be The Day,"
"Maybe Baby," "Oh Boy" and "Not Fade Away"
(Brunswick).

   "Peggy Sue," "Peggy Sue Got Married" and
("Annie's Been Working The) Midnight Shift" are
subtle allusions to and innocuous plays on the
infamous Hank Ballard and the Midnighters'
"Annie" series with their explicit sexuality.
Mainly, though, Buddy Holly dealt with the
mixed-up emotions of teenage love, eliciting
poignant, yearning pangs through his sobbing,
hiccup-syncopated vocals as in the incredible
drawn-out phrasing on "Peggy Sue" — "oh uh
Peggy, my Peggy Soo-ooh-hoo-ooh-ah-hoo-uh-
hoo-hoo" — that is so meshed with the guitar
it almost sounds as if his heart strings are
*literally* being plucked.

   English groups were the first to pick up on
Buddy Holly and a whole generation of young
English musicians was infected. On his 1958

tour of England with The Crickets, Buddy not only played his own hits but also introduced Little Richard, Bo Diddley and Chuck Berry. Holly showed a mesmerized audience that a mild-mannered, white singer could sing black man's blues and make it his own. In the audience at his concerts were John Lennon, Paul McCartney, and Eric Clapton (who later used two of The Crickets, Jerry Allison and Sonny Curtis, as back-ups on his first solo album). Six years later the Stones and a host of Cricket copycats were to take Holly's clear, clean sound and crisp drum beat and make it the basis for their own

translations. The Stones' first million seller was, in fact, Holly's "Not Fade Away" and Jagger (according to Keith Richard) even looked like Holly in the late fifties.

The greatest influence on Holly was probably Elvis, but it was Holly's vulnerable image that set him apart from typical rockabilly singers. He came on gently, though his voice had a tension, as if he were singing through clenched teeth. There was a coolness on the surface, but that almost meek Clark Kent facade with the glasses, tie and suit, seemed to be camouflaging *something* and one day that thing would be released.

# ROY ORBISON

IN THE FOUR YEARS BETWEEN "OOBY Dooby," an inane bopper that he still considers his worst song, and the wistful, wounded "Only The Lonely" in 1960, Roy Orbison's compassionate, intimate sound welled up like a tear trembling behind his perpetually shaded eyes. His songs expressed with almost excruciating pain the heartache of romance ripped apart, loss and inconsolable grief. His name and even his hometown — Wink, Texas — suggest that liquid sigh, frozen and polished into song.

Although Roy's father had picked a solid career in geology for his son, he'd always encouraged him to play guitar "as a hobby like." He got his first guitar in 1942 when he was six, and as the guys shipped out for overseas duty they'd stop by the house and do up some mournful country tunes before they said goodbye to their beloved west Texas oilfields, perhaps forever. These are Roy's first memories of music and as he says, "that's probably my life story . . . as far as people and music is concerned. A great good time was had by all before dying."

Saturday mornings he'd pedal down to the local radio station KVWC where he performed live and by his early teens he'd formed his first group, the Wink Westerners. While a student at North

Texas State University he backed up Pat Boone on his first effort, a song called "Two Hearts." It wasn't long before he left Texas as possibly the only singer to abandon geology for rock.

He formed another group to make his first stab at professional recording in 1956 at Norman Petty's studios in Clovis, New Mexico, where Buddy Holly would make his start a year later. Holly and Orbison came from the same part of Texas and not surprisingly, the sound Roy got from his custom-made Gretsch White Falcon with its Hawaiian pick-ups was very similiar to Holly's.

The two sides Orbison cut in Petty's studios, "Trying To Get You"/"Ooby Dooby," came out on an obscure label called Je-Wel. The record was eventually bought by Sun Records in Memphis, re-released and sold about a quarter of a million copies. Sam Phillips, the head of Sun at the time, was in the throes of rockabilly fever and in the habit of pulling out old Big Boy Crudup records, which Elvis had copied for his sound, then turning to his artists and saying, "That's how you're supposed to do it."

Roy could never quite get the hang of that "Sunsational" sound Sam wanted, though his Sun releases do sound a lot like Carl Perkins. His true genius, his vocal range, was never exploited at Sun, but it was there that he began developing

**Roy Orbison**

the "crying" ballad style despite the fact that the chief engineer at Sun, Jack Clements, specifically told him to stay clear of the "weepy ones." Unsuccessful at recording in the rockabilly style, Roy turned to writing songs for other people, penning huge hits like "Go Go Go (Down The Line)," for Jerry Lee Lewis, and early songs for the Everly Brothers — "Claudette," named for his wife, and "All I Have To Do Is Dream."

By the time he left Sun for Monument Records in 1960, he had not been performing or recording for close to three years. In the meantime, he had refined his voice into a crystal instrument with which he can hit E above high C, the peak that Caruso was famous for. With this range his pained words cracked into that cry which became a metaphor for every broken heart, a sound that seemed to puncture at the same time it healed. The ethereal climb of his voice which was to become his trademark appeared in 1961 on "Running Scared," his first number one hit.

For the next three years, he had a string of monster hits: "Crying," "Dream Baby," "Mean Woman Blues," "O Pretty Woman." In 1963 he got top billing on an English tour with the Beatles, but the hits were beginning to trail off, and two years later he moved on to MGM, where he had a few minor hits with "Crawling Back" and "Cry Softly, Lonely One," and starred in his only movie, *The Fastest Gun Alive*.

In spite of his fall from the charts, Roy Orbison has inspired a fanatical worldwide following, a congregation of wounded hearts who identify almost totally with the intensely personal pain he projects and for which he found the perfect equivalent at the top of his vocal range. His own life has been filled with tragedies enough, from the motorcycle accident that killed his wife Claudette in June 1966 to the death of his two children two years later in a fire. His songs are the matter of his life seen through the Frozen Tear. As he explained to Greg Mitchell in *Crawdaddy* magazine:

> The story behind "Crying" was, I was dating this girl and then we broke up — this must have been two or three years before I wrote the song. I went to the barbershop to get a haircut and I looked across the street and there was this girl that I had split up with. I wanted to go over and say, "Let's forget

*(Collection Alan Betrock)*

> about what happened and carry on." But I was very stubborn. So I got in the car and drove on down the street and got about two blocks away and said, "Boy you really made a mistake. You didn't play that right at all." I would say that I had tears in my eyes — I'll go that far — but whether I was physically crying or just crying inside, is the same thing. This is what I saw: I was alright for a while, I could smile for a while, I was feeling pretty good until I saw you last night.*

# GENE VINCENT

THE SECRET WAS ECHO, "FLUTTER" ECHO as it was known, and for the rockabilly sound of the fifties it was indispensable. Guided by visions of a cracking snare and country-oriented treble, Capitol Records had instituted a talent contest in 1956 with the express purpose of discovering the next Elvis Presley. After sorting through over 250 entrants, they chose Gene Vincent and "Be-Bop-A-Lula" as their brightest hope.

In a way, they were right. "Be-Bop-A-Lula," reflected and shimmered in a sea of echo, would prove a stunning debut for the young Vincent, instantly establishing him as a top ten artist. But he had none of Presley's animal grace, nor was he able to build on his initial success, creating instead an odyssey of personal and public torment that would haunt him for the rest of his life.

Gene had never had it easy. Born on the outskirts of Norfolk, Virginia, on February 11, 1935, Vincent Eugene Craddock was a poor boy who once used to shoot swans illegally for food. He dropped out of high school at fifteen, lying about his age to join the navy. Sent to Korea, he sustained a motorcycle accident that was to cripple his left leg. He refused medical suggestions to amputate the limb, and endured a limp and constant pain throughout his career.

Returning to Norfolk, Vincent resolutely set his mind to music, landing a spot on WGMS' "Country Show Time." It was at the station that he first heard about Capitol's search, and accompanied by a friend, Donald Graves, took an early train to Los Angeles. Though "Be-Bop-A-Lula" was supposedly written while perusing a Little Lulu comic along the ride, the truth is that co-writer "Sheriff" Bill Davis had paved Vincent's way by sending a demonstration disc of the song to Ken Nelson, an artist and repertoire man then at Capitol. The record eventually sold over three million copies, helped in no small part by Gene's rendition of it in the film, *The Girl Can't Help It*.

Vincent found his true focus in live performance, where he not only used his disability to advantage but often exploited it to the fullest. Unable to move in normal fashion, he would assume a rigid stance before the microphone, clutching at it as if for life. Dressed in black leather, a gaunt face chiseled in triangular edges, he presented a stark and tension-laden image, funneling his private damages into an emotive, sweat-stained performance that went far beyond light entertainment.

He was backed in this theatrical display by the Blue Caps, who had borrowed their name from President Eisenhower's omnipresent golf attire. They were all Virginians, and though none were as spiritually committed as Vincent, they showed little hesitation in leaping on the bandwagon, as their colorful names attest: lead guitarist Galloping Cliff Gallup, rhythm guitarist Wee Willie Williams, Jack Neal on bass and drummer Be-Bop Harrell. There was actually no reason to complain; at his height, Gene was working well over 300 dates a year, with mob scenes the rule rather than the exception.

If the hits weren't coming as quickly, Vincent's recording quality seldom flagged. He was working within a formula, but his enthusiasm was infectious, his voice an impeccable tenor instrument, his band excellent and dynamic musicians. The heavy-breathing "Woman Love," the B-side of "Be-Bop-A-Lula," resulted in a conviction for public lewdness and obscenity by the Virginia State Court (Gene, on the road, was convicted in absentia) and it was also banned by the BBC in England; others — like "Bluejean Bop" or "Lotta Lovin' " — caught the cruising essence of teenage life. Capitol began experimenting with Vincent after his early boom period, complicating arrangements and smoothing his approach, but it's safe to say they did more harm than good.

As his popularity faded in America, Vincent, like many other rockers, discovered a new audience in Europe. He toured regularly there in the late fifties and early sixties, having an immeasurable impact on a nascent generation

of pop fans. It was on one of these trans-Atlantic visits that he rode with his close friend Eddie Cochran on the latter's ill-fated journey to the airport. Vincent recalled later that he had taken a sleeping pill before the trip, and his relaxed state had probably saved his life.

He moved to London in the early sixties, and continued touring the Continent. He stuck steadfastly to the type of music which brought him to fame, guaranteeing the loyalty of his followers but inhibiting any chances for possible growth. Increasingly his stage appearances became erratic, fraught with psychic peril, and it was obvious that Gene was deteriorating both mentally and physically. Never strong, he seemed to be leaving a part of himself behind when he finished with a show; he became drained, nervous, overweight. Capitol quietly allowed his contract to expire, and in 1967 Gene returned to America for a leg operation.

For a while he dropped out of sight. Rumors abounded; he was working in a gas station somewhere in the South; he had changed his name; he was dead. He resurfaced in 1969 on the heels of the rock & roll revival, but intensely proud, Gene never liked the atmosphere of finale that surrounded such events. In a major comeback attempt, he recorded a misconceived country album for Elektra, and followed it by a surprisingly strong outing on Kama Sutra titled *Gene Vincent*. Braced by the Sir Douglas Quintet, the record brought Vincent powerfully into the present while not losing sight of his considerable history. Despite promise it didn't sell, and Gene retreated into depression.

He began drinking. On October 12, 1971, while visiting his family, Vincent died of a bleeding ulcer in Newall, California.

# EDDIE COCHRAN

HE LIKED TO GO TO THE MOVIES, PREFERABLY the drive-ins, with a load of his old friends and a six-pack of beer. A crack pistol shot, he was able to snuff matches with a Buntline at a hundred paces. He was five feet, eight inches tall, one hundred and forty-five pounds. He had small feet, size 6, and had a problem buying shoes. His favorite food was corn bread and

*(United Press International)*

beans. He liked to be home with his family, never enjoyed traveling that much, turned to the guitar for "companionship" when he moved to California. Dick Clark once forgot his name in the act of introducing him. His old manager and producer, Jerry Capehart, remembers that "there was nothing soft or fragile about him; he was a red-blooded American boy."

With more than fifteen years gone, the pieces of Eddie Cochran's life slide slowly into place. His career was relatively brief and understated, yet his legacy has held its own, an image of adolescence at bay that seems unchanged with the passage of time. Where others would sing of love's pain or pleasure, Cochran would concentrate on what being a part of teenage America was about, a unique spokesman who captured his moment so perfectly that the only way to fully recreate it would be to simply go back and play some (any) of his songs. His main character, put upon, always nagged, *bothered,* appeared trapped in a cage, his way toward freedom — via cars, girls, another five minutes of sleep — continually blocked off.

Eddie was born on October 3, 1938, in Albert Lea, Minnesota, the youngest of five children; the Cochran family was originally from Oklahoma City, Oklahoma, and he would always refer to it as his hometown. He began playing the guitar at the age of twelve, digging deeper into it when the family moved to California in 1953. By the fall of 1955 he had met Jerry Capehart at a music store in Bell Gardens, an association he would maintain for the rest of his professional career. Capehart, an aspiring songwriter, had been looking for someone to cut dubs for him. Eddie had been working the usual series of local shows in a duo with friend Hank Cochran (no relation), doing a mild form of rockabilly music. Shortly after, the Cochran Brothers (as they called themselves) went into the studio with Capehart to record their first single, "Tired and Sleepy," for the Ekko label.

It did poorly, and Hank soon left California for Nashville, where he would become a well-respected performer and songwriter ("Little Bitty Tear"). Eddie was intrigued with making a solid transition to rock & roll and stayed on with Capehart. The two collaborated for a while, and Eddie released another single, "Skinny Jim," for the Crest extension of their publishing company. By the beginning of 1956, Capehart was ready to go knocking on doors. Rock & roll was starting to become recognized as a commercially viable force, and most companies were frantically scrambling for competitive talent. Cochran met the president of Liberty Records, Si Waronker, and it was love at first sight.

Coincidentally, Eddie had also been offered a surprise part in *The Girl Can't Help It,* one of the best and most influential rock movies of the decade. It was originally thought that Liberty would use the song from the film, "Twenty Flight Rock," as Eddie's debut single. However, before it was released, the company came up on a John D. Loudermilk tune called "Sittin' In The Balcony," and after talking it over, Capehart and Cochran decided to go ahead. Hearthrob material, it was an immediate hit in the fall of 1956.

Eddie wasted no time in going on tour, meeting Dick Clark in Philadelphia not too many weeks after American Bandstand first went on the national air, hitting the top city deejays (Cleveland's Bill Randall, Howard Miller in Chicago, Boston's Joe Smith and Barry Kay out in Pittsburgh), making friends and accumulating fans.

The follow-up single, "Mean When I'm Mad," failed to come up to expectations, and when their next, "(Baby Let's Go To A) Drive-In Show," panned as only a regional hit, Eddie and Jerry began to feel worried. "Nothing really happened record-wise," recalls Capehart. "We were looking for some kind of feeling, but it just never came around in the right way." The only bright spot during 1957 was the release of *Untamed Youth,* a feature film starring Mamie Van Doren with Eddie in a prominent role. He can also be seen in *Go Johnny Go* (with Chuck Berry) and *Bop Girl.*

In March of 1958, he visited Capehart at the latter's Park Sunset apartment in Hollywood. They had a session scheduled for the next day,

but by the end of the night realized thay had nothing on their hands worth recording. Still, Eddie had a new guitar lick which started Capehart musing: "I knew that there had been a lot of songs about summer, but none about the hardships of summer. Of all the seasons, there'd never been a blues song about summer . . ." Forty-five minutes later, the tune was done. They went into the studio the next day, Eddie dubbing in a sonorous Kingfish voice, old school friend Connie "Guybo" Smith working the bass underneath. "Summertime Blues" was released in May, hit the charts in June and stayed there all summer.

Its success defined Cochran's personality, the promise of *"I'm gonna raise a fuss / I'm gonna raise a holler"* converted to *"No dice, son, you gotta work late. . . ."* * He followed it with a thematic extension, "C'mon Everybody," where the narrator brazenly invites his friends over for an illicit party, only to remain in constant peril of having his parents return home. Still, he shrugs it off. *Who cares,* bare feet a-slappin' on the floor, the chorus rolling with a sweep of acoustic guitar.

Stardom never seemed to have much of an effect on Eddie. Even after "C'mon Everybody" solidified his reputation, he seldom enjoyed being on the road. He had formed a band, the Kelly Four (so named because of Cochran's Irish ancestry), and began to be seen with a "steady" girl, Sharon Sheeley, who had written "Poor Little Fool" for Ricky Nelson. But the tours were long, immensely tiring one-nighters connected by a series of buses, trains, occasionally airplanes. Originally scheduled to join the tragic final circuit of Buddy Holly, Ritchie Valens and the Big Bopper, he took their deaths especially hard. Buddy, in particular, had been a close friend, and Cochran recorded "Three Stars" as a tribute. Increasingly, Eddie began to look forward to settling down, to getting married, to relaxing with his guitar and studio work.

There was to be another tour, though — this time to Europe and specifically England. Leaving in February, 1960, featuring Gene Vincent and English rocker Billy Fury, it blew the lid off the Continent. In Italy, they placed his face on national magazines opposite Brando, daring you to choose one over the other. In England, the fever was even more intense, front page news, the caravan followed everywhere by stricken fans (George Harrison, for one, trailing Cochran from town to town; for another, Georgie Fame on keyboards in his back-up band). By the time Sharon came over to join him in March, the tour had become a triumphal procession, snatching up audiences and leaving them dazed, irrevocably confirmed and sworn to the faith.

Cochran left for the airport on April 17, 1960, anxious to return home to visit his mother before returning for another ten weeks. "After this," he'd phoned her, "I won't have to go on the road anymore." He'd been visibly ill-at-ease lately; Sharon had found him in his room the week before playing Buddy Holly records, staring at the phonograph until she cautioned, "You'll only hurt yourself, honey." There were prophetic dreams, cryptic statements. He sat in the middle in the taxi, between Gene Vincent and Sharon. The car skidded on wet pavement, colliding with a lamp post by the side of the road. Eddie sustained multiple head injuries; he died several hours later without regaining consciousness, a legend once a star.

# DUANE EDDY

DUANE EDDY EARNED HIS MILLION DOLLARS worth of twang. Rejecting instrumental displays, speed or ornament, he concentrated totally on the audio signal of a vibrating string, passed through pick-up and amplifier, electronically processed and exaggerated. In so doing, he took the sound of rock & roll guitar and taught it a voice. It would be little wonder that his billing always listed "Twangy Guitar" as an equal member of the show, followed only then by his back-up band, The Rebels.

Before him, guitar virtuosos had been grafted from other musics — blues, country, jazz. A renowned Les Paul had paved the way toward insistent use of gadgetry, yet Paul was also a painstaking musician, a craftsman buoyantly set on expanding the tonal range of his instrument. Duane was the heir, accepting all technical breakthroughs as natural, building his fame not on prowess but on sound. If he could really play, his records hold little indication; nor did it matter. Far more than any other, he was the first pure rock & roll guitarist.

He began learning the instrument as a child in Corning, New York, where he'd been born on April 26, 1938. Chet Atkins was his long-standing idol, and young Duane was also interested in American frontier history and folk music, both fascinations given a boost when his family moved to Phoenix, Arizona, when he was thirteen. He left Coolidge High School there in 1954, and began playing for clubs and dances, meeting Lee Hazlewood, a local KCKY disc jockey, song writer, publisher and record producer; Al Casey, whose band he eventually joined; and manager Al Wilde.

Eddy had developed a technique of playing on the bottom strings of the guitar, echoing and fattening the sound with vibrato, and both he and Hazlewood recognized its potential use. They recorded "Movin' And Groovin' " as a demo in Hazlewood's studio and shipped it to the Philadelphia-based Jamie label in early 1958.

Jamie president Harry Finfer called in west coast producer Lester Sill to smooth off the rough edges, and in March of that year Eddy found himself with his first hit. It set the standard for his future releases. Over a muddy rhythm section, trading lines with a blaring saxophone, Duane played a deeply resonant single string melody, bending each note so that his solo swayed camel-back to its conclusion.

Duane Eddy on the set of *A Thunder of Drums,* his screen debut

*(Collection Peter Kanze)*

"The twang's the thang," he'd say if asked, and when he became a regular on the Dick Clark Show, it certainly appeared so.

Except for mood, the pattern varied little over the years. "Rebel Rouser," true to its title, added a series of Confederate whoops and hollers to its gunfire handclapping, notching Eddy's largest early seller. "Cannonball" exchanged claps for finger snaps; "The Lonely One" explored twang's sadder qualities. "Because They're Young" (from the movie of the same name, based on the novel *Harrison High*) featured lush orchestration, and he also had a small part in the film. Throughout, Eddy never diversified his approach, dogged in faithful execution. Despite such unflinching simplicity, his flair for writing melody kept his records sounding fresh, instantly recognizable and ingratiating. In 1959 and 1960, *Cash Box* twice named Duane Outstanding Instrumentalist of the Year.

Sill and Hazlewood helped him along by a creative use of studio techniques, designing landscapes to complement and direct his guitar. Duane never sang, a seeming handicap that hardly slowed his popularity. He traveled with Steve Douglas on sax, drummer Mike Bermani, and Ike Clanton, bass. For recording purposes, the group was expanded to his old friend Al Casey on piano and brother Corky Casey on rhythm guitar. Hazlewood would move to Hollywood in the sixties where he'd remember

the innate lure of lower strings to create the walking bass of Nancy Sinatra's "Boots."

Duane kept up the pace for a number of years, but by 1961 it was apparent that his sound had been assimilated to such a degree that it was no longer novel. With the urgings of Sill and Hazlewood, he moved to RCA-Victor and once more found chart happiness. "The Ballad of Paladin" (or, as Jamie noted when they attempted to cash in by rereleasing an early album, "Have Twangy Guitar, Will Travel") brought him back to prominence, and the double-diced "Dance With The Guitar Man" and "Boss Guitar" affixed more luster. "Guitar Man" introduced The Rebelettes, a female vocal chorus that Duane utilized heavily on his later recordings.

By then, he had surely outlasted his time. Already he was being instrumentally replaced by a horde of surf and guitar bands that were using him much as he had used the innovations of Les Paul. He attempted to compete with them briefly in "Your Baby's Gone Surfin'" and "Son Of Rebel Rouser," but he was chronologically mismatched. He ran through a stream of labels, surfacing nostalgically in 1971 to play a cameo twangy guitar on B. J. Thomas' "Rock And Roll Lullaby," at other times hiring himself out as a club musician behind song stylists. In 1975 Duane made a surprise comeback on the British Top Ten with "Play Me Like You Play Your Guitar," a hopeful augury of things to come.

# 4
# Stormy Weather

## THE R & B VOCAL GROUP

FOR THE BLACK VOCAL GROUPS OF THE fifties, rock & roll was the great emancipator. Stolidly confined to the rhythm and blues charts at the outset of the decade, they embarked on a series of accommodations and compromises which would eventually bring them to the heartland of mass appeal and taste. This absorption was not won easily, nor can it account for the thousands of rhythm and blues combinations whose careers were caught and held within the dynamics of the struggle. A solo artist might slip through on the force of his individual charisma and charm. Groups, on the other hand, diffused personality, often at the expense of racial stereotype, steepening and lengthening their uphill climb.

The postwar mood of the black vocal group was split into a pair of incompatible viewpoints. Gospel, primarily, and the funkier forms of jazz and blues, were directed solely at a race audience, while buffed, inoffensive harmonizers like the Mills Brothers and the Ink Spots provided soothing entertainment for the pop market. Such a rigidly artificial separation was certain to break down sooner or later, and so it did when the "bird" groups arose to fill the

nesting gap, the preliminary rustle of the Ravens.

Though the Ravens' material was mostly in a mild, pop vein (their first major R & B hit was, ironically, "Old Man River"), they set the *basso profundo* lead of Jimmy Ricks against the angelic high falsetto tenor of Maithe Marshall to create an air of depth and mystery previously unexplored. Their "new sound" was eagerly imitated and expanded, and in late 1948 Sonny Til(ghman) debuted his Orioles at the Apollo Theatre in New York. Nicknamed the Vibranairs when they would practice singing on Baltimore streetcorners, they were the first successful rhythm and blues synthesists. Raved *Cash Box*: "A new vocal quintette that speeds right into the top spot of the race disks this week and is really something to listen to . . . featuring a new, young tenor, Sonny Til, who spoons the lyrics of 'Barbra Lee' to a fare-thee-well . . . This disk's got 'it!' "

"It" made the Orioles the top group in the nation by 1950. With minimal accompaniment, they enveloped a cloudy harmony, introduced by chimes, a churchlike uplift so impossible to ignore that "Cryin' In The Chapel" edged its

Sonny Til of the Orioles

(Collection Peter Kanze)

way into the Pop Top 20 in September 1953, becoming the first R & B vocal group record to do so. Their earlier versions of "I Cover The Waterfront" and "What Are You Doing New Year's Eve?" were of equal breathless pitch, and until the death of guitarist Tommy Gaither in a one-nighter car accident caused them to withdraw from long-distance traveling, they were the pre-eminent model for the legions already lined outside record company doors, with names like the Swallows, the Wrens, the Robins, the Crows, the Cardinals, the Larks.

One of those watching this excitement with more than casual interest was Cleveland disc jockey Alan Freed. Leo Mintz, owner of the city's largest record shop, had told him of the sudden growth in sales of his R & B records, and soon Freed was opening his WJW show with the wailing theme of Freddie Mitchell's "Moondog Boogie," emphasizing its steady two-four by the smash of a hand against a telephone book. Freed wasn't the only outlet for rhythm and blues — there was a cross-country radio underground with such lights as "Jocko" Henderson and the original "Dr. Jive" — but Freed gave the music a new description, hoping

to remove it from racial classification, beaming his signal at black and white.

The catch-all phrase — rock & roll — did the trick. Morris Levy of Roulette Records attempted to place a copyright on it but gave up after two weeks "because it would have meant filing a thousand lawsuits." Freed always claimed it was more Mintz's idea than his, a combination of two R & B slang phrases perhaps borrowed from an obscurely titled record by Billy Mathews and the Balladeers in 1949. "Only the other day," Freed said in an interview from the late fifties, "Leo called me up and told me 'I had the foresight and you're making all the money.' " That he was. In March of 1952, Freed had staged a Moondog Ball in the Cleveland Arena; instead of the expected 10,000 capacity, over 30,000 poured through the gates and caused the show to be canceled. It was his first riot.

Before expanding to concert promotions and New York's flagship WINS, Freed took time out to involve himself in the record business. Later, the tangled favors of this period would recoil against him in the payola scandals, in which his alleged financial involvement in many of the records he helped make hits would return to ruin him. In the atmosphere of a witch hunt, arrested for "anarchy" and "inciting to riot" (in Boston), Freed maintained that money or no, he never played a record he didn't like. His discovery of the Moonglows in 1952 makes such a truth apparent.

The Moonglows was originally begun by Harvey Fuqua (whose uncle, Charlie Fuqua, had been a member of the Ink Spots), who gathered several of his friends from Louisville, Kentucky, and called them the Crazy Sounds. While touring the Midwest, the group — Bobby Lester, Alexander Graves, Prentiss Barnes, guitarist Buddy Johnson, and Fuqua — called up Freed for an over-the-phone audition. He liked their sound, changed their name to the Moonglows to fit his motif, helped them sign with the local Champagne Records and wrote both sides of their initial release, "I Just Can't Tell No Lie"/"I've Been Your Dog (Ever Since I've Been Your Man)." Though unsuccessful, the interchange of leads between Lester and Fuqua

The Moonglows

would be duplicated when the group later went into Chess Records' studios to cut their first major hit, "Sincerely."

Before that could happen, the Moonglows had to undergo seasoning. Freed brought them to Chicago and the pioneering Chance label, where they shared recording quarters with the Flamingos and the Spaniels. Chance would shut its doors in December 1954, but not before all three of the groups established themselves on the R & B charts to stay.

The Moonglows offered impassioned ballads on the order of "Just A Lonely Christmas" and "Secret Love," aptly backing them with "jump" B-sides ("Ooh Rockin' Daddy") in the standard of the day. The Flamingos, who had organized at a Chicago picnic under the guidance of brothers Jake and Zeke Carey (the additional members were Solly McElroy, Johnny Carter and Paul Wilson), glided to fame on "Golden Teardrops"/"Carried Away." The Spaniels (James "Pookie" Hudson, Opal Courtney Jr., Gerald Gregory, Ernest Warren and Willis C. Jackson), came from nearby Gary, Indiana, to open their first (and only) recording session for Chance with "Baby It's You." The restrained cooing of the "bird" groups gave way to a throaty harmony, instruments nearly inaudible on the slower sides, hot-blooded and frenetic on the faster ones. The R & B vocal group had found its voice.

Now they could deal with the problem of how to showcase that sound in a larger context. The Moonglows (still under Freed's direction) and the Flamingos signed with Chess Records, where they not only benefited from a better system of distribution (the Chess brothers, Leonard and Phil, were not averse to piling records in the backs of their cars and bringing them personally to one-stops and retail stores), but also signaled the beginning of a consciously commercial direction in their music. The Moonglows' debut record for the label, "Sincerely," was a sophisticated and polished rhythm and blues outing, promptly covered in an if-you-can't-beat-'em-join-'em pop version by the McGuire Sisters. Though this latter would eventually sell over a million copies, the Moonglows still managed to top the 300,000 sales mark. They became the most richly harmonic of the black groups — their blend brought to the high gloss of a fine classic car, touching embellished perfection in the "Ten Commandments Of Love."

The Flamingos' prominence was not as broad-based as the Moonglows in this period — they would reach their pop prominence with George Goldener's End label and "I Only Have Eyes For You" in the later fifties — but the Checker sides ("The Vow," "I'll Be Home," among others) found great favor. The Spaniels had moved to Vee Jay (joining the Dells and the Eldorados) immediately after Chance, their "Goodnight Sweetheart Goodnight" also outlasting a plague of cover versions to achieve some pop crossover. Their magnificent reading of "Stormy Weather" remains a collector's favorite, as do the intense gospel blow-notes of "You Gave Me Peace Of Mind."

As the fifties progressed, the R & B vocal group spun off into uncountable permutations. By 1955, recognizable city styles could be noted and easily identified. Philadelphia, through the Castelles ("Over A Cup Of Coffee") and Capris ("God Only Knows"), lavished the art of the falsetto tenor, carrying over to Detroit's Nolan Strong and the Diablos for "The Wind," one of the most immaterially vaporous records ever made. West coast groups seemed to kick their heels in a more bluesy manner, exemplified by the Four Deuces' strutting "W-P-L-J" (white port and lemon juice) and the Medallions' ode to a "Buick 59" (in 1954!).

New York's Harlem spawned a myriad of stunning ensembles. The Harptones, led by Willie Winfield, sculpted one of R & B's most enduring standards in "Sunday Kind Of Love," as did the Cadillacs with "Gloria." The Solitaires were a virtual supergroup, consolidating members from the Vocaleers, the Crows, the Concords, the Fi-Tones and the Mellomoods to formulate their series of epic sides, including the original version of "Walkin' Along" and a heavenly choir'd "The Angels Sang."

With such an abundance of talent, the black vocal group could no longer be regarded as an esoteric strain on the charts. Two combinations in particular, the Five Keys (featuring Rudy West) and the Platters (the expressive lead of Tony Williams), showed off the style's pop possibilities and maturation. Both had formed in the early fifties, the Keys out of Newport News, Virginia, the Platters from Los Angeles, the latter crafted and promoted by the dominant managerial figure of Buck Ram. Each had much success within the rhythm and blues world, but their shifts to Capitol and Mercury, respectively,

(Collection Peter Kanze)

The Five Keys

added an aura of graceful class to their recordings. The Keys peaked early, in 1956, with "Out Of Sight, Out Of Mind" and "Close Your Eyes," but the Platters lasted until the early sixties, when Williams decided to leave the group. Under Ram's guidance, their harmony tinged with Zola Taylor's feminine high registers, they were consistent hitmakers: "The Great Pretender," "Twilight Time," "My Prayers," "Smoke Gets In Your Eyes" and many others.

It was a sound equally accessible to sentimental adults and teenagers, yet the message of R & B in its more juvenile manifestation was probably no different from most rock & roll. The west coast "Earth Angel" by the Penguins and its east coast counterpart, "Gee" by the Crows, were early forerunners of the black doo-wop sound, but the Five Satins, from New Haven, Connecticut, put the 1956 seal on the style with the milestone "In The Still Of The Night." They'd begun in 1954 as the Scarlets, on Bobby Robinson's Red Robin label. After moderate acceptance, Scarlets' alumni Fred Parris and Richard Freeman added Bill Baker, Lewis Peebles and Parris' brother, Dick, to record "I Remember." Al Silver, who owned Herald-Ember Records in New York, heard the master, leased it and changed the name when he saw people going into record shops, asking for it by the first line of the song.

The singing was lighter, calculatedly adolescent, less thoughtful and more obviously catchy. The blurred gospel harmonies were schematized into a steady *shoo-doop-a-shoo-be-doop* — bridge, chorus and falsetto finish distilling the best of R & B formula. The Five Satins would never have another song with the universal invocation of "In The Still Of The Night"; by then, it didn't much matter. Groups like the Channels, the Heartbeats, the Cleftones and the Chantels were waiting their turn before the microphone. The golden age was at once over and begun.

*(Collection Peter Kanze)*

The Platters

*(Collection Ed Engel)*

The Five Satins

# THE DRIFTERS

IN EARLY 1953, BARITONE DAVID BALDWIN drew a slip of paper from a dish containing possible names for a vocal group. His old friend and once fellow member of the gospel Mount Lebanon Singers had just sent a telegram from California advising that he was leaving Billy Ward and the Dominos, asking for help in forming a similar combination. Baldwin gathered Will "Chick" Anderson, James "Wrinkle" Johnson and David "Little Dave" Baughan, and had them each jot down their choices for a likely title. When Clyde McPhatter arrived back in New York, he assumed control of a newly christened Drifters. None might have guessed that the casual appellation would not only outlive their own contributions to the group, but would go on to become a virtual symbol of the changing fortunes of pop rhythm and blues over the next two decades.

The Drifters' longevity spans a complex web of style, personnel and, at times, entire restructures, tied together by a single record label. At present, there are no less than three attractions claiming to be lineal descendants of the original Drifters, and all can back their inheritance with some degree of justification. Thirty-two individual vocalists, five guitarists, and well over a hundred recordings have passed through the Drifters' ranks, an odyssey that inserts their name in nearly every corner of rock & roll. They were not so much a group as an institution, a trademark of quality that attracted the best musical hopes of their several generations.

McPhatter was a product of the church, his father a Baptist preacher in Durham, North Carolina, before moving north to New Jersey during World War II. As a teenager, Clyde sang professionally with a quartet called the Mount Lebanon Singers, appearing in churches and in group competitions such as those held frequently in the Golden Gate Ballroom, the "Madison Square Garden of Harlem," where they would lock spiritual horns with the Selah Jubilee Singers, the Brooklyn Crusaders, the Harmony Five and others. Billy Ward, on the lookout for a lead singer with the pure tenor

tones of the Inkspots' Billy Kenny, asked McPhatter if he'd like to audition for a more secular group modeled on the popular "birds" of the day, the Ravens and the Orioles. Despite parental objection, Clyde joined Ward and his Dominos; by July of 1952, they were one of the top attractions in the country, had appeared at Carnegie Hall as well as the Apollo Theatre, and were the reigning stars of Federal Records in Cincinnati.

It wasn't gospel, and it wasn't blues, but another of the seeming hybrids that marked the birth of a new species. The Dominos are best remembered today for their raucous 1951 rendition of "Sixty Minute Man," but equally noteworthy was McPhatter's trilling lead on "Have Mercy Baby" and their immaculately paced versions of "The Bells" and "When The Swallows Come Back To Capistrano." Such an abundance of talent was bound to lead to internal disputes, and after a clash over billing and finances, McPhatter began training Jackie Wilson (later to become a star in his own right) as his replacement.

Ahmet Ertegun and Jerry Wexler of Atlantic Records had been watching Clyde for some time, and seized this opportunity to sign him and whatever group he wanted to bring along. They had in mind a more upbeat sound than the label's other popular rhythm and blues act, the Clovers, but when the first edition of the Drifters proved too light and buoyant for this approach, the group was hastily reassembled. Clyde picked two brothers, Gerhart and Andrew "Bubba" Thrasher, tenor and baritone respectively, whom he'd known from the Golden Gate Ballroom as the Thrasher Wonders, and Bill Pinckney, a utility voice assigned to formal bass when the original choice, Willie Ferbie, became too ill to continue.

This, then, was the classic Drifters. Though the sessions were carefully preplanned, Ertegun and Wexler's involvement was more supervisory than constricting, and they allowed the group as much room as needed. The mixture of blues and gospel was tightened even further than it had

The Drifters in 1964

been with the Dominos, a saucy strut to the rhythm section, a fragile lilt in McPhatter's voice. They were effectively shut off from the white pop market by programing barriers, except for the surprise seasonal appearance of "White Christmas," but their "Money Honey" and "Honey Love" made them immediate hits on the R & B circuit by early 1954. The songs were earthy, supple and sexy, and the Drifters fattened their appeal with an intricately choreographed stage show complete with strobe-like flashing lights.

Clyde was drafted in late 1954, a common interruption for those years, and Atlantic took advantage of his forced absence to begin changing him over into a solo artist. This left the Drifters without a leader, and for a time they utilized David Baughan, whose voice bore an uncanny resemblance to McPhatter's and could be counted on to faithfully reproduce the group's hits in live performance. He was soon replaced by Johnny Moore of the Hornets, himself drafted before he could exert much influence. This instability did nothing to help the Drifters' popularity, and manager George Treadwell began hiring and firing at will,

adding to the decline. McPhatter, stationed in nearby Buffalo, was meanwhile free to pursue his own ends. After his discharge in 1956, he came back to "Treasure Of Love" and undiminished glory, a far cry from his later decline and tragic death in 1972.

The Drifters' problem was more than transitory. Black music was undergoing great internal stresses, growing pains to meet the new pop demand for R & B, and even Atlantic had cast a hopeful eye toward the wider audience. Treadwell might have realized this, lacking confidence in the group's potential, or he might have just gotten tired of their apparent liability. As he owned the copyright on the Drifters' name, as well as a ten-year contract with the Apollo for their twice-yearly appearance, he fired what was left of the original Drifters after a show there in June 1958, leaving them for a group on the same bill, the Crowns.

It couldn't have been youth that Treadwell had in mind. The (Five) Crowns went back nearly as far as the Drifters, having existed in various permutations since 1952. Dock Greene and James "Poppa" Clark had been with the group from the beginning, while Elsberry Hobbs,

## The Drifters

Charlie Thomas and Benjamin Earl Nelson joined relatively late; Crowns' manager Lover Patterson had discovered Nelson singing in his father's restaurant in 1957. When the Crowns became the new Drifters, Benjamin changed his name to Ben E. King, after a favorite uncle.

For all intents and purposes, they effectively were the Drifters. Treadwell sent them (minus "Poppa," who was unmoved by the offer) on the road for seasoning, mixing the Drifters' old hits with newer group originals. When they came back to record, Atlantic placed the group under the veteran care of writers-producers Jerry Leiber and Mike Stoller, and with a single song, recorded at their first session, the ex-Crowns fulfilled their promise.

The use of strings on "There Goes My Baby" was not quite their primary introduction in a rhythm and blues context as is sometimes believed (the Orioles had used violins up to nine years previously, while the more recent — albeit white — Skyliners had crossed the charts with a symphonic "Since I Don't Have You"), but this spectral blend of Rimsky-Korsakov and Ravel was far more than basic sweetening. Centered around a strumming Brazilian rhythm known as the baion, Stoller later remembered they were pressed into experimentation because the session was going so badly. The resultant record always sounded to Stoller as if he were hearing two stations at once on the radio. Atlantic released "There Goes My Baby" half-heartedly, and was properly amazed when it broke into the top three in late summer of 1959.

The Drifters were a pop group now, and Leiber-Stoller acted accordingly. They drew on the best of New York's songwriters, first from Jerome "Doc" Pomus and Mort Shuman, later from Don Kirshner's Aldon stable. Pomus-Shuman supplied the Drifters' with "This Magic Moment" and "Save The Last Dance For Me," Latin rhythms with an overlay of romanticism, and the Aldon writers, who wrote best when given a specific outline, followed suit. Cynthia Weil and Barry Mann contributed "On Broadway" and "I'll Take You Home," and Gerry Goffin and Carole King came

up with their string of hits ("Up On The Roof," "Some Kind Of Wonderful," "When My Little Girl Is Smiling"). Compared with the spontaneous quality of the earlier Drifters, this was pop at its most calculated, filled with the hum and hymn of the city. As Leiber and Stoller worked over complementary textures and percussion, they were watched intently by a young apprentice named Phil Spector.

Spector would receive his chance when Ben E. King decided to go solo in 1961, taking with him the baion and a Spector-Leiber Drifters' vehicle, "Spanish Harlem." The group itself cautiously substituted Rudy Lewis from the gospel Clara Ward Singers to fill the void left by King, but this time there was none of the slippage associated with McPhatter's loss. The Drifters were far too well-established, their records polished to a degree that anyone might have sung them, and Lewis was an obvious talent. He led them through their greatest success; when he died suddenly in 1964, Johnny Moore, an ex-Drifter, returned to the fold and assumed his stance.

There had been other transfers as well. Leiber and Stoller eased themselves out of Atlantic to concentrate on their own publishing company and Red Bird label, handing the Drifters' reins to Bert Berns. Berns was an *aficionado* of Latin rhythms, and had little trouble retaining the group's distinctive sound, perhaps appending just the slightest hint of melancholia, the bittersweet ambience of "Under The Boardwalk." Recorded at the first session following Lewis' death, its immediacy was the closest the Drifters would come to their ancient gospel beginnings. By 1969, they were practically disbanded.

Or were they? Bill Pinckney has an "Original" Drifters in circulation; Charlie Thomas also has a Drifters, and he assures that they do "all the songs, all the hits." In 1974, Johnny Moore's Drifters scored a top ten smash in Britain, "Kissin' In The Back Row Of The Movies," strengthening their line of succession by the managerial presence of Treadwell's widow, Faye. Surely the name holds room enough for all.

# THE COASTERS

THE STORY OF THE COASTERS BELONGS AS much to the pairing of Jerry Leiber and Mike Stoller as it does to the individual members of the group itself. Exacting writers and producers, they guided the class clowns of rock through a host of comically droll situations, burlesque and mock heroic, the broad base of humor at its most ethnocentric. Outwardly simple, they blended the antics of Bulldog Drummond, Charlie Brown, Yakety Yaks, Jones and Poison Ivy; carefully concealed were the hours of meticulous studio work taken to create the Coasters' legacy, the precise timing and heightened imaginations involved.

It wasn't a sentimental "I Love You." Instead, Leiber and Stoller mined the social substrata of rhythm and blues, emphasizing slang and fashion, comedy moved from the drawing room to the pool hall. Leiber may have appreciated the talents of an Irving Berlin or Cole Porter, but as he told historian Charlie Gillett, "I tried writing straight love ballads but I never could, it never came out that way." Stoller appended, "We were the youngest ofays writing blues that we knew of."

The two had met as teenagers in Los Angeles, when Mike opened his front door in 1950 to regard the red-haired Jerry Leiber, with his one blue and one brown eye, looking for someone to set his lyrics to music. Stoller, a pianist, was uninterested until he found that the songs Leiber had in mind were blues, a form he could relate to through the boogie-woogie influence of Pinetop Smith, Meade Lux Lewis and Albert Ammons. As partners, they began making the rounds of L.A.'s jumping rhythm and blues scene, peddling their compositions to a wide variety of artists and labels, including the Robins and Jimmy Witherspoon (Modern) and Amos Milburn and Charles Brown (Alladin), the latter's "Hard Times" their first hit in February of 1952.

Leiber and Stoller's early work might have been a bit self-conscious in its slant of images toward the black market but their flair for rhythm and blues was evidenced by their lengthening series of hits and increasing absorption into the field. Federal Records, in particular, relied heavily on Leiber and Stoller's talents, and often they would not only write the song (for such as Little Esther Phillips) but follow it into the studio to guide production and arrangements. Their two best-known compositions from this period were Little Willie Littlefield's "K. C. Lovin'," a million seller seven years later for Wilbert Harrison under the title of "Kansas City"; and Willie Mae "Big Mama" Thornton's "Hound Dog," uncovered by Elvis in 1956 to the tune of eight million worldwide copies.

Tired of royalty complications and vague contracts which usually split their writing credits among a variety of "interested" parties, Jerry and Mike decided to strike out on their own. In February 1954, they began Spark Records, operating out of a small storefront on Crenshaw Boulevard, working with a group formerly under the Johnny Otis Show banner called the Robins. A holdover from the late

*(Collection Ed Engel)*

**The Coasters**

forties' "bird" combinations, the Robins were an established and versatile R & B act, and they fit easily into Leiber and Stoller's novel style. Their first record for Spark, "Riot In Cell Block No. 9," remains an acknowledged classic, a tale of prison rebellion underscored by the rapid fire of machine guns and piercing sirens.

"I was and still am, I guess, primarily interested in a kind of social satire," Leiber said later, "and a great source of material has always been the situation of the poor, the joke that the poor tell on themselves." The Flairs' Richard Berry, a major perennial on the west coast blues scene, was borrowed to provide suitably chilling narrative, charging the ostensible novelty record with deprettified realism. "Framed" amplified "Riot" 's implications, and during their stay on Spark, the Robins also performed more standard Leiber-Stoller fare: the sexually explicit "The Hatchet Man," ballads like "If Teardrops Were Kisses," and even a version of "I Love Paris."

Spark had neither the distribution nor the cash resources to break the label out of its west coast base, and when Atlantic Records offered to buy Leiber-Stoller's catalogue and services in late 1955, the duo quickly assented. It was one of the first independent production deals in the music business, with Jerry and Mike allowed to work on non-Atlantic projects. The benefits of this soon became clear, as the Cheers' "Black Denim Trousers And Motorcycle Boots" for Capitol became their first pop hit, backed by the nationwide success of another Robins' slice-of-life, "Smokey Joe's Cafe," under the aegis of Atlantic.

Leiber and Stoller were hot. The "Hound Dog" contact with Elvis Presley grew into a formal writing arrangement, and they dipped back into "Riot" 's prison genre for "Jailhouse Rock," as well as the more prosaic "Love Me" and "King Creole." The Robins weren't forgotten, and after managerial problems left only tenor Carl Gardner and bass Bobby Nunn from the original group, they added Billy Guy and Leon Hughes to form a new lineup known as the Coasters. The south-of-the-border feel of "Smokey Joe's Cafe" was retained for "Down In Mexico," but it was the group's third record for Atco, the double-sided "Searchin'/Young

Blood," that brought them securely to the nation's attention in the summer of 1957.

The Coasters' oft-quoted humor was not based so much on a punchline as on a scenario, reducing the narrator's plight to a single perfect metaphor split with accuracy and perception. From this base, Leiber and Stoller would range freely, elaborating an outlandish farce of manners. "Searchin' " took the apocryphal plea for lost or unfulfilled love into the realm of the detective story and the Northwest Mounties. "Yakety Yak" reduced the generation gap to "an unbroken, unheeded chain of commands" (Richard Goldstein). "Poison Ivy" might just as easily have been about the dangers of venereal disease as calamine lotion and late night "creepin'." Beneath the laughs, there was mindful heed of "the joke that the poor play on themselves." Charlie Brown's plaintive "Why is everybody always pickin' on me?" and "Wake Me Shake Me" 's "Swing down sweet garbage truck/And let your buddy ride . . ." contained their elements of pathos.

More lightweight were the outright spoofs (a cliff-hanging "Along Came Jones"), exotica ("Little Egypt") and arcania ("Shopping For Clothes"), as well as deserved respects ("That Is Rock And Roll"). Cornell Gunter (from the Flairs) and Will "Dub" Jones (from the Cadets) came in to replace the retiring Nunn and Hughes, and Leiber-Stoller built their voices into the group with scientific care. Compared with the pair's later magnificent work for the Drifters, the sound they produced for the Coasters was designed to be crisp and unadorned, many times utilizing only a four-piece rhythm section (with Mike on piano) and King Curtis' blistering saxophone. Not wanting their jokes to fall flat, they would repeat innumerable takes to preserve an elusive spontaneity, requiring a mixture of abandon and restraint, with the Coasters as on-call ham actors.

By the mid-sixties, Leiber and Stoller were concerned with the success of the Red Bird label (which they co-owned with George Goldner), and the Coasters marked time in the shadows. Red Bird would take the dramatically inclined novelty song to new heights with the emergence of the girl groups (the Shangri-las and the

Dixiecups, among others), but when that began to seem like too much of a business, Mike and Jerry closed shop in 1966 to begin where they started — writing and producing. Recently, they've placed their years of experience behind Flash Cadillac and the Continental Kids, Stealer's Wheel, T-Bone Walker and Peggy Lee.

On a smaller scale, the Coasters have kept going, much-requested at clubs and oldie shows, claiming a couple of ex-Cadillacs, Earl "Speedo" Carroll and Ronnie Bright, among their members after the departure of Cornell Gunter. There was even a short reunion with Leiber and Stoller in 1967. Just for old time's sake.

# HANK BALLARD AND THE MIDNIGHTERS

THE ROYALS WERE JUST ANOTHER MOODY ballad vocal group in the bottom echelon rhythm and blues charts of 1954 when Federal producer Ralph Bass suggested they try spicing up their approach. He also hinted that Henry Ballard, who had joined the group when baritone Lawson Smith went into the army, take the lead. With a self-penned tune named "Work With Me Annie," emphasis on *meat* and *gettin'*, Ballard helped open the fledgling world of rock & roll to gutbucket eroticism.

The only hitch, as it turned out, was that he would be the last to profit by it. Throughout his early career, Ballard seemed in the unenviable position of watching his greatest efforts turn to gold in other artists' hands. His "Annie" trilogy made him a star along the black circuit, but Georgia Gibbs filed off the cruder lyrical edges to sell a million copies of an asexual "Dance With Me Henry." And then, when Hank invented a dance called "The Twist" in 1960, Chubby Checker not only rode his brainchild to world-wide prominence, but managed to control it in a courtroom battle over subsequent rights.

The Royals had come from Detroit, where they were discovered by bandleader Johnny Otis one night in 1952 when they filled in for Sonny Til and his Orioles. Bass Sonny Woods, in fact, had once served as valet to Til, and had sung in practice sessions with the group. He was joined by tenor Charles Sutton, Lawson Smith, lead singer Henry Booth and guitarist Alonzo Tucker. Otis brought them to Cincinnati's Federal-King empire and arranged their first recording contract.

Their sound was typical of the era, gospel harmonies backing teardrop vocals over a spare instrumental array. The Royals were good enough at it, but seemed destined to become lost in a myriad of similar sounding combinations. They are best remembered today for excellent versions of "Every Beat Of My Heart" and "The Shrine of St. Cecilia," but their change of direction was presaged by the uptempo "Get It," which featured Ballard's throaty pleading vocal for the first time.

When owner Sid Nathan of King first heard "Annie," it's said he immediately reacted by ordering the group out of his studio, at which point the Royals returned to Detroit to disband. Actually, the story is probably more fancy than fact. King-Federal was no stranger to the bluer side of rhythm, having scored a huge chart success with Billy Ward and the Dominos' classic "Sixty Minute Man," along with such novelty items as the Checkers' "Don't Stop Dan," Todd Rhodes' "Rocket 69" and Bull Moose Jackson's "Big Ten Inch Record." Nathan rethought the matter when "Work With Me Annie" was released on a test basis, and the Royals were hurriedly called back to work.

To celebrate this change of luck, and to

avoid confusion with the popular Five Royales who had just joined the label after a stay on Apollo, the Royals changed their name in April 1954 to the Midnighters. Ballard was promoted to featured singer, and "Work With Me Annie" moved onto the rhythm and blues charts for seven months. In so doing, it caught the imagination of a host of inspired imitators. The resultant saga is only comparable in scope to the operetta James "Shep" Sheppard constructed — first through the Heartbeats and later the Limelites — for his star-crossed lovers from "A Thousand Miles Away" to "Daddy's Home."

Etta James was swift to answer with "Wallflower," beginning the polishing process that Georgia Gibbs would finish. The Champions told the story of how "Annie Met Henry," the El Dorados provided "Annie's Answer." Ballard himself continued the epic with "Annie Had A Baby" (the natural result of what happens when the "gettin' gets good") and cloaked in the "dance" question, added a disclaimer with "Henry's Got Flat Feet." Annie owned up in "Annie Pulled A Humbug," the family was extended in "Annie's Aunt Fanny," and Ballard summarized the whole tale with "Sexy Ways."

Despite his burlesque stance, Ballard made these episodes believable by reading each song in a sincere, even anguished tone while the Midnighters ooh-ahhed punctually behind him. He proved unable to break out of the rhythm and blues ghetto, however. By the time the pop market had extended itself to black performers later in the fifties, his material had fallen on repetitious times. In 1957, Lawson Smith rejoined the group when Charles Sutton left; the following year Norman Thrasher came in to replace Sonny Woods.

Ballard began tickling the pop audience in 1959, when his persistence paid off with "Teardrops On Your Letter" and a version of Wilbert Harrison's "Kansas City." The flip side of "Teardrops" was "The Twist," and after "Finger Poppin' Time" suddenly leaped into the top ten in early 1960, Ballard took full advantage. Chubby Checker had covered "The Twist" to noticeably good effect, and Ballard's own version was rereleased in a vain catch-up battle. "Let's Go, Let's Go, Let's Go" continued his chain of hits, the Ballard touch promising "a thrill on the hill," and he continued to sell well through 1962.

But the inordinate success of the Twist was

to overwhelm him, the originator, paid lip service to and forgotten. The Midnighters lost their momentum. Ballard's decline was slow and certain; by the late sixties he was playing small clubs to unfamiliar and inattentive crowds. Henry Booth died in 1968, and Ballard dissolved the group not much later, saying it presented too many problems. In 1971 he found a home in James Brown's revue, cutting several singles and occasionally guesting on Brown's albums; more recently, he has recorded disco tunes for the All-Platinum label.

# FRANKIE LYMON AND THE TEENAGERS

AT AN AGE WHEN MOST OF HIS PEERS WERE still debating the merits of homework and stickball, Frankie Lymon was well on his way to becoming an international star. There had been other sub-adolescent combinations in rock & roll, gathered around a high soprano pitch and childlike vibrato, but the enormous 1956 success of the Teenagers defined the form, popularizing it both on the road and record, with "Why Do Fools Fall In Love?" For a group of Washington Heights youngsters not yet past their midteens, it was to prove both an exhilarating and devastating experience.

Sherman Garnes and Jimmy Merchant had met in the ninth grade at New York's Edward W. Stitt Junior High School. They joined with a pair of Puerto Rican friends from a few blocks northward, Joe Negroni and Herman Santiago, singing in hallways near their home and rehearsing for neighborhood talent shows. On one of these outings, they met a young mambo percussion section featuring Howie Lymon on congas with his brother, Frankie, playing bongos. After a rehearsal, Frankie came around to the classroom where the quartet was practicing and asked if he could join in a couple of songs. He was accepted immediately as a member, and the Premiers — as they were now known after a brief flirtation with the Coupe De Villes — began to work in earnest.

Frankie, then thirteen, was no stranger to music. His father had been a member of the gospel Harlemaires, and the Lymon brothers

were encouraged into forming the Harlemaires Juniors. Given his age (the other group members were relatively "old" at fourteen and fifteen) and his late arrival, place was made for him as background first tenor, with most of the lead work taken by Santiago. Like most of the

*(Collection Peter Kanze)*

**Frankie Lymon and The Teenagers**

amateur area groups, the Premiers emulated older performers, and soon added several titles by such as the Dominos and the Valentines to their repertoire. Their one original had come about by a fluke. While singing one night in a convenient doorway, a tenant of the building had handed them some poems written by his girlfriend. They leafed through them, chose one called "Why Do Birds Sing So Gay," and set it to music.

Legend tells us that Richard Barrett, lead singer of the Valentines, heard singing outside his window one night, startled to realize that the song — his own "Lily Maybelle" — was being performed in a Spanish accent. Intrigued, he rushed to the window, only to see several figures melting into the darkness, too shy to hang around for their idol's approval. Still, it's more likely that the Valentines and the Premiers crossed paths one night in Stitt Junior High, which both groups used frequently for rehearsal purposes. Whatever the circumstances, Barrett (even then moving into a behind-the-scenes industry position) offered to take them to the Valentines' company, Rama-Gee, and label owner George Goldner.

Goldner had been expecting a Latin group at the audition, but consented to listen when he noted Barrett's enthusiasm. Alternate versions have it that either Santiago fell ill, forcing Frankie — the only other member who knew the lyrics — to take his place or that Goldner picked Lymon out of the lineup and asked to see how the group sounded with Frankie out front. Goldner also shifted the emphasis of "Why Do Birds Sing So Gay" to "Why Do Fools Fall In Love."

After contracts were signed, complete with parental approval, the Premiers recorded their song in Bell Studios in the spring of 1955. They were supported by the Jimmy Wright Band, whose leader made the timely suggestion that the group switch their name to the Teenagers. Barrett stood in the control room throughout the session, counseling Frankie with much of his own vocal stylizations, teaching him to phrase, cup notes, make the most of his talent. It was a priceless education.

The record was held in the can for the rest of that year, while the Teenagers restlessly contented themselves with entering George Washington High School. Not wanting to have the disc lost in the Christmas shuffle, Goldner waited until January 10, 1956, to place it on the market. When school started after the holidays, Jimmy Merchant was walking down the hall when he heard a girl singing a familiar phrase. Stopping her, he discovered the record was being played on the radio. By February, the group had appeared in their first Alan Freed show, in Hartford, Connecticut, and "Why Do Fools Fall In Love" was preparing to stay on the charts until early summer.

The Teenagers were an instant sensation, choreographed by Cholly Atkins (influential dance director of a line that stretches from the Cadillacs to the Temptations) and buoyed by the ebullient stage personality of Lymon. At first they tried to work only on weekends, but as their fame spread, they took to a grueling trail of one-nighters. "I Want You To Be My Girl" solidified their sound and appeal, and they scored again with "I Promise To Remember." "I'm Not A Juvenile Delinquent" spotlighted them in the film *Rock Rock Rock*.

As the hits flowed, other groups in their mold sprang up, marked by *castrato* innocence: the Kodaks, the Clintonian Cubs, Butchie Saunders and the Elchords, Little Bobby Rivera and the Hemlocks. Even Frankie's brother Louie was swept into the storm, meeting Fury owner Bobby Robinson at the Apollo one night while watching the Teenagers and forming the Teenchords as a result. The final brother, Timmy, though rumored to be in both the Tellers and Tiny Tim and the Hits, only peripherally touched the field.

But throughout their life span, none of these groups could approach the success of the Teenagers. Not satisfied with barnstorming America, they traveled to England, selling out the London Palladium on two separate occasions and performing for Princess Margaret in the Queen's Chambers. Yet dissension brewed beneath the whirlwind surface. A classic case of too much, too soon, the rest of the Teenagers felt jealous and slighted by Frankie's dominant position. Originally they had all been equal;

(Collection Peter Kanze)

now the billing was headed by Lymon's name, and sometimes they were referred to as "his" Teenagers.

By spring of 1957, matters had reached such a head that a split seemed inevitable. Frankie was being groomed for a career as an all-around entertainer and the group chafed in his shadow. Manager Morris Levy made the fatal suggestion to divide the team, Lymon going off as solo artist and moving to the Roulette label. The group's final hit was a version of Ella Fitzgerald's "Goody Goody," followed by separation.

No one profited by the arrangement. The Teenagers found themselves in difficult circumstances after Frankie's exit, their drawing power greatly reduced. Lymon, on his own, fared little better. In 1958, caught by the pressure of his age and the complexities of his

career, he began to experiment with narcotics. He attempted to kick the habit in 1960, but lapsed when his mother died of cancer. The records he released sold badly, especially compared to the dominance of "Why Do Fools Fall In Love," and as his voice changed his popularity declined considerably. By the time a retired dancer named Sam Bray befriended him in 1966, Frankie was addicted and penniless.

Bray worked tirelessly with him, persuading him to clean up, taking over management and finding him exposure along the club circuit. Recording arrangements were again set with Roulette, and after the dark years, his luck seemed about to change for the better. Frankie apparently decided to celebrate the night before the recording session. At his grandmother's house in February 1968, he expired from an overdose of heroin. He was twenty-six years old.

# LITTLE ANTHONY AND THE IMPERIALS

SHOWTIME. THE IMPERIALS ARE TAKING turns, one after another, strutting to the stage apron to indulge "It's Alright" in choreographed splendor. Tracy Lord, tenor, shivers through an intricate series of leg movements. Bass Gloster Rogers and baritone Keith Williams set him off in rhythmic stride, second tenor Ernest Wright Jr. leaning over backwards to dance on his hands. Little Anthony stands off to the side, wiping his brow with a sparkling handkerchief, spitting toward the wings, cueing for a display of splits that will steadily build his way into a turbulent finale, band vamping, group in formation, waving as they disappear behind the curtain.

The sum and substance of Little Anthony's approach has changed only slightly over the years. His material has moved with the times, current soul medleys now mixed with the Imperials' standard selection of hits, but the drive and kinetic draw haven't slackened during two decades of making music. Anthony Gourdine isn't so little anymore — nor was he then — but his high, fluttery voice can still fold a song in celestial octaves, and he dances just as good as he sings.

Anthony grew up in Brooklyn's Fort Greene projects, attending Boys High School there. In 1954, this meant as large a course in extracurricular harmonizing as it did more practical subjects, and the school boasted such groups as the Velours and the Fi-Tones as a result. Anthony began singing with a neighborhood friend named William Delk, whom he'd met in church choir, and formed a trio with a Coney Island friend, William "Doc" Dokery. Competition in the school was so high that instead of a bass singer, of which there were none available, they had to settle on baritone William Bracy to fill out the group's lower registers.

They called themselves the Duponts, after the chemical company, and began to appear locally. When the Velours came out with "Can I Come Over Tonight," the budding Duponts took heart to make plans for their own recording career. After singing for close to a year, they were placed in contact with Paul Winley, who would later become an important producer among New York vocal groups, notably the Paragons and the Jesters. Winley recorded the Duponts at Regent Sound with a band including Sam "The Man" Taylor, Mickey (of Mickey and Sylvia) Baker and Dave "Baby" Cortez, and a song written by Anthony and the group called "You." It was commercially unsuccessful, so the group used Doc's father to get an introduction to Otis Blackwell, who brought them to the primarily jazz Royal Roost label.

The resulting record, "Prove It Tonight," also failed, but label owner Jack Hook, who similarly managed Alan Freed, placed them on a Freed bill at the New York Paramount. Regardless of the fact that they were never paid for the job, Anthony was dazzled, and spent much of his time wandering around in awe of the Cadillacs until he developed laryngitis on the third day of their engagement.

The Duponts broke up in the winter of 1956, and Anthony joined another neighborhood group called the Chesters, soon to become the Imperials. The only change in personnel was baritone Clarence Collins, who had to leave the lineup because of parental pressure about his studies, only to return years later as part of the "new" Imperials. A member of the "Japanese Sandman" Cellos recommended they speak to Apollo Records, who signed them shortly thereafter. In early 1957, with Anthony still a junior in high school, the Chesters' debut release took off — "Fires Burn No More," backed with "Lift Up Your Head," a song he'd written on the subway. Though it never developed enough steam to become a strong national contender, Anthony reminisced to *Record Exchanger* in the early seventies that "it was the first indication we could make hit records."

To that end, they revisited manager Richard

Barrett, who had been watching their career with some interest and proved willing to introduce them to George Goldner of the Gone/End conglomerate. Goldner was a major force in early rock & roll, an entrepreneur whose power built empires around the Chantels, Frankie Lymon and the Teenagers and many others. Not satisfied with the results of their initial session, Barrett and Goldner suggested a song called "Tears On My Pillow," which the Imperials immediately disliked. Goldner wasn't through, however. "Why don't you sing like you talk?" he asked Anthony. "You have a very childlike girl voice." Resisting an impulse to take physical vengeance on Goldner, Anthony complied. Three weeks later, after a group name change and the addition of a lovely flip side ("Just Two Kinds Of People"), the record was immortal. Alan Freed christened him "Little" Anthony one day on the radio, never realizing the direct lineage between the Duponts and the Imperials.

Anthony spent several memorable years with Goldner. The variety of his records during the time speaks well for both the group's versatility and their label's sense of direction.

"So Much" built on "Tears" and the naturally weepy quality of Anthony's voice, but its relatively poor showing in the charts prompted the novelty-exotic "Shimmy Shimmy Ko-Ko-Bop" and the barreling "It's Alright." They were never able to repeat the success of "Tears," though, and soon moved to Roulette. There was no change, and depressed about his music and the business, Anthony left the group for a half-hearted stab at a solo career.

Both factions appeared sporadically in the early sixties, re-forming in late 1963 when they were brought to Teddy Randazzo, a singing star with the Three Chuckles at the time of Anthony's ascendance and now in an artists and repertoire position within Don Costa's production complex. The result of that collaboration, "I'm On The Outside (Looking In)," brought the Imperials back into the spotlight with the same strengths as previously, sustained by a more sophisticated and modern sound. "Goin' Out Of My Head" quickly followed, as did "Hurt So Bad." It was a stunning comeback, and for a time Anthony considered dropping the "Little" from his name. He's replaced it since, older and wiser.

(Globe Photos/Larry Barbier, Jr.)

Frankie Avalon

(Magnum/Charles Harbutt)

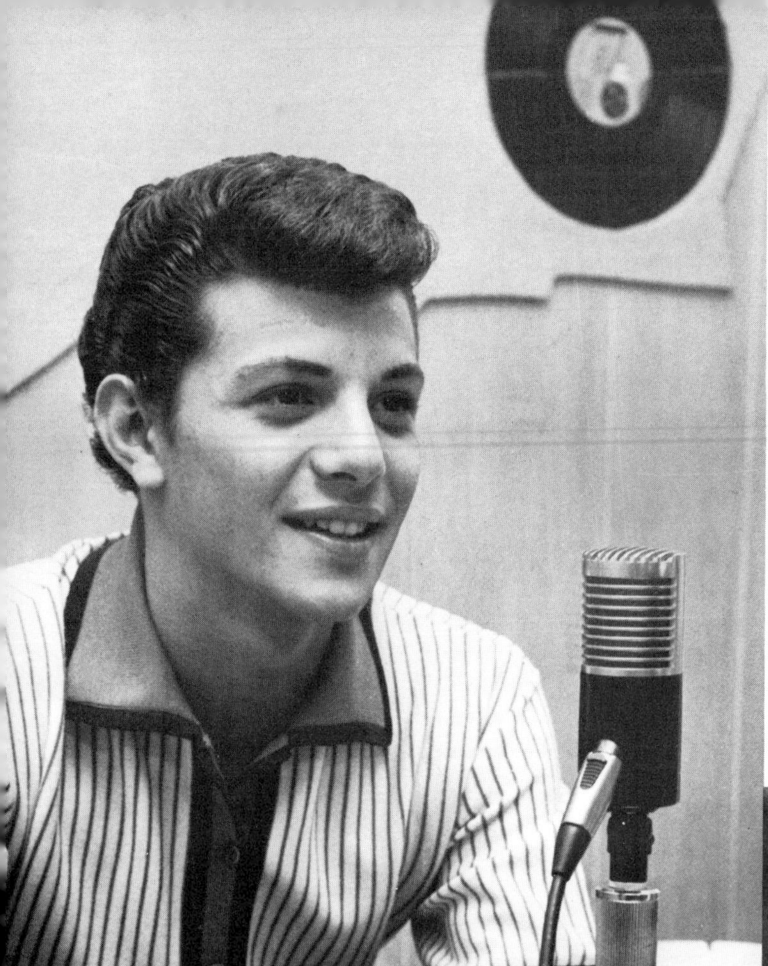

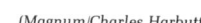

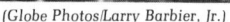

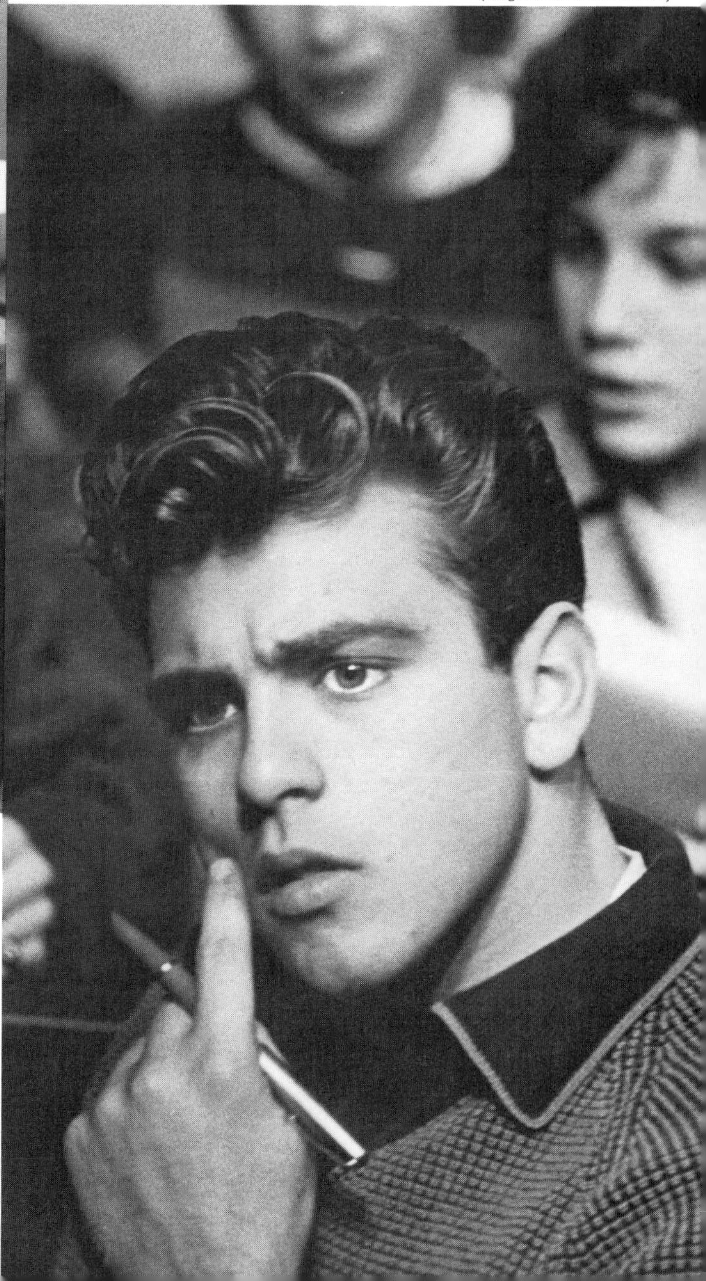

Fabian

# 5
# Beach Blanket Bop

## FRANKIE AVALON/FABIAN

THE TEEN IDOL WAS THE PUREST FLOWER-
ing of rock as image, and shrewd music
businessmen eagerly sought to find their own
versions of the boy (or girl) next door; visual
and personal appeal were the most important
qualifications, followed by any criteria of talent.
It hadn't always been thus — from Frank Sinatra
to Elvis, ability had generally preceded
adulation — but by the late fifties there were
enough ready-and-willing media to begin
generating a following long before initial
records were even pressed, supported by the
newly independent buying power of the
adolescent market.

With the right guidance, any artist,
authentic or readymade, could find his
successful niche. Many were genuine craftsmen
who regarded their fan clubs and attendant
glamor as necessary evils, or at best, harmless
diversions. Others (including cross-overs from
film and television) hovered somewhere in the
middle, participating freely in interviews on
favorite colors and ideal dates while retaining a
sense of creative enjoyment in their careers. Still
others were flagrant manufactures, programmed
for desirability and potential rise in body

temperature, a product to be air-brushed,
advertised, sold over the counter.

Of these latter, Frankie Avalon and Fabian
Forte were America's sweethearts. Their reign as
the nation's collective pulse beat was both lively
and fulfilling, as if in their total acceptance of
role they were able to rise above artifice to
become true stars. As in other classic dualities
(Elvis/Pat Boone, Beatles/Rolling Stones), they
represented the light and dark of the teen idol
business — Avalon the prettier boy, polite and
amiable; Fabian tougher, with more of the street
written on his features. Together, they set the
pattern of an epoch.

Francis Thomas Avallone had come first,
born September 18, 1940, in South Philadelphia.
His family was poor, at one point forced to
move to a single room in the home of relatives,
but by 1947 they were living in a tiny row
house on 22nd and Hemberg Streets, Frankie
attending nearby St. Edmund's School. When he
was eight he decided he wanted to be a boxer,
christening himself Kid Avallone and working
out at the Police Athletic League gym. After
seeing Mickey Rooney in a movie as a punchy
ex-champion, he quickly turned his attention to

## Frankie Avalon/Fabian

the second feature on the bill, Kirk Douglas' *Young Man With A Horn*. His father bought him a $35 silver trumpet two days later.

Avalon scored his first triumph at the President Theatre's weekly Talent Night; all of nine years old, he gathered a tiny band together to play weddings and "serenades." *The Horn and Hardart Children's Hour* liked Frankie, but not the group, and he won a savings bond for his troubles. He also guested on Paul Whiteman's *TV Teen Show*, winning a refrigerator and a console radio/record player. In 1950, he was dancing on bars for tips, and by mid-1951 had wormed his way into a party for Al Martino, where he boldly picked up a horn and entertained the assembled guests. Martino took Frankie to New York talent agent Jack Sobel, who in turn arranged a meeting with Jackie Gleason. Avalon played Gleason's favorite song, "Tenderly," and two weeks after found himself repeating it on the Gleason show.

He continued as a child prodigy with Garry Moore and Perry Como, did a stint as "The Boy With The Magic Trumpet" on the Pinky Lee show and worked regular dates with Ray Anthony's orchestra. When his cuteness faded, so did the jobs, and Avalon became a scuffling musician, playing with a neighborhood group called Rocco and the Saints.

Frankie was fortunate in one regard. Dick Clark's *American Bandstand* was focusing national television interest on Philadelphia, trailing scores of recording companies in its wake. Among these hopefuls was the young Chancellor Records, opened by Bob Marcucci and Pete DeAngelis, and they were looking for a singer. Avalon fit the bill, more or less, and in January of 1958 Chancellor released "De De Dinah," a novelty rocker built on Frankie's nose-clipped squeaky voice.

With *Bandstand* exposure and a quick follow-up in "Gingerbread," his popularity soared. Chancellor immediately put him to work on softer ballads, to increase his romantic stature, and Avalon was revealed as a modulated and not unpleasant tenor, as in the lovely "A Boy Without A Girl." "Venus" was his largest hit, fluorescent in purity, and "Bobby Sox To Stockings," "Just Ask Your Heart" and the

sing-song "Why" filled out 1959, his best year.

With Avalon established under DeAngelis' care, Marcucci returned to the streets of Philadelphia. On a late summer afternoon in 1958, he spotted a youth sitting on a stoop near Thirteenth and Ritner who reminded him of Ricky Nelson. The fifteen-year-old Fabian had failed choral classes at Southern High School, and couldn't believe the offer that was being made to him. Marcucci persevered, and soon Fabian was being coached after school each day, given vocal lessons and taken to see Frankie's area performances for pointers. "I was certain that Fabe was it," Marcucci remembered, "and that it was going to happen. But if it hadn't I would have looked for someone else and built him." At first the prototype was the razor-sharp Avalon, but two flawed discs later, Marcucci changed the chubbier Fabian into a casual sweatered ivy-leaguer. His next record, "I'm A Man," was a national hit, spurred in part by a story in *Motion Picture* which blurbed, "I Blew A Fuse Over Fabian!"

If anything, Fabian aroused an even bigger response than Avalon. Frankie had at least had some musical training, but Fabian (his last name was a closely guarded secret) came virtually unequipped. He hardly seemed interested in music, his later records ("Turn Me Loose," "Tiger," "Hound Dog Man" and "This Friendly World") selling on sheer nerve and Dick Clark's support alone. Probably this added rather than detracted from his appeal. DeAngelis left the company in protest; Marcucci counted his receipts. As for Fabian, he took over Number 20 of a bubblegum card series (the only performer to be so honored aside from Elvis, the Beatles, the Monkees and the Partridge Family), to answer whether he thought he had a good voice. "No, I don't," he replied truthfully on the card. "I don't think my voice alone has brought me success. I guess it's that I'm a kid singing what kids like to hear. I try to put to music what we teenagers feel in our hearts."

Such sentiments carried little weight with Scripps-Howard columnist Harriet Van Horne, who dismissed him as "a depraved cub scout," confessing to being "totally repelled by the strange, off-key wails of the strange, off-key lad called Fabian. Yes, I know that he is the nation's newest curly-haired darling. That he sells records by the millions. That he's not yet seventeen. And that he causes the earth to sway beneath the feet of maidens. Such is the state of our culture today.'' She was more right than she cared to imagine. By the early sixties, there were Jimmys (Clanton, Darren), Johnnys (Tillotson, Cymbal), Bobbys (Rydell, Vee, Vinton), Tommys, Mikes and Eddies, each neatly framed and wallet size. On the feminine side, Connie Stevens, Joanie Sommers, Annette, Sandra Dee and Jo Ann Campbell held similarly prim court.

Frankie and Fabian kept abreast of the field as long as they were able, but when their prominence eroded in the face of a newer style, they strategically retreated to motion pictures and, for Avalon, nightclubs. Fabian had always said he wanted to be an actor, but unfortunately, his only substantial dramatic role was as a psychotic thrill killer in the television series, *Bus Stop*, garnering him more notoriety than acclaim. Avalon progressed to a series of harmless American-International surfing musicals (*Beach Party*, *Bikini Beach*), in which he portrayed the mild young rebel whom Annette Funicello always managed to tame by the final reel. In one typical sequence from

Frankie and Annette

*(Collection Peter C. Kanze)*

*Beach Blanket Bingo*, Frankie coaxes Dee Dee (Annette) to his secluded beach house for an "unmarried honeymoon." He walks into the supposedly deserted premises to find a party in full swing; Dee Dee has cleverly invited all his friends to act as chaperones! "Not because I'm afraid of you, Frankie," she breathes, "but because I'm afraid of myself. . . ."

# PAUL ANKA

PAUL ANKA, THE GOLDEN BOY. WITH sultry bedroom eyes and a voice encompassing several octaves, he was in-the-wings ready, gifted with a certainty of talent and a divine right to the stage. There was never any question of whether he would make it; rather, it was just a process of marking the right time.

Anka was the most sophisticated of the teenage crooners that linked their names to rock & roll in the late fifties. It would eventually lead him to the world of nightclubs and more legitimate entertainment, but in the beginning he was successfully able to blend his adolescent

*angst* with traditional orchestration, an inherent maturity which wore well despite his youthfulness. Self-confident, aggressive and aware, he was, and still is, singularly free of the growing pains that tinged so many of his fellow hopefuls.

The sense of calm perspective this implies probably began for Paul as early as his Canadian childhood. Ottawa, Ontario, where his parents ran a profitable restaurant across from the Canadian House of Parliament, was a frequent stop for nomadic package shows of current stars, and Anka was a regular attender. He had been fascinated by music "as far back as I can remember," attracted by both rock & roll and its various counterparts, and on one memorable occasion had even broken backstage to pay homage to Fats Domino. There he encountered the show's impresario, Irvin Feld, who was so taken by the youngster's fast-talking assurance that he jotted down Anka's name and address for future reference.

Paul's earliest forays into show business had been as an impressionist, his rendition of Johnny Ray winning first prize at a talent contest in Gloucester, Massachusetts, when he was twelve. He sang in Canadian nightclubs and formed a group while at Fisher Park High School called the Bobby Soxers with schoolmates Ray Carrier and Jerry Barbeau. They

*(United Press International)*

were popular locally but Canada at the time was too remote to lead to better things. In the summer of 1956, he visited his uncle Maurice in California, where he found work as an usher at the Civic Playhouse, utilizing his spare moments to write songs. Shortly before he was due to return home to school, the rhythm and blues Modern label expressed an interest in his work, resulting in his first authentic record, "Blau-Wile-Deveest-Fontaine." It received some airplay, especially in Canada, but its major benefit was to reassure Anka about the potential of his career.

After meeting Feld at "The Greatest Show of Stars," Paul was encouraged to try his luck in New York. His parents were pressuring him to make a career decision (he had reluctantly considered law or journalism), but Anka eloquently pleaded his cause and his father gave him a hundred dollars to see what he could do in the ten days of his Easter vacation. On arrival, Paul looked up the Rover Boys, a popular singing group whom he'd met in the course of his travels, and spent the night sleeping in the bathtub of their hotel room. They recommended him to Don Costa, a respected producer/arranger at ABC-Paramount, and after hearing a song Anka wrote about his infatuation for an older girl, "Diana," Costa set contracts in motion.

"Diana" was a true story, inspired by eighteen-year-old Diana Ayoub of Ottawa, and Paul endowed it with all the deliberate fervor that his not-quite-sixteen years could muster. Irvin Feld, auditioning new releases at his chain of Washington, D.C., record stores in late May, caught this timbred quality, puzzling to himself the familiarity of Anka's name. When he remembered the enthusiastic youth from Domino's dressing room, he quickly added Paul to his upcoming extravaganza. The record was on the charts by July, Anka on the road beginning September 5, and after the tour was over, Feld allowed himself to be talked into becoming manager.

The ground rules were simple. "Whatever I say is binding," Feld told him in a post-Thanksgiving conference. "I don't want you to be a puppet; I want you to assert yourself, but in case of doubt my decision is final. And Paul,

## Paul Anka

I want you to be a real gentleman." But Anka couldn't have been better if designed by computer. His tawny Syrian features crossed international/ethnic borders. He dressed with subtle aplomb, never too showy, and he stared at the camera directly, as if unafraid of what it might reveal. He was personally solicitous and agreeable, feeling no qualms or inhibitions about performing.

He was also very much his own man. Anka's songwriting ability was undeniable, and Costa knew that only good could come out of encouraging him in that direction. There was a brief period of experimentation ("I Love You Baby"), but for "You Are My Destiny" they pulled out all the stops, a lush and passionate arrangement through which Paul's voice soared

cloudlessly. It was no different when he took a standard like "(All Of A Sudden) My Heart Sings"; far from being overwhelmed, Anka was one of the few young singers who was equal to full-scale orchestration and production.

Feld kept his part of the bargain by showcasing Paul in only the most prestigious of situations. The only time Anka had to share billing was once with Sophie Tucker. When Paul was past his eighteenth birthday and allowed to appear in nightclubs, Feld opened him at the Sands Hotel in Las Vegas. In June 1960, Anka became the youngest performer ever to appear at the Copacabana, his natural sense of personal style a sharp contrast to the frenzied preparations undergone by other teen idols.

Anka's string of hits continued through his

Paul with Diana Ayoub, 1957

*(Black Star)*

association with ABC, among them "Lonely Boy," "Put Your Head On My Shoulder," "It's Time To Cry" and "Puppy Love." The last was written to commemorate his much publicized romance with Annette, and she returned the favor by recording an album titled *Annette Sings Anka*. In 1962 he moved to RCA, where he retained a far greater control over his output than he'd had at Paramount, and concentrated on softening and maturing his image. It might have worked, had not the English Invasion caught him (as it did so many others) unaware, marooned far from the rock mainstream.

In accordance, Anka lowered his profile. Over the next years he concentrated on writing, granting Frank Sinatra the quintessential "My Way," giving Tom Jones a success with "She's A Lady." He served as patron for such budding singer-songwriters as John Prine and Steve Goodman, and ran a well-tuned publishing company. In 1974, Anka again became a recording artist in his own right when "Havin' My Baby" became the nation's number one song.

Pop writer Steve Kahn, in a 1961 Anka profile in *Tops in Pops,* once made what he thought would be a series of favorably outrageous predictions on Paul's future. "The year is 1975," he said, "Paul Anka is a ripe 34 years old. He has just broken international sales records of his own recordings . . . He is in every area of show business . . . the single most influential personality in the fickle world of entertainment." At least in substance, the statement stands as accurate prophecy. Paul Anka has never strayed far from the top.

# BOBBY DARIN

BOBBY DARIN WANTED TO BE A LEGEND BY the time he was twenty-five. He almost made it. "The key to me is I don't belong anyplace. I don't belong in the streets of the Bronx. I don't belong in high society or suburbia. I don't belong with beatniks and I surely don't belong in hotel suites. I know how to cope with all these environments, but I don't belong to them." In the end, it became his fatal flaw, a chameleon with no protective coloring of his own.

Darin was brash, outspoken and cocky, but he knew he was good at his chosen profession. He had to be; born Bobby Cassotto May 14, 1936, in the East Harlem section of New York, his childhood was torn between sickness and poverty. His father, a cabinet maker, had died before he was born, and the Cassotto family was held together by the will of his mother and brother-in-law. He suffered from rheumatic fever several times between the ages of seven and eleven, finally overcoming it sufficiently to enroll in the Bronx High School of Science. Bobby felt alienated from the more intellectual students the school attracted, and consequently spent most of his time alone, teaching himself to play drums, guitar, piano and vibraphone. After one term at Hunter College, he dropped out to devote himself to music.

His first professional experience was as a drummer to a thirty-one-year-old dancer, who found him in a Catskill Mountains' resort band. A tour to South America was discussed, but it soon developed that the dancer had more than rhythmic interest in the youthful Cassotto. Their affair lasted a year and a half; when it was over, Bobby felt himself irrevocably changed. "I never thought of life as a fight until I was eighteen," he told reporter Anita Ehrman. "I have never thought of it as anything else since. Before I met her, I said 'I want to.' Afterward I said 'I'm going to'."

He began by choosing a new name at random from the Bronx telephone directory. A chance candystore meeting with fledgling publisher Don Kirshner led to a collaboration writing songs and commercial jingles. Connie

# 61

## Bobby Darin

Francis' manager, George Scheck helped him sign to Decca, but a dispute over material convinced the company to drop him after a few trial records. In 1957, Kirshner brought him to Atlantic, where he persuaded company president Ahmet Ertegun to take a chance on the headstrong singer.

Atlantic's style was rhythm and blues. Their personalized approach had helped them become one of the most influential independent labels, but they had little experience in the pop field. Darin languished in obscurity. So sure was he that he'd shortly be released from his contract that he made arrangements to record for the rival Brunswick. Before that could happen, Ertegun took him into the studio, intrigued by the Fats Domino feel in a song Bobby had written with disc jockey Murray Kaufman's mother. It was a novelty tune, penned in twelve minutes, the narrator enticed from his "relaxin' in the tub" to a wild party downstairs. "Splish Splash" sold a million copies during the summer of 1958, and Atlantic quickly renegotiated while "Queen Of The Hop" (produced at the same session) provided an able follow-up.

Bobby liked to consider rock & roll as an art form, but he soon found he wasn't content to generate an endless succession of humorous slices of adolescent life. After "Plain Jane," he attempted to broaden the base of his sound; "Dream Lover" masked its traditional chordings and wish-fulfillment lyrics with strings and voices, hinting at his future direction. With "Mack The Knife," a Kurt Weill song then popularized by the Off-Broadway revival of *The Threepenny Opera,* he became an "all-around" entertainer, backed by a brassy, swing-oriented band, touted as a logical heir to Frank Sinatra. Several hits later ("Beyond The Sea," "Clementine," even "Won't You Come Home Bill Bailey?"), he seemed to prove the prophecies right, switching to Capitol Records in 1962 when Sinatra left to form his own Reprise label.

Darin may have helped to spearhead rock & roll's return to the pop mainstream in the late fifties and early sixties, yet he was not so much a teen idol as a teen interpreter. His rearranged

*(United Press International)*

versions of standards were at once contemporary and lively, and he was an astutely professional showman. He married Sandra Dee in 1960 (they were divorced in 1967), performed in a couple of movies (one, *Captain Newman, M.D.,* saw him nominated for best supporting actor in the year's Oscar awards) and continued recording, including an excellent live album cut at the Copacabana.

But he never fully integrated the dual audiences he was trying to reach, and his career soon began to feel the slowing effects. His often volatile personality failed to win the hearts of easy listeners, and after the Beatles and Rolling Stones washed over America, Bobby's tuxedo seemed irrelevant to most rock fans. He turned to country and western music briefly, then "Hello Dolly" and other show tunes; when that failed to work, he made his prodigal way back to Atlantic. There, learning the song note-by-note from Tim Hardin's original demo, Bobby had his last major hit with "If I Were A Carpenter." For a time it meant a new lease on life, and Darin commemorated it by shortening

his first name to "Bob." His new sincerity was supported by his addition of material by John Sebastian and Hardin to his club repertoire, and also by his own return to songwriting.

When he joined Motown in 1971, Darin appeared to have come to terms with himself, assuming his old nightclub stance with little of the sheer bravado that had characterized him previously. He was more relaxed, amused, comfortable in his surroundings. The possibilities of this new outlook were negated on December 12, 1973, when Bobby entered a Los Angeles hospital for treatment of a heart condition. It was a terminal reminder of his childhood illness, and he died in the early morning hours of December 20 after a lengthy operation.

# RICKY NELSON

THE RICKY NELSON STORY, OR HOW ERIC Hilliard Nelson came to the first *teenage* Heart Throb of Rock & Roll (he was only fifteen when he had his first hit in April of 1957) and rack up some 50 records in the top ten in the following ten years, sounds suspiciously like the simple, deceptively homey plots that appeared on the *Ozzie and Harriet Show* during its phenomenally successful fourteen-year run.

*Episode One:* Sometime in 1949, Lindsay, Bing Crosby's son ambles over to the Nelson's house for a game of tennis. During the afternoon Lindsay lets slip that he's going to be on his father's radio show. Ricky is eight at the time and Dave twelve. Up until now, both have been played by stand-in progeny on *their* parent's radio show *The Adventures of Ozzie and Harriet*. Later that evening at the dinner table, Ricky, taking the initiative as always, pipes up: "Dad, if we're going to take our own responsibilities like mowing the lawn and helping mom with the dishes and doing our paper route, how come we can't be ourselves with you and Mom?" Family discussion takes

place. David sensibly explains that they are old enough now and Ozzie, in his affable way, sees the point. Ricky and Dave become a permanent part of the show. Three years elapse. They make a TV pilot. Ricky and Dave look the part too. They continue to play themselves when the show is sold and casually become household names across the U. S. A.

*Episode Two:* Sometime early in 1957, Ricky has borrowed his dad's station wagon and is driving his date home. She turns on the radio. A popular singing idol (Elvis) is belting out his latest record. His girlfriend remarks that Elvis is the "smoothest cat around." Ricky looks crestfallen but recovers with True Troopers reflex: "Wait'll you hear *my* record, baby," he says, employing a well-rehearsed Presley pout. "Didn't know I was cutting a song, didya?" As he lets her off he lets her know, "I don't mess around, girl." An hour later at the Nelson home, Ricky has a chat with Ozzie. "Dad, I've just got to do it! I can sing, honest I can." Sings "I'm Walkin' " by Fats Domino, the only song he knows. Later that night Ozzie and Harriet talk it

(Wide World)

over. "After all, rock & roll is the biggest thing going with the kids," says Ozzie, weighing the possibilities, "and Ricky *is* a teenager." "Why don't you give him a chance?" Harriet adds conspiratorially.

A week later in a dance party sequence at the end of the show, Ricky appears singing half a dozen bars of rock & roll. Girlfriend tunes in, sees Ricky, passes out.

Within a week of its release, the song, "Teenage Romance," with a cover of Fats Domino's "I'm Walkin', hits the top of the charts, sells over a million copies. By December of 1958, Ricky has had 12 hit singles and made it onto the cover of *Life* magazine as "the teenage Top Throb." His "red hot platters just keep rollin' off the presses one right after another," said a contemporary Teenzine, "and his charming and easygoing style has eyelashes flickering in his direction."

The combination of television exposure — most of his subsequent hits were heard first on the *Ozzie and Harriet Show* — and image of the "boy next door" with dreamy blue eyes and acceptable teen outspokenness was irresistible. Unlike the rockabilly singers who preceded him and the Philadelphia greasers like

Fabian and Frankie Avalon who followed him, Ricky was palatable because he was, in somewhat the same way the Beatles were for another generation, neither country crude nor city-slick puppet. If not exactly your average white middle-class family in real life, the Nelsons, on TV at least, *were* your ideal All American Family.

His sudden rise to stardom was not just the merchandising of a teen icon; Ricky could actually sing, even if he couldn't exactly play a "fine Western guitar" as the liners to his first album boasted. He was backed up by really *great* country pickers: James Burton (who played with Elvis), Waylon Jennings and Merle Haggard, just to name a few. Ricky was best at mild rockers like "Travellin' Man" and "Be Bop Baby," even though he was no match for the original catalyst of his career, Elvis, on his cover version of "Have I Told You Lately That I Love You." "Poor Little Fool" made its way dreamily to the top of the charts in the summer of 1958, followed by "Lonesome Town," with its haunting, flickering echo. Ricky was never much of a "balladeer," which has saved him in his evolution from becoming mired in the lounge circuit of so many other rockers turned crooners.

Still, his soft, sensitive voice got him a part in a classic western (among other forgettable movies), Howard Hawk's *Rio Bravo*, where he shared a duet "My Rifle, My Pony, and Me" with Mr. Schmaltz himself, Dean Martin, sang a song to Duke Wayne and commissioned Johnny Cash to write one especially for him, "Restless Kid," which although never used is still a great song.

What saved Ricky from being a mere cipher in the rock & roll arena was his basic honesty, the *believability* of his sound. As his second album reassures us, "He is still modest, unassuming, and deeply appreciative of his success" and it probably was just that way. He was a kid who always outdid himself: at fifteen he was number five in the U.S. Lawn Tennis

Association; performed a trapeze duo with his brother in a traveling circus; "a cat, who from his crooner chores can beat a mean drum"; winner of trophies from dancing contests — and despite all these talents, you sense only *staged* arrogance, Presley "lip yoga," from him.

His current Stone Canyon Band has a modest California country sound. Though he's *Rick* Nelson now and his long hair and rock standard wardrobe make it clear he's changed and blended with the times, he's still your all-American boy, grown into the seventies. If he gets booed off stage occasionally by oldies fanatics at rock & roll revivals, it's because although he's sensitive to the changing times, what his fans want is Little Ricky, bringing 1957 back again.

# BRENDA LEE

SHE WAS BILLED AS LITTLE MISS DYNAMITE, all of four feet, eleven inches tall, and if the gritty power of her voice seemed incongruous with her dimunitive stature, Brenda Lee paid it no mind. "It was just natural," she smiles disarmingly. "That's what I'd always been doing. Singing to me was almost like eating."

Which might explain why those masters of grand cuisine, the French, found it so difficult to reconcile their eyes and ears when Brenda visited Paris' Olympia Theatre in 1959. On the morning after her debut performance, a disbelieving *Le Figaro* decided that instead of her stated fifteen years, Brenda was actually a thirty-two-year-old midget! She took it gracefully. "Oh, well, it was good publicity. . . ."

A copy of her birth certificate was quickly photostated and circulated, proving that, indeed, Brenda Mae Tarpley was born on December 11, 1944, in Atlanta's Emory University Hospital. A strict father had forbidden her to listen to the radio at home as a child, and she had to visit her aunt (also named Brenda) to receive musical encouragement. Entered in the weekly talent

contest of a local television show, *TV Wranglers*, she outfitted herself as a cowgirl and became a Saturday regular for three years.

"After my dad died, it became necessary for me to work," she recalls, "because I was the only one making any money. The little bit that it was . . . it was no great amount or anything, but it was better than my mother working eighteen hours in a cotton mill every day."

A disc jocky friend, Peanuts Faircloth, took her backstage at a Red Foley show in 1955 to ask for the favor of a guest spot. "Mr. Foley liked what he heard, and asked me if I'd like to come back to Springfield, Missouri, and do his network television show, which at the time was the *Ozark Jubilee*." By March 1956, Brenda was being managed by Foley's overseer, Dub Allbritten, and had signed with Decca Records under Owen Bradley's A & R supervision.

Even with a recording and performing career, Brenda found herself only slightly removed from other children her age, working mostly on weekends and after school. "I never really took it that seriously . . . I was just having

# 65

## Brenda Lee

a good time. I went to school in Nashville, and they're used to people in the entertainment business. Most of the kids I was going to school with I'd known for years. When I did have a hit, I was no different than anyone."

An additional factor might have been the time it took that initial hit to reach her. Brenda's first record was a version of "Jambalaya," and in 1957, she bottomed the charts with "One Step At A Time" and "Dynamite" (the source of her nickname). It was not until the early weeks of 1960 that she generated real excitement, when Ronnie Self, a writer from Springfield, gave her "Sweet Nothin's" and its follow-up, "I'm Sorry." Taken together, the two songs displayed Brenda's talents to the fullest. She could growl

*(United Press International)*

and belt with the best ("Nothin's"), as well as place a country teardrop in her voice for a sentimental ballad ("I'm Sorry"). Except live, where the odd effect could hardly remain unnoticed, her singing transcended the barrier of age; sweet almost-sixteen though she was, when Brenda opened her mouth, she was a woman.

Between 1960 and 1963, she racked up thirty-one singles in the Top 100 chart, establishing an international renown to match her local significance. On March 29, 1961, Brenda Lee Day was declared in Georgia by Governor Ernest Vandivar. "I Want To Be Wanted," "Fool #1," "All Alone Am I," "Losing You," the seasonal appearance of "Rockin' Around The Christmas Tree" — each added another coating of gold to Brenda's reputation. She was preserved in wax at Madame Tussaud's. When the hits began to taper off in the mid-sixties, she began covering popular contemporary songs and working club dates and Las Vegas. In late 1970, *Memphis Portrait* returned her to her country roots, and she's been a staple ("Big Four Poster Bed") in the Opry arena ever since.

Despite her apparent switch from pop, Brenda has never categorized herself. "I've always just felt that I sang what I liked, the material that best suited me. I hate for them to say 'this girl is country' and she can't be anything else, or 'that girl is pop' . . . I think if it's good, then it's everything.

"I've always been accepted in both fields. As far as my singing goes, I think I'm improving every day. At least I hope so. I pick the best songs that I can and do the best job that I can."

Is there a difference between the private and public Brenda Lee? "When I come off the road," she emphasizes, "I leave the road on the road. I leave show business completely out of my life. I have to. I have two lovely children and a wonderful husband . . . when I'm home, I want to be at home. My marriage has lasted and been successful, and I feel that's the only way it can be."

There are no highlights. "Of course, things like the Command Performance for the Queen of England stand out in your mind, but everything I've ever done in my career means something to me, no matter how big or small. Every little high school gym, every auditorium, every little town, every big town . . . it's all been great.

"It's what I've wanted to do. It's my life . . . I wanted to be accepted doing it and I have been. I'm very happy. I wouldn't change any of it, for anything." Amen.

# PAT BOONE

FOR EVERY ACTION THERE IS A REACTION; Pat Boone was the antithesis of rock & roll. White bucks vs. blue suede shoes, he provided a congenial foil to such youthful threats as Elvis, and for a time his popularity actually rivaled that of Presley's. Boone was almost too good to be true, a God-fearing Christian with a wife and daughters, steadfastly continuing his education despite hit records and movie offers, heart-warming and unflappably sincere. His wholesome image was no sham. Randy Wood, president of Dot Records, called him "the first teenage idol that Grandma can dig!" and though the two might have once seemed mutually exclusive, it's likely Pat did much to soothe troubled parents over the effects of this new, untamed music.

He was conceived in the best American tradition, allegedly the great-great-great grandson of pioneer Daniel Boone, born in Jacksonville, Florida, on June 1, 1934, as Charles Eugene Boone. At the age of ten he sang pop tunes on Saturdays at the Belle Meade Happiness Club in Nashville. By eighteen, he took first prize in an East Nashville talent contest, but it would be more important to him

## 67

### Pat Boone

that he was twice voted "Most Popular Boy" at David Lipscomb High School. Not only did he serve as student body president (his future wife, Shirley — daughter of country singer Red Foley — was secretary), but Pat also reigned as captain of the baseball team, school newspaper cartoonist and a member of the Inter-High School Council in the city of Nashville. On Sundays, naturally, he sang with the church chorus.

His trail soon led to the Ted Mack Amateur Hour, where he won three times and qualified for the finals in Madison Square Garden. Before he had a chance to appear, he began moving up in a similar contest sponsored by Arthur Godfrey. As soon as he was declared a Godfrey winner, Mack disqualified him from further competition. Boone, at the time attending North Texas State College, became a regular on the Godfrey show. In the fall of 1954, he was signed to Dot Records, and by March of the following year went to Chicago to cut his first record, "Two Hearts, Two Kisses."

It was not the most obvious choice. Wood might just as easily have converted Pat into a straight country or pop singer, but judging the new teen market and gauging its implications, he raided a rhythm and blues hit by the Charms for Boone's debut release. The refined cover version was an expected smash, and Pat followed it with "Ain't That A Shame" (from Fats Domino's "Ain't It A Shame"), "At My Front Door" (the Eldorados), "Tutti Frutti" (Little Richard), "I'll Be Home" (the Flamingos) and "Long Tall Sally" (again Little Richard).

The practice was common, and Boone wasn't the only white performer to profit from black creativity. Still, it was even then regarded as not quite legitimate, and disc jockey Alan Freed refused to play Pat's records in deference to the originals. By this time, however, his career was well established, and it was a simple matter for Boone to move into more traditional areas.

In 1956, he signed a million-dollar contract with Twentieth Century Fox for seven movies; one of the stipulations forbade the company to interfere with his college education. Enrolled at

*(United Press International)*

Ike and Pat Boone kick off
National Bible Week, 1959

(United Press International)

Columbia University, he was working toward a B.S. degree in Speech and English, and he eventually was graduated *magna cum laude* in June of 1958. His films were strictly family entertainments, *Bernadine, April Love* and *State Fair*; Pat never so much as kissed the heroines in these epics, lavishing more of his attention on the theme songs. By the age of twenty-three he had four children, a television show (*The Pat Boone Chevy Showroom*), nine gold records and his own production company, Cooga Mooga Inc. One of his singles, "Love Letters In The Sand," remained in the charts for over eight months.

Boone took his success casually, the deserved product of faith and perseverance, but in reality much of his appeal lay in the fact that he was safe and familiar, a throwback to an earlier tradition when crooners wore suits, combed their hair and were taught to say "sir" and "ma'am" at every opportunity. Pat's collegiate looks and inexhaustible popularity guaranteed him a fruitful adolescent following, and for those who wanted the fringe benefits of rock, well, he was so much easier to *deal with*.

As a teen spokesman, he could be very much the older brother, understanding, sympathetic, experienced. His philosophy, revealed in two best-selling books, *'Twixt Twelve and Twenty* and *Between You, Me and*

*the Gatepost*, was fundamentalist common sense, and with his own innate belief to back him, he avoided condescension and false piety. He discussed parental relations ("They're people too"), dating (" 'Making out' in all its forms spells danger to the lightheartedness, the gaiety, the fun of young love"), popularity, self-analysis, choosing a career ("a very special teenage land where every twist and turn presents a challenge and an opportunity"), politics ("our Four Freedoms against their totalitarianism") and "us, you and me" ("We're not gonna let 'em down"). Interspersed was a family album of Boone snapshots, from formal portraits to Pat tucking his daughter Laury into bed, living proof of positive thinking.

The realignment of morality at the turn of the sixties would undercut Boone's foundation severely. Suddenly old-fashioned, he no longer seemed relevant even as contrast; rock & roll was rapidly losing its air of notoriety. He tried dramatic roles, in *Journey To the Center of the Earth* and *The Yellow Canary*, along with bigger production musicals (*Mardi Gras*), but there was little of the old box-office excitement. He came back briefly with a novelty hit in 1964, "Speedy Gonzalez," and then tried a fling as owner of the Oakland Oaks basketball team. Today the Boone family records as a unit. *Between You, Me and the Gatepost:* "That's *real* marriage magic."

# 6
# Scopitone

## DION AND THE BELMONTS

STAG AND DRAG. AMIDST FURTIVE CIGA-
rettes, the boys' bathroom at Theodore Roosevelt
High fills with smoke and the tiled echoes of
"Sunday Kind Of Love," "Stormy Weather,"
"Gloria," safely shutting out the more sedate
dance orchestra so thoughtfully provided by the
P.T.A. Snapping fingers, hitting notes. Closing
eyes. "Hey, youse guys are good . . . j'ever think
of making a record?"

Doo-wop was the white equivalent of the
black vocal group sound, spreading radially
from New York City as rock & roll became
formal music. It was as much inspiration as
imitation, tightening gospel harmonies into
steady triplets, transcribing formless ooh's and
ahh's into precise, onomatopoeic statements,
nonsense syllables of a language all their own.
For a time it seemed as if every streetcorner and
neighborhood boasted residential favorites, and
"turf" was as religiously guarded a concept as
in the delinquent wars of the period.

Dion and the Belmonts were neither the first
nor the last of this outcropping, but it was their
mid-1958 recording of "I Wonder Why" that set
the seal on the foundling style. Opening with a
chimed four-part chord, interlocked by falsetto
and bass, Dion's gallant lead and the group's

diddy-wop backing seemed to disregard the
song almost completely, relying instead on vocal
tricks and illusions for effect. This had partially
come about because of forced *a capella*
rehearsing, usually in stairwells or convenient
subway stations, but it also owed no small debt
to the music's pronounced emphasis on sound
rather than substance, the human voice as naked
instrument.

The Belmonts had all grown up in the
Bronx within a few blocks of each other and
chose their name from a prominent avenue
running through the borough. Dion DiMucci's
early ambition was to be a painter, but at age
twelve he began making appearances playing
acoustic guitar and singing "Jambalaya." A
group called Dion and the Timberlanes passed
by briefly·in early 1957 with "The Chosen Few"
on Mohawk; late that year they were replaced by
Dion and the Belmonts, with Fred Milano,
Angelo D'Aleo and Carlo Mastrangelo. The
predominance of Italian names in the group was
hardly coincidence. Early rock & roll was
primarily working class in its instincts, and
during the fifties, the largest melting pot of
urban second generation immigrants on the east
coast were *paisanos*, utilizing the music as

much for prestige and social mobility as aesthetic pleasure.

By February 1958, the Belmonts had transferred to Laurie Records and were ready to embark on a string of nine chart hits over the next three years, including Rodgers and Hart's "Where Or When" and Pomus-Shuman's "A Teenager In Love." The significance of the teen idol explosion out of Philadelphia was not lost on group manager Sal Bonafede, and he carefully steered attention toward Dion, thus avoiding the anonymity granted such as the Mystics, the Passions, the Regents and the Elegants. When Angelo entered the navy in late

1958, he was not replaced, pushing Dion even further into the limelight, a move formalized in October 1960 when a solo career was launched with "Lonely Teenager."

Dion had not had much chance to generate a personality within the framework of the Belmonts, but on his own he elaborated a freewheeling, restless character caught in perpetual motion. He was the moody stranger, gone before you knew he'd arrived, leaving a chain of broken hearts and wishful dreams in his turbulent eddy. He was a runaway ("Lonely Teenager"), "The Wanderer" meeting his match in "Runaround Sue," episodically torn between

*(Collection Ed Engel)*

*(Collection Peter Kanze)*

"Little Diane," "Sandy," "Ruby Baby," "Donna The Prima Donna."

Ernie Maresca of Laurie was responsible for much of Dion's direction at this critical juncture, having come in contact with the Belmonts as a songwriter shortly after the success of "I Wonder Why" (his "No One Knows" was the group's follow-up). He wrote "Runaround Sue" and "The Wanderer" with Dion, retaining the Belmonts' feel by employing another local group, the Del-Satins ("Teardrops Follow Me"), for vocal backing. The amalgam was pop doo-wop, much as Buddy Holly had been verging on pop rockabilly; the Belmonts, alone, could make no such compromise. Retreating to their own Sabina label deep within the doo-wop underground, their later records — "Tell Me Why," "Don't Get Around Much Anymore," "I Need Someone" and "I Get Around" — are dateless expositions of the street corner sound.

That the life Dion was singing was reasonably close to the life he was leading became apparent soon after he switched labels to Columbia in 1963. He got off to a fine start, closing the year with "Drip Drop" in the top ten, but it would be his last major hit before he fell sway to drug addiction. It led to a prolonged self-imposed exile in Florida, followed by gradual and painful recovery. Dion was a marked man, aged overnight. He recalled those times in a frank talk-song addressed to drug-users, "In Your Own Backyard," the drift of conversational monochrome: "I been sitting here thinking," he began,

> *about when I started in drinking. I went on to dope, surely did change my life . . . I lost everything near and dear to me, namely my children and my wife. My idea of having a good time was sitting with my head between my knees. I knew everything there was to know. I didn't need any of that junk that was going 'round . . . I can quit . . . let me finish what I've got . . . then I'll get my feet back on the ground. We're all losers in that game. Thank the good Lord I've had enough. You don't need to be stoned to grow a friend. I can do anything I want to do. It's got to start In Your Own Backyard . . . \**

Dion was one of the lucky ones. He came back to a 1968 hit on Laurie, "Abraham, Martin and John," his own mortality and rebirth confirmed in "the good they die young" imagery of fallen martyrs. Now a guitar-carrying folkie, he still pays spot visits to the Belmonts as they work the revival circuit. Far from attempting to conceal his origins, he brings the spirit of his old songs alive with love and admiration. He is redeemed from the fate of the old men he used to photograph as a hobby. The camera clicks; you just turn around and they're gone.

# JOHNNY MATHIS

HIGH ABOVE SUNSET STRIP, A BILLBOARD salaciously celebrates The Immaculate Voice:

FEEL LIKE MAKING LOVE? TRY JOHNNY MATHIS. MILLIONS HAVE.

Five grey images of Johnny Mathis prance ecstatically beneath the huge letters. It is not the personality of Johnny Mathis, but the Voice, an almost disembodied sound, that is the aphrodisiac which has penetrated the ears of countless melting lovers around the world (Johnny sings in six different languages). This voice moves like a feathery wand, transforming tacky motel rooms and chintzy bedrooms into Arcadian boudoirs charged with sensuality. Johnny Mathis' propaganda plays on the most frequently heard remark about him: "More people get laid listening to Johnny languidly spinning on the turntable than to any other singer." Sex at 33 RPM. Johnny Mathis is the

## Johnny Mathis

master of pillowtalk crooning, an insinuating cupid who creates an ideal erotic ambiance.

Insured, humidified, vitamized and atomized, the voice is spoken of almost as an autonomous entity. "IT" has sustained "drawing card appeal for two decades." "IT" has been with Columbia Records for almost 14 years. Johnny himself modestly refers to "IT" as "his best friend." The owner of "this incredible musical instrument" as Mr. Gold, current head of Columbia A & R characterizes "IT," is painfully shy and lives almost as a total recluse in his Hollywood mansion, which was built for Jean Harlow. Little is known about his private life save for an occasionally bizarre entry in a gossip column like Jack O'Brian's "Voice of Broadway": "Johnny Mathis, who adores daintier things, decided peacocks would be more decoratively protective than watchdogs at his California ranch because they scream while dashing about gracefully. The first night they were eaten by coyotes."

He is almost invisible; neither black nor white, male nor female. His voice is feminine in timbre but directs itself to women. Loaded with innuendo while remaining innocent, lonely and ambivalent, Johnny sings from the utopia of the voyeur, his notes mingling in the caresses of lovers, on albums like *Open Fire*, *Two Guitars*, *Faithfully, Close to You*, while he carries on his romance with his own voice. "I would definitely put him in the legendary category," says his agent Fred Dale, "at least for the next couple of generations."

"I think I can say my style has done pretty well for me through the years," Johnny says bashfully. Johnny's style, the inimitable "Mathis mystique," is essentially rock mood music. There is a curious parallel in the careers of Elvis and Mathis. They both broke about the same time, Johnny with "Wonderful, Wonderful" and Elvis with "Heartbreak Hotel," both careers tapered off in the early sixties (Mathis disappeared after the traumatic death of his mother in 1963) and both made comebacks in the late sixties. "At the time I was as relative to Elvis as he was to me," Johnny explains. "When the kids tired of Elvis, they wanted to hear me. Elvis and I worked as a sounding board for one another."

Johnny Mathis' style is really a re-creation of the smouldering style of torch singers of the forties and early fifties — Lena Horne, Billy Eckstine, Sarah Vaughn, Nat King Cole, Johnny Ray — filtered through his own melting vocals and presented to a new audience. It was in the jazz clubs along San Francisco's North Beach that he began to develop the faultless phrasing and haunting tones that wash over the lyrics of all his songs. He grew up listening to "My Blue Heaven," and tried to emulate the jazz-tinged standards, but his ambition was not originally to be a singer.

He was born September 30, 1935, one of seven children of domestic servants to a Bay Area millionaire. While in San Francisco State College, he entertained thoughts of becoming an Olympic track star, excelling at hurdles and the high jump despite a "missing bone" in his lumbar region.

He was discovered singing one Sunday night at the Blackhawk Club by an aggressive agent named Helen Noga who coralled a convention of Columbia Records executives into

(United Press International)

listening to her find, then at the famous "hungry i" coaxed pianist Erroll Garner into singing a couple of songs with Johnny. One of the Columbia execs, George Avakian (who happened to be a cousin of Miss Noga's) was so impressed he wired the New York office immediately: HAVE FOUND PHENOMENAL 19 YEAR OLD BOY WHO COULD GO ALL THE WAY STOP SEND BLANK CONTRACTS.

Needless to say, his hunches based on Miss Noga's nudges proved phenomenally true. Two of the songs cut on the first session with Mitch Miller — "Wonderful, Wonderful" and "It's Not For Me To Say" — became mood music monsters. He is the only popular singer to make it into the Guinness Book of Records for his feat of staying in the *Billboard* Top 100 Album charts for 400 consecutive weeks with *Johnny's Greatest Hits*, and of his other albums (some 60 of them which have never dropped below half a million in sales) 20 are already gold. He is second only to Sinatra in the total number of albums sold over the last ten years. He is the first "album artist" in the pop/rock field. People didn't just want specific songs by him, they wanted the Mathis *mood*, and they bought his albums as a background to do other things against.

The voice that created the astronomical hits seemed to emanate from his own wounded self. He projected vulnerability. As he said, "Singing to me was always like standing on stage naked, nerve endings and all." A further hangup about it's "not being masculine to get up on stage and sing love songs" aggravated his stagefright to such a degree that he became addicted to amphetamines, taking four dexamyls a day plus vitamin injections administered by a "helpful" doctor. Convulsions left him alternating public appearances with bouts in the hospital until he finally forced himself away from his "treatment" to maintain his sanity. He now uses hypnosis and a glass of wine to soften the still painful exposure.

If clichés, as Freud has said, are the profoundest form of human communication, then Johnny Mathis' classics like "Chances Are," "The Twelfth Of Never," "Shadow Of Your Smile," "Love Is A Many Splendored Thing" have spoken eloquently to the millions who bought them. As he says on his "personalized" commercial for the TV package of his hits, *Warm and Tender*, "It's the kind of music you like to listen to when you're with someone you love. These songs sum up what life is really all about — love."

# JAY AND THE AMERICANS

WHILE ENGLISH GROUPS WERE WORKING on fifties rock & roll and blues in the early sixties, American teenagers Kenny Vance and Sandy Yaguda (aka Sandy Deane) were trying to capture the sweet, falsetto harmonies of the Harptones, the Moonglows and the Dells. The Harborlites (so called because they lived in Belle Harbor) began in 1959 with two records on an obscure Brooklyn label called Jaro — "Is That Too Much To Ask" and "Ticka, Ticka Tock." Nothing happened with them, and Kenny and Sandy began looking for a lead singer. As chance would have it, John "Jay" Traynor, a stand-in singer with the Mystics who felt he

was not accepted by that group, was looking for another spot. Since both groups had the same manager, Jim Gribble, the three got together, adding an old friend, Howie Kane.

The four of them headed for producers Jerry Leiber and Mike Stoller, who had a fantastic track record with R & B vocal groups like the Drifters, Coasters and Ben E. King, and a deal with United Artists. United Artists had just finished producing the movie version of *West Side Story* and offered the boys heavy promotion if they recorded "Tonight" from the sound track. On the tape of "Tonight" it sounded like a lead singer, backed by a vocal

studio, Kenny heard a new Drifters record, "Only In America," and wanted, given the group's name, to record it. When Atlantic vetoed the Drifters version (in 1963 you couldn't have a black group singing about becoming President), The Americans, using the Drifters' music track, changed offending lyrics like "Only in America . . . do they make you sit in the back of the bus . . . " and released it in August, 1963. It was as antiseptic as the national anthem and was greeted with widespread acceptance.

They followed it up with "Come A Little Bit Closer" in late 1964 and "Cara Mia," a favorite oldie of Jay Black's, in mid-'65. They had a hit at the end of that year with Neil Diamond's first song "Sunday and Me."

Jay and the Americans were a hot American group when they appeared, along with the Chiffons and the Righteous Brothers, on the Beatles' first American tour. "It was during intermission" Kenny remembers, "when we hear this unbelievable roar, it practically blew the room away. It must have equaled the roar that went up when Babe Ruth hit that 60th home run. . . . The Beatles were here and from that day on everything changed in rock — money, personal appearances, everything."

Everything except Jay and the Americans, *the* cleancut group, in their alpaca sweaters with white dickies and their choreographed act. For another ten years, the group continued to do their oldies and other peoples oldies, as if time stood still.

Jay and the Americans did attempt some changes in their style in the mid-sixties when they started writing their own material, sort of hip urban songs like "Living Above Your Head" and "French Provincial." "From 1966 to '69 we were barely eking out an existence," Kenny says, "working toilets in New Jersey and running through producers to try and find our way back. We met up with Tommy Kaye and decided to do an album of oldies, a sort of tribute to the way the guys felt about the fifties R & B groups, recording it white but feeling it soul."

It was a weird time warp, a revival of a revival of a revival. "This Magic Moment,"

group, so Jerry Leiber, who was into spoofs at the time, suggested Binky Jones and the Americans as a name for the group. They settled for Jay and the Americans. "Tonight" sold about 50,000 records locally, but hardly touched the Ferrante and Teicher version. It was their second release, "Dawning"/"She Cried," which became a hit after a west coast deejay locked himself in the booth and played the flip side "She Cried" for four hours straight.

After the first hit, the group went through a lot of changes. Singer Howie Kane, also working as a mortician, couldn't work on Sundays, when Murray the K had his Coney Island shows, so he dropped out along with Jay Traynor. Marty Sanders from the Empires joined the group on guitar and introduced Kenny and Sandy to another ex-Empire, David Blatt. Blatt accommodatingly changed his name to Jay Black, and at this point Jay and the Americans took its classic form.

One afternoon while rehearsing in the

originally recorded by the Drifters in 1960 got Jay and the Americans their biggest hit of all in late 1968 selling some two million copies, and they followed it up with another oldie, "Walking In The Rain." When they appeared with Frankie Valli, the Four Tops and Martha Reeves and the Vandellas at Richard Nader's Rock Revival in 1971, the response was ecstatic. "They went crazy," says Kenny, "banging and screaming. We knew we were back."

Kenny, Sandy and Marty finally quit the group in 1974, but Jay Black and the Americans still continues. Somewhat older than the others and the most conservative of the group, Jay has resisted all changes, tenaciously sticking to the belief that staying the same can sometimes pay off. He will be playing rock revivals, Las Vegas lounges for as long as people want to hear it the way it was.

Rock & roll was a low lying scene before the Beatles came, and afterwards, the vivid visual impact that the English groups presented almost eclipsed Jay and the Americans. They continued to have hits, but they were almost invisible. Like the Four Seasons, only the voices had presence. However, Jay and the Americans come from the mainstream of American music that somehow got buried in the English avalanche. "We always felt we were valid, we had as much heritage as the Stones. It just never came into focus that way," says Kenny. But somehow that response they were looking for, as he sings on his solo album, never quite came —

*Cause we were looking for an echo*
*An echo to our sound*
*A place to be in harmony*
*A place we almost found.**

*"Looking For An Echo" by Richard Reicheg © 1974 Warner Brothers Music Corp. All rights reserved. Used by permission.

# THE FOUR SEASONS

IT STARTED AS A JOKE, FIFTEEN MINUTES tacked onto the end of a recording session. The Four Seasons had been languishing for nearly two years in Bob Crewe's expanding production factory, and rather than grant a requested release, Crewe had relented and taken them into the studio. When Perry Records showed interest in the resultant master, there was talk of changing the record's name to "Perry" as a promotional gimmick. The overkill would not be necessary. With Frankie Valli's falsetto geared to crack chandeliers throughout America, "Sherry" had all the gimmick it needed and more. The artificially high voice could no longer be relegated to religious-inspired slow leads or gentle cooing in the background. After its novelty introduction, Valli threw it over all manner of song, suitable for any mood or emotion. So successful was he that when the Beatles came to America in 1964, they found only two other groups with the resources to challenge their supremacy, both masters of the falsetto: the Californian Beach Boys and their east coast counterparts, the Four Seasons.

Many who assumed the Seasons to be newcomers on the music scene might have been surprised to learn that the group had an extensive history as the Four Lovers, achieving minor prominence in 1956 with "You're The Apple Of My Eye" (which took them to the Ed Sullivan show) after a long stint along the northern New Jersey lounge circuit. All the members had been born either in or around Newark, and it was there that Valli (formerly Castelluccio), Nick and his brother Tommy DeVito, and Hank Majewski gathered a quartet very much in the style of other white pop groups of their day, the Crew Cuts, the Ames Brothers, other "Fours" like the Aces, Coins and Lads.

Though they played their own instruments — the DeVitos were guitarists, Hank

The Four Lovers

a bassist, Valli a brush-stroke drummer — they stuck fairly close to traditional standards like "My Funny Valentine" and "My Mother's Eyes." As their surnames suggested, they appealed to an insular ethnic audience, ingratiating themselves with versions of "Come Si Bella" and a ribald "Italian Cowboy Song." RCA Records likely discovered them one night en route from the Silhouette Club in Newark to the Broadway Lounge in Passaic, and under the direction of Herman Diaz, boosted them on their short spurt to fame.

The Four Lovers were never able to follow "You're The Apple Of My Eye," and were soon back where they'd started. Hank left in search of "a new sound," joined Chang Lee and the Zaniacs, and was replaced by Nick Massi (Macioci), a bass player from another local group, Hugh Garrity and the Hollywood Playboys. When Nick De Vito decided to try the greener hills of Las Vegas, his position was filled by Bob Gaudio, a former member of the Royal Teens, on organ.

As the transition was made from Four

## 77

### The Four Seasons

Lovers to Four Seasons, individual members of the group would often participate in session work through their acquaintance with George Goldner. In the late fifties, Goldner had released a record of "Come Si Bella" by Frankie Valli and the Romans, and after they'd met Bob Crewe, Goldner put out the Four Seasons' debut, "Bermuda," on his Gone label.

Crewe himself was a writer turned performer turned producer, a former child model who had helped pen "Lucky Ladybug" for Billie and Lillie, and Freddie Cannon's "Tallahassee Lassie." When Valli recorded as a solo for Okeh under the pseudonym of Frankie Tyler, Crewe wrote "I Go Ape" for him in collaboration with Frank Slay. After leaving Goldner, the Four Seasons were making the rounds with their demos (mostly Gaudio's material) when they ran into Crewe again. Mutual interests were discussed, and the Four Seasons signed with him for three years.

Luckily, negotiations with Perry Records fell through, and Crewe placed "Sherry" with Vee Jay, one of the best known independents in the music business. In August of 1962 it began a darting climb to the number one position, followed two months later by the similar rise of "Big Girls Don't Cry." There was time out for a Christmas exercise, "Santa Claus Is Coming To Town," and then back to number one with "Walk Like A Man." Within the space of six months, the Four Seasons had become one of the most powerful groups in America.

As far as Crewe was concerned, it was pure commerce, a punchy pop sound made distinctive by Valli's piercing shrill. The verses would carry the song until its chorus, and then Frankie would reach into his upper registers for his patented dog frequencies. Charles Callello worked the required arranging miracles (he had sung with Valli and the Romans), and Crewe and Gaudio split the writing chores. Royalty litigations prompted them to leave Vee Jay after "Candy Girl," and in their new home on the Philips label, the Seasons continued their winning ways.

Slowly, a lyrical and production style emerged. Falsetto was a natural for expressing longing or pleading, and with Gaudio leaning

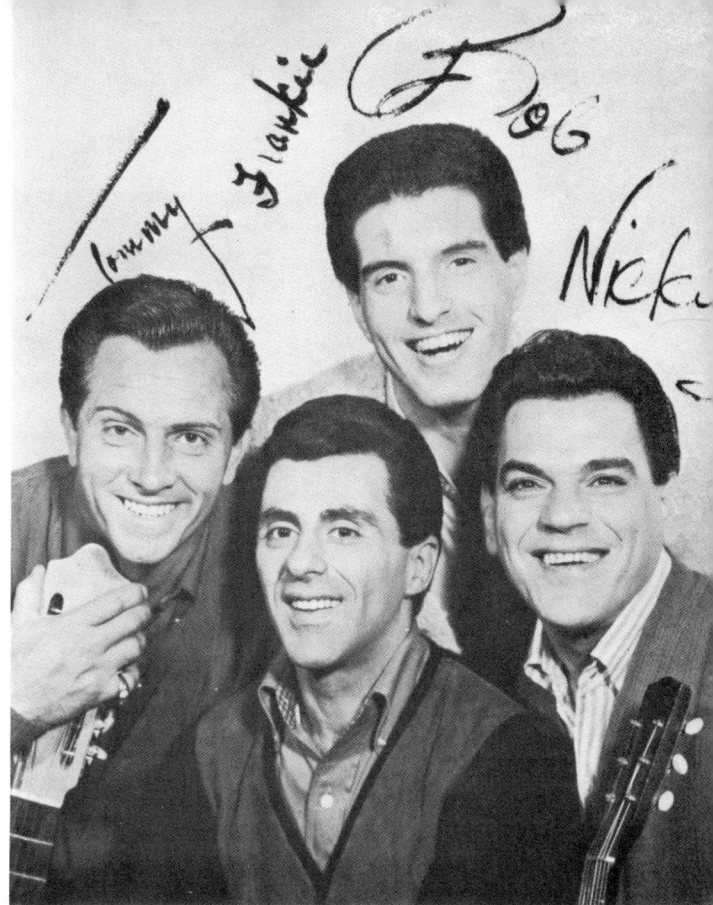

(Collection Alan Betrock)

toward grandiose production, Frankie was frequently placed on the tormented shores of unrequited love. In "Dawn," the classic "Rag Doll," "Big Man In Town," matters of class and personal pride created an unbridgeable chasm, filled only by a constant succession of gold records. By 1966, the Four Seasons were so hot that Frankie Valli could not only support a solo career ("Can't Take My Eyes Off You"), but thinly disguised as the Wonder Who they covered Bob Dylan's "Don't Think Twice," as Rose Murphy might have done to delightful and lucrative effect.

The middle sixties spelled consistent success. There was seldom a time when a Four Seasons record couldn't be found in the Top 10. Primarily singles artists, however, they began to worry that the more progressive music then in gestation would pass them by. Gaudio joined forces with singer-songwriter Jake Holmes, and the Four Seasons embarked on a new direction. *Genuine Imitation Life Gazette* was a brave album attempt at illuminating the problems of urban strife. It took several months to record, but sold poorly in comparison to their more mainstream hits. The group stepped back to consider the possibilities. Massi had left in 1965 because of the pressures of constant traveling; DeVito retired in 1970, and Gaudio left to pursue his own interests the following year.

Thus, as Frankie Valli and the Four Seasons, the "group" became a headlining regular at Evenings of Solid Gold. There they might have stayed, content to share memories with fans, had not "My Eyes Adored You,"

credited to Frankie Valli, become a national hit in 1975, followed by the 1976 triumphal reappearance of the Four Seasons with "Oh What A Night" (Dec. 1963). Many who assumed Valli to be a newcomer on the music scene might have been surprised to learn that he once had an extensive history as lead singer of the Four Seasons.

# THE RONETTES

"MY SISTER MADE A PHONE CALL," ABsently floating a hand in the air as the time slides, "we were supposed to do background for somebody. She dialed the wrong number or something, and it was my husband on the phone. And so he says 'Who's this?' and she said 'Who's *this?*' and he said 'I'm Phil Spector' and she says 'Well, I'm one of the Ronettes,' and he said that he'd heard about us.

"At that time we were doing Murray the K shows, we were called his dancing girls; and he asked her if we would be interested in doing a background session for one of his groups — I think it might've been the Crystals or one of them. So she said sure, and we met the next night in a studio on Fifty-Seventh Street, he wanted to hear how we sounded. And you know, we never did get to do that background. . . ."

Thus was begun one of the most fruitful collaborations of rock & roll's early adolescence. Phil Spector was the boy wonder of the record business. He had started with the Teddy Bears and "To Know Him Is To Love Him," moving through an apprenticeship with Lieber-Stoller to his own production company and label, Philles, building a mountainous wall-of-sound studio technique that was far in advance of anything in its time. He was after grandeur, three-minute pop segments in which every note was gauged for maximum explosive potential. He would take eight pianos, record them separately, and then combine the whole to a single, depth-laden

keyboard track. He would overdub vocal choruses until he had a virtual choir, arraying percussion instruments so that the song vibrated to a dozen inner rhythms. He was a genius and he knew it.

But his artists had always seemed to lack something vital. Though he brought out their best, utilizing voices as pieces in a puzzle — Curtis Lee with "Pretty Little Angel Eyes," the skin-tight Paris Sisters, dusky-voiced Lala of the Crystals — they never seemed to inspire any fervor on their own. His chance meeting with Veronica Bennett changed all that, as fate provided this Pygmalion with his ultimate Galatea. Under his tutelage, she became the reigning queen of a girl group explosion in the early sixties that also contributed the Chiffons, the Shangri-las and the Shirelles to the fantasy-ridden consciousness of record-buying America.

They were beautiful, saucy street flash dripping with exotic sensuality. Led by Ronnie, the Ronettes had grown up along Manhattan's West 149th Street, two sisters and a cousin, learning three-part harmony and basic vocal techniques after classes at George Washington High School. Estelle was the older sibling, and had gone on to a year of drama and dance studies at the Bergof Drama School as well as a year of fashion design at the Fashion Institute of Technology. Along with Nedra Talley, they began singing whenever their grandmother would lock them in their rooms as punishment.

## 79
**The Ronettes**

(Collection Peter Kanze)

## The Ronettes

It was somewhere around 1961 that the group — then called Ronnie and the Relatives — met their first manager, Philip Halikus, who turned a record deal for them with Don Kirshner's Colpix label. They did an album's worth of material for him under the production hand of Stu Phillips, most of which was stereotypical girl-group Top 40, back seat titles like "What's So Sweet About Sixteen," "I Want A Boy" and a lovely number called "Good Girls" which coyly promised drive-in passion in exchange for true love.

Colpix never bothered to promote any of the Relatives' product while the group was with them, and the girls were left to fend for themselves. They sang in New York's famed Peppermint Lounge for a while, and also made spot appearances with disc jockey Murray the K in his holiday shows at the Brooklyn Paramount. After meeting Spector, their career picked up sudden momentum. With their hair piled in beehives, wearing the shortest of skirts, their eyes encircled with kohl, they captivated Spector, and he was even more delighted to discover they could actually sing. Dragging them in to meet engineer Larry Levine, he immediately set to work on "Be My Baby."

Phil Spector

The sessions were grueling affairs. In the studio twelve to fourteen hours a day, dubbing instrument over instrument, it was a far cry from anything the Ronettes had yet been accustomed to. "It was like night and day compared to Colpix," says Ronnie. "With Phil, I knew that he was out to make hit records. I would go there and listen to the band and everything — because of the union, the performer had to be there and stand in the booth — but I wouldn't sing. And then, after Phillip finished with the band, they would leave, and then he could turn out all the lights in the studio and I would sing. In the dark."

The results were some of Spector's best remembered moments, imbued with a glowing warmth unreachable through any of his other artists, including such later contenders as the Righteous Brothers, Bob B. Soxx and the Blue Jeans, Darlene Love, Ike and Tina Turner and even the Beatles. The records he cut for the Ronettes took him to the pinnacle of his art, a canyon of sound set against the surprising intimacy of Ronnie's powerful voice. The fact that he would soon make her Mrs. Phillip Spector only heightened the emotion implicit in every line.

Of all the material the Ronettes did with Spector, Ronnie picks out "Walking In The Rain" as her favorite. "It took only one take, that song. I wanted to do it over again, and Cynthia [Weil] and Barry [Mann], the ones that wrote it with Phillip were there, and I said lemme do it again, you know once you feel it out you figure you can do it better the second time. They said, 'Nope, that's it, that's what we want,' and that's how it went out."

There was never any question of creative room with Spector. By and large, Ronnie did as he instructed, and for both it turned out a satisfactory arrangement. There were three gold records in all, and perhaps because Phil carefully regulated their output, the Ronettes seldom made a bad disc; among their better known classics are "Baby I Love You," "The

Best Part of Breaking Up," "Do I Love You," "Born To Be Together." Traveling to England, they placed high in the music polls, and were immediately put on a pedestal by some of the newer "beat" groups then gaining prominence, notably the Beatles and the Rolling Stones.

Spector, especially after the marriage, found it hard to separate Ronnie's public from her personal life. He forbade her to go on the 1966 U.S. Beatles tour, drafting another of her cousins to take her place. As his own disenchantment with the music business grew, most pointedly with the failure of Ike and Tina's "River Deep Mountain High," he withdrew from the musical mainstream. It was not a particularly happy time.

When Spector came back in the late sixties through A & M, he made an attempt to get the Ronettes' career refueled with a song entitled "You Came, You Saw, You Conquered." Though by then only Ronnie remained, he put it out under the name of the Ronettes, feeling its chances might thus be improved; the record never moved more than a couple of feet off the ground. Her next attempt at chart success, "Try Some Buy Some," was written by George Harrison and produced while Spector worked on the *All Things Must Pass* album. Ronnie never liked the record much, her vocal lost in a haze of swirling mandolins. "But Phil Spector and George Harrison together, how can you say you don't like a song?"

Finally, her reclusive life in Spector's twenty-three-room Los Angeles mansion became too much to bear. "I started to feel that something was missing," she allowed on the eve of her 1973 comeback, "and I knew it was the stage." Under the urgings of Estelle's husband, Teddy Vann, she gathered a pair of Ronettes (both Nedra and Estelle were too settled to return to the hit-or-miss life of continual performing) and began appearing in clubs and oldies' shows throughout the country, including a stint with Dick Clark in Las Vegas. She has also begun recording again, hoping to expand her career to movies and television.

# THE SHANGRI-LAS

GEORGE "SHADOW" MORTON SITS IN THE dim winter light of a Long Island bar, talking about the craft of producing. "It ends at the recording board," he says, swirling his glass on the table top. "It's what happens after the board gives all it's got to give. A producer makes a hit because he deals with a quality of the people that sit in the studio that are capable of making hits, and then he counts on a lot of things. He counts on the situation, he counts on energy, he counts on a little bit of God, he counts on a little bit of luck, a little bit of music. . . ."

Morton cocks his head. "I don't consider myself a good producer. I consider myself one of the best producers." And at least until the waitress brings another round, nothing more needs to be said.

With the *femme fatale* Shangri-las, Morton found raw material that was almost too good to be true: unconscious, innocent, cute with a naïveté that seemed to work at cross-purposes with the hard-core nature of his material. If the Ronettes were the royalty of sixties' girl groups, the Shirelles their unwilling ladies-in-waiting, the Shangri-las were the handmaidens that made good, rising from virtual kitchen scullions to the rank of pop cinderellas. "They were the wildest chicks that ever walked a street, bar none today," he laments, almost wistfully, "the kind of girls who could never be appreciated in 1960 but will always be appreciated in 1970. They pulled off more shit, in front of more people. . . ."

His involvement with the group came about almost casually, the by-product of a semi-dare from writer Jeff Barry. Morton's adolescent singing group, the Gems, had backed a singer named Ellie Gay at local high school dances in the early sixties. Discovering that she was the same Ellie Greenwich who was rapidly becoming a successful writer, he hitched-hiked into New York in 1964 with a dollar in his pocket to offer his services.

"She was polite, she played me some of the records they had just made. Not wishing to offend an old friend, I said they were nice, and that irritated Jeff Barry. He had been sitting there all the while, just strumming away at the piano. We didn't exist as far as he was concerned. Very cool. Finally he turned to me, he wasn't missing a beat on that piano, and he said, 'You think that's a *nice* record?' I said yeah. He said, 'Do you think you can make a *better* record?'

"We went on like that for about an hour, kind of cat and mouse. Blah, blah, when can you have it ready? I say, 'Well, this is Thursday, I'll have it ready for you by Tuesday.' He says,

'I'll give you a month.' I say, 'No . . . I only need until Tuesday.' Finally I left. I had no idea what I was getting into, but now I had to come up with something."

Shadow was not without his options. An east coast disc jockey named Babalu — Bob Lewis'. We'd like to do anything.' I said fine. I from Queens who had made a couple of fruitless records, first as the Bon-Bons and later the Shangri-las. Composed of sisters Mary and Betty Weiss, and "lifelong" friend Mary Ann Ganser (whose twin, Margie, sometimes sang with the group as a floating fourth member), they had done little more than play various club dates in Manhattan. At one, they were reportedly so nervous that when the owner rapped on their door and shouted "you're on!" Mary Ann raced for the stage only to discover she had forgotten the slacks to her outfit in her haste.

"So as fate would have it, I got a phone call

*(David Dalton)*

# 83

## The Shangri-las

Shadow Morton

from these girls, who were the Shangri-las. Mary Weiss called, and she said, 'We haven't done anything since the last time we saw you at Bob Lewis'. We'd like to do anything.' I said fine. I called up a friend of mine who had this basement studio, his name was Joe Monaco, and I said, 'Joe, listen, I got this company who's interested in making a record, and I got this group.' He said terrific. Then I got hold of this friend of mine named George Sturman who knew musicians, and I told him Sunday afternoon we're going to make a record. It's all set up.

   "Comes Sunday afternoon, we're supposed to be in the studio by 2:00, and I get in the car by 1:00, and on my way to the studio I realize I don't have a song. I didn't know what we were going to be doing. So I think about this tune on the way to the studio, I walk in, say hello, go to the piano, take two fingers, say 'You sing this, you play this.' I record that and on Tuesday I bring it in to Jeff Barry."

   Who, Morton assures, hasn't moved from the piano stool in all that time. Barry looks over, says "I see you brought something." Plays it. Listens carefully. Asks if he can play it again. Then takes it down the hall to play for some "other" people. "I was starting to get nervous all of a sudden. This wasn't a game any longer. Up to this point I could still walk out, could still say 'what do these people know.' Now I began to think it might be for real."

   An impression justified when a pair of contrasting colored eyes ("Mr. Jolly Blue and Brown," as Morton used to call him) looked in and their owner, Jerry Leiber, offered him a hundred dollars a week, clear.

   The record was "Remember (Walking In The Sand)." Ellie Greenwich remembers that the version Shadow brought in was close to seven minutes long with an introductory narration. Suitably pared, with a few Mira sound effects additions, it proceeded to storm the charts on the fledgling Red Bird label, which Leiber-Stoller and George Goldner were utilizing as virtual house representative for their resident writers and producers.

   It was to be the first of many such successes, not to mention a lengthy, rocky and

ultimately endearing relationship with the Shangri-las. Morton's records were constructed like film scripts, catty dialogue alternating with strikingly visual plots and a healthy, creative use of stereotype. He took folk heroes on the order of motorcycle hoodlums, teenage runaways, teases and flirts, and graphically presented them in a way that seems even more of a breakthrough now than it did then.

   "Here's what went on. The Shangri-las' record came out, and two months later you got three girls from Cambria Heights thrown into the *da-da* spotlight, right? The first show they ever did . . . I went to them, I said listen, you girls gotta do a show. They said we can't do a show, we don't know how to sing any other songs. What'll we do? So we rehearsed a strip act. They stripped off half their clothes, down to the garter, the old thumb on the garter routine, *boing* to the audience, and everybody went crazy. That's how they got by, in the beginning." He shakes his head. "You don't find chicks like that anymore. They loved what they were doing and they got off on it."

   Morton led them every step of the way, scoring them with his vision of custom ecstasy: "Leader Of The Pack," "Give Him A Great Big Kiss," "I Can Never Go Home Anymore." "Mary was the lead singer, but Mary was not necessarily the best singer in the group. Her sister Betty was a better singer, but Mary had the sound — we're not talking about talent, we're talking about sound."

Music hovers somewhere in the distance. "The best way to record them — and okay, Mary, you can sue me for this one — was to put the group down, and then I would go into the booth, or stand close enough to Mary to sing the song in her ear!" He laughs sharply, a cackle that rises from the back of his throat like a prolonged wheeze. "Really. I mean, you gotta understand the times. You weren't expected to find three white girls out of Queens who were accustomed to singing. I mean, they sang good, and they knew harmony, but to tell them phrasing, or to tell them soul. . . . My records were basically acting records, and Mary had to learn to deal herself as an actress. That made it hard for them."

The record company wasn't helping matters either. When Morton had informed Jerry Leiber that the next side he'd be cutting for the Shangs after "Remember" would be a song called "Leader of the Pack," Leiber advised him to forget it, that the label would never release it. More, after the record was finished, the Shangri-las said they'd sue if the disc came out.

"I was being paid a hundred dollars a week; who had total control? I had total conviction. Two weeks later I sent him the master. He had total control; but I can do whatever I want. Screw Jerry Leiber, much as I love him. They said you can't deal with records like that, you can't make heroes out of guys in black leather jackets. I say why not? I wear a black leather jacket. You tellin' me I'm a bum, I can't be a hero?

"So the record came out. Two weeks after it came out it was something like number twelve on the charts, and then you get all these phone calls of congratulations. The same old story."

Despite such day-to-day traumas, Morton recalls the years at Red Bird with affection, particularly because of Goldner. "It was like a family thing. George, he kept that together, he managed to make it a fun-loving group of people, and he was a king in his own way. There were a lot of times when, say, there'd be a session on the Dixie Cups, or the Jelly Beans, and I would show up, and Ellie and Jeff . . . everybody seemed to end up at the studio at the same time. That's how most of those records were made, and that's what made them so great."

On their own, the Shangri-las expired in personal tragedy and lack of direction. Morton went off to guide the recording careers of Janis Ian, the Vanilla Fudge, Richie Havens (whose first album bears his imprimatur) and, more recently, the New York Dolls. He respects his earlier work, but doesn't care to live with it. He doesn't even own copies of his records. "The important thing is to create: traveling there, not being there. To see the path, to walk the path, to be the path." Get the picture? (Yes we see).

# LESLEY GORE

BLINKING BACK THE TEARS AND PETULANT-ly asserting her given right to cry at her own party, Lesley Gore earned the sobriquet of Everygirl in a field beset by exceptions to the rule.

She had none of the blatant sexuality of the early sixties' fem-groups (it would have been unthinkable to see her as a member of Reparata and the Delrons), nor the itty-bitty pout assumed by many of her sympathetic solo forebears, a Linda Scott or a Kathy Young. Neither was she an adult, a woman in the sense of Connie Francis, Timi Yuro, even — and who would've thought it? — Annette Funicello. Many claimed to be the girl next door, but Lesley actually was the neighborhood big sister, a typical teenager as conscientious in her studies as her social life.

Her songs reflected this rise from innocence, soap operatic, themed with a seasonal coming of age. She might be found on the phone, talking

to the quarterback of the school football team. They'd been together since sophomore year, and when they went to Seaside Heights last weekend he won her a big blue teddybear to sit on the corner of her chenille bedspread. It's her birthday and she's got her best party dress on. He'll be coming by at eight. She reaches up to fondle his ring, looped on a gold chain around her neck.

Lesley might be in for a rude recorded awakening when Johnny walked into the party holdings hands with Judy, but the instantaneous success of "It's My Party " would more than mitigate her loss, entering the charts nine days after her seventeenth birthday in May 1963. She had been at a friend's get-together when someone playfully suggested she put her vocal talents on a demonstration disc. She did just that, and Mercury Records liked what they heard, assigning her to the tutelage of arranger-producer Quincy Jones. Almost instantly, the belle of Tenafly, New Jersey, had the number one record in the country.

Through "It's My Party" and her subsequent hits, Lesley matured rapidly. If her first thought was helpless jealousy at seeing Judy with Johnny, she could soon savor the fruits of revenge when he returned in "Judy's Turn To Cry," much to the relief of an anxious America. This musical version of advice to the lovelorn continued with "She's A Fool," in which Lesley was able to view an affair gone bad from the inside. By "You Don't Own Me," she was ready to assert her independence, the flip side coincidentally titled "Run Bobby, Run." Finally she could become confident, with a shrug-of-the-shoulders acceptance: "That's The Way Boys Are" and "Maybe I Know."

Lesley was much the same off-record as on. Attending Dwight School for Girls in Englewood when her recording career broke, she chose to continue her education at Sarah Lawrence College, majoring in literature, recording only on weekends and semester breaks. She had tried to study music, but "I realized that the music students and I were too different from each other. I understood commercial music and that was a hindrance up there. They never taught the students that, as a performer, you had to please

*(Collection Richard & Lisa Robinson)*

the audience. The music department was probably putting me down for looking at music in a commercial way, but I knew that their attitude was wrong for me."

Career arrangements were kept within the Gore family, Lesley's father handling business, her mother answering fan mail and her grandmother supervising her fan club. Though she had to pass up tours and television offers to pursue her studies, she nonetheless found time to appear in the famous *T.A.M.I. Show,* an in-concert film with the Rolling Stones, the Beach Boys and James Brown, as well as cameo appearances in *Girls On The Beach* and *Ski Party.*

Lesley continued to have hit records through 1967, but removed from the trials of adolescence, she lost some of her over-the-counter appeal. "California Nights," produced by Bob Crewe, was a welcome change from a predictable succession of standards like "Sunshine, Lollipops And Rainbows" and "Look Of Love"; her tastes were changing as well, evincing an interest in the meeting ground between jazz and pop. She worked in nightclubs and summer stock, and took the youthful guerrillas of the later sixties in stride. "There are things that need to be done. My concern is that things not be done in violence or anger, but be done intelligently and cleverly."

Ever the voice of reassurance. As if in recompense, Lesley Gore's loyal fan club has yet to disband, much to her grandmother's pleasure.

# CHUBBY CHECKER

"THE TWIST IS A VALID MANIFESTATION OF the anguish, frustration, and uncertainty of the 1960's," the *Saturday Review* once theorized in a contemporary account, "an effort to release some of the tension which, if suppressed or buried, could warp and destroy."

Chubby Checker used to tell it a different way. "First and simply," he wrote in *Ebony,* "the Twist is great fun. If you watch a group of people doing the Twist, you will notice that all the faces are smiling, laughing or singing along with the music. "Better yet, try it yourself!"

America listened and learned. While half the population strained to pretend they were stubbing out a cigarette with an extended front toe, the remainder worked an imaginary towel across their backs, wearing such essential accessories as Twist socks, Twist sweaters, Twist skirts, Twist cufflinks and tietacks, most of which came engraved with a telling CC. Tom McAn sponsored a line of Twister shoes. A maker of spaghetti introduced a model called the Twist. And as the blissful sound of chiming cash registers mingled with the slightly delirious shuffle of a new national pastime, the question of whether there would have been a Twist if not for Chubby Checker asserted itself against the inevitable, would there have been a Chubby Checker if not for the Twist? Surely Ernest Evans, as Chubby was named before Mrs. Dick Clark saw him as a young Fats Domino, had no hint of the tempest he was about to unleash. Previous to the Twist, he was just another twenty-year-old singer from South Philadelphia, newly graduated from an occupation as a butcher boy (chicken plucker), trying to work his way through the promotional mazes of show business.

He had touched solid ground in mid-1959 with a novelty record for Parkway called "The Class," featuring high-speed imitations of many of the day's stars — Elvis Presley, Ricky Nelson, the Chipmunks, even Fats himself — but it wasn't until nearly a year later that he began to make his presence felt on a national level. Hank Ballard had scored in the summer of 1960 with another of his famed *double-entendre* suggestions, "The Twist," and Chubby quickly followed it with a cover version aimed at a whiter, more pop-oriented audience. The dance

(Wide World)

# 88

## Chubby Checker

(also known as the Hump) had caught on with the teenagers, replacing the fading Slop, and both rode the wave for as long as possible, Chubby garnering the major portion of sales and celebrity. As Ballard passed back into his home rhythm and blues market, Checker, under the guidance of managers Kal Mann and Henry Colt, kept exploiting the dance theme, following "The Twist" with such catchy instant replays as "The Hucklebuck," "Ponytime," "The Fly," "Dance The Mess Around" and others in the same vein.

Yet when the October 21 issue of *The New Yorker* hit the stands in 1961, it slowly must have dawned on Chubby and his handlers that only the merest surface had been scratched; that, indeed, the ride had yet to begin.

" 'Been trying for weeks to get into Peppermint Lounge,' " Cholly Knickerbocker quoted Times Square correspondent Our Man Stanley, " 'Hot spot of West Forty-Fifth Street where new dance step known as The Twist has fantastic following. Place always jammed. Huge lines outside. Finally made it last night after hour's wait. Exhilarating experience.' "

Excitement rampaged down Fifth Avenue. Chubby's version of "The Twist" re-entered the charts in November 1961, went to number one for an unprecedented *second* time, and before anyone could catch their breath, precipitated a full force stampede. In the Peppermint Lounge, the famous and near-famous fought their way to the stamp-sized dance floor, eager to see and be seen doing the brand new sensation "just a'sweepin' the nation." On a good night, Porfiro and Odile Rubirosa could be noticed dancing neck and neck with the Duke and Duchess of Bedford. The Bruno Pagliais' matched afterbeats with the Senator and Mrs. Javits, pausing only briefly to eye the wriggling figure of Tennessee Williams. High society abandoned its charity balls for the liberation of a Twist party. The mania spread across the country, then worldwide. For a time, it seemed as if *everybody* was going 'round and 'round, up and down. . . .

And Chubby? Despite hard-nosed competition from Joey Dee ("Peppermint Twist"), Killer Joe Piro, Oliver Twist and anyone who recognized an inviting coattail when they saw it (who can forget Pudgy Parcheesi?), Checker was the undisputed king. He leapt to his task like a born leader, a *coup* at any Beautiful People party, a movie star through *Twist Around The Clock*, ringing up $10,000 a week from personal appearances alone.

If he ever had a sense that the bubble could burst, he never let on. To the end of his days with Parkway, he continued turning out variations on his greatest triumph, creating a body of work that even today has to stand as a landmark of choreography. When the dream faded in America, Chubby took his steps to Europe, where his popularity always bordered on the extreme. There was a brief try at a comeback here in 1969, when he spent five weeks on the charts with the Beatles' "Back In The U.S.S.R.," but even then the heights once his by a simple matter of grace were under a different chain of command. Today he makes the rounds of the various rock & roll revivals, sells oldies albums on television (his "made in the shade" commercial is a classic of the genre) and still can dance up a storm. Limbo, anyone?

# 7
# The Big Three

## THE BEATLES

IN 1963 A BENIGN BUT HIGHLY CONTAGIOUS virus began spreading throughout the British Isles. In October it reached Sweden and by January of the following year, Paris. A month later the U.S.A., had fallen under its sway, then Copenhagen, Amsterdam, Hong Kong, the whole of Australasia. The victims, fainting, pupils dilated, holding their heads in rapturous agony, alternately weeping and shouting with joy, desperately attempted to unite themselves with the carriers of the infection in a supersonic scream of ecstasy. Their cry announced the arrival of a new species: With the Beatles a new age had begun, with new creatures in it.

According to the testament of John Lennon, this unlikely chain of events began in Liverpool sometime in the late fifties, when a man on a flaming table appeared to him in a vision saying, "You are the Beatles with an A." Another version says that on the afternoon of June 15, 1956, John and his skiffle group, the Quarrymen, were playing at a wedding held at Wolton Church where he met Paul McCartney. They became the Nurk Twins and thereafter "bad boy" John encouraged "good pupil" Paul to play hookey and write songs like "One After

909" which turned up more than ten years later as a track on *Let It Be*.

Paul went to school with George and by 1958, John had reluctantly admitted "Little George" to his group which was now called "Johnny and the Moondogs." A year later they got their first gig at the Casbah and met their first drummer, Pete Best. By 1960 they were the Silver Beatles (a play on Buddy Holly's Crickets) and were performing at the legendary Cavern when they got an offer to play at the Indra club in Hamburg's seedy Reeperbahn.

In Germany they made their first record on Polydor, backing singer Tony Sheridan, (an album subsequently re-released as *The Beatles First*). A turning point in their career occurred on October 28, 1961, when a certain Raymond Jones walked into NEMS (North End Music Stores) and requested a record by the Beatles. The proprietor, young Brian Epstein, was not exactly a follower of Liverpool's thriving Beat Groups (The Swinging Blue Jeans, Rory Storme and the Hurricanes, Pacemakers, etc.) but curiosity and fate led him to the dingy, sodden, packed atmosphere of the Cavern where Jones said he'd first heard them. A few days later, after

The Beatles with Ed Sullivan, 1964

negotiations at a milk bar, Brian became the Beatles' manager. He liked the lads' hair-dos (or "hair don'ts," as John called them) which they'd acquired in Germany, courtesy of Astrid Kirchener, girlfriend of early Beatle member Stu Sutcliffe, but he persuaded them to trade in their Gene Vincent-style black leather for Teddy Boy jackets with velvet collars. The next six months were very discouraging. Record contracts were rare, and none of the record companies were interested in the fifties rock & roll the Beatles were playing. Finally in June 1962, Epstein telegramed The Beatles, who were then back in Hamburg sharing the bill at the

Star Club with Little Richard, that they had an audition with George Martin, a producer at EMI. Martin persuaded them to record their own compositions, and in July they cut, among others, "Love Me Do" and "P.S. I Love You," which slowly made their way up the charts in the fall.

1963 was the year of the Beatles in England. In January they'd made it to the top of the Mersey Beat poll. "Please, Please Me," recorded the previous November, came out the same month and gave them their first number one hit. Besieged by mobs as they rehearsed at the Palladium, watched on the telly by 27 million

# 91

## The Beatles

pairs of eyes (more than had viewed the Coronation), hounded by journalists for trendy tidbits and Liverpuddlian anecdotes, they replaced royalty and religion as icons.

The zany, cheeky "Fab Four," with their gelatinous accents, Scouse slang, effervescent good spirits, quick wit ("On the next number," said John at the Royal Variety performance, "would those in the cheap seats clap? The rest of you can rattle your jewelry") and pernicious puns came like barbarians from the north and sacked London. (John: "You can sack Rome, or you can sack cloth or you can sacrilege, or saxophone . . .") They had four more hits in England that year.

What caused Beatlemania (a reaction to the Kennedy assassination? The fall of the British Empire? Genetic mutation?) It is an almost unanswerable question, but how it came to originate in such an unlikely place as Liverpool is less difficult to explain. Like New Orleans, which also produced a profusion of music, Liverpool is a seaport, absorbing a wide variety

of influences. It was the first place in England where American records got played. Also, it is a city of rock & roll gangs. Soon after *Rock Around the Clock* was shown there, gangs began forming, and eventually the gangs centered their attention around their favorite local groups. They had their own clubs and even their own music paper, *The Mersey Beat.* So fierce were loyalties to these tribal totems, that in August 1962 when Ringo Starr left Rory Storme and the Hurricanes and replaced Pete Best as the Beatles drummer, riots broke out; Brian Epstein feared for his life.

The stars of the fifties had almost all been solo singers, but with the Beatles, group mania began, bringing out the Animals, the Stones, the Kinks, etc. The group was a self-contained unit, a collective identity that the audience could share in. The Beatles were the first of these collective organisms — one for all and all four one — who fused themselves together through their harmonies. In their early songs they deliberately encouraged participation in

*(Joe Pope/Strawberry Fields Archives)*

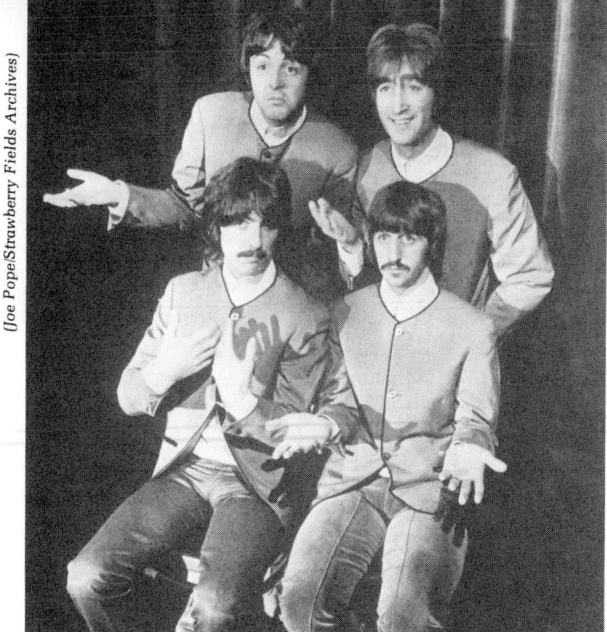

their musical family, by making their songs into a dialogue with their audiences — "Love Me Do," "From Me To You," "Do You Want To Know A Secret?," "All My Loving," "I Want to Hold Your Hand" — to which their fans responded with screams of recognition.

> REPORTER: "How do you find America?"
> JOHN: "Turn left at Greenland."

"Love Me Do" and "Please, Please Me" had been released in late 1963 on two American labels, Swan and Vee Jay, and had made virtually no impact at all. "I Want To Hold Your Hand" — first aired on WMCA Radio at 12:50 P.M., December 29, 1963 — was released by Capitol the following January, along with a

massive publicity campaign of 5 million stickers saying "The Beatles Are Coming." The Beatles climbed the charts in an unprecedented three weeks. When they stepped off the plane at Kennedy airport in February 1964 they were greeted by 10,000 delirious fans. Their effect was instantaneous. As they passed through customs, boys ran down the stairs combing their pompadours into bangs and shaking out their ducktails. Deejays began recording the temperature in Beatle degrees, time in Beatle seconds. Everything was transformed overnight in their image. There were Beatle eggcups, wallpaper, dolls, T-shirts, wigs, nighties, watches and winklepickers.

Essentially, the Beatles were giving back to America a lost American music. Rock & roll had formed the largest part of their 6- to 8-hour sets at the Star Club and the Cavern, but they never thought of it as old music or nostalgia. For them it was part of the rock continuum, and in their re-creations and imitations, they reminded us of the vitality and timelessness of the best rock & roll. On *Beatles '65* they devoted an album to their rock & roll roots, and on *Help* Paul conjured up an uncanny duplication of his idol, Little Richard, in "I'm Down." On their last album together, *Let It Be*, they were still using Carl Perkins, Chuck Berry, Jerry Lee Lewis and Fats Domino as a sort of rock catechism to get into their own music.

John, Paul and George had been playing together for four years before they made their first record, and it was this long preparation that gave them such command of their own musical language. The collaboration with George Martin gave them the ability to make the first lasting innovations in rock in a decade. The balance of personalities, musical and psychological — Paul's bitter-sweet ballads, John's wry humor and word play — provided a constant momentum, and because both wrote words *and* music, a more complex and varied sound evolved than with the Stones. *Rubber Soul*, released in December 1965, was the first album entirely written by John, Paul and George, and they had begun to expand musically and lyrically. John had confined his wickedly surreal mind to his Joycean books, *In His Own Write*

On the roof for *Let It Be*

(Joe Pope/Strawberry Fields Archives)

and *A Spaniard In The Works*, but after meeting Dylan in New York he released his impish images into his songs, which grew more personal, starting with "Norwegian Wood," gradually becoming almost hermetic, in "She Said, She Said," "Strawberry Fields," "Across The Universe," "I Am The Walrus" and "Come Together." With the sitar on *Rubber Soul* they started to expand their musical vocabulary as well, and on *Revolver*, possibly the most innovative rock album ever made, harpsichords, brass and violins were introduced along with the backwards tapes and multiple tracking that eventually led to the electronic experiments of "A Day In The Life." *Revolver* was a total collaboration with George Martin, giving a fifth dimension to their music through his arrangements and production. By allowing them

to expand without any technical or musical barriers he opened up practically unlimited possibilities.

It was George Martin, who had played in the brass bands on Sundays in St. James Park, who suggested the marching band theme for Sgt. Pepper, their psychedelic masterpiece for which they were canonized by Timothy Leary as "the Four Evangelists from Liverpool." Just when everything seemed to be getting better all the time — they were the four most famous names in the world, "more popular than Jesus," as John blurted out, and were seeking the light with the help of the Maharishi — Pepperland began to fall. First came Brian Epstein's death from an OD of barbiturates. When the Beatles stopped touring, his universe had fallen apart. Without "Daddy," as Paul called him, the

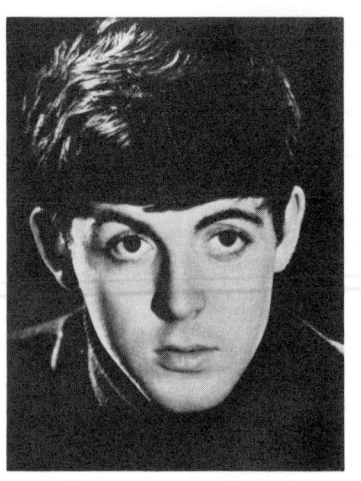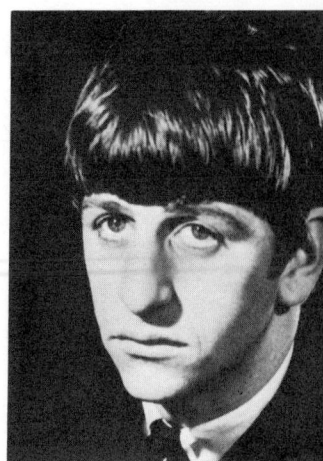

Beatles fell prey to business megalomania, psychedelic clichés, transcendental tautologies and internal feuding. By the time of the white album in 1968, John, Paul, George and Ringo were no longer writing songs *together*. They had effectually split up long before the final break in January 1971.

The sixties was the Beatles' decade. It began with them and they grew up with it. They radiated an incredible optimism that in its spontaneous exuberance, energy and imagination approached a child's vision of the world where everything is transformed into play. It was as if through the theatre of their albums, John's wordplay songs, their hide-and-seek movies, their refusal to take anything seriously, they were attempting to solve the problems of the world by playing their music and through their *make-believe* they made us believe it could be done.

# THE ROLLING STONES

THEY HAVE PARTICIPATED IN AND PRO-voked the transformation of the morals and manners of their generation so effectively that to future social historians the Rolling Stones might actually seem to bear out reactionary ravings that they are the ringleaders of an international conspiracy of rock & roll punks to undermine Western civilization with drugs, music, polymorphous sexuality and violence. But myths involve complicity. As Mick Jagger, the pied piper of this revolution, said, "All this stuff about my leading and perverting them . . . we just sort of went along together, didn't we?"

The Stones have been the primary catalysts in creating an adolescent lifestyle without precedence by grasping the repressed elements of society and expressing its confusions and frustrations with outlandish exhibition. What they sang about and projected on stage became the blueprint for a new society within society, fantasized about since rock & roll began. If the Beatles initiated it, it was the Stones who amplified it and stretched it to its logical conclusion, and if their effect has been less universal than that of their polar twins, the Beatles, it has also been more insidious because it is more difficult for society to absorb their antisocial stance. The Stones have always delighted in their role as outlaws, even when it meant the banning of their songs, censoring of album covers (the toilet graffiti on the original *Beggar's Banquet*) and even jail sentences. Their punky arrogance makes them the aristocrats of the new morality. "We are not old men," Keith Richard told the court disdainfully when asked

(16 Magazine)

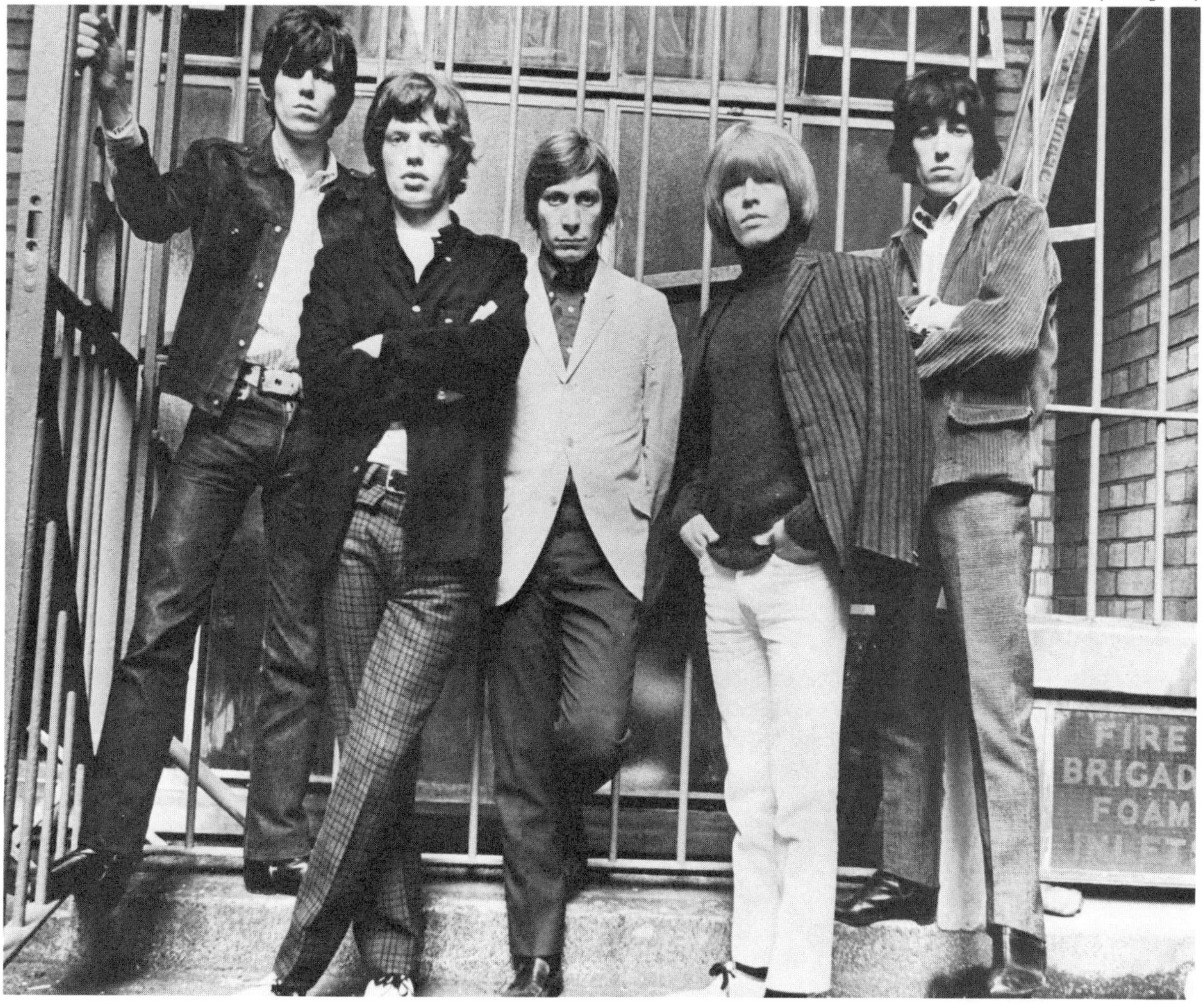


(Collection Peter Kanze)

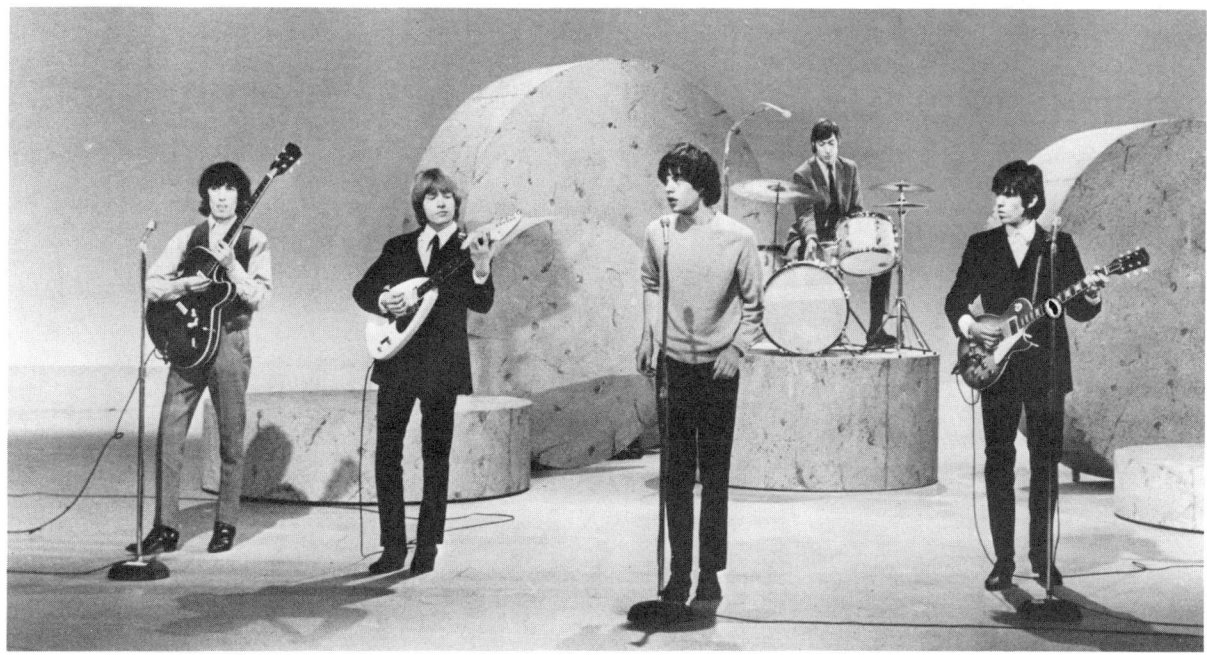

about the presence of a nude girl at the "drug party" for which he was being sentenced, "we are not concerned with your petty morals which are illegitimate."

As street fighters for the new sensibility, the instrument the Stones used to pry themselves and their subculture away from traditional morality and convention was the liberating monster reeking of barely concealed menace and sexuality latent in rock and blues. When English groups discovered bluesmen like Howlin' Wolf and Muddy Waters and resurrected the rock & roll of Chuck Berry and Bo Diddley, for social and emotional reasons they found it easy to identify completely with them and made explicit what was only implicit in R & B and rock & roll. Because they were not inhibited by the social and racial pressures which the black musicians worked under, working-class lads were able to take its hip, aggressive and sensual stance and make it into a social force.

R & B had always been suspect by the English musical establishment, who favored jazz — especially traditional jazz — and it was this bigotry that was the occasion for the Stones getting together for their first professional performance early in 1963 at the Marquee Club, standing in for Alexis Korner's Blues Incorporated. The Stones, as yet unnamed and minus Charlie Watts, had been playing together since the previous summer. The original nucleus, Mick, Keith and Brian Jones had first gotten together at a pub called The Bricklayers Arms at the end of 1961, all sharing a taste for raunchy R & B, rock & roll and blues. Brian, as the only "professional" musician of the three (he had played with a number of blues groups like the Ramrods and Blues by Five, of which Charlie Watts was later a member) became the original leader of the group. Keith was a hard-core rocker and talented layabout who had gotten into old blues at art school, Mick, who had come from the same town of Dartford, site of the fourteenth-century Peasant's Revolt, was seriously pursuing studies at the London School of Economics, although he had been singing with Blues Inc. since 1960. Mick had been a mimic since childhood, always the loudest in his class: "When it came to singing nursery

Brian Jones backstage

(David McCabe)

rhymes, when I didn't know the words I'd make them up." Charlie and Bill Wyman, who formed the Stones' driving rhythm section, started out in jazz, but after exposure to Alexis Korner acquired a taste for R & B too.

In February 1963, the Stones began to really start rolling as the resident band at the Crawdaddy Club in the Station Hotel in Richmond, attracting their first fanatical followers. In May (after some unsatisfactory attempts at IBC Studios) they cut their first two singles at Olympic, "Come On" released in June, and the Beatles' "I Wanna Be Your Man" for Decca. In the fall they went on their first English tour with Bo Diddley and the Everly Brothers.

By early 1964 they had established themselves on the English charts with "I Wanna Be Your Man" (backed by the first of the Stones' incredible mood songs, "Stoned"), "Not Fade Away/Little By Little," and an EP containing "Poison Ivy," "Bye, Bye Johnny," "Money" and "Not Fade Away." With the help of their manager, the quintessential mod and pop propagandist, Andrew Oldham, they were imprinting their image as "the group parents love to hate." The National Federation of hairdressers offered them haircuts, police dogs went berserk at their concerts, girls flew off balconies, and soda bottles touched by Mick were being hawked as sacred objects. In June they began their first U.S. tour, and the second trip, although they were still relatively

**The Rolling Stones**

unknown, gave them a chance to show their contagious effect on American audiences by successfully following James Brown, the Supremes and Jan and Dean on the *T.A.M.I. Show*.

The Stones remained a cult group, and as with all such groups were pushed by a small fanatic group of fans until the summer of 1965, when they established themselves almost instantaneously with "Satisfaction," *the* classic rock song. Opening with Keith Richard's menacing fuzz tone riff and sung with an insinuating, calculated slowness by Jagger, its smouldering sound sums up the frustrations of the sixties in an emotional language. Loosely based on Martha and the Vandellas' "Dancing in the Streets," it is a bitter, ironic blend of blues, R & B and rock that the Stones had been working on since 1962. The synthesis created a disdainful tone that was to become the epitome of their songs. Their album *Out Of Our Heads*, recorded at the legendary Chess Studios in Chicago, came out the same year. Its white funk R & B sound was the culmination of the first phase of the Stones' career. R & B had never been done better by a white group; the Stones had an instinctive "feel" for it. Although other English blues singers like Eric Burdon and Stevie Winwood had voices closer to those of the black R & B singers, Jagger's nasal style of singing was more evocative: he was able to make it personal and identifiable, instead of a mere facsimile. But the Stones's obsession with R & B presented some problems for their writing which had been mainly limited to uncanny re-creations of blues and soul in songs like "Little By Little," "Heart Of Stone" and "The Last Time." It wasn't until *Aftermath*, their fifth American album (which came out at the same time as *Revolver*), that the Stones produced an LP of entirely Jagger/Richard compositions.

In the early compositions, the lyrics had been simple and repetitive and the sound deliberately derivative, but on *Aftermath* and *Between the Buttons* the Stones entered their most bizarre period. Conjugating a verbal ambiguity inspired by Dylan and social themes from the Kinks, their songs took on a surrealistic quality, focusing on a weird collection of types:

*(Joann Jiminez)*

Mick Jagger

**The Rolling Stones**

neurasthenic bitches, suburban pill-poppers, discotheque dodos and slumming heiresses. They developed an expressionistic precision for examining confused relationships, disturbed emotional states, and made an art of arrogance and egocentricity. "Under My Thumb" is so vicious it manages to justify itself by its own outrageousness.

By the end of 1966 Mick and Marianne Faithfull were the models of a perfect mod couple, and the Stones were replacing the Beatles so rapidly as trendsetters that Mick had to tell his faithful followers, "The lines around my eyes are protected by a copyright law." They were also becoming targets. They were an open threat, flaunting a new and menacing lifestyle. A month after the release of "Let's Spend The Night Together" in January 1967, both Keith and Mick were arrested on flimsy evidence for the possession of drugs, and in June were sentenced to one year and three months respectively. A lead article in the London *Times* turned the tide in their favor and in July they were released. Unrepentant as ever, they released the sneering "We Love You," which opens with a jail door slamming, and in December put out the drug-drenched futuristic *Their Satanic Majesties Request*. This late psychedelic album is considered by many to be the most pretentious and baroque of their efforts.

Along with Dylan and the Beatles, the Stones stopped touring between 1966 and 1969. It was their most confused period, and for Brian it was fatal. Already broken from the strain of constant touring, he began to disintegrate. He was in and out of hospitals for nervous exhaustion, and following his first bust in October 1967, the police pursued him ruthlessly "like when a hound dog smells blood," as Keith put it. The harrassment and brutality had turned this once tough little Welsh bull into an irridescent ghost made barely visible by the drugs which sustained him. When the Stones decided to go on tour again in 1969, Brian was in no shape to travel. On June 9 he officially quit the group and was replaced by Mick Taylor from John Mayall's Blues-breakers. In less than a month he was dead, drowned in his swimming pool.

With Brian gone a certain amputation took place and a dimension of the Stones' basically monolithic sound was lost. It was Brian's complexity and diversity — his satanic sitar on "Paint it Black," the dulcimer on "Lady Jane," the recorder on "Ruby Tuesday" — that gave a subtle inflection to the elemental sound of the Stones' songs and created a counterpoint. As the only other "performer" in the group, Jagger was pushed into a solo stance and undermined the collective force of the group.

It is their economy — Keith Richard's pure treble guitar as shrill as the voice of electricity, balanced like a knife edge on the relentless solid rhythm section of Charlie Watts and Bill Wyman, combined with the sexual innuendo of Jagger's voice out in front — that creates the critical emotional mass of their music. Their approach permits them to reconnect instantly with their roots without resorting to nostalgia. Simple as direct current, their basic attitude has been "It's Only Rock 'n' Roll But I Like It."

Although no less "artificial" than *Satanic Majesties*, the Stones regained their bearings with the rambling acoustic styles of *Beggar's Banquet* and resurrected their "mythic readymades" now fermented with humor and salacious detail. The most fantastic apparition to appear at the Banquet is Lucifer himself in "Sympathy For The Devil," an exultant hymn to

Keith Richard

(© 1976 Bob Gruen)

The Rolling Stones, 1976,
with Ronnie Wood

the dark forces. The Stones began to redefine their old amped-up selves in "Jumpin' Jack Flash," a version of their own fantasy history as singers of the blues, extracting its essence from their old favorites, Chuck Berry, Bo Diddley and Howlin' Wolf.

America to the Stones has always been an erotic and violent landscape, fantasized out of the potent images of R & B. But by 1969, after Charles Manson and the murder at their Altamont concert, the chilling visions of "Midnight Rambler" and "Gimme Shelter" they had summoned up on *Let It Bleed* were becoming alarmingly real.

The history of the Stones after the bluesy synthamesc-spiked *Let It Bleed* is the history of a different kind of band, as they began experimenting with rock forms outside their old R&B roots, developing more layered and complex recording techniques, adding the horns of Bobby Keyes and Jim Price to *Sticky Fingers,* and adapting the styles of their rock contemporaries like Santana (on "Can't You Hear Me Knockin' ") and Van Morrison ("Winter" on *Goat's Head Soup)* in the same way they had once used Delta Blues and Soul. Jagger's voice even shifted in resonance from a deliberate imitation of black singers to almost a twang, beginning with their monster hit single, "Honky Tonk Women." The masterpiece of this period is the double *Exile on Main Street* album, the most intimate of all their albums, as well as

the most emotionally explicit.

Once known for their monolithic blues and soul transformations, in the 1970s, the Stones became almost chameleonlike in their synthesis of styles. If the output was occasionally thin, as on the burnt-out *Goat's Head Soup,* following their 1972 tour, or the corporate Stones' statements of *It's Only Rock and Roll,* or the concept band on *Black and Blue* with its moveable Stone components, they remained as calculated and unpredictable as ever.

The power of the Stones' hieroglyphic songs and hypnotic performances — their satanic stance, pansexual hedonism, drug fetishes and politics of delinquency — is that they *are* fantasies dreamt up by the dark princes of rock & roll, mental tigers awakened from the deepest layers of rock geology. The songs seem so real because the Stones, at one remove from both the sources and the consequences, are capable of embodying them so totally, thus creating rock's most sensual and convincing theatre. To Mick's outrageous, polymorphous and campy music hall ventriloquism Keith's lethal guitar lends authority and intensity, and together make Mick into some beautiful sequined monster of his own imaginings, prancing, lurching, flaunting himself in a narcissistic fury as if driven by the fevers of electricity to look at himself in every face in the crowd. And we, by sheathing ourselves in him, experience through the Stones the projections of what we are about to be.

# BOB DYLAN

"I SEE THINGS OTHER PEOPLE DON'T," Dylan once said about himself. "I dissolve myself into situations where I am invisible." Dylan's progress has been a serial enigma, his oscillating personality making him the most elusive presence in rock. Each successive phase of his career has given rise not only to a radically different type of music, but what amounts to a new Dylan, as if he consisted of an overlay of images each transparent through the next, fused and connected to each other only by his own mysterious and dynamic current: the earnest singer of dustbowl ballads and protest hymns in work clothes; the flashing rock star with shades, aureole of hair, amphetamines and seething irony; the bearded patriarch, teller of mystic tales; contented country gentleman, and starcrossed troubador of the seventies.

"Dylan," said a friend from his early folk days in New York, "was someone who was continually inventing himself." His many metamorphoses began in the summer of 1958 when he created his first identity: Bob Dylan.

He was born Robert Allen Zimmerman in 1941 and grew up in Hibbing, Minnesota, a mining town renowned as the site of the "biggest hole made by man." In high school he formed his own group, the Golden Chords, imitating Little Richard and Buddy Holly. He went to the University of Minnesota but dropped out after a year to play in the campus coffeehouses around Dinkytown. He began replacing his background with his own mythology, variously claiming to be an orphan from Oklahoma, an itinerant carny worker, a bass player with Bobby Vee, or Bobby Vee himself.

In the fall of 1960, while singing between strippers at the Gilded Garter in Denver, he found a personal model in the wandering dustbowl singer Woody Guthrie. Guthrie, with his frontier idealism and his drifter's ways, was a romantic figure, and his idiosyncratic talking-blues suited Dylan's adenoidal style of nonsinging. "Guthrie," Dylan said, "was my last idol. My future idols will be myself." He totally absorbed Woody Guthrie's vision of folk poetry and it enabled him to create songs which had the quality of traditional American music.

Early in 1961 he hitchhiked to New York to see Woody Guthrie (who was dying of Huntington's disease) and began hanging out around Manhattan's Greenwich Village folk scene. By April he'd landed his first professional job at Gerde's Folk City. Basically Dylan was an eclectic, sifting, borrowing and grafting on material and styles from musicians like Dave Von Ronk, Ramblin' Jack Elliott, Eric Von Schmidt and Danny Kalb.

His early songs — "Talking Bear Mountain," "Picnic Massacre Blues" (from a newspaper item) and "Talking John Birch Paranoid Blues" were pure Woody Guthrie, but by 1962 he'd fused a number of elements together into an uncanny reconstitution of traditional folk music. He was not averse to taking old folk tunes and gluing his own words onto them. By pinning the lyrics of his early songs to recognizable folk melodies — "Scarborough Fair" for "Girl From The North Country" and "Lord Randall" for "A Hard Rain's Gonna Fall" — he endowed them with an additional authenticity.

Dylan was ideally synchronized with the protest movement of the sixties. His songs, unlike those of many folk singers, seemed to propel the movement by their immediacy, while in turn the movement itself became a vehicle for Dylan's rise to fame. The song which established him as the most important writer in the protest movement was "Blowin' In The Wind."

Dylan appeared on a number of blues and folk records playing harmonica (including the title track of Belafonte's *Midnight Special*) before putting out his own album for Columbia in March 1962. Although Bob Dylan was comparatively successful, he was known first as a songwriter who sang his own songs in a weird voice. In June 1963, Peter, Paul and Mary released a version of "Blowin' In The Wind" which sold more than 300,000 copies in the first two weeks and became the anthem of the protest movement. When Dylan appeared at the

**101**
**Bob Dylan**

(Jenny Shatzberg)

Bob with Pete Seeger, Greenwood, Mississippi

Newport Folk Festival a month later he was hailed as the visionary poet hero who was orchestrating the "youth revolution."

Although he was by now the acknowledged Crown Prince of Folk, Dylan had begun to suspect the literal-mindedness of protest songs which saw life only in "lies of black and white." To the naive question "which side are you on?" he answered, "which side can you be on?"

Dylan's later protest songs, like "Masters Of War," "With God On Our Side" and "The Times They Are A-Changin'," with their hymnlike grace, gave depth and substance to the feelings of hopelessness and desperation that so many kids were experiencing and which Dylan shared. The incredible density of "A Hard Rain's Gonna Fall," written at the time of the Cuban missile crisis, came from Dylan's fear that time was running out.

By the time he was making his fourth album, *Another Side of Bob Dylan*, he had exposed the paradox of protest — "I'd become my enemy in the instant that I preach" — in "My Back Pages."

Misgivings about commitment to causes also came from his certainty about himself as an artist. Bombarded by the poetry of Allen Ginsberg and the French symbolists, his lyrics became more elliptical, ironic and surrealistic. But it was not this new figurative language or his bitter personal vision, but the defection to rock that made Dylan a Judas to the folk movement. Rock was considered commercial,

inane and a sellout by folkies. Dylan broke out as a rock star on *Bringing It All Back Home;* the title referred to his rock beginnings and also became his first million selling album. He had been impressed with what the Animals had done to two folk songs from his first album, "House Of The Rising Sun" and "Follow Me Down," and when the Byrds in early 1965 came out with a rock version of "Mr. Tambourine Man," Dylan saw how rock could shoot electricity through his epic images and convert them into neon icons.

"My words are pictures," he said, "and rock is gonna help me flesh out those pictures." Despite the fact that he had come out with *Bringing It All Back Home* in March and in June "Like A Rolling Stone" was playing over top 40 radio, when Dylan stepped on stage at the Newport Folk Festival in July with a solid body

**Bob Dylan**

electric guitar and launched into "Maggie's Farm" his "betrayal" seemed to come as a shock. They booed him off the stage and he kissed them goodbye with "It's All Over Now, Baby Blue."

Joan Baez, with her militant stance, had done a lot to promote Dylan during his early career. They had became the King and Queen of folk music, which made his defection to rock seem especially cruel because it shattered the romantic image they'd created.

Ironically it is on his identity as a rock singer that Dylan's reputation depends and it was on the albums he made between 1965 and 1967 — *Bringing It All Back Home*, *Highway 61 Revisited* and *Blonde On Blonde* — that he created his masterpieces of electric poetry. Nevertheless, Dylan remains one of the oddest rock stars around. None of the giant figures of sixties rock had good voices, their imperfections guaranteed their authenticity, but Dylan's raspy howl, once described as "the sound of a prairie dog caught on barbed wire," was an eccentric, rusty instrument that made a virtue of imperfection and gave his penetrating images a ferocious personal edge that was impossible to ignore or mistake.

He had a habit of barely rehearsing his material and recording in few takes. He gave his songs a startling intimacy and immediacy by leaving in out-of-tune instruments, wrong notes and by adapting his phrasing to loping speech patterns like "How does it feel?" and "Something is happening but you don't know what it is, do you?"

Dylan broke the three-minute barrier for singles on "Like A Rolling Stone," and introduced country music along with a number of other regional styles into the bloodstream of rock. While Dylan brought with him a subtlety of language from folk music, he made his lyrics part of a rock tradition by amplifying what Chuck Berry had begun. What Dylan called his "chains of flashing images" fit perfectly into the fragmented idiom of rock.

If Dylan had alienated the original folk audience in 1965, he created in its place an even more fanatical audience. It was impossible for him to fulfill the expectations he had created, to continue the precedent of innovative quality he set on albums like *Blonde On Blonde* and *Highway 61*. He had put a permanent revolution into motion, and so much importance was attached to everything he said that friends feared it was becoming dangerous for him to appear on stage. Dylan's albums were listened to as if they were seismic readings from an impending apocalypse.

In the summer of 1966 he suffered a near-fatal motorcycle accident near his home in Woodstock. For two years the oracle was silent and when he re-emerged it was as a grim figure of an Old Testament prophet, speaking still in parables, but the images were stripped bare, epitomized in the chilling vision of "Along The Watchtower" and symbolized by the monochrome cover of *John Wesley Harding*. The austerity of the album had an instantaneous effect on the hothouse climate of psychedelic music. The folk hero John Wesley Harding was a favorite theme of Woody Guthrie, and as Dylan returned to his roots, the two other titans of rock — the Beatles and the Stones — looked back on theirs with *Let It Be* (originally titled *Get Back*) and *Beggar's Banquet*.

Unlike the Beatles and the Stones, Dylan looked on rock & roll and R & B as the Old Testament of rock for which he would write the new gospel. For his text he developed vivid electrical connections by juxtaposing paradoxical images. It is fair to say that songs like "Get Off Of My Cloud," "Jigsaw Puzzle," "I Am The Walrus," "Strawberry Fields" or "Come Together" would not have been written without Dylan's example.

His genius was to conjure up and make visible the American Dream as nightmare through his attack on the tyranny of logic and morality, and to let us see it not simply as his own vision, but as though his were the only eyes that could really see it. He became the catalyst for the mass adoption of the underground. The Woodstock pop festival was an unspoken homage to the visionary poet from a generation who had used his ideas as maps.

If his move into country music and his association with Johnny Cash on *Nashville Skyline* were unexpected, they came from a genuine impulse; Hank Williams had been his boyhood idol back in Hibbing. Dylan recognized country music as the genuine legacy of white folk music, what he somewhat cynically referred to as "the last area of authentic American music left for us to dig up." The album contained a couple haunting songs, "I Threw It All Away" and "Lay, Lady Lay," but it was more country and Dylan than an attempt to mimic Nashville.

Next came the ironically titled *Self Portrait* (containing mostly songs written by other people), the lethargically optimistic *New Morning*, followed by *Planet Waves*, which contained some bizarre interpretations of his own material on the "live" tracks. This dismal period has been compared to Rimbaud's self-imposed exile in Abyssinia, but unlike Rimbaud, Dylan had a generation to contend with who obsessively confused the messenger with his message, and waited patiently at the foot of the mountain for his next commandment. Unlike the anonymous hero/victim of "Like A Rolling Stone," Dylan was no longer invisible. A million eyes watched him even in retreat and waited for the secrets they felt he was hoarding.

On *Blood On The Tracks* the lonely intensity, missing from his albums since *Blonde On Blonde*, seemed to have returned. As he exposed the pain of his private life, the separation from his wife Sara ("Shelter From The Storm," "You're a Big Girl Now"), the tortured confusion of his early days on the road ("Tangled Up In Blue"), the imagery was no longer surreal and illusive. He had crafted a vernacular, a language that was functional, almost simplistic. On "Idiot Wind" the old fury had awakened as he converted his personal vacuum into an epic image of national futility. On *Blood On The Tracks* the "old Dylan," so often invoked, was back "alive as you or me," but the effect of this resurrection had the eerie

quality of a time warp as if the album belonged chronologically somewhere between *Bringing It All Back Home* and *Highway 61 Revisited*.

On the following album, *Desire*, he literally seemed to be returning to his own beginnings with an actual protest song ("Hurricane Carter") and an example of the American hero-made-myth ("Ballad Of Joey Gallo"). But as hauntingly resonant as some of the songs are on this album, especially his hymn "Sara," it pales beside his great albums of the sixties. There is a decline in the evocativeness of the language (he actually shares writing credits with Jacques Levy on many of the songs), and a woeful manufacturing of overblown symbols instead. Performances came off better, though they lacked innovation. In 1975 with the secretively planned and clandestinely executed Rolling Thunder Revue, he seemed to be trying to return to the simpler more communicative relationship with his audience, taking along his buddies from the old folk days, Joan Baez, Ramblin' Jack Elliott and Bobby Neuwirth.

From his solitary growlings to his enigmatic utterances as oracle of an angry god to the troubador's tales of the seventies, Dylan has always possessed the ventriloquist's gift. His genius has been to animate a seemingly infinite cast of selves and others, to populate his ongoing epic with elements drawn from history, movies, the blues, the Bible, literature, politics, comic strips, newspapers, cliches, the circus, police blotters, casual conversations and the driftwood of the unconscious. As long as he kept his jealous inner core camouflaged, it would generate the voltage for that hoard of angry and wounded clones of himself. It allowed him to imagine so many different Dylans that he has created a sort of Dylan on Dylan effect where he speaks so articulately to and through others because they too are himself.

# 8
# Blow-Up

## THE ANIMALS

THE SULPHUROUS COAL MINING AND IN-
dustrial belt of England is often referred to as
"The Black Country," and it was from these
"dark satanic mills" that the "blackest" of all
English R & B groups emerged.
Newcastle-on-Tyne, hometown of the Animals
and Eric Burdon, who became spokesman for
the group and its only surviving member, is a
drab, "grotty" colliery town straight out of D. H.
Lawrence. Here, working-class toughs like Eric
had little to look forward to besides a bleak life
of drudgery and Saturday night booze-ups.

The hopelessness of this oppressive, soul
destroying atmosphere kindled in belligerent
war babies like Burdon and his mates a
smouldering resentment which seemed to have
no outlet. But Newcastle-on-Tyne was also a
seaport and like Liverpool or New Orleans, a lot
of music was channeled through it. It was the
music from the R & B records brought back from
the States by merchant seamen that the Animals
were to weld into a blunt instrument for venting
their pent-up aggression and frustration,
vindicating their lower-class background by
identifying themselves almost totally with the
plight of black Americans and their music.

The group's surly stance and scruffy
working-class garb, and the attitude of their
"cocky Geordie" lead singer, Eric Burdon,
bristling with hostility, won the Alan Price
Combo (as the group was originally called) their
nickname, "the animals." They proudly adopted
it as the name for the group.

Alan Price, the group's organist, had
originally formed the nucleus of the group with
Bryan "Chas" Chandler on rock bottom bass and
John Steele on drums. After teaming up with
Eric Burdon and Hilton Patterson (who changed
his name to Valentine, presumably because he
was the heartthrob of the group), they began
playing a mix of skiffle, jazz, and Bo Diddley at
local pubs and clubs. Mickie Most spotted them
at the Club-A-Go-Go (it was one of Mickey
Most's first production ventures — he went on to
produce Donovan and T. Rex) and he typed up a
contract then and there on a sheet of Mike
Jeffries' stationery. (Jeffries was the club's owner
who went on to produce Hendrix.)

Their first release in late 1963 was "Baby
Let Me Take You Home," a reworking of an
obscure Dylan track and it immediately made
the British top 20. But it was another song that

### The Animals

Dylan had also done on his first album, "The House Of The Rising Sun," that became a worldwide smash and made the Animals equal to the Stones and the Beatles in their initial impact. In 1964 Eric Burdon was voted the Best White Blues Singer of the Year in the *New Musical Express* poll, and Brian Jones, of all people, called him "the best lead singer in Britain."

The group wanted to make bluesy records, which they did effectively, like John Lee Hooker's "Boom Boom Boom" and their own "I'm Crying," but their producer Mickie Most pressured them to record more commercial material, hence a rare blend of raw blues and Tin Pan Alley evolved and out of this fusion came possibly their best song, "We Gotta Get Out Of This Place." It seemed almost tailor-made for them by professional songwriters Cynthia Weil and Barry Mann, who had written hits for the Righteous Brothers and the Crystals.

In the summer of 1965 internal problems began to develop in the group, culminating in the departure of Alan Price, who nevertheless had a fairly successful career on his own with his jazz-inflected pop songs like "I Put A Spell

On You" and "Simon Smith And His Amazing Dancing Bear," and the 1973 score for the film *O Lucky Man*. After Price left the Animals, they continued to have hits — "Don't Bring Me Down," "Don't Let Me Be Misunderstood," "When I Was Young." But Price was right when he said, "They never had a million seller after I left." While Burdon could still belt them out, the original effectiveness of the Animals came from the counterpoint between Alan Price's soulful Ray Charles inspired organ playing and subtle arrangements played off against Eric Burdon's raw vocals.

This loss of Price left the remaining Animals vulnerable to Burdon's gullibility and endless reshufflings of the group. In San Francisco he seemed to become totally derailed, writing chamber of commerce lyrics and after-the fact songs like "San Francisco Nights," "Monterey" and "Sky Pilot." But Eric himself never quite managed to take it over the Rainbow Bridge.

By 1969 the Animals were completely disbanded, and Eric turned to his old self-professed ideal of becoming a "white nigger," forming an all-black group called War,

*(Collection Peter Kanze)*

DAVE ROWBERRY  ERIC BURDON  CHAS CHANDLER  HILTON VALENT

with which he had a worldwide hit, "Spill The Wine," before leaving to do it on his own.

Inadvertently Eric's runty punk sincerity, the backbone of the original Animals, now became a liability; singing the blues wasn't enough for him. While other English invasion groups postured, inflected and re-created American R & B, Eric, earnest as ever, made it his life's ambition to "Paint It Black." His original and valid equation — working-class hero-black man's burden — became an unintentional seesaw between guilt and total identification with the black singers he was so faithfully duplicating and therefore exploiting.

What seemed to be missing in the later history of Eric Burdon *and* the Animals, as they came to be called, was not just imagination or even Alan Price's organ, but an almost total lack of a sense of humor that made Eric himself into a musical joke as he evangelically promoted every manipulated fashion, becoming a parody of what were obviously genuine impulses. While the press was fond of ridiculing Eric for his crusades, more generous spirits sympathized with the Burdon who protested on his 1965 hit, "Don't Let Me Be Misunderstood."

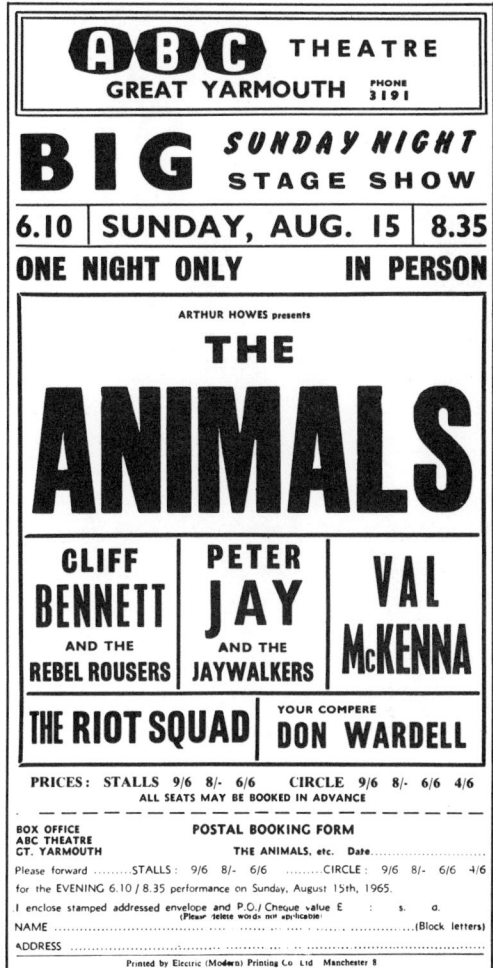

*(Collection Alan Betrock)*

# THE WHO

THE TEEN DREAM LIES AT THE CORE OF rock & roll and no group has explored, projected and interpreted the turbulent substances of teenage craniums with such relish and consistency as the Who, an English group that became the undisputed mod band of the mid-sixties. Mods were young working-class lads full of an incipient violence that would find its perfect expression in the performances of the Who.

The group began as the Detours in 1963. Pete Townshend (on banjo) and John Entwhistle (on trumpet) had been in a Dixieland jazz band together in school, and when they joined up with a local roughneck, Roger Daltry, they began playing top forties numbers at local pubs, wearing matching red jackets. Townshend had acquired a taste for John Lee Hooker, and persuaded the band to play blues; they got themselves some scruffy gear and changed their name to the Who.

Shortly thereafter a new image, another new name and a new drummer popped up. One night while they were playing at the Oldfield Hotel in Greenford, Keith Moon staggered up on stage and challenged the group to play with him. After totally demolishing the other drummer's kit he was hired on the spot. Under the influence of "mod miracle man" Pete Meaden, they adopted the name the High

The Who at Shepherds Bush Bingo Hall, 1964

Numbers, and cut their first single, "I'm The Face"/"Zoot Suit" for Fontana which quietly faded away.

With the arrival of competitive groups like the Yardbirds, the Who abandoned blues and switched to slicker Motown material. By 1964 they had also found film producers Kit Lambert and Chris Stamp, who would help focus, package and propel the group to international stardom. They became the Who again and had three instant hits in England in 1965: the classic "My Generation" (originally a slow talking blues spoof with no key changes), "Anyway, Anywhere, Anyhow, Anywhere" and "I Can't Explain." Although they still played a lot of Motown/James Brown material, they were now evolving their own relentless driving sound, based on fifties American hard rockers Eddie Cochran, Gene Vincent and Johnny Kidd and the Pirates, and a punky stage stance that reflected the irruptible attitudes of their Mod following at suburban London dancehalls.

"Ours is a group with built-in hate," Townshend liked to say about the Who when the group hit the stage of The Marquee Club at their Tuesday night rave-up, their energy demonically coiling as they escalated the decibels to a deafening crescendo. "I'll be getting really musically involved and some

stupid girl with 'Freddie' tattooed on her front will come up and scream 'Ringo.' You feel like smashing her with coke bottles.''

It was at some point in this year that Pete Townshend, doing one of his aerial leaps, slammed his guitar neck against the low ceiling of the Railway Tavern, ''got a tremendous buzz from it'' and proceeded to smash it to pieces. He thus created the first of their ritual apocalyptic destructions, the drum-demolishing, smoke-bomb climax that was to become a nasty habit that they were compelled to re-enact at almost every performance for the next five years.

The Who remained a cult group in the United States, until the 1967 release of a novelty song, ''Happy Jack,'' and an intensive publicity campaign by New York deejay, Murray the K. Their legend had preceded them to the States, and rockers got a first tantalizing taste of them at Murray the K's Easter Show at the Paramount, but it wasn't until later that year, at the Monterey Pop Festival, that American audiences got the impact of their ferocious, flamboyant act with its remarkable climax.

They had their first American hit with ''I Can See For Miles'' in 1968. In the vacuum created by the absence of the Stones, Dylan and the Beatles from concert performances, the Who gathered momentum as the last of the great British hard rock bands. By this time the Mods who had spawned them were becoming an endangered species, and the Who themselves had mellowed considerably. Somewhat influenced by the satirical, sartorial Kinks with whom they now shared producer Shel Talmy, the Who had become almost whimsical and reflective, turning out wry tales like ''Whiskey Man,'' ''Tattoo'' and ''Pictures of Lilly'' told with nursery rhyme simplicity but spiked with biting morals. In songs like ''Substitute,'' with synthetic man as its hero, Townshend began to add his unflinching insights to the slashing guitar and startling harmonies which operated like parallel razorblades. On the equally ironic, but less mordant *The Who Sell Out* — the first fully realized concept album — they continued their mockery of twentieth-century commercial fantasies.

The Who's pop parables suggested the shape of things to come, especially the two compassionate mini-operas, ''A Quick One While He's Away'' and the mystically tinged ''Rael.'' Townshend, brooding on the philosophy of Meher Baba (an Indian mystic who had not spoken for 20 years) next created rock's first kunstgesamstwerk, *Tommy*, an opera about the celebration of innocence. The hero is a deaf, dumb and blind boy whose tactile genius makes him into a pinball wizard, and then an avatar whose religion is an ecstatic expression of direct experience. *Tommy*, which was eventually made into a film by Ken Russell, has been described as ''the finest extended thematic structure any rock group ever pulled off,'' and it propelled the Who to a position in rock very different from their image as rock & roll punks. As an antidote to the artistic respectability of *Tommy*, they released their next album, *Live At Leeds*, which more than any others evokes their sheer instrumental force and the cathartic effect of their stage presence.

The Who are the longest-lived of all English rock bands, and in 1974 to commemorate their tenth anniversary and a decade of delinquency, they made a cyclical return to their origins on *Quadraphrenia*. The album is dedicated to ''the kids of Gildhawk Road, Carpenters Park, Stevenage Newtown and to all the people we played to at the Marquee

*(Collection Ira Robbins)*

and Brighton Aquarium in the summer of 1965,'' but it is less a celebration than an exorcism of Mod. "It's about growing up," said Pete Townshend, adding wistfully, "at the end of the album, the hero is in danger of maturing."

The real horror for the Who is that the spectres of their old anthems have come back to haunt them in the form of self-parody. Trapped in their self-created image their rituals turn into musical masturbation. They are doomed to repeat themselves, stuck in a groove like a record eternally spinning on a turntable, "I am going round and round, I am going round and round," as Townshend on *The Who By Numbers*.

Unlike the climax of their act, the Who cannot disappear in a cloud of smoke in the ultimate rock gesture of autodestruction. It's unlikely they will just "f-f-f-fade away" either; their indelibly vivid image is almost hypnotically stamped on their generation. They have the best moves in rock. Manically in synch with their sonic landslides and violent crescendos, their faces and bodies are distorted by the sensory overload: Pete leaping ecstatically as he slashes his guitar with razor sharp chords; Moon with a face like an exploding pudding, lunging, buzzing and crashing over his drums; Daltrey lethally whirling the microphone, a smouldering doll-like punk behind blue eyes and baby curls; and, perhaps most sinister of all, John "the Ox" Entwistle, lurking catatonically like some Frankensteinish assistant behind his bass.

Intuitively manipulating the grammar of rock in abrupt spurts of energy they express the tension, resistance, dreamily violent sensuality and uncontrollable alternating currents of city life. As long as adolescence symbolizes this flux, fury and fantasy the Who will remain its purest and most eloquent interpreters.

# HERMAN'S HERMITS

PETER BLAIR DENIS BERNARD NOONE WALKS over to the hotel door, inserts a soda bottle in the latch-hole and with a swat of his palm cleanly slices off the cap. "The old Holiday Inn trick," he grins. "You never forget it."

The face hasn't changed much since the days when its classic lines set the tone for Herman's Hermits. The hair seems blonder, a shade longer, the eyes more subdued and confident. He can register under his own name now, the echoes of hysteria lost in some nostalgic crevice of his past.

"I never expected to be a teen idol," he remembers, "because the kind of songs we did in the act didn't seem to be the kind of thing that would draw screams. I always tried to head the band away from that kind of thing. That's why we changed our name from Pete Novak and the Heartbeats. I thought Herman was a name that couldn't be screamed."

Nonetheless, mid-sixties fans found it rather easy to peal away at his concerts, and by the time Herman's Hermits were nearing the end of their line, a sixteen-year-old Noone had probably amassed enough audience decibel power to deafen most of the semi-civilized world.

Riding on the wave of English fever mounted by the Beatles, the Manchester-bred Hermits were perfect for their time, delving (at least for Americans) into Britannic exotica like Henry the Eighth and "luv"-ly daughters while posing none of the artistic paradoxes that the new transatlantic music would soon foster. In particular, Noone seemed tailormade for an early adolescent mirror, a mouthful of gleaming teeth set off by an engaging and perky personality.

His saving grace was always that he had a strange depth, despite the apparent superficiality of his image, which out of the spotlight's glare manifested itself in an absorbed reverence for American rock & roll and trivia, mingled with a

**Herman's Hermits**

sure knowledge of where exactly he was heading. Contrary to popular belief, Noone (with producer Mickie Most) made all the decisions for the Hermits, defining their style with a rigorous and — in retrospect — sharply creative hand.

"I'm a very lucky kind of guy. Everything was always falling into place for us. 'I'm Into Something Good' was the first record I ever made, and nobody liked it. It got turned down all over. By the time we finally got it on the market it was a number one smash: 400,000 copies. They still come around to me saying 'I can't believe I turned that record down.'"

The Hermits — including Karl Anthony Green, Keith Hopwood, Derek Leckenby and Barry Whitwam — traveled to America early in 1965, a move which insured their reputation. It was also the turning point for Noone himself.

"The only reason Herman's Hermits came to America is that I'd read all the Mickey Spillane books and wanted to walk down avenues, and see Little Anthony at the Apollo. The first time I was here I hiked from the Manhattan Hotel on up to Harlem. It was just a fantastic experience.

"I went on the Dick Clark Caravan of Stars. It was the first time I met black people in my life. Actually met them, sat next to them on the bus and all that. Things like that just didn't happen in England. We went to bars in the South where they couldn't go in . . . and in Georgia, *I* wasn't allowed in the bars. It grows you up pretty quick."

The Hermits lasted until a more mature brand of progressive pop edged them off the charts. Today, Noone is on the comeback trail, though he likes to think it merely a continuation of where he's been all his life. He rounded out the phase of his Hermits career over a nationwide British Rock Revisited tour in which Noone and Co. were the only passable signs of life, and recently signed with Casablanca Records to release a series of singles with a hopeful roadshow to follow.

"I'm essentially doing the same sort of thing as when I started out at fourteen," he explains. "In the Hermits our act was always based on my comedy, and my way of talking over a song and then singing it. Still, we couldn't really present

*(Collection Richard & Lisa Robinson)*

the songs as I originally foresaw doing them. 'Mrs. Brown,' for example, used to open with a three-minute dialogue between the boy and the mother. You couldn't do something like that when everyone was going crazy all around you.

"I have a lot more room in which to move in my present situation. I can chat, I can set things up properly . . . I like to construct a song so that the audience knows what to do, where to get involved, where to clap. I'm the only guy left who's doing that. I can stand on the stage and not be embarrassed about it. At my shows I put everybody on the same level as me, and when you've got them singing along and having a good time, people leave and feel like they haven't seen a show, but that they've been *in* a show."

Happily married, sharing his time between Los Angeles and London, Peter admits life has tamed considerably since he was a star-struck youngster. "I never used to sleep, eat . . . the only reason I'm probably still alive is that I met my wife just at the right time. I was really messed up then. It straightened me out; for the first time in my life I have time to think."

His taste in music hasn't changed, however, the intervening years only serving to underscore his personal taste. "I'm very interested in those records that tell a story. Not the usual boy meets girl, have a bash type things, but those you have to listen all the way to the end to find how it turns out. Something like 'Silhouettes,' or 'Dandy.' I feel very close to those records. They're a story and they're total. They have motion. You could make a cinema in your head of them.

"I'd like my current single to get a little footing, and then for there to be a market for the album. There never was that for the Hermits. We just made albums of singles."

# THE KINKS

WHEN THE KINKS APPEARED ON THE trendy English tv show *Ready Steady Go*, thrashing about in red hunting jackets and frills, laying on their lurching rock hard ("You Really Got Me"), like a motley pack of slightly bemused mock aristocrats singing gutbucket blues, they had already suggested the shape of Kinks to come. Their foppish stance, part self-parody and part satire, has become the matrix of all their music — a sly irony which does not allow them to take themselves any more seriously than whatever they are satirizing. What could be more absurd than a bunch of English schoolboys from the North London suburb of Muswell Hill affecting the raunchy Chicago southside R & B sound?

With lyrics as repetitious as the go-stop-go rhythm itself, the Kinks' first hit was bludgeoning in its implicity, punctuated only with a breathless solo by Dave Davies. "You Really Got Me" was number one in England shortly after it was released in July 1964 and leapt into the American Top Ten too. The vocal harmonies delivered in a flat whine against a raw percussive beat were an unprecedented sound in rock and began a slew of rock & roll and R & B hits for the Kinks: "All Of The Day And All Of The Night," "Tired Of Waiting For You," "Set Me Free," "Who'll Be The Next In Line?" It hardly mattered that they sounded almost exactly alike. "G, F, B flat — those three chords were my life," Ray Davies once said. The repetition contributed to their frenzy and had its own fascination — it was hypnotic.

As an art student, the lanky Ray Davies, leader and *Kronicler in residence* of the Kinks, had started out playing Sonny Terry and Brownie McGee type folk blues in the Dave Hunt Band. His younger brother Dave had his own group, the Ravens, and when the two bands merged, they began getting gigs in then jazz-infested clubs like the Picadilly, with the

*(Globe Photos)*

help of that patriarch of English blues, Alexis Korner. In one of these dives, they were discovered by producer Shel Talmy, who got them on the Pye label. Their first two records "Long Tall Sally" and "You Still Want Me" were flops.

Having established themselves as a gutsy rock band with "You Really Got Me," their devoted followers were alternately stunned, irritated and delighted when in late 1965 they released the first in a series of social documentaries: "A Well Respected Man" was delivered in a vocal style as dry as a glass of sherry. It brought the Kinks to their second and most critically acclaimed style, as the vaudevillian historians of rock, and it easily made the top twenty. So did its sequel, "A Dedicated Follower Of Fashion," a little bit of mod mockery at the expense of London's trendies. Their beautiful, reflective and resigned river reverie "Sunny Afternoon," got them their third number-one single in England. For some reason, many of their more extraordinary records from this period, "Dead End Street," "Waterloo Sunset" (inspired by Terrence Stamp and Julie Christie in *Far From The Madding Crowd*) and "Days," made little impression. With the ironic,

compassionate scrutiny of Dickens and the clownishness of the music hall, the Kinks began collecting short stories about the British way of life, on albums like *Face To Face*, *Something Else* and *Village Green Preservation Society*.

Ray Davies once remarked that the decline of the British Empire could adequately be dealt with in one fifteen-minute song. In a slightly less presumptuous manner, he preserved its waning days in one 45-minute album, *Arthur*. Here he recorded with an entomologist's zeal the habits and mores of the mothlike denizens of his beloved Muswell Hill. It is a wistful, evocative study of these exotically drab specimens dreaming their magnificently dull dreams, "Greyness is beauty in boredom,"* says Ray cryptically. It is the saga of Arthur Morgan and his family, living out their comfy cozy life in a house called "Shangrila" — all the houses have names because they all look the same — with the telly, slippers, gooseberry tart picnics and chintzy Cinderella snobbery ("She Bought A Hat Like Princess Marina"). While it is a biting satire of bourgeois pretensions and smug self-satisfaction, Ray Davies is a

*Copyright © Rolling Stone magazine, January, 1973.

Ray Davies

*(Collection Barrie Wentzell)*

compassionate chronicler. In curious blend of tenderness and irony, he identifies with his creatures as if slipping secretly inside them to discover their "small quiet radiance."

*Arthus* is a perfect counterpoint to the Who's *Tommy* or *Quadraphrenia*, as if these blind molelike lives provoke the violent autistic or double schizoid conditions of the Who's heroes. The legacy of the British Empire lives on in these contented people, pompous as an Elgar march and complacent as Victoria Regina herself.

Fascination with kinky themes led to another hit single, "Lola," the first song overtly about a transvestite. The Kinks are one of the longest-lived of all British groups and have built up a fanatical following sometimes referred to as Kink Kultists. After Warner Brothers released

*The Kink Kronikles*, they vociferously demanded the release of *The Great Lost Kinks Album* and when Ray, ragged from exhaustion, abdicated in July 1973 from the group, the outcry in letters and the press was so loud that two weeks later he dutifully resumed his place in Kinkdom.

In their sensitive, sensual déjà vu vignettes, the Kinks seem as interested in preserving absurd delusions in vinyl as they do in tearing them down. Their lyrics, lucidly flickering in the declining rays of the British Empire, have an autumnal iridescence. Ray Davies once described his elusive, whispy vocal quality to Jonathan Cott in typically whimsical vein: "I once made a drawing of my voice on 'Sunny Afternoon.' It was a leaf with a very thick black outline — a big blob in the background — the leaf just cutting through it."

# THE BEE GEES

IN LATE SPRING OF 1967, WHEN EVERY NEW record from England was received with the same urgency as the first transatlantic phone call, deejays began playing a record by a "mystery group" called the Bee Gees. With its understated melancholy guitar opening, voices swelling into a sea of strings and its dreamlike images of existential suffocation, many people jumped to the conclusion that the song, "New York Mining Disaster 1941," could only be the work of those groundbreaking geniuses, the

Beatles. This seemed especially convincing when it was learned that the group was managed by none other than NEMS, who had launched the Fab Four.

Shortly after "New York Mining Disaster" became a hit in America it was revealed that the initials B.G. did not stand for any Beatles Group, but for the brothers Gibb — Maurice, Robin and Barry — a highly versatile group capable of sounding like any number of other people: Procul Harum, the Everly Brothers, Moody

**The Bee Gees**

Blues, the Byrds or an English boys choir, not to mention their uncanny mimicry of the Beatles. In addition to all the impersonations, these sonic chameleons had their own distinct personality, distinguished by Bill Shepherd's subtle arrangements and ingenious orchestral dynamics. The Bee Gees' spooky, echo-laden harmonies and strange, brooding lyrics gave their sound an unmistakable quality. Four months after "New York Mining Disaster" surfaced at the top of the American charts, this sound was still evident in their follow-up, a middle of the road ballad, "To Love Somebody," which emerged from under some 26 instruments with a close to glutinous quality.

They became consistent AM hitmakers with

"Massachusetts," "World," "Words," "I've Got To Get A Message To You" and "Lonely Days," one after another in an unending stream of boundlessly lush ballads varied in sound by the use of soul horn arrangements, pounding piano climaxes (as on "Lonely Days") synthesizers, ominous drums and the tumultuous chanting on the bizarre "Every Christian Lion Hearted Man Will Tell You."

In an age when aggressive casualness on stage was the emblem of integrity for most groups, the Bee Gees, immaculately groomed in tastefully modish suits and ties came on like puppets. ("Nothing is spontaneous in our performances," Robin says deadpan, "the visual impression and staging are more important than the sound we're laying down.") They were clean and sweet enough for mums, yet sensitive enough to adolescent agonies to appeal to teenagers, Robin's quavering voice, blissfully falling back on the nectarous horns and strings that seductively encircled poignant ballads about lonely people. Their performance had a cheap mystique; the curtain rises after the third song to reveal a 20-piece orchestra in tuxedos and black gowns.

The Bee Gees are mechanically professional and proud of it. They had been in show business for 20 years, beginning their career in 1955 when Robin and Maurice did prefilm entertainment Saturday mornings at the local British Gaumont Theatre in their hometown of Manchester. When the family emigrated to Australia three years later, they soon got their own show on Brisbanes SKQ radio station. By the end of 1960 they had their own weekly TV show called "Cotties Happy Hour."

In the mid-sixties they became perennial pop stars making it into the Australian top ten with songs like "Wine And Women." When their song "Spicks And Specks" made number one in January 1967, it gave them the money to try their luck in England. Although this song was only a minor hit in England, Robert Stigwood of NEMS (who was managing Cream and later Slade), signed them almost as soon as they stepped off the boat and they began a series of marathon recording sessions out of which emerged "New York Mining Disaster." Despite the mammoth party held to launch it in London, this song was not a hit in England — which makes its bizarre presentation in the U.S. a little less "mysterious."

Despite the subterranean title of their hit, the Bee Gees were anything but an underground group. The "hip" press bristled at their Rolls Royce, religion, anti-drug pieties and waxwork worship of the "British Heritage." When the brothers Gibb returned in 1971 after a two-year absence from internal feuding and "excessive pressure," their re-emergence was greeted with what one critic archly called "a cosmic yawn." They "appeared" to be just the brainwashed bourgeoisie the Kinks were always complaining about, dripping in marzipan, grown glib on the greed of fantasy-starved fans, turning out songs like music boxes (they wrote some 2,000 in a period of ten years, and "Lonely Days" was whipped out in a mere ten minutes). But the songs of the Bee Gees are freakish creations. Their verbal dexterity is like that of a child locked in a room until he finishes his song: playing with building block words, stacking them in surreal configurations and coloring them with soft crayon sounds. They create a tension in their lullabies by playing close to the nerves of fantasy.

Like the mutant children in *The Village Of The Damned*, the Bee Gees' superstraight appearance belies the eerie quality of these doll-like entertainers and their songs. "They write all their lyrics phonetically," explains Stigwood, "because they never learned to spell," perhaps accounting for the alfabetik name: B.G.s.

# TRAFFIC

ON APRIL 1, 1967, FOUR YOUNG ENGLISH musicians, Stevie Winwood, Chris Wood, Jim Capaldi and Dave Mason, moved into a rustic cottage on the Berkshire Downs as funky as a sharecropper's shack and there began to create a soulful, jazzy, psychedelic and whimsical music. The idyllic Berkshire cottage was part of Traffic's image. What could have been more propitious for these four musicians than to be deep in the ruminant English countryside where there was nothing to do except get stoned, and make music? They had purposely sought out this nurturing grove of sanity far from London's trendy ways for their inception; it was a timeless

**Traffic**

space as populated with spirits as English folklore and as fantasy-filled as a boy's adventure book.

Expectations for the group were high. The nucleus of Traffic was the then nineteen-year-old "Mozart of British soul," Stevie Winwood, whose R & B hits with the Spencer Davis Group were so uncannily soulful that at first black American stations put them on their playlist unaware that they were hearing a white band from the Midlands of England. Winwood's lead vocal, which sounded like a young Ray Charles, actually came from a frail, introspective teenager who had been playing professionally with his brother Muff since he

was in grammar school. They got together with a student, Spencer Davis, and a drummer, Pete York, and formed the Muff Woody Jazz Band, which later became RBQ and eventually, the Spencer Davis Group "for want of a name." They played a weird mix of blues, jazz and "stuff from Tangiers" to somewhat nonplused British Railway Workmen's Clubs and local dives. Chris Blackwell, a young producer who imported ska or blue-beat (later to become reggae) records from his native Jamaica, saw the group and signed them to his Island Production Company in 1964.

Their first effort, John Lee Hooker's "Dimples" which came out in March 1964, was

(United Artists Records)

eclipsed when John Lee released his own version of the song while on a British tour. Three subsequent singles also failed to make it on the charts but with the fourth, "Keep On Running," released in February 1966 on Decca, they made it to number one in Britain. Two other hits followed, "Gimme Some Lovin' " and "I'm A Man," the latter written by Winwood and Jimmy Miller (later producer of both Traffic and the Rolling Stones). By 1966 Winwood was such a celebrity that a North London cafe was offering "Poached Eggs Stevie Winwood and Toast Spencer Davis" on their menu.

Despite its success, the Spencer Davis Group was not Stevie Winwood's cup of tea. The format was not flexible enough for the kind of music he could hear in his head and he started jamming with a couple of friends from Birmingham, drummer Jim Capaldi and a flutist named Chris Wood who was playing "what I thought was jazz" with a group called Locomotion. Capaldi and Wood had both played on "I'm A Man." Capaldi introduced Stevie and Chris to Dave Mason, with whom he'd been playing drums in a group called the Hellions.

Birmingham (pronounced something like "burning gum" with a cold, in the thick Midland accent) seems like an unlikely place to spawn so many groups (later the Move developed there, too) but as Stevie says, "It's very much like Chicago with its own heavy musical scene. West Midland people are definitely characters, they're the people Tolkein based his Hobbits on." If Birmingham had its own special flavor, the atmosphere of the Berkshire cottage, which contributed no little part to Traffic's mystique (not to mention their music), was a very powerful force. For almost a year, on and off, the four wove some of the most inventive, swirling, yearning music to come out of rock, a blend of jazz, sound effects and blues, with Chris Wood's fluttery flute coiling around the evocative words and Winwood's incredible yet restrained vocals, and organ and guitar.

Their first single, "Paper Sun," with Dave Mason playing a subtle sitar, came out in June 1967 and was an instant English hit. It was followed in September by Mason's composition "Hole In My Shoe," a sort of child's opera of humor and wonder, which made it to number two in England. When their album *Mr. Fantasy* was released in the U.S. early in 1968 with its Hendrix-type riffs on the title tune, and Winwood's intricate beautiful phrasing, Traffic had fulfilled everybody's expectations. It was so inventive, experimental and diverse that it seemed incredible all these fantastic fragments could be held together. But by this time, Dave Mason, one of the group's most lyrically inventive members, had already departed. For the next four years Mason turned up intermittently, contributing songs to the next three Traffic albums and jamming with them on the so-called "documentary" live album, *Welcome To The Canteen*, while pursuing his own career on *Alone Together* and *It's Like You Never Left*.

Whatever the reasons that caused the split in Traffic, its reverberations can be heard in the songs written by Capaldi, Winwood and Mason on their second album *Traffic*, and their final studio effort together, *Last Exit*, which sounds like the internal dialogues of a group lyrically diagnosing its own symptoms ("Feelin Alright," "Means To An End").

In 1969, shortly after *Last Exit*, Traffic broke up. Stevie began jamming with Eric Clapton and Ginger Baker of recently disbanded Cream, and along with Family bassist Ric Grech formed the hype-ridden Blind Faith which made one album, did one predictably superstar tour and then splintered. In January 1970, more than a year after they broke up, Winwood, Capaldi and Wood got together to re-form Traffic, and in July they came out with the jazz-inflected *John Barleycorn Must Die*. The improvisations on the album were tight, the lyrics had an almost foreboding tone, but subsequent albums suffered from aimless interminable Traffic jams and "noodling," and experimental collaborations, most recently with The Red Theatre.

From the very beginning, Traffic had been one of the most successfully eclectic bands, because of their ability to absorb material and transform it. Stevie had always been aware of the necessity of musical form to offset Traffic's diffusion — "It's the limitations that give things character."

# THE YARDBIRDS

(Collection Peter Kanze)

Yardbirds I

WHILE THE YARDBIRDS ARE GENERALLY remembered today as having provided a training ground for three of rock & roll's finest guitarists — Eric Clapton, Jeff Beck and Jimmy Page — the contribution of the group as a whole cannot be overlooked in any survey of the music's rise to maturity in the mid-sixties. Inordinately experimental, tearing apart the fabric of their songs to introduce foreign and often radical breakthroughs, they presaged much of what would become the standbys of progressive rock. In their hands the guitar solo was first transformed to an end in itself, eastern instruments and scales began an acculturation later to result in Ravi Shankar's appearance at Woodstock, and feedback and electronic mayhem were established as the accepted norm.

As with most innovators, however, they were never in a position to reap the fruit of their labors. Unable to satisfy the conflicting demands made on them from either the pop or avant-garde sector, they were constantly beset by management, personnel and record company manipulation. "We were all immature," said Jim McCarty when it was over. "It was an education, it was growing up, it was . . . I don't know. The Yardbirds never quite made it, did they? They missed out slightly. If we knew then what we know now, we could have been one of the biggest."

Not that they had done particularly badly, compared with most of the other groups that had grown from London's bustling R & B underworld in the early sixties. The revival had been sparked out of traditional jazz circles, giving way to a wholehearted absorption of American rhythm and blues by numerous British musicians. Given a focal point when Cyril Davies and Alexis Korner opened the Ealing Rhythm and Blues Club in March 1962, the scene would soon birth the Rolling Stones, Zoot Money, Graham Bond, then-unknowns Jack Bruce, Ginger Baker, Georgie Fame, the Pretty Things, Long John Baldry and many who would never be heard from again: Gary Farr and the T-Bones, the Cheynes, the Downliners Sect, Ray

Anton and the Peppermint Men.

The Roosters, featuring a crew-cut guitarist named Eric Clapton, were typical of these R & B groups, heavily influenced by Bo Diddley and John Lee Hooker. At about the same time, in late 1963, the Metropolis Blues Quartet was evolving into the Yardbirds, with former art student Keith Relf on vocals and harmonica, bassist Paul Samwell-Smith, rhythm guitarist Chris Dreja, drummer McCarty and guitarist Tony "Top" Topham. Topham's parents were against him playing professionally, and "Slowhand" Clapton was brought in as replacement.

The group was immediately successful on the expanding R & B circuit. After the Stones had outgrown their residency at the Crawdaddy Club in Richmond, the Yardbirds took over their weekly slot. Club owner Giorgio Gomelsky assumed their management, and an inkling of how they must have sounded at this point in their career is available from a live Sonny Boy Williamson album on which they provide subtle if unspectacular accompaniment.

On their own, it was quite a different story. While remaining faithful to initial inspiration, the Yardbirds slowly built their own style,

## 120
### The Yardbirds

Yardbirds II

Yardbirds III

called the "rave up" and prominently displayed on *Five Live Yardbirds*, recorded at the Marquee Club in 1964. It was an early form of rock jamming, building more on the music's inner rhythms than on basic melody; Clapton has remembered that it partially came about because of his inability to play standard melodic lines. The results were electric and dynamic, with standard material like Chuck Berry's "Too Much Monkey Business" and Howling Wolf's "Smokestack Lightning" taken on long, physical rides, sliced by harp and guitar, moving continually faster in geometric precision.

Commercial prominence was neither forthcoming nor expected, but after the failure of their first two singles, "I Wish You Would" and "Good Morning Little Schoolgirl," the Yardbirds began to think seriously of changing directions.

# 121

## The Yardbirds

This was too much for Clapton, who considered himself a strict blues guitarist, and he left the group at the end of 1964. "It was only after I'd been with the Yardbirds for almost eighteen months that I started to take my music seriously," he said. "I was all screwed up about my playing . . . I realized that I wanted to be doing it for the rest of my life, so I'd better start doing it right." He retired from performing briefly, working in the construction field before joining forces with John Mayall's Bluesbreakers.

The Yardbirds had wanted to replace Eric with session guitarist Jimmy Page, but were unable to match the money he was making at the time. Page referred them to Jeff Beck, a veteran of the Tridents and a dozen other groups; Relf thought he was a passable instrumentalist, and advised him to play like Clapton. Jeff acquiesced for a while, but the differences in their styles — Clapton was heavily rhythmic, Beck more the accomplished soloist — meant that the Yardbirds' sound would gradually undergo revision.

It was just as well. By 1965, even the Stones were changing their bedrock roots into more pop forms, leaving Chuck Berry behind to follow their own musical instincts. The Yardbirds had found a song written by a young Manchesterian named Graham Gouldman, "For Your Love," and Gomelsky inveigled the Yardbirds' record company into releasing it. It was a far cry from R & B, sweetened with bongo drums and a harpsichord, but the record was a major hit on both sides of the Atlantic.

The Beck-Yardbirds represented the group at their highest peak of creativity, unpredictable and generally miles beyond the activities of their contemporaries. "Heart Full Of Soul" and the droning "Evil Hearted You" continued the minor key tradition begun with "For Your Love," and Jeff was enhancing his guitar playing with all manner of distortion and hardware. With "I'm A Man," released in October 1965, it was obvious something very new and unusual was happening, Beck's guitar and Relf's harmonica dueling in a final coda of disintegrating noise.

The group continued turning out hit after hit, but their increasingly adventurous use of the studio was frowned on in several circles. Their record company, for one, would have liked to keep the Yardbirds more within acceptable boundaries. The band was incorrigible, however, and they continued in their exploratory ways, combining East and West in "Over Under Sideways Down," adding social relevance with "Shapes Of Things." On the *Over Under Sideways Down* album (which was, strangely, the only studio album to be released in England by the Yardbirds), they utilized Gregorian-like chants, outlandish percussion instruments (an Australian wobble-board), and Beck's full range of guitar appliances. If it occasionally seemed as if they were using the songs more as convenient hooks for speculation than first-rate material, the group's attempt to expand their horizons could not be faulted.

Internally, things weren't going as well. The band's inability to fully develop an audience resulted in numerous arguments, usually arraying Relf and McCarty on one side and Beck on the other. Samwell-Smith felt pressured in the middle, the Yardbirds' now-chaotic music going against his meticulous grain, and he exited to pursue an interest in producing. Jimmy Page, bored with session anonymity, was recruited to fill the empty bass position, with the intention of switching places with Dreja and eventually to play co-lead with Beck. The possibilities were endless, and after appearing in the Antonioni film *Blow-up*, where they took a leaf from the Who scrapbook to destroy their equipment on stage, Beck and Page combined for the Yardbirds' most futuristic effort, "Happenings Ten Years Time Ago," re-creating a guitar war-zone complete with howling sirens and feedback explosions, Relf cackling and muttering underneath.

It proved too rich a mixture. The song was a relative failure on the charts, especially surprising since the Count Five, from San Jose, California, had taken a blatant Yardbirds imitation named "Psychotic Reaction" into the top ten not two months earlier. Instead of the expected alliance, Page's presence brought out Beck's latent dissatisfactions. Always moody, he began missing concert dates, to the point where the group was forced to ask him to leave. Or he quit; Beck had had enough anyway. He released two singles on his own in late 1966, "Hi Ho Silver Lining" and "Tallyman," and debuted the Jeff Beck Group in March 1967, with singer Rod Stewart and bassist Ron Wood, both later Faces.

Page was now in full command, but he was given little opportunity to take advantage of it. Though the group was more formidably alive than ever, their record company was convinced Beck's departure meant the end of the Yardbirds (Relf's stymied attempt at a solo career provided little solace). For the *Little Games* album, producer Mickie Most was brought in to make the band commercially promising, much as he had with the Nashville Teens, the Animals and Herman's Hermits. It was not a good match, despite the intentions, and Most lost the group's personality in cover versions (Manfred Mann's "Ha Ha Said The Clown") and inappropriate novelty songs (Nilsson's "Ten Little Indians"). The old Yardbirds could be heard only in snatches, on "Drinking Muddy Water" (a retitled "Rollin' And Tumblin' ") and Jimmy's acoustic showpiece of "White Summer."

Matters worsened. When "Goodnight Sweet Josephine" folded, Relf and McCarty began seriously thinking of departing the group. They continued touring, making their final visit to the United States in spring of 1968 (their last recorded statement was, appropriately, another live album, from the Anderson Theatre in New York with the band in enthusiastic if slightly awry form). Page and Dreja attempted to continue as the New Yardbirds, but after a short tour of Scandinavia to "fulfill commitments," Jimmy took the pieces back to England to form Led Zeppelin. Relf and McCarty, with Samwell-Smith producing, begat the classically based Renaissance; Keith later went on to play with Medicine Head and Armageddon before his untimely death from heart failure in May 1976, while Jim recently surfaced with a group called Shoot. For his part, "Sam" would guide the career of Cat Stevens to notable fortune. Dreja took the easy way out. He became a photographer and is quite happy today, thank you.

# CREAM

CREAM WAS THE FIRST OF A NEW SPECIES — the high-voltage superblues group. By channeling their "amplified heat" through traditional blues, they created a clean, lean, sensual sound which fused their audiences together in a virtual cult of electricity, with Eric Clapton as its god. Clapton was the nucleus of the group with his genius for exploiting the technology of the electric guitar and his ability to sustain notes to the breaking point. Cream's audience became so addicted to their massive doses of current that at their final concert their devotees screamed "God save the Cream!"

Formed in 1966, when the Stones were still into co-ordinated casuals, Cream presented themselves as flamboyant bohemians: Ginger Baker in his old RAF jacket; gnomelike Jack Bruce in antique market silks; and Clapton with his homage to Bob Dylan hair and psychedelically decorated guitar. Their stance was that of the pre-Haight Ashbury English underground whose attitude toward blues was purist. They demanded that their music be taken seriously. Cream's esoteric leanings were responsible for excavating a legion of forgotten or obscure American bluesmen, names which would be recognized before 1966 only by avid blues aficionados: Big Bill Broonzy, Robert Johnson, B. B. King, Buddy Guy, Blind Boy Fuller through them became part of rock mythology.

Cream's mastery of their instruments brought a new complexity to rock. Jack Bruce's whirlwind bass configurations, borrowed from

## 124

**Cream**

Bach and jazz, were so sophisticated he could often sound like a lead guitar. Baker's drum dynamics and multiplication of African-based rhythms made it possible for him to play the first tolerable extended drum solo in rock on "Toad." Finally, Clapton's mastery of a variety of blues styles, most notably his "twinging" borrowed from B. B. King, earned him the title of "god" of English blues musicians.

While still in his teens, Clapton had been in the pioneering English R & B group the Roosters, playing Chuck Berry, Bo Diddley and John Lee Hooker. But as their approach veered toward top 40 material, Eric's tastes became more refined, and he left in 1963 to join the Yardbirds. Two years later he was playing with John Mayall's Bluesbreakers, with whom he

recorded the classic album of the same name. John Mayall's somewhat purist group was a breeding ground for young blues musicians (Mick Fleetwood and Mick Taylor, among others, came out of it) and it was through Bluesbreakers that Jack Bruce and Eric Clapton got to know each other. Before joining the group, Bruce had worked with Ginger Baker in the seminal R & B band, Alexis Korner's Blues Inc., and they both stayed with it when it evolved into the Graham Bond Organization. "I had thought about a tie-up with Jack and Ginger for months," Clapton said on the formation of Cream in July 1966, "but I thought it wasn't likely to come off. For a start I felt Ginger was just too good for me to play with, too jazzy. Then he approached *me*, and to my surprise I

*(Don Paulsen)*

Eric Clapton in the studio, recording *Disraeli Gears*

found that he was a really solid rock drummer at heart."

Although they had a couple of successful singles ("Sunshine Of Your Love," "White Room"), Cream was the first group to make it with albums rather than hit singles, and the albums sold furiously based on a word of mouth reputation and exposure on the new underground FM stations. Cream was possibly the most influential hard rock group of the late sixties, and their departure left a vacuum that was obsessively filled by a host of heavy metal groups. So consuming was the demand for the superblues they had created, that Clapton, Bruce and Baker often found themselves in groups that were virtually parodies of Cream: Ginger Baker and Clapton in Blind Faith; Jack Bruce in West; Bruce, Laing and Baker in his Baker Gurvitz Army.

Their sound was structured around a repeating run of heavily syncopated ascending and descending chords. While these three superstars were able to create stunning raunchiness on their first two albums, *Fresh Cream* and *Disraeli Gears*, their deliciously indulgent jams soon became destructive as they began to dissolve back into their separate spheres. Bruce's ability to play lead lines on his bass, which had created an exciting tension and counterpoint with Clapton, had become destructive by their third album, *Wheels of Fire*, where on live tracks like "Spoonful" he steps all over Clapton's lead in an effort to outdo him. By 1968 it had become obvious that this group of leaders could no longer hold together under the strain of ego clashes, and in the same year they dissolved.

With the exception of Clapton's classic "Layla" with Derek and the Dominoes, none were as effective in their subsequent roles as they had been in Cream. Bruce cut solo albums and joined Tony Williams' Lifetime jazz quartet with John McLaughlin; Baker formed Airforce and rejoined Clapton briefly in Blind Faith; and Clapton has settled for a somewhat anonymous career as a solo artist after numerous group collaborations (Plastic Ono Band, Delaney and Bonnie, etc.).

In spite of Ginger Baker's thrashing possessed fury, Cream even at its most ferocious, gave off a cool controlled energy characterized by Clapton's icy soaring leads and apparent detachment from the waves of high voltage blues he was beaming at his audience. If their playing often seemed to lack the expressiveness of blues musicians like Hendrix, what they were conveying was the beauty of the form of the blues, and it was an intuitive feeling for this form that they perfected. As Jonathan Cott wrote in *Rolling Stone:* "Bruce, Baker and Clapton purified their approach to their music as far as they could, went as far as they went, and wound up repeating their perfections like a snake swallowing its tail."

(Collection Peter Kanze)

# 9
# Can I Get A Witness?

## B. B. King

BLUES NOTES HANG EERILY IN THE AIR AS
B. B. King squeezes long whooping wails from
his guitar. His action on the guitar is fluid and
casual, but he picks each note precisely,
vibrating, bending, "twinging" the strings to lay
bare their shrill, mordant edges; *naming the
pain.* His eyes closed, his head tilted back, he
seems stung by the notes as he disturbs them
from their ancient beds on the fret board which
must be as familiar to him as his own mind. He
appears to be fused onto his apple-red stereo
Gibson, which he calls "Lucille." (She's the
seventh one he's had and they all share the
name he gave to the original. The name came
after a typical event when his guitar narrowly
escaped going up in smoke after a joint he was
playing in burned down because of a fight over
a girl named Lucille.)

The audience at Madison Square Garden
had come to see the Stones, and although B. B.
got second billing on the tour, the audience
listens reverently to the King of the Blues.
Anyone there who's ever read an interview with
Eric Clapton or Mike Bloomfield already knows
that this is the source of the style on which most
of the white superblues guitarists have built a

unique mix of blues, jazz improvisation and
gospel strains. His audience now is almost
entirely white. Blacks have turned their backs
on the blues, considering it a painful reminder
of the rural past of plantations, poverty and
oppression. It has "lowdown" connotations
which are much less attractive than the more
uplifting soul music and progressive jazz which
replaces pathos with pride.

"When I go to a jazz club sometimes the
M.C. will say 'B. B. King, the well known blues
singer is in the audience tonight'," says B. B. a
little bitterly. "And the way he says 'blues' you
know he really means 'nasty.' I'm a blues singer
all right. And I don't mind being called a blues
singer just so long as the tone of voice is right,
you know. When a lot of people say "blues
singer" you know they're thinking of some
ignorant lush moaning in a gutter some place."

In his 25 years on the chitlin' circuit of
small black clubs, B. B. has crusaded for the
redemption of the blues, which in legend and
fact has been traditionally associated with
two-time losers, rootless drifters and double
murderers: bluesmen like the demonic Robert
Johnson poisoned by a jealous girlfriend, whose

(Magnum/Bob Adelman)

spectre is still traveling the South on ghostly Greyhound buses, or the sexually arrogant shouters of the Chicago blues like Muddy Waters and Howlin' Wolf, who hark back to a more primitive form of blues, or unbelievers like the wry old Texas philosopher Lightnin' Hopkins. B. B. wants to pry the blues loose from its negative image. To him it's an art rather than a way of life, which is the way most people think of it. His style is smoother and more sophisticated than the percussive Chicago bar blues that heavily influenced English groups like the Stones in the early sixties. In his insistence on "sanctifying" the blues with his virtuoso playing, he sacrifices some of the intensity which is an essential ingredient of the blues.

B. B. taught himself to play guitar on his uncle's sanctified preacher's guitar while the elders ate dinner. His falsetto singing style basically derives as much from gospel singers like Sam McCrary of the Fairfield Four as it does from R & B style of Roy Brown. With the possible exception of Muddy Waters, who influenced all the younger electric blues guitar players in the Chicago area in the late forties and fifties, B. B. is King of the blues. His singing is more elaborate and dramatic than the gravelly, laconic delta blues. Unlike many country blues artists or even the urban blues singers, B. B. King is not merely another blues legend to be recorded for the Library of Congress. He is one of the most popular of urban blues singers because he has constantly experimented, synthesized and recombined diverse elements, developing a dialogue with different styles that has made his sound genuinely contemporary without compromise. His incorporation of different styles can in part be attributed to the fact that B. B. has, unlike most blues singers who spent all their lives in one area, spent most of his life on the road (his home is still a motel room) and picked up bits and pieces from the places he passed.

B. B. got his start in Memphis, where he formed a group called the Elkhorns. His first professional job was at the Sixteenth Street Grill in Memphis, and soon he was given a ten-minute spot promoting a bloodbuilding tonic called Peptikon on WDIA, a radio station in West Memphis. His spot became so popular that his time was extended to an hour-long show. It was over local radio station broadcasts rather than in clubs that B. B. like Sonny Boy

## B. B. King

Williamson and others, slowly accumulated a wider and wider audience. He acquired the name B. B. while working as a deejay for WDIA, where he was known as "The Blues Boy from Beale Street." Ike Turner, who backed him for awhile, later became a record company scout, and in 1948 signed B. B. to the Bihari brothers RPM label on which his first hit, "3 O'Clock In The Morning," was recorded.

Although he says Gene Autry was also an early influence, he essentially codified the style of T-Bone Walker's smooth Texas blues and Ellmore James' slashing bottleneck. He saw in them a seed that he could nurture and expand: "When I heard T-Bone Walker with his electric guitar, I said to myself 'Man that's me.' I know I feel a lot of things I never say."

B. B. was born in Itta Bena, Mississippi, the eldest of four children in a family of sharecroppers. His mother died when he was nine. They had plenty to sing the blues about. "We worked from 'kin to can't,' which means from the first hour of daylight when you can see till the last hour when you can't." His family didn't approve of his singing "blues songs." They felt it was disrespectful and sacrilegious. So around the house he sang church spirituals and gospel hymns, while in the fields or in the woods he sang the blues of Robert Junior Lockwood, Sonny Boy Williamson, Blind Lemon Jefferson, Lonnie Johnson and his cousin, Bukka White.

He began to get into the blues seriously when his boss on the Indianola plantation bought him an eight-dollar guitar from Sears. In 1943 he went into the army, and after the war moved in with his cousin Bukka White, a blues slide guitarist. It was at this point that he began developing his famous "twing" effect on the guitar. Unsuccessful at imitating his cousin's bottleneck style, he worked out a parallel sound by vibrating his finger on the frets of his guitar, five times on each note to simulate the sound of the slide guitar. This produced a kind of trilling that gives a haunting emotional vibrato to his sound. Traditionally, the guitar in blues is played as an accompaniment to the lyrics with solo breaks, but since B. B. found he could not sing and play at the same time, he was forced to develop a sort of fluid dialogue between his voice and guitar, which alternate with one another; first Lucille "singing" then B. B.'s voice completing the phrase begun by the guitar. By adapting Django Rheinhardt and Charlie Christian jazz improvisations, he was able to extend Lucille's voice. "Stay close to the melody, extend the progression a little but do it with feeling — bend it, pull it, tease it, get everything you can out of that one note," B. B. says about his slinky strings. Throughout the fifties and early sixties he had a string of minor hits on the R & B charts, "Sweet Little Sixteen" and "Sweet Little Angel," but the blues had to cross the Atlantic before it was received by a mass white audience. It was English blues freaks like Eric Clapton and later the American adrenaline blues of Mike Bloomfield that introduced B. B. King's style, which might be called the spasms of single-note fretting, to white audiences. Although white blues players picked up their million-dollar riffs from B. B., they didn't include his sense of humor, evidenced in such tunes as "How Blue Can You Get" and "Nobody Loves Me But My Mother (And She Could Be Jiving Too)."

It took B. B. some 22 years of playing one-nighters on the chitlin' circuit to make it with his "lowdown" blues, and part of the sadness of his masterpiece "The Thrill Is Gone" is that although he's finally been accepted there's still a hint of nostalgia for the Beale Street catfisheries and the pain he's left behind.

The blues is "an aching old heart disease" but it's also an exorcism, and in the classic tradition of the blues, B. B. uses the form to let out the tension. But the final cry is one of triumph rather than defeat. He says about the ultimate Blues, the blues behind the blues:

> You could say that the blues keeps me one step ahead of the blues . . . and the pressure is like a spell. But I know this; I've never played what I hear inside, I get close but not there. If I did I'd play the melody so you'd know what it was saying even if you didn't know the words. You wouldn't know when I stopped and my voice began.*

*Reprinted by permission of ABC Records, Inc.

# BOBBY BLAND

(Magnum)

"BLUE" IS TAKING HIS TIME, LONG-NAILED fingers wrapped around the microphone, the crowd shouting encouragement, a droplet of sweat — or is a tear? — carving a path down his fleshy cheek. *"Mmmm . . . I went down to St. James Infirmary . . ."* Melisma spreads several notes over the space of each single word. The horns serve as call and response, doleful in their mourning, a funereal backdrop.

The blues that came out of Memphis after World War II were markedly different from those channeled through the black migratory capital of Chicago. Emphasizing showmanship and polish in place of the Windy City's more traditional rural electrification, Memphis' musical cross-currents allowed its artists a greater choice and sophistication of form. Without changing their stance, they could often participate in the commercial overlap of rhythm and blues; indeed, in the early years, many forged the very basis for that introduction, witness a 1948 aggregation called the Beale Streeters, starring Roscoe Gordon, pianist Johnny Ace, at times Junior Parker and B. B. King, and a young vocalist named Robert Calvin Bland.

Bobby was born in the small town of Rosemark, Tennessee, about thirty miles from Memphis, where he grew up to the sounds of popular gospel quartets like the Dixie Hummingbirds. Ira Tucker of the group used to help him with his singing, and when he was eighteen, Bland journeyed to Memphis and the Beale Streeters. He was also very much influenced by the music played by B. B. over his WDIA radio show. Bobby, who occasionally worked as King's chauffeur, was discovered in due process by Ike Turner, who took him to Modern and his first recordings, though Bland had to enter the army before much could come of it.

Another disc jockey from WDIA, James Mattis, decided to take advantage of Memphis' talent boom by forming a record company, Duke, signing Johnny Ace and, later, Junior Parker, (whose "Mystery Train" for Sun carried over to Elvis Presley). The Duke label was soon sold to Don Robey's Peacock complex, the most successful black-owned record company before Motown, located in Houston. Robey saw Bland at a talent show at the Club Matinee there, and taking advantage of Bland's military status, recorded "Army Blues" and "A Letter From A Friend In Korea."

At first, Robey's mainstay hope had been Johnny Ace, the potential of whose 1954 hit, "Pledging My Love," was sadly truncated on Christmas eve of that year when he lost a game of Russian Roulette between shows at the City Auditorium in Houston. Duke's specialty was a pop reworking of gospel and blues — Little Richard had cut some early sides for Peacock, as well as Big Mama Thornton — and they concentrated their focus on Bland and Parker. Junior was initially the bigger star, and as they shared bills across the country during the middle fifties, Bobby had to work simultaneously as Parker's valet and driver.

When Bland began hitting in 1957 with "Farther Up The Road," their positions were reversed, Bobby assuming leadership of the big band.

The larger sound was a vital factor in Bland's development. Unlike B. B., who could effectively rely on his guitar for dialogue, Bobby interplayed with the various facets of his band, stepping back to exchange phrases with his guitarist, his saxophonist (or other hornman), his back-up singers. In contrast to the four- or five-piece Chicago groups, any improvisation had to be firmly regulated within set charts and arrangements. The guiding force behind this was trumpeter Joe Scott, who led the band and coached Bland himself.

"In the studio Joe was strictly business," Bland told San Francisco journalist Joel Selvin. "I went along with his decisions on things because he . . . he taught me a helluva lot that I didn't really know. I didn't know anything about the music field at all. I just knew I had a voice, but I didn't even know how to handle that really. He used to show me different things and he'd sing — he can't sing a lick — but he could always get his point over to me 'cause I knew what he wanted. And if a word was pronounced wrong, he'd have a way to come and tell me and not to make me feel bad or anything like that."

Scott's tact with Bland and careful attention to recording began paying dividends toward the end of 1960. Despite such successes as "Cry Cry Cry," "I Pity The Fool," and "Call On Me," the atmosphere of the recording studio seemed to intimidate Bobby somewhat, and often many takes were needed before he caught the right edge on his vocal. Though he never overtly took the mannerisms of a gospel singer (as did, for instance, Sam Cooke), he used the form's dynamics for much of his impact. In "Turn On Your Lovelight," his best known effort, the instruments fall away to a surging drum solo, Bland a revivalist preacher exhorting his congregation. His voice was physically strong, capable of raging bursts of energy or the rich, mellifluous tone of a crooner.

This sense of deliberation carried over into Bobby's stage show, where it remains today, as involving and forceful as ever. The band plays a few selections to set the mood, and then Bland's warm-up man, Barnett Williams (replacing Al "TNT" Braggs), comes out to raise the pitch to fever level. Bland seems at once helpless in the face of all this, evoking a sympathetic appeal, and very much the fount of lonely experience, a personal tributary of hurt. There is no remoteness. He sings from where he's always stood, two steps from the blues.

# SAM COOKE

RHYTHM AND BLUES WAS A STRICTLY black music when Sam Cooke came on the scene, newly released from the industry ghetto of "race" records, infringing on the white-dominated pop charts solely through the most dedicated of efforts. As R & B veered to meet the demands of this unprecedented marketplace, beset by sweetened cover versions and limited airplay, it was forced into a continual struggle to retain its natural identity; notably successful performers like the Mills Brothers and Nat King Cole were worlds removed from their roots. It was not until the early sixties that "soul," a legitimate commercial marriage between blacks and the top 40, would become viable, with each side given its full credit, respect and due.

The change, beginning as rock & roll fortified its hold on the nation in the late fifties, pivoted around the figure of Cooke, the son of a Chicago Baptist minister. He had started singing in church, one of eight children who became members of their father's choir as early (at least for Sam) as age six. When he was nine, he formed a group called the Singing Children with a brother and two sisters, appearing for free will

(Collection Alan Betrock)

began to evolve many of the stylizations later to characterize him as a pop singer. A pure, effortless master of the phrase, switching to falsetto and back again with an unbroken sweep of his throat, he also provided his voice with depth and strength, so that the effect was never coy or flimsy. His control was impeccable, and as the line of Stirrers' hits stretched toward 1955, it was inevitable that Sam would soon begin to think of the expanding pop market. He had already recorded a secular song under the name of Dale Cook, "Lovable" (from the Stirrers' gospel version of "Wonderful"), but Specialty owner Art Rupe remained unconvinced of his potential.

Producer "Bumps" Blackwell had no such myopia, however. A veteran of Little Richard's similar transition, he bought both his and Cooke's contracts from Specialty in 1956 with the idea of linking with Bob Keene's Keen label. The results were immediate and gratifying, with Sam's "You Send Me" breaking number one in the early weeks of 1957. Cooke followed it with a string of lesser hits, including "I'll Come Running Back To You" and "Love You Most Of All," and then established himself as a major artist with "Everybody Likes To Cha-Cha-Cha," "Only Sixteen" and the vibrant "Wonderful World."

Cooke's work with Keen stabilized his creative stance, straddling in equal measure the divergent worlds of rhythm and blues and its pop counterpart. Compared with the more ethnic Soul Stirrers, Sam made necessary compromises according to the dictates of the day, most notably in choice of material. The songs were bright and catchy, the themes inoffensive, adolescent and familiar: "Everybody Likes To Cha-Cha-Cha" was built from a dance craze, "Wonderful World" set a high school parable rejecting book learning for the diploma of love. It was Cooke's voice that added the vital difference, treating each line as an airborne vehicle to be embellished, highlighted, sustained.

After three years with Keen, Sam received an extremely attractive offer from RCA, and transferred there in 1960. Hugo (Peretti) and Luigi (Creatore) took studio care of him and

offerings at neighboring churches. By the time he graduated from Wendell Phillips High School, he was a formal member of the gospel Highway Q.C.'s, named after the Highway Baptist Church and serving as a talent farm for the Soul Stirrers, one of the most popular gospel quartets of the forties.

The Stirrers had been around since the mid-thirties, when they had begun as a high school glee club in Trinity, Texas. In 1950, lead tenor R. H. Harris decided that fifteen years of the road was more than enough, and he was replaced by young Cooke, then eighteen years old. The group moved to the Specialty label, and with Sam's developing semi-yodel providing vocal embellishment, gained a second lease on life. Over the next five years they became the most prominent of gospel combinations, Cooke not only retaining their older faithful but attracting a younger, more energetic audience.

It was while with the Soul Stirrers that he

after a slow start (with "Teenage Sonata," a Jeff Barry composition and one of his finest songs), broke through with "Chain Gang" late that summer. RCA's approach was understandably closer to pop than R & B, but Sam persevered much as he had with Keen. "Cupid," "Twistin' The Night Away," "Bring It On Home To Me," "Another Saturday Night" — all were treated to the lithe Cooke touch. He seemed able to take any material, self-penned or otherwise, and render it priceless, dotted with bejeweled movements and intricate flourishes.

Realizing his potential, Sam began to branch out. He formed SAR Records with manager J. W. Alexander, whom he'd met in the Highway Q.C.'s. Between 1960 and 1962, the label fostered several hit acts, including the Sims Twins ("Soothe Me"), the Valentinos (whose "Lookin' For A Love" would prove an updated smash for lead singer Bobby Womack over a decade later) and Johnnie Taylor. He toured England in 1962 with Little Richard and Jet Harris, and by June 1964 had erected a 100-foot sign atop a building in New York's Times Square to herald his arrival at the Copacabana. "Sam's the biggest Cooke in town," it read.

In light of all this activity, Cooke's sudden death on December 10, 1964, seems even more inexplicable than it did at the time. According to newspaper reports, Lisa Boyer, twenty-two, of "British-Chinese background," told police that Cooke had "kidnapped" her after she had accepted an offer of a ride home from a Los Angeles bar. When Cooke forced her to accompany him to his motel, she grabbed most of his clothes and fled when he went into the bathroom. In hot pursuit, Cooke, clad only in a topcoat, entered the motel office, where he accused the manager, Mrs. Bertha Lee Franklin, fifty-five, of harboring Miss Boyer. He struck Mrs. Franklin twice with his fist, and she shot him three times with a pistol. The girl was found in a nearby telephone booth after the shooting, and the incident was later ruled "justifiable homicide" by a coroner's jury and corroborated by lie-detector tests.

It was a sad anticlimax to a notable career. Cooke's influence remains not only in the musical strands he helped knit together but the many performers who claim his legacy. Otis Redding dedicated "Shake" to his memory; Smokey Robinson, Johnny Nash, Clyde McPhatter and Al Green share his mantle equally; artists such as Rod Stewart and Cat Stevens have seen that his published catalogue does not go unnoticed. Still, there might have been so much more.

# RAY CHARLES

RAY CHARLES DOES NOT FIT EASILY INTO the mythology of rock. He can't be classified exclusively as a jazz pianist either, or gospel/blues shouter or soul singer, and he moves with ease into country music, Jimmy Webb territory, Beatles covers, standard middle of the road ballads and show tunes. These moves are still viewed with suspicion by his early fans who see the classic orgiastic gospel-soul rocker, "What I'd Say," as the height of his art.

But Ray, like Charlie Pride, who duplicated his innovations years later, grew up listening to the country western music of Hank Williams, Roy Acuff and Hank Snow, and had begun his career mimicking the torch songs of Nat King Cole. "The only reason," he once said, "that I haven't made a Christmas album, is that I couldn't find enough material." It's not that Ray can't discriminate, it's simply that he doesn't discriminate. He is the consummate musician, who X-rays every song, with the supreme confidence that he can see the soul buried deep in the simplest ballad — "Man, 'Stardust' has soul" — and he has the precision, technique, affection, insight and voice to unearth its soulful core. His many transitions in style are probes and reflections of his essence, as he says, "I've got to hear *myself* into a song." He simply refuses to say categorically where *his* soul resides, just as his "attack" on a song is never obvious. No note is attacked straight. It is stretched, moaning words into musical phrases, or tightened by biting hard on certain syllables, and leaves without ever having committed itself to a single meaning.

Ray's ability to lend credence to the most banal song as well as brewing up a gospel frenzy or revealing the terror of the blues is a personal vision. It allows him to see fragments of his own experience in any kind of music and expose it to the rawness of his voice, filed to a pained edge by a life of incredible hardships which drove him to heroin addiction at the age of seventeen. His brother drowned in a washtub behind their "shotgun shack" when Ray was four and already blind from glaucoma because his parents could not afford an operation. He lost his father when he was ten, and when his mother died five years later, he was shipped off to the St. Augustine School for the Blind and Deaf.

He learned to play piano in the general store in Gainesville, Florida, and within a year he ran away from the school and joined a dance combo in nearby Jacksonville. Close to starvation, he asked a friend to find the farthest point on the map, borrowed some cash, got on a Greyhound and was gone. Once in Seattle, Washington, he talked his way into a talent contest at an after-hours bar called the Rockin' Chair and although he lost, got himself a job. Later, playing an Elks Club party, someone told him he sounded like Nat King Cole, and in order to maintain himself he began imitating that style, though his own idols were gospel-tinged bluesmen like Louis Jordan and Roy Brown.

In 1948, he made his first record, "Confessin' The Blues," with an L. A. label called Swingtime, but because of a union ban it was never released. Between 1949 and 1952 when Ahmet Ertegun of Atlantic records saw him and bought his contract for $2,000, Ray had performed as a solo at the Apollo, backed Ruth Brown and formed the Maxim Trio — the first black act to be sponsored on Pacific Northwest TV — with whom he recorded some 40 sides.

On signing with Atlantic, Ray formed his own septet, and played the clubs, constantly refining his gospel-blues style. In 1954, when he was playing at the Peacock Club in Atlanta, he phoned the New York based company and told them he was ready to record. Although his producer, Jerry Wexler, has described recording Ray "like putting a meter on fresh air," the first session took place under incredibly cramped conditions (they recorded at a local radio station and had to stop every 15 minutes for news broadcasts). In spite of this, it was an historic event in the history of music, out of which came "I Got A Woman," "Greenbacks" and "Come Back Baby."

It was his fusion on these tracks of the climactic cadences of gospel on to a blues head that gives Ray the credit for inventing soul sound. While the influence of blues had made itself felt within the church (as in Rosetta Tharpe's singing or "Professor" Alex Bradford's piano, which heavily influenced Ray), his act was unprecedented in popular music and he carried it off with his usual confidence and sureness of touch. He took Clara Ward's "This Little Light Of Mine" and turned it into "This Little Girl Of Mine" and Whitaker's "How Jesus Died" into "Lonely Avenue," translating them note for note. Both blues and gospel singers seemed outraged at his new synthesis. "He's cryin' sanctified" said bluesman Big Bill Broonzy, incredulously.

Although Ray's unique mix was created while he was on Atlantic, it was when he moved to ABC in 1959 that he began to have his big series of hits, beginning with "What I'd Say," "Let The Good Times Roll," "Georgia On My Mind" (his biggest hit), "Hit The Road Jack," "Unchain My Heart" and "One Mint Julep." In 1961 he recorded his ground-breaking *Modern Sounds in Country and Western Music* volumes I and II, from which came "I Can't Stop Loving You" and "Born To Lose," among others. He continued to have hit singles such as "Busted," "Crying Time" and "Yesterday" through the late sixties, and formed his own label, Tangerine.

To Ray, the spirit in the dark, shared by gospel and soul, does not belong to anyone and is *only* present when it is shared. In a metaphor strange for a blind man Ray compared soul to electricity. "We don't know what it is but it's a force that can light up a room." To watch Ray is to witness a rare fusion of sex, religion and rhythm, and to see an audience turned into a congregation. Urging his piano on in block chord progressions and backed by the Raelets, whose repeated responses to his holiness shouts over and over create a cumulative effect, Ray Charles releases his soul in its purest form. As Purvis Spann said, "When you're thinking about pure things, you're thinking about the soul of things."

# OTIS REDDING

"I FIRST MET HIM IN 1962," SAYS STEVE Cropper who co-wrote two of Otis's hits, "Fa, Fa, Fa, Fa, Fa" and "Dock Of The Bay," and arranged and played on most of his sessions. "At the time Otis was sort of a road manager, singer and driver for Johnny Jenkins and the Pinetoppers. They'd come up to Memphis to cut a bunch of sides and Otis was just sitting in a corner of the studio all day long and every once in a while he'd get up and say, 'Man I sure would like to cut a song!' So after we'd finished cutting Jenkins there was about 40 minutes left and we said 'OK let's see what this guy's got.' "

Thus almost accidentally began the rise of possibly the greatest and most loved soul singer of the sixties. The song was "These Arms Of Mine," which Otis had written two years before, and which ended up selling some 800,000 copies. It was not only the beginning for Otis, but of a new funky Memphis-based soul sound that came out of an experimental mix of gospel, the laid-back but punchy R & B of Stax-Volt instrumental groups, Booker T and the MG's and the alternating current of the Markeys' horns, and opened the door for Sam and Dave, Arthur Conley and numerous other soul singers.

In contrast to the smooth urban soul of Motown or Gamble and Huff, Otis developed a rougher unrehearsed style that was effective just because it was so unfiltered. What he put down on record was what actually took place in the studio (Stax-Volt, Otis' record company, had only mono equipment up until 1966). The immediacy of a song like "Respect" derives in part from being written in a day, arranged in 20 minutes and recorded on the first take. Otis was known to cut an entire album in a couple of days, capturing his high voltage energy on the spot. "When I go into a studio to record a song," Otis said of his approach, "I only have a title and maybe a first verse. The rest I make up as we're recording. We'll cut three or four times and I'll sing it different every time . . . we cut everything together, horns, rhythm and vocal, cut six songs in five hours." This spontaneous method had a huge influence on both soul and white rock. Following Otis, Aretha Franklin and Wilson Pickett came to Memphis to record many of their biggest hits with the Stax rhythm group to achieve that laid-back sound, and subsequently the Allman Brothers and the Rolling Stones followed them to get some of those Memphis licks to stick to them.

Although many of Otis' songs were raw and hard driving, the impression his records leave is one of a gentle singer; his ear was subtly tuned in to what producer Willie Mitchell calls "Memphis time," what became the trademark of Stax-Volt sound. "The time here," Mitchell told *Rolling Stone*, "isn't so much a metronome; it's more personal. Even the singers . . . all sang lazy . . . if you remember Otis Redding's records, they'd be playing behind the tempo just a little bit and all of a sudden everybody . . . would kind of *sway*."

Otis was as effective on fast songs as he was

**137**

**Otis Redding**

on ballads. The B side of his first hit, "Hey, Hey, Hey," is typical of the crude, shouting, Little Richard style Otis started out with and later converted into the breathless energy of numbers like Sam Cooke's "Shake" and "I Can't Turn You Loose." Otis idolized Little Richard (they both came from Macon, Georgia) and from the almost pure Little Richard imitation of "Shout Bamalama" that he recorded for Bethlehem in 1960, he slowly evolved a fluid intimate style combined with anguished rasping vocals that characterize singles like "Mr. Pitiful," "Respect" and "I've Been Loving You Too Long," cut in 1964 and 1965. It was the tightness of the Stax-Volt bands that he recorded with — Duck

Dunn's looping bass lines, the subtle splicings of Steve Cropper's guitar and the Markeys' surging riffs — that helped him to develop his distinctive style of skipping every alternate beat and then coming down hard on it.

Otis' version of the Rolling Stones' "Satisfaction" (a song heavily influenced by his own idiosyncratic drawnout phrasing) was almost a parody of this Gotta-gotta-gotta style of singing, but it got him his first exposure on pop stations. In 1965 and 1966 he had a number of top 40 hits — "I've Been Loving You Too Long" with its tremulous, reverential vocal floating on a slow soaring rhythm, "Fa, Fa, Fa, Fa, Fa" and the plangent and pleading, "Try A Little

*(Stax Records)*

## Otis Redding

Tenderness" — but it wasn't until his appearance at the Monterey Pop Festival in 1967 that he began to break through to a pop audience. The same year he displaced Elvis as top male vocalist on the Melody Maker poll and was on his way to establishing himself as the Crown Prince of Soul when a chartered plane he was traveling in crashed into an icy Wisconsin lake.

One of Otis' ambitions was to fill the vacuum left by Sam Cooke's death in 1964, and in spite of the hard-driving quality of many of his songs it was the fundamental gentleness that he shared with Cooke that distinguished him from most urban soul singers. Otis did not start out in gospel but developed a blend of gospel and R & B that gave his songs their convincing quality and sustained momentum. More than any other soul singer, Otis managed to communicate the intimate, encouraging, sustaining power of gospel and translate its fundamental faith into an international

emotional code. One of the reasons he was successful lay in his own personality; a vulnerability that projected through all his vocals made him accessible to both black and white audiences, where more aggressive singers like James Brown and Wilson Pickett could not reach.

"Dock Of The Bay" was Otis' first number-one record, but he did not live to see it climb the charts. Its wistful lyrics, gentle lilting motion and refined tension make it the essence of his art and life to which his death lent a special poignancy. It was a country mellowness that made his songs especially eloquent and universal. As Steve Cropper told *Hit Parader*: "My original feeling for Otis wound up to be my final feeling, he was a pure man. His love for people showed in his songs. He was always trying to get back to his baby — or he missed her, she was the greatest thing in the world. His approach was always *positive*."

# 10 Four On The Floor

## THE MOTOWN SOUND

IT WAS EVER MORE THAN A RECORD LABEL. At its zenith, during a span that dominated most (if not all) of the sixties, the hit factory of Motown charged and defined the state of rhythm and blues art, offering black identity through multiracial discipline, individual independence subordinated to the needs of a vast, insatiable audience. Berry Gordy, Jr., a self-defined "Mr. Hitsville," had absorbed his lessons well on the Detroit assembly lines; in the manner of Henry Ford, he conveyed a belt of sleek, chromed models from initial blueprint to final showroom display, overseeing production to suit every taste and pocketbook. Motown's approach was total, educating their performers in a virtual charm school, indoctrinating them in the "Sound of Young America" until their family heritage was unquestioned, beyond reproach.

Gordy built slowly and knowledgeably, relying on his proven instincts and the talented songwriter-producers he hired to convert fancy into chart fact. Unlike the sporadic, underfinanced and inconsistent black-owned companies that preceded it (often relying on outside distribution and ethnic support), Motown was a full-blooded corporation, promoting and delivering its own without regard to stigmatized barriers. Its social significance, turning the color wheel to face an opposing direction, was only heightened by the general excellence of its product, mixed for transistors and three-inch speakers, a brilliant synthesis that aligned beat and chambered chorus in unmistakable emphathy.

Most accepted stories of Motown's origins begin with Berry Gordy borrowing several hundred dollars to leave a Detroit car plant and form the Tammie (Tamla) record company. While surely a graphic representation of Berry's working-class roots, the story jars considerably with the string of hits he had amassed as an independent producer prior to 1959. He wrote for Jackie Wilson ("Reete Petite," "Lonely Tear-drops," "I'll Be Satisfied"), Marv Johnson ("You Got What It Takes") and advised William "Smokey" Robinson of the Miracles, whose first efforts he helped lease to major companies like End and Chess. Detroit had never been known as a record center — its foremost representative, Jack and Devora Brown's Fortune network, operated out of a small, dusty storefront — but the Falcons' 1959 smash of "You're So Fine"

## The Motown Sound

convinced him that there was a large potential within the city itself. His sister Gwen formed the Anna label (named after another sister) and by January 1960 had netted preliminary rewards with Barrett Strong's "Money," which Gordy had co-written. Soon after, in June, "My Beloved" by the Satintones appeared as Motown 1000.

The early years of Tamla-Motown belonged to Smokey Robinson, whose Miracles not only established the company as a major force (with "Shop Around") but musically set the succession of styles to be embellished in later administrations. As delicate a writer as he was a performer, Robinson attributed much of his inspiration to Gordy, and has remained a staple of the company to this day, serving as vice-president and solo artist. Between 1960 and the emergence of the Supremes four years later, he accounted for a majority of Motown's success, working with the Marvelettes, Marvin Gaye, Mary Wells and the Temptations, as well as boosting the Miracles to becoming one of the most visible and prolific attractions in the pop market.

Robinson wrote with intelligence and sophistication, underplaying his lyrical hand to

The Miracles

*(Collection Peter Kanze)*

Berry Gordy, Jr.

*(Collection Richard & Lisa Robinson/Neal Preston)*

separate the contradictions between fantasy and reality. He was at his best within the sad, sweetly-taken ballad, the milky quality of his voice flirting with heartache and devotion, reversing images one over the other: "The Hunter Gets Captured By The Game," "What's So Good About Good-Bye," "My Girl" and "The Love I Saw In You Was Just A Mirage." When called on to write more uptempo material, he responded with a broad grin, "Mickey's Monkey" and "Goin' To A Go Go," the Miracles stepping lithely around him.

Robinson was not the only bright spot. Motown had shown a willing grasp of formula nearly immediately — the Contours' "Do You Love Me" carboned the Isley Brothers' "Twist and Shout" — and Gordy's drive to firm the label's personality soon found him altering the existent pop theorems to his own uses. Like the New York producers of the time — Leiber and Stoller, Phil Spector — he realized that

**The Motown Sound**

precognition was not to be camouflaged but rather singularly pursued in quest of a Sound. In consequence, Motown threw all its energies behind their 45's, concentrating statements in the smallest, most accessible form possible. Once made familiar to the public-at-large, Berry felt that the texture of each Motown record, no matter how dissimilar or varied, would subliminally clear a path toward the potential listener.

Of the first batch of performers chosen to represent this developing Sound, Gordy perfected the techniques of discovery and manipulation into an ongoing format. His artists were generally unknown, and depending on their pliability, were given greater or lesser attention in the studio. The Marvelettes, discovered at a local talent show, had the company's first number one single in "Please Mr. Postman," but though they continued scoring hits through several years, they seemed to be passed over in favor of other, less specifically typed artists. Loyalty was also a factor: Mary Wells, after several appreciable successes ("My Guy," "Two Lovers") expressed interest in freeing herself from Motown's restrictions and has seldom been heard from since.

The Temptations typified the Motown philosophy, weathering several incarnations and switches in personnel with remarkable resilience over the years. Otis Williams, Eddie Kendricks, Paul Williams, Mel Franklin and Elbridge Bryant had sung variously under the names of the Primes and the Distants, but it was not until David Ruffin (originally signed as a solo artist) replaced Bryant as lead singer and Smokey Robinson became the group's main producer that they began making an impression. Ruffin had a voice almost as fluid as Robinson's, matched by the equal strength of the other members, and the Temptations benefited from much of Robinson's best material. He wrote specifically for their tailored, urban sense of cool, the classic "My Girl" to "Since I Lost My Baby." "I'd always liked them and liked their sound," Robinson said of his initial involvement, "because they always reminded me of a church group, the soulful sound, from the high tenor to the low bass."

A future direction was hinted at when an Eddie Holland-Norman Whitfield composition titled "Ain't Too Proud To Beg" roughed up their image. Whitfield stayed with the Temptations, assuming prominent control in the later sixties, but Holland's moment had arrived. Along with the production team of Bryan Holland and Lamont Dozier, he helped to usher in what is generally regarded as Motown's golden era, beginning with Martha [Reeves] and the Vandellas and reaching their greatest heights with the Four Tops and the Supremes.

Martha Reeves typified the in-house quality of Motown's grooming. She began as a secretary in the company's A & R department, but her singing career was launched when she filled in as a back-up singer on recordings for Marvin Gaye and Mary Wells with two friends, Annette Beard and Rosalind Ashford. Finally she was offered a contract of her own. Working with Holland-Dozier-Holland, the Vandellas first touched the charts in April 1963 with "Come And Get These Memories," quickly following up with "Heat Wave," "Quicksand," the exuberant "Dancing In The Street" and "Nowhere To Run." The songs were straightforward and rambunctious, tempoed by a relentless four-beat pattern that allowed Martha full vocal volume, emphasized by the Vandellas' alliterative enthusiasm.

The same sense of restrained ferocity was the keynote of the Four Tops' recordings, led by Levi Stubbs and supported by Abdul "Duke" Fakir, Lawrence Payton and Renaldo "Obie" Benton. As with the Vandellas, Holland-Dozier-Holland sought to contain Stubbs' explosiveness within a cordoned production style, conceptualizing the raw nervous energy of "Baby I Need Your Loving," "I Can't Help Myself," "Standing In The Shadows Of Love" and "Reach Out I'll Be There" into deliberate, commercial statements. The Tops, veterans of a long recording apprenticeship before they reached Motown, were more than willing to align themselves with Gordy's guiding principles, but willingness, as least as far as the Sound was concerned, was not enough. In the search for an ultimate formula, artistic strength was necessarily replaced by

(Don Paulsen)

The Temptations

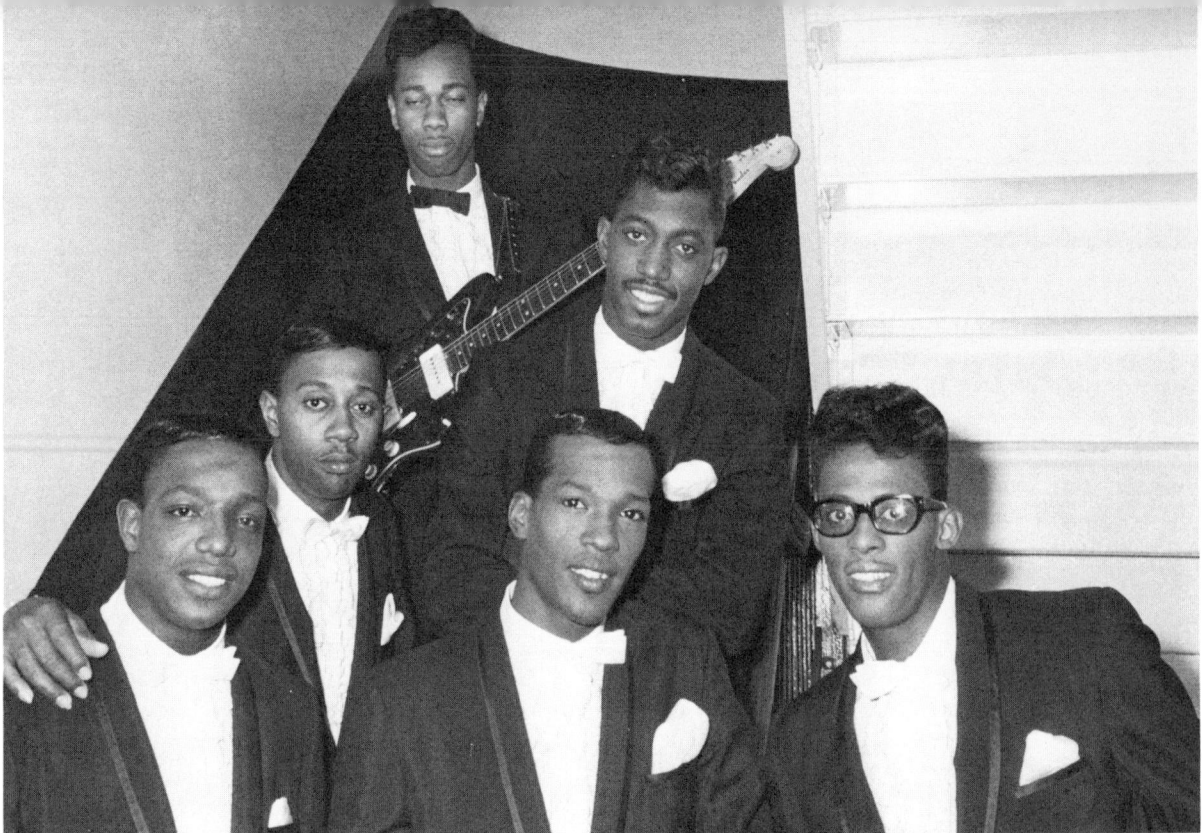

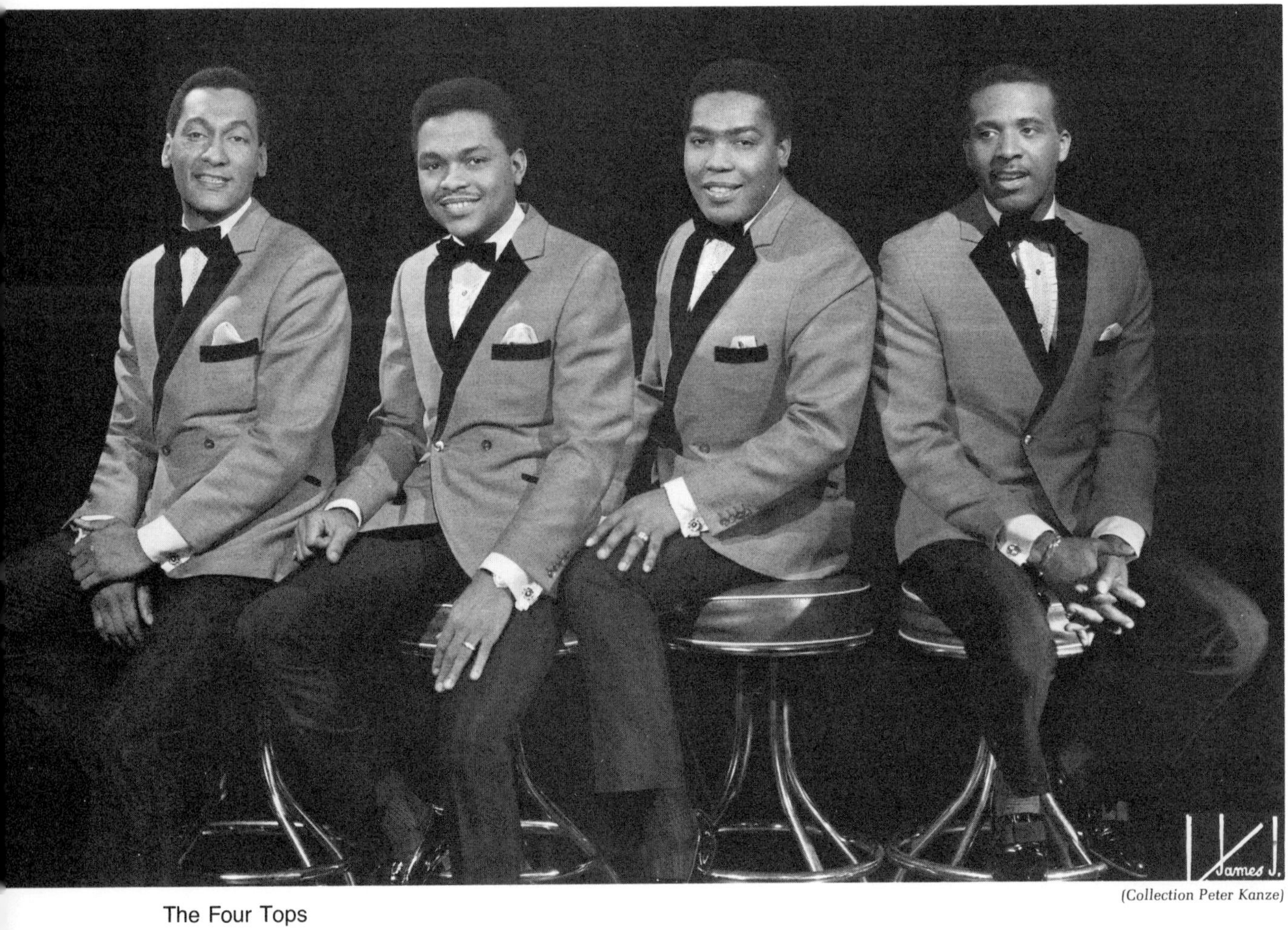


(Collection Peter Kanze)

The Four Tops

The Supremes

Stevie Wonder

submissiveness and malleability, and with Holland-Dozier-Holland unwilling (or perhaps unable) to channel these groups into more diversified areas, their recordings soon became predictable and rudimentary.

The Supremes were better suited to this type of approach. The quintessential Motown combination, they were molded by Holland-Dozier-Holland into gamine-like purveyors of soul, wide-eyed and breathy. They were a trio from the Brewster Housing Project in northwest Detroit, introduced by Eddie Kendricks to enhance the then-Primes, as the Primettes. Their early releases were in the mode of a softer Marvelettes, but with "Where Did Our Love Go" in June 1964, Diana Ross, Florence Ballard and Mary Wilson were transformed into all their new name hinted. Having perfected studio technique through the Vandellas and the Tops, Holland-Dozier Holland turned their attention to the shaping of artists. The gritty tension of "Heat Wave" gave way to a smooth, effortless pitch, removed from blandness by the sultry tenderness of Diana's vocal intimacy.

The records were slick, impressively conscious of their arrangements and hooks (the Motown rhythm section is one of the unsung heroes of modern rhythm and blues), and H-D-H ran their operation like a glorious machine. The spare use of Motown instrumentation suffered little in its expansion to orchestral depths, and through a string of ten number-one singles and several top-ten contenders, the Supremes were rigorously abstracted, glossed, rebuilt in the archetype of Gordy's Motown Sound. Holland-Dozier-Holland further elaborated as they went along, churning the group through "Baby Love" and "Stop! In The Name Of Love" to the more ornate "You Keep Me Hanging On." The last represents a high-water mark for the Supremes and their producers; following its success in 1966, even the formula showed signs of limitation, as Holland-Dozier-Holland took solace in shock gimmickry and fad effects (the mechanical overtones of "Reflections").

It was a problem that was predictable in light of Motown's leaning toward singles and obedience. While attention was paid to performing careers, artists were encouraged to

move in the direction of nightclubs and acceptable "family" entertainment. On their albums, which were seen more as vehicles for further circulating singles than as complete portraits, the result was shallow recuts of show tunes and pop medleys; live, between succulent hits, equally inappropriate material was showcased. Often performers were given a hit — Gladys Knight and the Pips' "I Heard It Through The Grapevine," Brenda Hollaway and "Every Little Bit Hurts," Jimmy Ruffin's "What Becomes Of The Broken Hearted" — and then seemingly forgotten, left to lie fallow. Others were regarded as perennial second liners, a Junior Walker or an Edwin Starr, and despite an average spacing of hits, were made to feel at home in their niche.

By subordinating artist development to

Marvin Gaye

(Don Paulsen)

The Jackson Five

(CBS Records)

corporate growth, Motown found itself unbalanced, potentially troubled should misfortune strike the writing and production staff. Such was the case in 1967, when Holland-Dozier-Holland left the label to form their own company, creating a vacuum that was not helped by a subtle shift in Motown's previously inviolable stature as industry frontrunner. Music itself was changing, absorbing Gordy's breakthrough to raise a host of new contenders in the realm of black pop, felt most apparently through Memphis' Stax Records, sporting Otis Redding, Sam and Dave, Booker T and the MG's. In a business once ruled by producers, the artist was again regaining control, and Motown's rigid proclivities tumbled in the public's favor.

Gordy was placed, for the first, in the position of pursuing trends. He admirably acquiesced to the situation, diversifying even as he continued to make money. Diana Ross was separated from the Supremes, and after a short attempt to funkify her roots ("Love Child"), reappeared as a glittering show business queen, culminating in her intense portrayal of Billie Holiday in the film and soundtrack of *Lady Sings The Blues*. The Temptations were formally deeded to producer Norman Whitfield, and in the absence of David Ruffin, he streamlined their rhythms to total danceability, grafting socially persuasive lyrics in a freewheeling array. It was a debt owed to Sly Stone if not to Whitfield's unique genius (brought to patented perfection in his 1972 masterpiece of "Papa Was A Rollin' Stone").

The Greening of Motown, as it came to be called, also reacted favorably on an artistic level. Both Stevie Wonder and Marvin Gaye, associated with the company for several years with a commensurate lineage of hits, were suddenly given the power to choose their own directions. Unleashed, following divergent paths, they became by the early seventies two of Motown's most highly regarded innovators, superstars whose early frustrations only heightened their creative desire and commitment.

The confidence this augured was especially fitting for Stevie Wonder, whose multi-instrumental talents had often gone begging at Motown. Blind since birth, he had been signed up at the age of twelve. Gordy's search for a pint-sized Ray Charles was rewarded by "Little" Stevie's first hit single, "Fingertips," a live exhibition of his crowd-pleasing capabilities recorded at the Apollo. His maturity was taken in stride with "Uptight (Everything's Alright)" and "A Place In The Sun," jazzily preened with "For Once In My Life" and "My Cherie Amour." Entering self-production with the *Signed, Sealed and Delivered* album, he embarked on a discovery of personal worth, a mist of subdued *rightness* that brought him to the realizations of *Music Of My Mind, Talking Book, Innervisions, Fulfillingness' First Finale.*

Wonder's technical judgment was flawless and his composing abilities boundless, encapsulating the gregarious pull of disco-rock ("Superstition") to torching ballads ("All In Love Is Fair"). His voice attacked notes from above and below, stretching and snapping them back into place, pounding his keyboard with uncanny precision.

Gaye similarly came into his own, shedding his previous career with not a glance backward. Marvin's hits had been among the most pronouncedly pop of Motown, beginning with "Stubborn Kind Of Fellow" in 1962. Once a temporary member of the Moonglows, his light vocal mannerisms prompted many producers to frame him in steady beatific swingers like "Hitch Hike" and "Pride and Joy." Only in his duets with Motown starlet Tammi Terrell (following earlier successes with Mary Wells and Kim Weston) was he allowed to draw on his considerable emotional resources. Their best-known collaboration, "Ain't No Mountain High Enough," was written by another of Motown's up-and-coming production teams, Nick Ashford and Valerie Simpson.

The untimely death of Terrell touched Gaye deeply, and when he came out of seclusion, it was with a new sense of purpose. *What's Going On* was not the stereotyped realism of the later Temptations; he offered a world view unseamed by instrumental transitions, a symphony of the black urban experience percussed softly and hypnotically. Gaye was one of the luckier ones. Many Motown artists unable to adjust to this change in values, especially those who relied on production support, were forced to seek refuge outside the label. For Gladys Knight and the Pips, Martha Reeves and the Four Tops, the relocation proved a boon, as each breathed greater life into non-Motown careers.

Yet the family pattern, bolstered through marriage — Gaye to Anna Gordy, for instance — remained intact. Even when Motown left Detroit for Los Angeles in the early seventies, it retained the corporate identity Gordy had implanted. The tight unity of the Jackson Five, brothers and sisters from Gary, Indiana, only confirmed the strength of the company as a whole, polished and professional, with leader Michael not far removed from his preteens. The Jacksons' riotous stage show coupled with Motown's never-forgotten flair for making records opened the Sound to a new, budding audience. Old combinations were reshuffled — Eddie Kendricks was boosted to solo prominence; the Supremes returned to the charts again — and branching out, Motown began signing white artists on a regular basis. Indivisible, as Gordy might say, with liberty and justice for all.

# 11 Atlantis

## THE VENTURES

THE LIGHT IS SHINING IN THE GARAGE
again tonight. There is the sound of a record
stopping, echoed from another source, starting
again. A hand laboriously forms another
unfamiliar chord, lifts the needle back to the
scarred groove, listens intently: a guitar lesson,
circa 1964. In a scene to be repeated throughout
the world, a west coast instrumental quartet
named the Ventures is providing scholarly
introduction, a contribution more important to
rock & roll than the dozen or so hit
instrumentals that will eventually carry their
name.

"Who knows," mused then-drummer Mel
Taylor, "how many groups out there began with
a Ventures record?"

The list is probably endless. The Ventures
may not have been the best of their
contemporary lot, but any challengers — such as
the Surfaris and the Chantays — lacked the
sustained ability to slide past their primary
foothold. The Ventures never stopped, album
after album and tour after tour, and even when
their music faded, satisfied to take current hits
and homogenize them into a basic guitar over
rhythm sound, that which they represented
carried their reputation, as it has to the present
day.

The Ventures were a particular product of
their time. In the fifties the pop music door had
swung open to allow an influx of untrained
street musicians, but the outgrowth was mostly
confined to vocal combinations. Instrumentalists
were expected to be highly skilled, able to
sight-read, proud of their technical knowledge
and anxious to show it off. Leads were generally
centered on the piano and saxophone, and
guitars — except in selected rockabilly
hands — were tightly reined to counterpoint
rhythmically around the edges.

By the early sixties, the guitar explosion
that had begun with the advent of Elvis Presley
was beginning to make itself felt on a local
level. It was coupled with the growing idea that
a rock band did not necessarily have to study for
years to step out in public. With a basic three
chords at the ready, a group could form and be
on stage by the following weekend; it was an
irresistible temptation, and millions of budding
virtuosos took the six-string hint.

When the Ventures arrived in this hotbed of
enthusiasm with "Walk — Don't Run," a better
piece of central casting couldn't have been
provided. Themselves amateur musicians, Bob
Bogle and Don Wilson had worked hod-carrying
on a Seattle construction project for three

*(Collection Greg Shaw)*

months before discovering their mutual interest. Noticing a guitar in the back seat of Bob's car, Don suggested they jam one Sunday. Their association progressed from there to a hotel in Pullman, Washington, where they traded ideas and were encouraged to make a tape of their music. Don's mother, Jonie Wilson, took it around to record companies with scarcely a nibble, retaliating by forming her own label, Blue Horizon Records.

Bogle and Wilson continued at their day jobs for the time being, rising at 5 A.M. to work at the construction site and then continuing at a local club until one in the morning. Deciding to become serious, they added bassist Nokie Edwards and drummer Howie Johnston, picked jazz guitarist Jimmy Smith's "Walk — Don't Run" and pressed 5,000 copies of their first single. A local radio station, KJR in Seattle, converted it into an area hit, spurring nationwide interest

from Dolton Records, a subsidiary in the huge Liberty system. By the end of summer 1960, the disc had sold a million copies.

"Walk — Don't Run," along with its follow-ups "Perfidia" and "Ram Bunk Shush," quickly became standard repertoire with the new band generation. The Ventures sensed this appeal early on and, acute businessmen as well as performers, moved to fulfill demands. At first they were content to provide living models, manuals in the form of simple, easy-to-play standards. This would soon evolve into a series of guitar and bass instruction booklet/records, as well as a sponsored line of Mosrite guitars which the group and friend Semie Mosley had designed over a ten-year period.

Mel Taylor came in to replace Johnston in 1963, when the latter was injured in an auto accident and advised to retire from the road. The group had already begun to travel heavily, making excursions into Europe, South America, even Japan, where their reception was every bit as strong as in the United States. Carrying their guitar gospel, they were virtual electric missionaries, and their record sales reached into eight figures. Every so often, just to show they hadn't lost touch, the Ventures would deliver a hit single when it seemed most becoming. In 1964, they struck with "Walk—Don't Run '64"; five years later the theme from "Hawaii Five-O" climbed into the top five.

Creatively they were just following trends, but by then it didn't matter. *In Space* took them along the fringes of psychedelia; *Underground Fire* was likely progressive; there were Christmas albums and live albums. Jerry McGee replaced Nokie Edwards, John Durrill was added on organ, Mel Taylor made way for Joe Barile, Nokie rejoined the group. Their *Tenth Anniversary* album reprised the decade's greatest hits, and they've passed several milestones since then, pausing only briefly to sit back and chuckle whenever they realize the song they're instrumentally covering has been done by someone who probably learned it all from the Ventures, one night in a long-ago garage.

# JAN & DEAN

WHAT STARTS OUT AS SIMPLY COMIC HAS a way (especially in California) of turning out sort of cosmic, as Jan and Dean, those clown princes of rock & roll found out. From their first vinyl gag "Jenny Lee" to that mysterioso business of "Deadman's Curve" they were "the funnybone of rock & roll, the ganglia of schlock and humor," as David Marsh diagnosed them in his liner notes. As Marsh suggests, what "endeared Jan and Dean to their hard core fans was their absolute refusal to acquire the garb of pretension. . . ." They were in it for the party, that one last ride on the green curling surf. Their career came to an abrupt end in April 1966, when Jan Berry slammed his Stingray into a parked truck and suffered severe brain damage.

Here, in Dean Torrence's own liner notes for the *Jan and Dean Anthology Album*, is how it all began:

> We both made the varsity football team in our last year at University High and by chance happened to get team lockers next to one another . . . it wasn't long before a bunch of us on the team discovered that the sound in the shower room was the best echo around. Group songs were popular that year, and a bunch of other guys started singing the songs of the day in the

*(Collection Peter Kanze)*

# 150

## Jan & Dean

(Don Paulsen)

*University High shower room: "Get A Job" by the Silhouettes, "At The Hop" by Danny and the Juniors, "Tell My Why" by Norm Fox and the Rob Roys.*

*The football season ended which meant that the showers were now being used by the baseball team, so the group, now called the Barons, had to start practicing in the boys' restrooms.* *

Jan Berry was a joker, a master thief (he "borrowed" the auditorium mike for their rehearsals), an electronic whiz (simulating that ineffable shower room echo by creating a tape delay on two tape recorders) and a certified wise guy (he had an IQ of 185). But if Jan was the Charlie Brown of West Los Angeles University High School, Jan's jokes were, well, almost serious. "He rarely did anything for fun," explains Dean. "He had four or five rationales for everything he did. There would even be a rationale for the accident." Jan has recovered sufficiently to be back recording a solo album again, but he is in a semi-aphasic condition, and we may never know what put-on was behind the put-on that got them their first hit record, "Jenny Lee," in the spring of 1958. They'd made it in Jan's garage for a friend's party as a joke and ended up with a recording contract.

Everybody at the party said it sounded like a real record, and Arwin records when they heard it thought so too. They put it out and *holy moly* if it didn't make it to number three nationwide.

Through Sam Cooke, Jan had met Lou Adler, who became their future producer. It was to be an historic relationship, their joint ingenuities developing what later became the California sound: soft layered vocal harmonies, multi-tracked voices and sound effects, all backed by a group of advanced session musicians — Hal Blaine on drums, Leon Russel (who played keyboard for Jan and Dean until 1963) and Glen Campbell among others.

It wasn't until they were working on "Linda," 10 singles and 3 labels later in the Fall of 1962, that they hit upon the sound which became the surfing sound, trademark of the Beach

*Reprinted by permission of Dean Torrence/United Artists Records.

Boys and Jan and Dean. Liberty hadn't given them much of a budget for the album. Jan and Dean had to do all the background vocals themselves with lots of multi-tracking on two four track recorders. On one take Dean sang lead in a falsetto voice just like a girl. If it weren't for that androgynous vocal effect we wouldn't have the Beach Boys, the Byrds, Love, Buffalo Springfield and Crosby, Stills, Nash & Young (which is almost all of California right there). Dean put it this way on the liners for *Greatest Hits Volume Two:* "I said, do you really think you can get me to sing like a girl . . . But Spleen he said in his easy going voice (not the one he sings with) I'll give you some milk duds and some gum if you just warble some high notes for me."

The reaction was truly torrential: "Linda" sold nearly a half million copies. So it wasn't so bad sounding like a girl after all. And as fate would have it, enter the Beach Boys. "The Beach Boys opened up the surfing field, they got the sound from us, we got the beaches and wheels from them," Dean says matter-of-factly about this historic exchange. While hanging around Western Recorders, Brian Wilson (the apotheosis of Beach Boy mystique) was tooling around the piano and the song just happened to be that sybaritic vision of the surfer's dream dreamed aloud, the two girls for every boy of Surf City. This was the male teen dream even for landlocked mods, Boston boppers and midwestern teenagers; the ultimate California equation "Summer Means Fun": cars cruising, chickadees, pendeltons, woodies, St. Christopher medals, "shootin' the breeze," the "asphalt aisle," baggies, and madras.

"Linda" was followed in early 1963 by their biggest hit, "Surf City," written for them by Brian Wilson, and a string of surf drag smashes: "Honolulu Lulu," "Drag City," "The New Girl in School" and "Dead Man's Curve."

"Drag City," a typical Jan and Dean novelty nugget which was a goof on "Alley Oop" broadened the topics that could be treated. Subject matter now consisted of such items as a drag-racing old lady ("The Little Old Lady From Pasadena"), "Sidewalk Surfin'," a senior citizen car club, a taco wagon, "Batman," and "Popsicle."

Today Dean, who is a graphic artist with his own company, Kittyhawk, is almost scrupulously casual about it all:

"The lifestyle of the beach was the key to our music, the California sound was almost more of a lyric. We never started off with what are we going to write about, but mostly just from the images like the "Little Old Lady From Pasadena" came about when I was watching this Dodge Commercial on TV. . . . That was what was so beautiful about *Endless Summer*, just sounds and images."

# THE BEACH BOYS

IN THE BEGINNING . . . WERE THE BEACH boys. Under the avalanche of the English Invasion, the Psychedelic Apocalypse, supersonic guitars and flash, it is almost forgotten that this longest-lived of all rock groups was the true innovator of the new age of rock. Not only did they begin the revival of fifties R & B, their harmonies gave voice to a new generation and established the sense of *community* central to the whole of sixties rock.

These messengers of the Aquarian Age were an unlikely collection of teenagers from the Angelino suburb of Hawthorne, California: the Wilson brothers — Brian, an introspective giant dreaming in his lonely room, Carl, cherubic and precocious, and Dennis, a fearless California primitive — their cousin, Mike Love (who later became chairman of the board for New Atlantis), and a next-door neighbor and budding folk singer, Al Jardine. They began harmonizing together at family get-togethers, and gradually

drifted up to Brian's room where they could sing their teen favorites, the Four Freshmen's classic "Their Hearts Were Filled With Spring," the Everly Brothers' "Dream" and novelty numbers like "Short Shorts." At first they sang *a cappella*, then about a year before the group got started, Brian picked up the piano, Carl, a mere thirteen at the time, learned some guitar chords from John Ross of the Walker Brothers and Al taught himself some elementary chords on the stand-up bass, popular in folk groups at the time.

Dennis didn't play anything but he was the one to supply the words. An obsessed surf freak with all the beach badges — bleached hair, hurachi sandals, Pendleton shirts and a Woody — Dennis hung out a lot at the Rendezvous Ballroom where Dick Dale wailed on his surfin' guitar and he just kept bugging and bugging his brothers about the new kick. "Let's do a surf kinda idea," he would say.

(Collection Peter Kanze)

Brian Wilson

(Collection Alan Betrock)

One weekend while their parents were on vacation south of the border, they rented some instruments with the food money, and, as Brian says, "As if by magic the future took its course." A week later Al had an audition with a publisher who wanted him to tape some folk songs as demos and Al took Dennis, Carl, Brian and Mike along for support. "We sang our song called 'Surfin' for him," recalls Brian. " 'Hey, that's that surfing fad, isn't it?' He flipped for the idea, and said he would like to cut it. So he threw away the folk thing and went with our surfing idea. And his wife Derinda flipped, they both said, 'Hey that's going to be a hit for you guys.' And he gave us Pendletons and told us to dress like surfers. We were going to call ourselves the Pendletons, for the shirt. They were surfer shirts, real wooly long sleeves. Well, you know real funky and when they put the record out, we saw the label and it said the Beach Boys. We said, 'Who did that?' We hated it but we had to go with it."

"Surfin' " was recorded in about ten minutes, in the studio where "Pink Shoelaces" was cut,

and featured Brian on "drums," the bottom of a plastic garbage can. It got heavy play on KFWB in Los Angeles and made it to number three in the local charts. They performed their first concert at the Richie Valens Memorial Hop in Long Beach on New Year's Eve, 1961. Candix Records folded the next year and they moved to Capitol where they had their first smash hit, "Surfin' Safari." Taking the melody from Chuck Berry's "Sweet Little Sixteen," it broke on a hot day in June 1962 and established them as a potentially big group.

Initially their music was as simple as the things they wrote about, surfing, cars, girls, school, but by their third album, *Shut Down*, released in March 1963, they were entering new terrain. *Teenset* called it "the top selling teen angled LP of the year that fired off the starting gun of roaring hot rod platters." The guitar as car as sex machine they had picked up from Chuck Berry ("Maybelline," "You Can't Catch Me") but the Beach Boys accelerated the cult and localized it as exclusive teen terrain. On "Shut Down" and "Little Deuce Coupe" the

**The Beach Boys**

technical lingo is straight out of the body shop.

Brian had taken over production of their records on *Shut Down* and despite, or perhaps because all of them were still in their teens, the group began developing the most sophisticated teen sound to be generated by any rock group at that time. It was physical, sensual and smooth; they were working a formula with genius. Beginning with "Don't Worry Baby," "I Get Around" and "Help Me Rhonda," the rhythmic gear shifts were becoming more innovative, and the production was getting thicker and more complex. Goofing on the record ("I'm Bugged At My Old Man") and elaborate sound effects ("Amusement Parks U.S.A.") became part of the philosophy of "Fun, Fun, Fun." On *Summer Days* (June 1965) they were attempting to transfer atmospheric qualities to vinyl, "a concept of different feelings you have in the summer," as Mike Love described it. Meanwhile Brian was developing a wistfulness and expressiveness on "In My Room" and "Back Of My Mind" that was indicative of things to come.

Confronted with hip culture feedback and the larger than life personalities of the Beatles and the Stones, Brian decided to withdraw from touring with the group. In April 1965 he was replaced on stage, first by Glen Campbell and then Bruce Johnston of Bruce and Terry. While the group was on tour in Japan, Brian began work on his masterpiece, *Pet Sounds*, writing and producing all the tracks himself. "*Rubber Soul* had just come out," he says about its genesis. "I had time to think things out. I wanted to make an album that would stand up in ten years. I thought of it as chapel rock, commercial choir music." Brian idolized Phil Spector's massed quality of sound but on *Pet Sounds* he surpassed Spector in subtlety. Its ethereal tonal colorings contrasting textures of sound, narcotic sensitivity and pure angelic vocals achieved Brian's desired Sistine Chapel effect. Its sheer iridescent density is the star of the album. Layer on layer of sonic whispers, hypnotically fused, transport the listener "on warm, swelling waves of sound to a place where time passes slowly in a gentle celebration of innocence." "Wouldn't It Be Nice," "Don't Talk (Put Your Head On My Shoulder)," "I Just

Wasn't Made For These Times" deal subliminally with an intimate space between adolescent reverie and the threshold of growing up.

Brian, employing a legion of studio musicians and electronic effects, spent four months in five studios laying down the tracks, leaving the vocals open until the rest of the group returned. They were totally unprepared for Brian's innovations and were not flattered that they had become "the performing part of Brian Wilson's mind." The departure was too radical — the previous album, after all, had been the "live" *Beach Boys Party* — they felt it would be disastrous to their image, and "why mess with the formula?"

In a sense they were right, *Pet Sounds* was their greatest achievement, but it was also the first of their albums that failed to become a million seller. And this created an insecurity in the group that was to undermine all the Beach Boy's future output. Unlike the audiences of Dylan and the Beatles, Beach Boys fans were not ready to follow them in their experiments. What was worse, Capitol was so opposed to it that they agreed to issue the album only if they could release simultaneously a *Best of the Beach Boys* repackage. Capitol at the time was concentrating almost exclusively on the Beatles, and consequently short-circuited the only American group that came close to rivaling the Beatles in scope and mass appeal.

The Beach Boys sound was of a generation waking up. The music brought into focus a new class, the children of suburban America, who had appropriated the artifacts of rock & roll culture of the fifties. They expressed themselves through these common denominators: teenage love, cars, novelty and the search for the perfect wave. The beach replaced the rooftop and under the boardwalk as the stage for teen rituals. There was surf music before the Beach Boys but it was instrumental primarily, played and listened to by "greasers and ho-daddies." In the context of the Beach Boys' songs, hot rods and surf boards became symbols celebrating a new freedom in a cult of the Endless Summer.

The Beach Boys have always been hampered by their image. Bruce Johnston aptly described them as "the Doris Day of rock

(Collection Alan Betrock)

groups." Because of their apolitical, clean-cut stance and their squeamishness about dealing with anything but the most innocuous material, they became branded as creators of "decadent fluff," mindless hedonists addicted to the fetishes of the American Dream. Although they introduced elements that would turn into trends, the Beach Boys still kept one foot in the fifties. They are often criticized for their lack of relevance, but it is the very timelessness of *Pet Sounds* that ten years later makes it eminently more enjoyable than most albums made in the late sixties.

As the first self-produced group, they were prodigious innovators; they founded the "California Sound" (the Byrds, the Mamas and the Papas, Crosby, Stills, Nash & Young), were creators of the first concept albums (beginning with *Shut Down)* and masters of the subliminal sound — "Wind Chimes" and "Meant For You" have the unconscious quality of something drifting through your mind. Finally, the single "Good Vibrations," a pocket masterwork whose three minutes and twenty seconds took longer to make than the whole *Pet Sounds* album, is still the trippiest of all psychedelic songs.

The Beach Boys continue to turn out great soft rock, most noticeably their tribute to R & B, *Wild Honey,* and the Looney Tune *Smiley Smile* which followed. After *Pet Sounds* Brian kept pushing the limits, collaborating with Van Dyke Parks (notably on the singles "Heroes And Villians" and "Surf's Up"), toying with the sound effects of twenty musicians playing hammers and saws, the Moog droplets on "Cool Water," frogs, birds, crunching carrots on "Vegetables" (written with Paul McCartney).

Like the true California innocent that he is, Brian relentlessly pursues the ineffable sound in back of his mind. As he said about his long withheld masterpiece "Surf's Up," "I wanted it to have the sound of heaven."

# THE BYRDS

THE BYRDS ENCAPSULATED THE MID-sixties' compulsion to make everything new, to force back every boundary. The New Age required new sounds, new signs, a new language, new myths, and what could've been more perfect than the Byrds' own fantasy of themselves: Space Cowboys! Didn't they write Earth's first love song to a quasar ("CTA-102")? And who but cybernetic Roger McGuinn would drag a pet laser (Ruby) about with him for companionship? In flashes and vibrations, they brought us acid Newspeak. Early Byrds' fans found only colors to describe them. The harmonies of their soaring vocals and the overtones of the 12-string guitars all buzzed and droned like the whine of liquid oxygen.

It's hard to believe the recorded life of the original group barely spanned two years, but during that time they crashed one sonic barrier after another: the first political protest song in "Turn, Turn, Turn"; the first serious country song in sixties rock, "Satisfied Mind"; Bach in the bridge of "She Don't Care About Time"; electronics in "CTA-102"; the infamous raga rocker, "Why"; and, of course, the first psychedelic song, "Eight Miles High."

John Lennon once asked McGuinn why they didn't wear outfits on stage. "We lost them," he said. "I wish we'd lost ours," said Lennon. That attitude was to become the dominant underground style for both audiences and performers: levis, casual stage manners — even turning your back on the audience during a jam. The Byrds' own casualness on stage, however, was almost always contrived. Ill-at-ease with their image — McGuinn's granny glasses and Crosby's mustache tended to look a little glued-on, like Sgt. Pepper patches — they often overacted (as in Crosby's famous Kennedy assassination speech at the Monterey Pop

Festival), distorted their volume (this is rock & roll, baby) or tried to look bored. Most of this came from a folk-rooted embarrassment about how to behave on stage, and is graphically described in their triumph of self-consciousness: "So You Want To Be A Rock & Roll Star."

The Byrds' first hit in 1965, "Mr. Tambourine Man," was the first American response to the English invasion, the first call-back on the transatlantic rock cable. Where the English groups were basically dealing with mixes of folk and fifties rock & roll, the Byrds had discovered a whole new territory with electrified folk music. The idea of the Byrds came to Roger McGuinn while watching *A Hard Day's Night*, and after a return visit to the film to check out what kind of guitar George Harrison was playing (a 12-string Rickenbacker), he began adapting traditional folk music to an electric sound. But his adaptations, like Dylan's, were very specific, and while he was working on this new sound on a solo gig at The Troubador in Los Angeles, Gene Clark and David Crosby heard him and the three of them

formed the nucleus of the original Byrds.

All three had a background in folk music. McGuinn began playing at The Gate of Horn, a folk grotto in Chicago, later worked as a banjo player for the Limelighters, and had accompanied The Mitchell Trio and worked with Judy Collins. David Crosby had been a folk singer with Les Baxter's balladeers, and Gene Clark, who was to write most of the original material on the first two Byrds albums, also came out of a folk music background. The three of them found Chris Hillman (who was playing mandolin in a bluegrass band) and persuaded him to pick up a Japanese bass. When Crosby found Mike Clarke playing bongos on Venice Beach, the original Byrds were formed. The producer of all their early singles and LP's was Terry Melcher, the son of Doris Day, who also produced hits for Paul Revere and the Raiders, Pat Boone, Wayne Newton and others.

Since they were consciously modeling themselves after the Beatles, their manager, Jim Dickson, originally gave them the name the Beefeaters (after the bottle of gin he happened to

**The Byrds**

be drinking at the time). Their first single, "It Won't Be Wrong," simply disappeared. They changed their name to the Byrds and Dickson persuaded them to record Dylan's "Mr. Tambourine Man." By then they had perfected the vocal harmonies that became their trademark, but only McGuinn was competent enough to play on the session, and studio musicians (among them Leon Russel), were brought in in place of the other four Byrds. The record was an instant hit. It was the catalyst that drove Dylan to pick up an electric guitar. The Beatles themselves began writing Byrdsongs: "Nowhere Man" and "If I Needed Someone."

The input of the Byrds' music was the disparate elements of traditional folk music, blues, country and western, John Coltrane's jazz, Eastern music, Dixieland, bluegrass and electronic sound. But it was essentially one sound, the thickly textured instrumental sound of the guitars, combined with choir-laden harmonies of the vocal parts. McGuinn wanted "weird harmonies" reminiscent of the dissonant modal chords of Appalachian music, and told the others in the group to look for them. The Byrds' sound was a California sound, music of the new land, a portable music with vocal harmonies that suggested the collective spirit of a nation moving West.

As progressive as they were, when their extraterrestrial single "Eight Miles High" came out in 1966 and was blacklisted because it was considered a drug song, the Byrds began to lose confidence in themselves. When it fell out of the top 40, making it a commercial disaster, the already aggravated personal conflicts within the group were compounded — this was a pre-underground era and failure to make it on the charts seriously undermined a group's musical authority. As the original members began to drop away (Gene Clark had already left because of his fear of flying), the idea of the Byrds began to dissolve. When David Crosby left the group in 1967 it was all over. Crosby is cited as the major irritant in the Byrds, but it was the *tension* between Crosby and McGuinn that had made the original sound, and without it the New Byrds were no longer five-dimensional.

Chris Hillman, like Gene Clark, had caught

(Columbia Records)

country fever at the close of the sixties and made three subtle nouveau country albums with the Flying Burrito Brothers, as well as two single albums on his own. He ended up playing with Stephen Stills' Manassas and then forming his own group with Souther and Furray. David Crosby, as everyone knows, went on to become a millionaire with Stills, Nash and, eventually, Young. By 1968 Roger McGuinn and Mike Clarke were the only original Byrds remaining in the group, and a year later McGuinn was the only remaining Byrd. However, he kept on recruiting Byrds as if the group were some sort of religious order.

Each new incarnation of the Byrds was greeted with expectation, but once the original group had disbanded and the sound dissipated, duplication was out of the question. There were fewer and fewer surprises, and even the innovations seemed forced. Nostalgia, blandness and cowboy posturing took over. As McGuinn said to Dylan at about this time, "Country music is the last authentic American sound we've got left to rip off." The Byrds were not wholly foreigners to country music. Gene Clark was from Missouri and Chris Hillman had been a bluegrass freak, and "Satisfied Mind" is credited as being the first country and western rock song of the sixties. But it wasn't until Gram Parsons joined the Byrds in 1968 that these leanings got out of hand, what McGuinn described as "Japanese."

Parsons convinced McGuinn that their "imitation Dylan songs weren't working too well . . . . I wanted to take the sweetness and down-home feeling of country and western and create goosebumps and make a little catharsis." Camouflaged in their new sound, the Byrds even made it to The Grand Ole Opry, but their version of country and western had the charm of old postcards and these Byrds could never project the original personae that everyone was looking for, which was perhaps buried in McGuinn himself, the keeper of the vision.

When the five original Byrds reunited briefly in 1972 to record an album, their return was greeted with great expectations, as if through some time warp they could bring back that idyllic time they had helped create some seven years before in a science fiction fantasy: reunion at the Telstar Corral. Gravity surrounded them in a familiar envelope as a yucca-embossed arm set the controls that would ease them out of orbit. They'd been away a long time on their intergalactic trails but how could they misinterpret Mt. Shasta's soft contours on their holographic scanner? Their descent is soundless except for the "rrrrrrrr . . . . . er" of the humming retros tuned to Roger McGuinn's soul sound. On the ground a group of ecstatic fans are breaking out into a wave of dolphin chants . . . .

# BUFFALO SPRINGFIELD

THE BUFFALO SPRINGFIELD ENVISIONED themselves almost self-consciously as an *American* band, setting themselves apart from English rock groups by creating a specifically Californian blend of rock and folk music. Essentially what they did was to weld the acoustic intensity and harmonic overlays of folk music onto a rock chassis to produce a flexible musical machine which was capable of absorbing a wide range of different styles: Latin, soul, country, hard rock and ballads. But the inflection was uniquely their own.

Given the aggravated personal climate of the group, its continual shifts in managers and producers and almost schizoid manner of working in the studio, it is amazing how complex and polished their recorded sound came across. Aside from the telling lyrics it would be hard to guess that the group was being torn apart from within. Unlike the Byrds, whom they often resembled in timbre and attitude, they did not simply precipitate folk music into rock; instead, they wed them to each other but allowed the instruments to retain their individual qualities, juxtaposing the mellow voice of acoustic instruments against the searing wail of electricity.

The geographical backgrounds of the members of the Springfield were as different as their individual musical tastes. Steve Stills (variously from Texas, Florida, Louisiana and Costa Rica) brought with him a taste for soul sounds, Latin rhythms and smooth folk harmonies; Neil Young, from the wilds of Winnepeg, infused the group's sound with slashing lead guitar lines and ferocious crystal poetry; while Richie Furay (Yellow Springs, Ohio) wrote the group's lovesongs and later, with Jim Messina, its soft ballads. Dewey Martin, who came out of the country folk group the Dillards, added a tinge of bluegrass and a Memphis back beat, while another Canadian, Bruce Palmer, underpinned this musical crew with his supple inventive bass. These inputs of personality and interweaving of influences created a rich musical mosaic when they

**Buffalo Springfield**

meshed during the incredibly brief period the Buffalo Springfield was together. It also, inevitably, produced tensions which the group could only contain for so long before it finally split them.

The founding members of the group got together by accident, literally running into each other in an L.A. traffic jam when Richie Furay spotted a hearse with Ontario license plates. "I bet that's Neil Young," he said to Steve Stills.

They'd both recently come from New York where they played together as the Au Go Go Singers, and it was from Greenwich Village that Richie knew Neil. Bruce Palmer, also in the hearse, had been in Neil's Toronto group the Squires, and the four of them got together, found themselves a manager who got them drummer Dewey Martin and named themselves after a tractor on a Beverly Hills lawn. Within a few weeks they were playing a six-week gig at

(Collection Peter Kanze)

The Whiskey a' Go-Go on Sunset Strip.

As untogether as they were initially (Bruce Palmer's bass had three E strings from a guitar tuned down), they almost immediately established a loyal local following. Their presence as a smoking live band never really got transferred to vinyl, but left an indelible impression on their audiences: Richie bouncing about the stage, Steve smouldering and smoothing out the harmonies, Neil, the Hollywood Indian, a "midnight double scorpio" glowering in his fringe jacket, Bruce coolly turning his back on the audience, and the whole group surging up to the microphones on cue. Eventually the legendary "guitar wars" between

Steve and Neil became part of their mystique, an attraction in itself even if it was to be fatal to the cohesion of the group.

Their first single, "Nowadays Clancy Can't Even Sing," on Atlantic's ATCO label, was a song Neil had taught Richie in New York, which had accidentally been released as the A side instead of Still's more pop "Go And Say Goodbye." To make matters worse, "Clancy" was denied air play because it contained the word "damn." The group was floundering even before it had begun, and playing gigs like Redondo Beach, where they opened the show for the Turtles, which hardly seemed encouraging. Things seemed to be crumbling in

L.A. There were riots going on on Sunset Strip. Steve Stills retired to Topanga Canyon to contemplate the sound that was going down and wrote his subtle, elliptical "protest" song, "For What It's Worth," which incorporated an ingenious protest against protests ("people carrying signs that mostly say hoo-ray for our signs").

If it was equivocal, "For What It's Worth" was also obviously sympathetic (besides being a great song) and to young Angelinos the Springfield became the disseminators of defused dilemmas, and consequently *the* hot new group.

By September 1967 they had three hits simultaneously in the L.A. charts: "For What It's Worth," "Rock 'n' Roll Woman," and a ten-minute version of "Bluebird," which deejay B. Mitchell Reid had unearthed. But by the time they had established themselves as a major national group, they were disintegrating fast. Bruce left, then Neil Young quit the group at least twice before finally leaving to devote himself to his own solo albums. In June 1967 he did not even show up at the Monterey Pop Festival to play with the Springfield. There were other problems too. Neil was often physically ill, the result of a vicious police beating, and the intense hostility between him and Steve reached the breaking point. Though they performed their last concert in May 1968 at Long Beach, for almost a year the group had existed only on record, individual members often going into the studio separately to cut tracks that were later put together for albums that appeared under the group name.

Not that the Buffalo Springfield ever tried to cover up the fierce internal irritations or pressures of their life as a group. Many of their best songs are revealing autobiographical pictures of the white heat interior of the life of a Rock Star: "Mr. Soul"; the mini opera "Broken Arrow," with its ironical opening screams lifted from the Beatles' L.A. concert; the more personal "On The Way Home," directed at Steve Stills; Richie Furay's indictment of Neil on "Child's Claim To Fame," answered by Neil in "I Am A Child"; the premonition of "Out Of My Mind."

The spectrum of sound that the Springfield generated at their best was an eclectic yet integrated music that was to provide the model for most of the west coast groups of the early seventies, not to mention the groups that arose out of the fragments of the Springfield itself — Crosby, Stills, Nash & Young; Steve Still's Manassas; Poco; Loggins and Messina; Souther, Hillman and Furay. With the exception of Neil Young's violent, narcissistic, introverted solo albums, none of these groups even equaled the energy and intensity of their original. In fact, it was the myth of the shattered Buffalo Springfield that lay behind the mystique of the groups that grew out of its remains.

# CROSBY, STILLS, NASH & YOUNG

JIMI HENDRIX ONCE DESCRIBED THE COLlective sound Crosby, Stills, Nash & Young make as "tinkling Western sky music." With their pure high harmonies, translucent guitars, and the pastel tones of their vision of the rosy apocalypse, their music does suggest the soft polychrome colors of a desert twilight, with the first four stars of the seventies rising like crystals above the horizon.

CSN&Y's melting music is a synthesis of the folk, rock and pop styles. On their solo acoustic sets and plugging into current rock fusions on the group jams they blended an optimistic commercial sound, in spite of the prevailing "downer" lyrics. Their first album, *Crosby, Stills & Nash*, made it simultaneously onto the top 40 listings as well as infiltrating underground and easy listening stations, even sneaking onto *Billboard's* soul survey at number 35! Yet their songs were sprinkled with enough drug/

## Crosby, Stills, Nash & Young

revolution references ("Marrakesh Express," "Chicago") to make them into the sweet hippie anthems that their audiences sipped like nectar.

It was at the Monterey Pop Festival, just after Neil Young had left the Buffalo Springfield, when Steve Stills asked David Crosby of the Byrds to play in his place, that the core of the future group was formed. The Springfield had always been fans of the Hollies, and in 1968, when Graham Nash, came to L.A. on tour with the Hollies, Stills and Crosby (who'd both by now left their respective groups) got together with him and sang a few songs together. After a couple more harmonious singalongs, the three started talking about the possibility of forming a new group, though it seemed unlikely Graham Nash would leave his position as leader and principal songwriter of the Hollies.

How organically this trinity worked can be gauged by the fact that within a month of studio time they had laid down both sides of their first album, *Crosby, Stills & Nash*. Its near perfect production, sumptuous arrangements, precise harmonies and guitar overlays won them the dubious honor of being possibly the first group to be faulted for producing an album that was "so perfect" it lacked spontaneity.

It was evident even to Steve Stills that some element was missing, and having recruited Dallas Taylor from Clear Light, and a Motown bassist, Greg Reeves, into the group, the gap was even more obvious. Stills needed another lead

guitarist to "hit from" who would complement his playing and give the group the driving sound it needed. Ironically, since it was the notorious guitar wars between Stills and Young that had fractured the Buffalo Springfield, Neil Young was chosen as the missing link.

Neil Young provided the tension CS&N sorely needed, and despite Crosby's revolutionary ravings, he also brought a conscience to the group with his stark aura and songs like the Appalachian marching hymn "Ohio." Young gave a dissonance and ambiguity to the group. He sharpened its image, especially on stage and in his solo songs, and provided a looseness and simplicity to the production of their albums, while not noticeably altering the group's basic sound. What prompted this "loner" with his werewolf visions to leave his lair for CS&N's child's garden of flowers can be understood in part by the mutual benefit derived — without him CS&N could not long have extended their sweet, wistful laments without sounding cloying, and, as a consequence of his incorporation into the group, Young's two previous solo albums and the subsequent *After The Gold Rush* and *Harvest* all sold over a million copies.

CSN&Y has been described as "Music from Big Ego" — all the members, excepting the diplomatic Nash, are well-known megalomaniacs—but it is the differences not the similarities that give a group its character. They

*(Michael Putland/© London Features International Ltd.)*

Steve Stills

Neil Young

Graham Nash and David Crosby

merged in 1969 for the first of their Million Dollar Bashes at the tribal gathering of Woodstock, though with legal care they deliberately used their linked names as the group's title. Despite their titanic personalities, Crosby, Stills & Nash were ideal blenders, submerged even in the groups they came out of; their practice of opening their shows with solo sets of "wooden" acoustic music and building up with a series of little highs, left enough room for each member to maneuver. In spite of the care taken to sustain the studied informality they projected on stage, the group dissolved not because of the Stills/Young tensions but, as Nash gently explains, "It was between Stephen and me . . . over a lady."

In the Spring of 1971, after several abortive attempts to put back the pieces under the palms of Hawaii and beneath the redwoods of Northern California, the four reunited briefly and were, predictably enough, ecstatically welcomed back. They were, after all, leaders of the California children's crusade — their harmonies stirring a collective soul in soft painless idylls with the illusion left just intact enough to make it believable. The current that flows "free and easy" between the group and its audience, lapping back and forth in litanies of innocence, is what propels the CSN&Y mystique — as the four of them set sail in their "Wooden Ships" to the Land of Nod.

# THE DOORS

THE PROJECTOR ROLLS, FLICKERING ANCIENT bits of film: a meeting on the beach, two heads bent to the ceaseless peristaltic motion of the waves; the Doors onstage, Morrison lifting his face to the light, a leathered lamb; maced in New Haven; the numbing solace of alcohol, the release of poetics, shaman exposed, lizard flicking tongue — "the culmination, in a way, of our mass performing career"; a death of Marat, mojo rising.

This, then, was the end of the night. They could lay no claim to past or future. The Doors existed in the cruciform of Los Angeles present, a canvas in yellow and black, lashed to the mast, speared by the heart. William Blake presided at their baptism. "There are things that are known and things that are unknown; in between are doors."

James Douglas Morrison seldom acknowledged his backgrounds, unwilling "to involve anyone unless they want it." Born December 8, 1943, he was raised by naval parents in the port town of Alexandria, Virginia, bouncing through several colleges before he gravitated toward UCLA and the study of cinema. "There's no authority on film," he commented on his choice in the Lords' *Notes On Vision*. "Any one person can assimilate and contain the whole history of film in himself, which you can't do in other arts. There are no experts, so, theoretically, any student knows almost as much as any professor."

The same might be true of rock & roll. In July 1965, he began talking about music to Ray Manzarek, a classmate who dabbled in keyboards with a club band called Rick and the Ravens. Morrison recited to him the lyrics of several songs he'd composed, one of which was "Moonlight Drive," whose sand-and-surf imagery prompted "Screaming" Ray to contact jazz drummer John Densmore. Two months later, with Manzarek's brothers Rick and Jim on guitars, the Doors had completed a twelve-song demo for possible record company approval.

A "tantalized" talent scout at Columbia Records, Billy James, was impressed by their potential and signed them to a short-term contract. The company never followed through, and the Doors went back to playing Sunset Strip nightclubs. Robbie Krieger, a jug-band import, joined to replace the Manzarek brothers, and the group was hired as the house band at the Whiskey a' Go-Go for a period of four months. As the Doors grew in musical maturity, Jim extending and improvising an omnipotent stage personality, they harvested a considerable following. Elektra president Jac Holzman saw them at the Whisky during their tenure and overcame initial hesitation to begin serious negotiations. By the fall of 1966, the Doors were recording their debut album.

"I have never been as moved in a recording studio," remembered producer Paul Rothschild later in a 1967 article in *Crawdaddy*. "I was impressed by the fact that for one of the very first times in rock and roll history sheer drama had taken place on tape." *The Doors* presented as complete a statement as the Doors themselves were capable of, each track unveiling another facet of Morrison's polygonic personality. If "Back Door Man" established his erotic credentials, "Soul Kitchen" enhanced them, the garish California neon of "Twentieth Century Fox," set next to Brecht-Weill's "Alabama Song (Whisky Bar)" of another age. "Light My Fire," minus its long instrumental release, was the obvious single, while "The Crystal Ship" offered passage to realms unexplored, the "Other Side" so inscrutably prescribed in "Break On Through."

The album's tour de force, "The End," had begun innocently as the Doors' show farewell, stretched by Morrison into a molten fresco of travel-weary images and faces. "C'mon, baby, take a chance with us," he cajoled, outlining terrors real, imagined, pulsing with phosphorescence and decay. He walked through hallways beyond the range of vision, confronting the Oedipal embrace of "Father I want to kill you . . . Mother I want to . . . ," the beast language of primal instinct. "I felt emotionally washed," Rothschild told

Jim Morrison

John Densmore

Robbie Krieger

Ray Manzarek

*Crawdaddy's* Paul Williams. "There were four other people in the control room at the time, when the take was over and we realized the tape was still going. And all of us were audience, there was nothing left, the machines knew what to do."

Morrison and the Doors leaped to fame overnight. Immediate darlings of the underground, they broadened the base of their success when "Light My Fire" hit the AM charts in the summer of 1967; Jim's brooding sensuality seemed equally at home in the pages of *Vogue* as in *Sixteen* magazine. In performance, Morrison outdid himself again and again, conceptualizing his brazen aura, weaving about the stage, pressing himself against the microphone, working himself into rabid frenzy. He appeared unconscious of harm, climaxing each show as if it were his last.

Times wouldn't always be so good to the Doors. Pinioned by the respective demands of their dual audiences, the one demanding hit singles, the other "art," the Doors were never able to combine these demands to their own satisfaction. Morrison made few concessions to commerciality for its own sake, but the fact that this was underrecognized throughout much of the group's creative career created, in retrospect, many needless problems. Morrison, especially,

seemed to feel alternately trapped and emboldened. Consumed by the idea of music as ritual, he both accepted and thrust maddeningly at its boundaries. "It's kind of like human sculpture," he admitted to Jerry Hopkins in a

*(Neal Preston-Andy Kent)*

**The Doors**

*Rolling Stone* interview. "It's like art, because it gives form to energy . . . a custom or a repetition, an habitually recurring plan or pageant that has meaning. It pervades everything." Yet too often his attempts at creating mood would be jarred by asensitive shouts; if he decided, on the other hand, to "just push a situation as far as it'll go," there was similar uneasiness in spectacle.

The awareness brought by this quixotic dilemma surfaced as early as the Doors' second album, *Strange Days*. The poetry was more formal ("Horse Latitudes"), the swagger more overt ("Love Me Two Times"), the surrealistic patchwork of "The End" transferred to the strident invocations of "When The Music's Over." But the Doors, like most of their generation, had to decide what to do with the world once it was theirs. In a sense, that turning point had been passed with "Light My Fire."

Morrison, seeking to heal the rift, only exacerbated it. In *The Unknown Soldier*, a 1968 single with accompanying film, he sacrificed his cinematic self to the cry of "The war is over!" surviving onstage to herald the good news. Only it was never that easy. Too simply could he become the fool, drunk and disorderly; also, to be sure, he could become the blessed poet. A long epic took shape, "The Celebration of the Lizard," though only the studio fragment of "Not To Touch The Earth" was actually released. The music gained texture and ornamentation; Morrison scooped deeper into his fantasies, rich and loamy, a rite of natural fertility. Perhaps the struggle was also inward, the pretensions of a pop star rebelling against the pretensions of an artist. Perhaps it was too early to understand that one need not conflict with the other.

Whatever its causes, Morrison's behavior became more erratic, reaching a head in March 1969 when he was arrested during a concert in Miami's Dinner Key Auditorium for "lewd and lascivious behavior in public by exposing his private parts and by simulating masturbation and oral copulation." The more serious charges were later dismissed, but Morrison was dangerously marked in the eyes of promotors. It was just as well; the Doors needed rethinking.

Their hit singles — "Tell All The People," "Touch Me" — had kept up, as had the quality of the albums (some of their best work was yet to come: *The Soft Parade* with its Gantryesque "pe-ti-tion the Lord with pray-uh," *Morrison Hotel*'s Rock 'n' Roll look backwards, *Absolutely Live*'s rendition of the complete "Lizard"). Still, Morrison knew it was time to take stock.

"I think of myself as an intelligent, sensitive human being with the soul of a clown which always forces me to blow it at the most important moments." he told *Rolling Stone*, being more than candid.

Unable to find a solution within the Doors, Morrison looked without. *L.A. Woman* would be their seventh and final album for Elektra, and more relaxed, the group decided to record it in their own basement studio. Though he seldom drank less, Jim appeared settled, publishing a book of poems, *The Lords and the New Creatures*, freeing his means of expression in other, privately circulated volumes, such as *An American Prayer*, 1970.

There were fewer moments than he knew. *L.A. Woman* was his swan song to Hollywood, "Riders On The Storm" emphasizing his restlessness, the temporality of nonexistence and removal. Having broken through to the other side, Morrison found himself stranded, with no return passage. Acquiescing, he left California to take up residence in Paris with his wife Pamela. The Doors began working as a three-man unit in his absence. After attempting to carry the name without Morrison, John and Robbie later formed the Butts Band, Ray carving a niche for his own steadfast solo career.

Morrison kept in touch while he stayed in Paris, talking to old friends and business associates over the telephone. A respiratory ailment had kept him reasonably subdued, and he was writing voluminously. On July 3, 1971, he rose early to take a morning bath; Pamela found him there, "a half-smile on his face," dead of heart failure. The news was withheld from the public several days, until Morrison could be buried quietly in the poet's corner of the Père Lachaise cemetery in Paris. "There was no service," related manager Bill Siddons. "We just threw some flowers and dirt and said goodbye."

# 12
# Binary Stars

## JIMI HENDRIX

THIS IS NEWARK, THE NIGHT AFTER MARTIN Luther King's assassination. Jimi Hendrix is playing the Symphony Theatre to a crowd of white, modishly dressed hippies. "Oh, it's so boring up here," shoulders roll, a laconic twitch, swinging his Stratocaster around in howling protest. He glances down at his watch. "Ho hum, another twenty minutes to go . . . ."

The concert skitters to anticlimax. Jimi takes off his guitar, framed in slow motion, tangential. He looks at the audience once, as if to freeze their strain beyond the footlights, their voyeuristic desire flushed with excitement. He closes his eyes in acceptance, lifts the machine, and with no sense of incipient melodrama piledrives it into the wooden slats of the stage. It lies there, a scarred instrument of resignation, waiting for the curtains to finally close. Nor is there an encore.

As an artist, Jimi Hendrix robed himself in paradox and frustration. If he had been anything less than a pure musician, he might have been able to sidestep the web of his image; but bursting on the scene at the 1967 Monterey Pop Festival with a fully realized, uniquely cataclysmic blend of theatrics and technical

wizardry, he found himself without the logical room to maneuver granted more pedestrian performers. It was a conflict that was to follow him in several variations throughout his meteoric life, setting the backdrop for both his greatest triumphs and moments of despair.

He was born James Marshall Hendrix in Seattle, Washington, on November 27, 1942. The son of a landscaper, he passed a comfortable, middle-class childhood in a predominantly white area, leaving school when he was sixteen. At ten he pretended that a household broomstick was a guitar until his father gave him a real instrument a year later. He joined the army in 1963, entered the paratroops and made a total of 25 jumps. Injured on the 26th, he was discharged, and moved inexorably into the world of rhythm and blues road shows.

It was a dues payment Jimi would remember with mixed feelings. While it did give him an opportunity to consolidate the guitar knowledge he had picked up in the army, sharing stages with the likes of the Isley Brothers and Little Richard, he felt burdened and enclosed by the often tiresome mechanized role he was expected to play. "I was always kept

**Jimi Hendrix**

in the background," he once told *Melody Maker*'s Chris Welch, "but I was thinking all the time about what I wanted to do. I used to join a group and quit them so fast. I dug listening to top 40 R & B but that doesn't mean I like to play it every night."

Hendrix made his break in late 1965. Changing his name to Jimmy James, he organized a band called the Blue Flames and began appearing along the circuit of semi-rock coffeehouses dotting New York's Greenwich Village. He toiled at the Cafe Wha for a span of months, took a step upwards to the influential Cafe Au Go Go, and finally sensed his luck

about to turn when ex-Animals' bassist Chas Chandler volunteered to become his manager and take him to England.

It's not hard to see what Chandler immediately sensed as so powerful in Jimi. His songwriting was at best undeveloped, his ruffled and studded personality still embryonic. Yet his stage presence ran rampant, garnished by a consuming display of gnawing his guitar, all the while constructing runs of remarkable fluidity and grace. He was a craftsman who liked nothing more than to lay back and play formal blues (as the definitive "Red House" will attest); and a master of sound effects, utilizing

(Reprise Records)

electronic gimmickry with a kind of brazen openness. Electricity was never mere amplification for Hendrix, but rather the unfolding of an alien terrain to be roamed at will.

Chandler and co-manager Michael Jeffrey put their pieces together carefully. The idea of a black guitarist breaking and entering white ranks could only be looked on as natural in England, in a country where American blues artists were lionized long after they'd been forgotten in their homeland; and Chandler-Jeffrey sweetened the mix further by dressing Jimi and back-up musicians Noel Redding (bass) and Mitch Mitchell (drums) in all manner of exotic finery. Jimi would become a sinister and sensual figure, with catlike violence lingering beneath the surface of a foppish dandy. It was a duality of stereotype, and it worked.

He was a front-row sensation wherever he went, a visual and tonal assault that left club audiences gaping. The band, christened the Jimi

Early Jimi Hendrix with the Isley Brothers

### Jimi Hendrix

Hendrix Experience, played a debut performance with Johnny Halliday in Paris, then moved to conquer London. By the beginning of 1967 their first single, "Hey Joe," had entered the English charts. Their major introductory British tour started in March, the first guitar burned shortly thereafter. The rapidly congealing underground claimed him as their own. His initial album, *Are You Experienced*, quickly became the *de rigeur* waxing of that hopeful spring.

Jimi's reputation slowly filtered back to America, and he was asked to join the bill for the upcoming Monterey Pop Festival. There, in the midst of intensely stellar competition, he carved a triumphant set out of sheer determination. At first nervous, he found secure footing with "Like A Rolling Stone," dropping to his knees to torch his instrument in the midst of a raging "Wild Thing." The crowd erupted. Hendrix was home and through the gates. Unbeknownst to Chandler and the group, Jeffrey immediately flew to New York to sign the Experience to play on an incipient Monkees tour. As thousands of preteen fans looked on uncomprehendingly at Forest Hills Stadium, Chandler and Jeffrey took reward when a hastily conceived tale of mass protests by the Daughters of the American Revolution was widely reported to have "banned" Jimi from the show.

Nothing could stop him. *Are You Experienced* was released in America to general accolades, "Foxy Lady" to "Purple Haze" to "The Wind Cries Mary," and before the year was out he was a familiar and highly regarded face on the tour circuit and record racks. Feedback became a common household word. He was absorbed into the pop whirl with growing furor, and there were times when it looked as if the passion of legend might have the potential of outracing its subject.

For Jimi, at least, it quickly became a hollow victory. His first album had promised a new wave, a total portrait in which artist and music were fused in indelible presentation. But once the preliminary breakthroughs had been made, the gold records on the wall, the soldout crowds wildly cheering even the most rudimentary efforts, a vital momentum seemed to melt away. Unchallenged by either his

backing musicians (who, in fairness, were tightly leashed by Hendrix) or his audience, he had only himself to rely on for artistic spur. He found it a difficult road to travel.

Jimi called it "pop slavery." Management quarrels erupted. His public notoriety resulted in troubles with the police, first in Sweden and then later in Canada, where he was arrested for possession of drugs (the charge was later dismissed). As his personal quandaries mounted, his music seemed at a virtual standstill. While Jimi never made a bad album (most are acknowledged classics), he foundered on a lack of good material, his style and virtuoso approach often not enough to pull him through unscathed. *Axis: Bold As Love*, his second release, programmed a refinement of *Are You Experienced*, and the double-set *Electric Ladyland* proved even more spotty. Jimi appeared searching for a new vehicle, less contrived and artificial, a more organic direction to frame his guitar intricacies and free-form lyrics. It was only through other people's standards — Dylan's "All Along The Watchtower," Jimi's sonic rearrangement of "The Star Spangled Banner" — that he eased enough to fully play what was on his mind.

The Experience dissolved in late 1968, due in part to Jimi's dissatisfaction with his progress. Jeffrey and Chandler had exited earlier the same year. On his own, he drew away from concerts and recording studios, preferring the informal atmosphere of guest stopovers and afterhours jamming. With the pressure off, his live appearances took on new fire. More often than not he would let another musician — drummer Buddy Miles, for instance, at a 1970 New Year's Eve bash at the Fillmore East — handle the showboating.

He built a new studio, Electric Lady, and prepared to lay tracks for a series of future albums. Jimi was taking his time, gathering his resources, waiting until he felt he had something worthy of laying before the public. After an opening party for the studio in New York, he flew across the ocean to play the third Isle of Wight festival. He was tired, the band (by this time featuring old army buddy Billy Cox on bass) made an effort, but the performance was

## 171
### Jimi Hendrix

ragged. A short European tour faltered in Germany, and when Cox became ill Jimi returned to London. Though disappointed, he spoke hopefully of his coming directions, feeling he'd turned full circle at last.

By then, it was too late. On Friday, September 18, 1970, he was found unconscious at the apartment of a girl friend, Monika Danneman. Pathologist Donald Teare noted that the cause of death was suffocation due to "barbiturate intoxication." No hint of suicide was turned up, and from the buried tapes now seemingly uncovered every day, there is no basis for even idle speculation. Each casual jam, each song-in-progress shows a new range of music Jimi was attempting to absorb, from jazz to soul and forms beyond, to find a place for himself and his guitar. To kiss the sky, excuse me.

(© Baron Wolman)

# JANIS JOPLIN

*(© Jim Marshall)*

TWO STARS EMERGED OUT OF THE Monterey Pop Festival. Until then unknown, they became not only superstars of rock, but symbols which embodied the aspirations of the psychedelic generation.

Janis Joplin and Jimi Hendrix were the proof of the acid vision of the late sixties, an impossible optimism which believed that time could be reversed to the rural funkiness of a simpler era, or projected into a utopian future/present where the ugliness, apathy and materialism of the world would be dissolved in a solution of wishes and dreams. Janis and Jimi seemed almost magically equipped to fulfill this vision, Hendrix beaming interstellar signals through his supersonic guitar while Janis came on with an earthy, elemental raunchiness that had more than a little of the legendary quality of blues belters, riverboat queens and Daisy Mae.

But of all the fantastic impersonations conjured up in that psychedelic summer, Janis' still seems the most fantastic, and also the most real. She was as superreal as an acid flash of the Garden of Eden and as irresistible as R. Crumb's innocent, sensual and nubile giantesses for which she was the model. When *Cashbox* described her as "a mixture of Leadbelly, a steam engine, Calamity Jane, Bessie Smith, an oil derrick and rotgut bourbon funneled into the twentieth century somewhere between El Paso and San Francisco," they were talking about *that* Janis. In the beginning, it was just an extension of her irrepressible personality, but after she became a star it was required of her. The media ate it up, her audiences loved it and finally she came to demand it even of herself, a broad parody of her real drives and energy. The illusion she created was so perfect that many imagined she really was some sort of Faulkner character, a genuine product of the ruminating, exotic southern landscape that produced Howlin' Wolf and Tennessee Williams. But little except her own romantic dreams prepared her for the mythic role she was to play in rock.

She was born the eldest of three children in the smoky, humid oil refinery town of Port Arthur, Texas, and grew up with a background hardly more exotic than any other middle-class, suburban kid in the fifties, passing through a somewhat lumpish childhood into a painful adolescence (her mother once explained her weird dressing as an attempt to hide the fact that she was overweight). Ill at ease in the suffocating atmosphere of Texas in the late fifties, she came to hate everything and everybody around her, and her resentment was cruelly returned when she was voted the Ugliest Man on Campus at the University of Texas. Then she read about Jack Kerouac and "all those other degenerate dope-smoking uglies" in *Time* magazine, made up her mind to become a beatnik and split for San Francisco. A friend who ran into her at the time described her as a rundown crazy speed freak, "the kind you see on the street with the little fine polished crescent of dirt around their eyes." Soon she was reluctantly back in Texas recovering from a heavy addiction to methedrine. Wondering what to do next with herself, that Voice which became the compelling force of her life came

Big Brother and the Holding Company, 1967

along and grabbed her one rainy afternoon while she was singing along with some Odetta records in an abandoned lighthouse.

It told her she was a singer, and she began performing with a bluegrass group called the Waller Creek Boys in an old gas station that had been converted into a country music club. Meanwhile back in San Francisco, rock was gradually replacing folk music and jazz, and homegrown rock groups began experimenting with what was to become the San Francisco sound. A fellow Texan, Chet Helms, was a key figure in this scene and when the group he was managing, Big Brother and the Holding Company, began looking for "a chick singer" he remembered the pudgy little girl with the gravelly voice he'd heard in Austin and dispatched Travis Rivers on a mission to find her and bring her back. "Travis just scooped me up," Janis recalled when asked how her momentous musical career began. "He said 'Go get your clothes I think we're going to California.' Halfway through New Mexico, I realized I'd been conned into Big Brother by this guy who was such a good ball. . . . I was in space city, man, when I got together with the group for the first time. I'd never sung with electric music and drums and I was scared to death. I got on stage and started singing, whew! what a rush man. All I remember is the sensation — what a gas! the music was boom-boom-boom! and the people were all dancing, and the lights flashin' and I was up there singin' into this microphone and gettin' it

on and I dug it so I said 'I think I'll stay boys.' "

The combination of Big Brother, that band of blond long-haired Injuns with their spacy sounds, and Janis' down-home blues was almost too good to believe, and along with the Grateful Dead, Jefferson Airplane and Country Joe, they formed the nucleus of San Francisco's hierarchy of hip. From here on, Janis' life flashed by breathlessly, a whole lifetime slipping by in four meteoric years, as tragic and intense as any blues lyric. If you could stop the film anywhere along the way, it would have to be there in Panhandle Park of 1966, or on one of the High Days of San Francisco's psychedelic celebrations, like the summer solstice when Janis appears in her purest crystal state belting out blues from the bed of an old truck carrying the sound equipment. Her hair is triangular with electricity and she is weighed down by as many bangles as an Ibo bride, swigging away from a bottle of Southern Comfort between sets as she belts out her gutsy blues like a raunchy mother goose ladling nursery rhymes to groups of ecstatic, stoned kids swimming in the wake of a dream from which they do not wish to wake. At those moments, she was the *child* of San Francisco and embodied everything in that morning of a new world which paradoxically expressed itself in the ancient sorrows of the blues.

It was after Monterey, their high point as a group, when things began to show evidence of a strain. Big Brother felt Janis was on a star trip. "She was into making it like an Aretha Franklin

or Marilyn Monroe," as Dave Getz, the group's drummer, described it, "and there was no room for us in that scene." For her part, Janis felt the group was goofing off, not rehearsing enough and satisfied to play their old standards like "Down On Me" over and over, indefinitely. Worst of all, Janis was being told that Big Brother really was not good enough for her and if she wanted to really make it, the band would have to go. Insecure at the best of times, and sensing an urgency about herself and her music, she finally gave in to her worst fears, and a year and a half after Monterey at a concert for the Family Dog in San Francisco, Big Brother and Janis parted company.

They had recorded two albums together which still seem like the best records of that time, the all-night parties for the Hell's Angels at the Avalon Ballroom and endless afternoons playing in Golden Gate Park. Even the shoddily produced first album, *Big Brother and the Holding Company*, now seems evocative simply *because of* its primitive quality. And *Cheap Thrills*, with its Crumb Cartoon Cover featuring a cyclopic Jim Gurley tripping in the desert, Janis juicing, freaks at the Fillmore freaking, talking 2s, and a Hell's Angels' seal of approval, perfectly expresses its appetizing table of

contents: "Piece of My Heart," "Turtle Blues," "Combination Of The Two" and "Ball And Chain."

Big Brother perhaps wasn't the greatest band in the world, but together with Janis they formed a family, and the hip community and San Francisco in particular never forgave Janis for splitting it up. They could not see that Janis was looking for a way for her music to develop. She idolized Otis Redding's piston-like gutsy precision and wanted to fuse herself onto that mainstream of soul music. Early in 1969 she began assembling a group with the standard soul horn section which turned out to be a pale imitation of Detroit and Memphis R & B bands. Her second band was so anonymous that it never even got named, although Janis, putting on her critics, jokingly referred to them as the Joplinaires.

Where Big Brother had been a unit, the second band was merely a professional back-up band, but they failed to impress even the soul musicians they modeled themselves on. The disastrous reception the group got at the Memphis Sound Party in December of 1969 was typical of reactions to Janis' new group. While Janis was with Big Brother she had the San Francisco seal of approval, and in the hip music

death on his own vomit in a similar drug "suicide," it seemed as if the lid had been sealed shut forever on the millennial dreams of the psychedelic era. Her death seemed totally incomprehensible. She had just completed recording what is probably the best album of her career, *Pearl*, had a hit single on the charts with "Me and Bobby McGee," she had finally got together the ideal group in the Full Tilt Boogie Band, found the love of her life and was planning to get married. What more could she have wanted?

And yet that was always the problem with Janis. As her old friend Country Joe MacDonald said, "Her game was running out because her dreams were coming true." It was a paradox Janis understood only too well but somehow that only made it worse. She colorfully referred to this sorry state of affairs as the Great Saturday Night Swindle; she felt that this cosmic con trick was at the core of everything, the reason the blues will always be around.

"You got to remember to spell it with a 'K,' Honey," she said about her own great "Kozmic Blues" that seemed to sum up the whole predicament for her. "It's too down and lonely a trip to be taken seriously, it has to be a Crumb cartoon like "White Man," I mean it'd have to be, but the Kozmic Blues just means that, no matter what you do man, you get shot down anyway . . . .

"I remember when I was a kid they always told me, 'Oh you're unhappy because you're going through adolescence, as soon as you get to be a grown-up everything's going to be cool.' I really believed that, you know. Or as soon as you meet the right man or if only I could get laid, if only I could get a little bread together, everything will be all right. And then one day I finally realized it ain't all right and it ain't never gonna be all right, there's always something that's gonna go wrong."*

In the end, her body too confused to go on, her colossal optimism continually disappointed, she collapsed. She had extended the blues, it seemed, as far as it could go, and then followed its doomy notes herself still grasping like some giant child for the dreams of sensuality and ecstasy.

community they could do no wrong, but now she was a lone target. The very things that had made her such a sensation at Monterey were now used against her. "She doesn't so much sing a song as strangle it to death right before your eyes," wrote one critic.

If the faceless lineup was never a group, most of them were competent musicians, and the one album that came out of her association with them, *I Got Dem Ol' Kozmic Blues Mama*, produced a great hit single in "Try," the incredible "Work Me Lord" and a jazz-tinged pathetic self-portrait in "Little Girl Blue." A year after they'd got together, Janis split with the new group and disappeared to the jungles of Brazil with "a huge bear of a beatnik" to recuperate and kick a heavy heroin habit that she had contracted while with Big Brother.

When Janis died alone in her motel room in Los Angeles in 1970 at the age of twenty-seven, just a few months after Hendrix had choked to

# 13
# The Scene

## THE BLUES PROJECT

THESE ARE THE ORIGINALS, THE ONES WHO placed their debut album on the charts without benefit of a hit single, who fused the idea of the rock group as musician with the reality of the extended solo, who formally welded the bond between electric and acoustic. The Blues Project undertook a soldering of form that had previously only been hinted at in the mid-sixties. Their reputation spread by word of mouth and evangelical zeal, they became the first underground rock band to deal from a position of strength, a catalyst for an entire generation of progressive insights, the seeds of revolution in their making.

Together, they were an accident of fate that was nonetheless inevitable. Rock had outgrown its stigma for serious musicians, its expansive possibilities leading to immigration from related musical fields, especially folk, blues and jazz. The resultant hyphenation was at first cautious, content to add amplification to the traditional forms; when the Blues Project entered the picture in mid-1965, there was a drastic change of perspective. Whatever musical sources they chose to draw on were perceived from the vantage point of rock & roll, rather than vice-versa, and if the blend made their music

"respectable" in some quarters, it also turned the tide on a majority of accepted pop stereotypes.

Each Project member contributed his share to the collation of this new sound, their differing backgrounds kneaded into an all-encompassing mix. Danny Kalb was a folk guitarist, who had learned at the knee of Dave Van Ronk and extended his roots into finger-picking blues. Steve Katz stemmed from a different area of folk, apprenticing with the Even Dozen Jug Band, a good-timey brand of classicism that fit easily into their appearance on network television's *Hootenanny* show. A versatile drummer with jazz inflections, Roy Blumenfeld was taken with the melodic rhythms of Elvin Jones. Andy Kulberg was trained in the classics, a flautist who admitted "I play the bass as if it were a flute." Of them all, Al Kooper provided their closest link to rock & roll. A session musician and song writer, he had begun his career in the late fifties as part of the Royal Teens ("Short Shorts").

The initial spark for the group stemmed from Kalb, who heard Tim Hardin one night in the Night Owl Cafe backed by an electric band. Kalb was a respected accompanist on the

Greenwich Village folk scene (he played second guitar on Phil Ochs' first record), and absorbed the hint to begin working with a small trio in January 1965. By March, he had borrowed the name of the Blues Project from an Elektra anthology of urban blues artists in which he had had a part, adding Blumenfeld on drums (they'd met at Kalb's New Year's Eve party of that year), bassist Kulberg (a friend of Roy's from N.Y.U.), guitarist Artie Traum and singer Tommy Flanders. Traum soon left for Europe and parts unknown, and Katz, a fellow frequenter of the Fretted Instrument folk shop, was invited to replace him.

Kooper had a more complex history. Already in possession of a number one hit as the writer of Gary Lewis and the Playboys' "This Diamond Ring," along with an enviable session reputation through his work with Bob Dylan (the nourishing organ of "Like A Rolling Stone"), it might have seemed as though the last thing he needed was a band of young hopefuls around his neck. But he wasn't proud of the Lewis record, and his supportive role with Dylan was limited, as he later remembered,

"playing as I imagined Dylan would if he played the organ. I wasn't doing anything of my own, in my own way." Hired to enhance the Project's sound at an early test recording session, he stayed to contribute his keyboards and occasional guitar.

The group took up residence at the Café Au Go Go on Bleecker Street, building a following over the fall while their record company, Verve-Folkways, vacillated on how best to handle them. When Au Go Go owner Howard Solomon decided to celebrate Thanksgiving week with a massive blues show, the decision was made to record the group live; it proved the wisest of choices. Morally supported by the presence of Muddy Water, John Lee Hooker, Otis Spann and a dozen others on the bill, *Live at the Café Au Go Go* was a seminal album, capturing the Blues Project on the rise, as excited about their music as the capacity crowds who came to cheer them along. Very much Kalb's and Flanders' showcase, the material ranged from straight electric blues ("Spoonful," "Back Door Man") and straight electric folk ("Catch The Wind," "Violets of Dawn") to various hybrids, "Alberta" 's stately balladeering watched over by the flat-out manic drive of Bo Diddley's "Who Do You Love." The music's flashy exuberance and skidding lack of control (especially Kalb's blurred-note guitar) were unmistakable rock hallmarks.

The mysterious Flanders soon left for a solo career, but the Project's momentum was hardly slowed. There were other white electric blues bands in circulation, most notably Paul Butterfield's aggregation out of Chicago, starring Mike Bloomfield on guitar, and John Hammond Jr. had been pioneering in the field for years with his Hawks, but the Project were more than re-creators. "We are aware of that tradition and we draw on it," said Kalb, "but as a group we aren't imitative. If we do a 'Two Trains Running' [Muddy Waters], it's a 1967 'Two Trains Running,' never a 1947 version." In this, the example of the Yardbirds might be noted and remembered.

The consciousness fostered worked like a mainspring, wound ever tighter until the Blues Project came along to set the mechanism in motion. *Live at the Café Au Go Go* by its very presence necessitated a need for alternate radio and alternate music, tools to guide a growing alternate life style. Within the Project Kooper seemed to sense this change the fastest, and his influence slowly grew to replace Kalb as the dominating force.

*Projections*, an intellectualization of *Live at the Café Au Go Go*'s synthesis, was no less spectacular in its impact. The group may have been showing off to some extent, but it was only to be expected, given the heady excitement of their new-found freedom. Kulberg's echo-plexed "Flute Thing," the frenetic "You Can't Catch Me," a lush "Steve's Song" and a buoyant "Wake Me, Shake Me" — all seemed pulsing with overflow ideas and possibilities. Such crowding, in fact, led to the Blues Project's sudden demise. After a *Live At Town Hall* which reprised *Projection*'s greatest hits, they broke up in the summer of 1967.

Kooper was the first to leave, and he made his mark in several fields: organizing supersessions, producing for himself and Columbia, birthing the horned-rock Blood, Sweat and Tears in a landmark first album. Steve Katz was with him on that latter project, keeping the post-Kooper band going to the strains of mass popularity and enormous success. The Blues Project's rhythmic heart — Kulberg and Blumenfeld — went to California to form Sea Train, carrying it through several generations before Blumenfeld left to join Kalb in a later edition Blues Project back in New York. And Kalb, one of the first influential lead guitarists in a then-barren field, had tussled with a host of personal problems before finally coming out on top, making a graceful acoustic duet album with Stefan Grossman, leading his new Blues Project through its tilting course until he came to rest as a solo performer.

They got back together in June of 1973 to celebrate a return and reunion, the seven-year-itch of a locust's swarm. It was more than nostalgia, "Two Trains Running" for the encore, a final interlocked bow to say goodbye.

"Folk-rock," chuckles Al Kooper, laying down his guitar after the final ascending figures of "Fly Away" have left the stage. "How soon we forget."

# THE LOVIN' SPOONFUL

WITH THEIR CIRCUS OF INSTRUMENTS — banjos, dobros, fiddles, concertinas, clarinets, washboards, kazoos and slide whistles — the Lovin' Spoonful *looked* like the Loony Toon music they played. Zany Zally Yanovsky, the Kibbutz Kid from Canada in fur coats, cowboy hats and a toothy hillbilly grin, was the irrepressible comic relief; "Four Eyes" John Sebastian, blissfully hugging his auto harp, angelic as Harpo, purred out the Spoonful's gentle music, to the twist band beat of Joe Butler, "The Big Noise from Speonk," beaming behind his drum kit; and the lanky laconic Steve Boone was on bass. It was old-fashioned "good time" music, jug-band blues, barbershop harmonies (in their trademark candy-striped T-shirts) and folk frequencies retuned to rock — soft, sweet, funny and "groovy, like an old time movie."

John Sebastian, the gentle leader and songwriter for the group was, like his father, an accomplished harmonica player. He had accompanied Dylan at Gerde's Folk City, put the "harp" tracks on Tim Hardin's first album, and done sessions with Jesse Colin Young and Tom Paxton. In 1963 he joined the Even Dozen Jug Band (later to become the Jim Kweskin Jug Band) with Maria Muldaur. Then as Pooh and the Heffalumps with Felix Pappalardi (later Cream's producer and member of Mountain) and Eric Jacobsen (the Spoonful's future manager) cut a single for the Laurie label. One side was a sort of surf song called "Lady Godiva" but it was the flip side, a Sebastian song called "Rooty

# 180

## The Lovin' Spoonful

Toot," that suggested the type of folk-jugband-rock that was to become associated with the Spoonful.

Sebastian got to know Zal Yanovsky when he played harmonica on an album by the Mugwumps with Mama Cass Elliott and Papa Denny Doherty. Yanovsky was a Canadian folk singer who'd played with Denny in a Toronto group called the Halifax Three. Steve Boone brought in his bass from a four-piece swing band that played mobster lobster joints on Long Island, and Eric Jacobsen called in Joe Butler (replacing Jan Beukner) from an imitation Beatles band, the Sell Outs, to complete the group. While the group worked on their sound in the basement of the Albert Hotel, Jacobsen laid out his last $790 to cut "Do You Believe In Magic"/"On The Road Again." None of the record companies were interested, but by 1965, the Spoonful had become celebrities at The Night Owl, visited by Phil Spector, the Byrds and Dylan. *Hit Parader* headlined them on the cover: THE LOVIN' SPOONFUL WILL BE AMERICA'S NEW IDOLS, and soon record companies began coming around, and in one week they got two offers. They decided in favor of Kama Sutra Productions, which formed a record company around them, while giving Elektra Records four outtakes from their first album as a consolation. MGM distributed Kama Sutra, and this tie-in later gave the Spoonful work writing scores for *You're A Big Boy Now* and *What's Up Tiger Lily?*

In August 1965 "Do You Believe In Magic" was released, and made it into the top ten, as did its follow-up, "You Didn't Have To Be So Nice." "Daydream" and "Did You Ever Have To Make Up Your Mind" both got to number two, and with "Summer In The City," with its cacophonous sound effects, pneumatic drills, auto horns, they had their first number one record in July 1966.

The songs which followed were more wistful — "Rain On The Roof" and "Darling Be Home Soon." With "Six O'Clock," released in April 1967, the group's sound began to change — it was their last top twenty hit. This was not so much due to a shift in style as a moral issue which arose from the group's name. The group had named itself from a line from

*(Globe Photos /Gene Trindl)*

Mississippi John Hurt's "Coffee Blues." Intentionally or not, it suggested drug overtones, and when the Byrds' "Eight Miles High" was denounced for contributing to a "moral crisis" pop music seemed to promote, the Spoonful was another "source" which came under careful scrutiny. When Zal Yanovsky was busted for possession of marijuana and "collaborated with the authorities" to avoid extradition to Canada, the Spoonful were both condemned by the straight press and ostracized by the hip community.

In July 1967, Zally left the group (he later cut a solo album, *Alive And Well In Argentina*) and was replaced by Jerry Yester. Without Zally, the Spoonful seemed to have lost both its magic and its heart. Sebastian's songs, notably "Money," began to take on a darker hue and a year later, he too left the group to pursue a low-keyed solo career. The group continued a while longer as Joe Butler's Lovin' Spoonful.

The daydreams of "goodtime music" were dissolving in any case from other causes (the Mamas and the Papas broke up the same year). Though its "magic" and whimsy could not withstand the heavy voodoo of the lysergic deluge, the Spoonful bottled for posterity the high-spirited essence of the times in their effervescent songs: the hypnotic "Daydream" with its twenties tap-dance percussion; the delicate dilemma of "Did You Ever Have To Make Up Your Mind" and "Do You Believe In Magic," which evoked the feeling the group projected, a childlike faith in the power of rock. "The magic's in the music and the music's in me."

# THE (YOUNG) RASCALS

AS THE BEATLES PREPARED TO TAKE THE stage at Shea Stadium in August 1965, a short, cryptic message was flashed across the scoreboard, courtesy of promoter Sid Bernstein. "The Young Rascals Are Coming," it heralded, and though the overall impact might have been lessened in the ensuing mania, manager Bernstein was even then readying to prove his point. Today the Hamptons, he might have said, tomorrow the world.

They never just walked on a stage. They literally slithered in front of you, Dino snapping his head and twirling sticks, Felix waving and rocking back and forth, Eddie with the toys and tanbourines, Gene playing the fattest guitar in five states. The Rascals were the quintessence of blue-eyed soul, the first unabashed rock band to claim a massive rhythm and blues heritage, raised in the dancing discotheques of New York. If they weren't to become the American Beatles, as Bernstein hopefully foresaw, they could at least aspire to the next best thing, which was the American Rolling Stones. Until their tangents got the better of them too early in their career, the Rascals came close enough to matter.

The members had surprisingly similar backgrounds, having kicked around lounge and club undercircuits as reliable and steadily working musicians. Keyboardist Felix Cavaliere had studied medicine for two years at Syracuse University before he took to the road, judging that "my heart was in a different place." His earliest group, the Escorts, also contained Mike Esposito (later to be a prime force in the Blues Magoos) and Neil Diamond. He met drummer Dino Danelli on a Las Vegas jaunt with singer Sandy Scott, and vocalist Eddie Brigati and guitarist Gene Cornish during a stint with Joey Dee's Starlighters. Though Dee's twisting days were numbered by then, the star of the Peppermint Lounge made a final, indelible impression on the Rascals' sound.

Joey had called Felix from Europe, saying that his organ player had just left the group and would Cavaliere like to take his position? "When we went on stage for the first time,"

## 182
### The (Young) Rascals

remembered Felix, "the first thing I saw was a Hammond B-3 organ. I had seen them before but I had never touched one in my life. But naturally I couldn't let Joey know this. I sat down and played. I don't know how good or bad it sounded, but we got off alive." More than that, the big Hammond's overt richness would provide a comforting foundation for the Rascals' early work, orienting the band away from the predominantly guitar tonal textures of other groups.

"Felix came up with the concept of our sound," Gene agreed. "He said we'd base everything on the organ. It would be a blanket. The drums and guitar would be the rhythm. Together, the organ and guitar would be one complete sound as an orchestra. I had to rethink my whole style of playing."

In early 1965, Felix, Gene and Eddie began discussing plans for a group. Dino was working with a band at the Choo Choo Club in Garfield, New Jersey, with David Brigati (Eddie's brother and an original Starlighter), and Eddie used to regularly stop by to sit in on a few numbers. Danelli was recruited to complete the foursome and they played the Choo Choo until spotted by the owner of the Barge, in the Long Island jet-set resort of Westhampton. Dressed in Lord Fauntleroy collars, peaked caps and knickers, their stagy theatrics were matched by dramatic readings of little-known R & B classics.

"We were all influenced by Ray Charles," said Dino "We were trying to get R & B really out into the open where it should be. What we did was to go up to Harlem and browse through the record shops, looking for artists you would never find on a pop top ten chart. We'd do them on stage and people would get knocked out, thinking they were our songs because they'd never heard them and they were really great. It all comes from rhythm and blues."

The concept was blue-eyed soul, but rather than assimilating R & B in the Apollo revue tradition of the Righteous Brothers and the Magnificent Men, the Rascals operated from the context of a white rock & roll band. Their spunky drive soon spread over Long Island, alerting socialites and record companies alike, and the Rascals became the darlings of that

South Shore summer. By fall of 1965 they had moved into regular appearances along Manhattan's disco circuit, a gamut of clubs from the Phone Booth to Scott Muni's Rolling Stone, signing with Atlantic Records after a mini-bidding war. There was local success with their first release, "I Ain't Gonna Eat Out My Heart Anymore," and number one status with their second, a livid remake of the Olympics' "Good Lovin' " in March 1966.

Felix would later disown the record, saying "It wasn't us. The first Rascals album was hard, soul, push, let's-knock-the-brains-off-everybody kind of music. It was our interpretation of other people's records. 'Good Lovin' ' was written by someone outside the group. But I'm very proud to say that a lot of groups copied us. That's the highest form of flattery. They grabbed our instrumentation, our harmony and our interplay between instruments. That meant we must have

*(Collection Peter Kanze)*

had something going for us and it gave us the courage to try things of our own.''

So while Action House bands like the Vanilla Fudge, the Vagrants, the Rich Kids and the Hassles were telling their drummer to baton the sticks, their guitarist to buy an overweight Gretsch, their lead singer to shake fistfulls of maracas and go *"thenk you"* after every song in a high voice as the organist spun around in his chair, early 1967 saw the Rascals thinking about removing the "Young" from their name. "On our new single there isn't any organ," said Gene at the time, "there is no guitar and there are no regular drums. There's a bass, a harpsichord, a piano, a conga drum, tambourine, vibes, a harmonica, a vocal and birds.''

"Groovin' " brought out both the best and worst in the Rascals. Probably their most infectious record, it also pointed them toward cocktail jazz, the essential lightness of the song somberly weighted by Felix's voice. The lyrics were almost too timely, and when the Fauntleroy costumes were exchanged for beards, beads and nehru jackets, a Long Island

Orientalia set their image at odds with itself. Eddie's comment, "We feel that we have to project something that is not only nice to hear but something that is beneficial to the people who are listening to it,'' may have coincided with the expansive time, but it wore badly in the hands of the Rascals. They became simplistic, softer, obviously conscious of their extra-musical significance.

Though they continued having hits (the Rascals *always* made great singles — "People Got To Be Free," "Carry Me Back," "See"), they were never able to regain the excitement of their youth. Felix in particular pursued his metaphysical leanings, and when the Rascals left Atlantic for Columbia in 1972 with him as the only remaining original member, he formulated a serene jazz setting for his spiritual experimentations; he's since returned to a more straightforward fold. Gene and Dino came up with a lively Bulldog and "No" in 1973. Eddie, with the help of Felix, put together a recent (1976) version of "Groovin'." Even the Young Rascals had to grow up someday.

# TOMMY JAMES

IF TOMMY JAMES MAKES SUDDEN THANKFUL reference to "the man upstairs" in the course of his conversation, it's only because fate provided him with ample cause. A scuffling midwest musician in 1965, spending his time between spot work as Junior Walker's guitarist and a horn act in Chicago named the Coachmen, he watched in astonishment as a song he'd recorded and forgotten five years previously became a worldwide "overnight" sensation.

"I freaked," he admits, not a little wonder remaining in his voice to this day. "I'm sitting home, out of work, on a Saturday afternoon, and I got a call from a promoter in Pittsburgh who wanted to know if I was the singer. I have no idea how he got my number. He told me I had a number one single with 'Hanky Panky' and I

almost hung up the phone. It was that close. The following week I was working in Pittsburgh with the hottest record in town. I couldn't believe it. It was like watching a movie with someone else playing my part."

Tommy recovered from his initial shock long enough to move to New York, launching one of the most consistent and underappreciated careers in the history of pop records. Tommy was not an innovator, nor did he anticipate any grand changes in the cultural or social climate. Instead, he merely turned out hit single after hit single, each carefully planned for maximum car radio impact, building on his creative instincts so that his records never seemed dated or musically unaware. Many *nouveau*-progressive rockers tended to regard him as naïve and superficial for paying so much attention to the top forty, but Tommy never let that stand in his way. Throughout, he proved himself impossible to categorize, changing styles deftly and with apparent ease, a "one-hit wonder" with fourteen gold singles and a pair of similar albums, backed by some fifteen years of hard-won experience.

As Thomas Jackson, he was born in Dayton, Ohio, on April 29, 1947, growing up in various locations around the Midwest. He was given a ukelele when he was five, and by the time he touched seven he'd pictured himself as a guitar-playing singer — "A rock & roll star." An only child, admittedly spoiled, he soon developed a need for mass approval. "Let's face it, to be a performer . . . it's a legal form of exhibitionism. You have to be crazy to get up in front of twenty thousand people and take a chance on blowing your cool. It's fun to sing, to write songs . . . but I guess the next step would be getting shot out of a cannon."

His family bought him a Stella guitar when he was nine, and he taught himself to play. Not having any instruction books, he would tune the guitar to an open chording and move one finger up and down the neck. The Jackson family never tried to discourage him, and their hopes were somewhat rewarded when young Tommy sang the McGuire Sisters' "Sugartime" in a statewide talent contest and won. By the time he was eleven and living in Niles, Michigan, he had formed his first band, debuting downstairs at the local American Legion. He made $21.00 that night, making sure to receive the money in singles. "I spread it all out on the davenport," he recalls. "I spread 'em end to end, then I turned them sideways, then I got George Washington's face to go all in one direction. . . ."

In 1960, Tommy was working at a local record shop and leading a group called the Shondells when Jack Douglas, a disc jockey at nearby WNIL, approached him with the idea of making some masters. They went over to the station's studios and cut a song called "Hanky Panky," an early composition of Jeff Barry and Ellie Greenwich which Tommy had first heard performed by another area band. Douglas opened his own label, Snap Records, and with

limited airplay sold 20,000 copies of the disc within a small tri-state area.

James quickly became the neighborhood pop star, but he doesn't remember it as an especially pleasant period in his life. "It's not easy being green," he says simply. "Quite honestly, that's a pretty heavy trip for a thirteen-year-old. It would probably have been extremely awkward if the record had happened when it was recorded." As it was, Tommy had some breathing room. The record came and went, except for occasional jukebox play, and Douglas subsequently lost his job over it.

By all rights, the matter should have ended there. But shortly after Tommy graduated from high school in 1965, he began spotting regional breakouts of "Hanky Panky" in the trade magazines. Station KDKA in Pittsburgh had begun playing it as an oldie, and someone in the area had picked up the demand to release it as an unauthorized bootleg. At first Tommy didn't think it was his record; after witnessing the excitement in person, there was no disputing the fact.

"I had mixed reactions. Sure it's great to have your name on a hit record . . . but this was from 1961, and it was bad for 1961. It was like going back to kindergarten. I was playing with a jazz group, and I was quite proud of my musicians. I had to give all that up, go back to playing tinkertoys after I'd completed an erector set."

"Hanky Panky" was rock reduced to its bare essentials, a simplistic catchy tag-line over the most familiar of I-IV-V progressions. The master was sold to Roulette Records, who took it to the coveted number one slot in the summer of 1966. Unburdened by the Shondells (who'd broken up years before), his voice a full half-octave lower than his hit, Tommy was faced with a decision. "I didn't know whether to play what I was into at the time, or try to stretch it." He opted for gradual movement, holding his own until he met Bo Gentry and Richie Cordell, who joined him in a writing and production capacity.

The hits began to tumble, "I Think We're Alone Now" to "Mirage" to "Mony Mony." James had happened on a sound and it appeared

unbeatable, bass guitar pressed forward into the speakers only to be broken by a wave of pipeline chorus. The style was picked up in preteen form as "bubblegum music," personified by such groups as the Ohio Express and the 1910 Fruitgum Company. Tommy took it bitterly. "They made a joke out of it, exploited it to the point of absurdity. It was insulting to both artist and audience."

Possibly as a reaction, Tommy decided to produce himself. In 1969, "Crimson And Clover" spoke of his developing maturity, gifted with a lyric that conveyed more mood than message. It was to lead into his best year; "Sweet Cherry Wine," "Crystal Blue Persuasion" and "Ball Of Fire" kept up the pace, and the *Crimson and Clover* album bore liner notes by Hubert H. Humphrey, whom Tommy had worked for during the 1968 presidential campaign. But it was all abruptly pulled to a halt in February 1970.

James had a pill problem. "I remember they used to hand them out like they were nothing. So many of my friends were strung out, and they just couldn't understand why." It finally hit home in Montgomery, Alabama, where Tommy collapsed on stage. Faced with a life or death decision, he retreated to an upstate New York farm to calm down.

"We were really at our peak, and I deserved just exactly what I got. There's like a six-month period of my life that's a total blank to me. . . . I stared at walls for a year. I quite literally forgot how to do anything, how to write songs, how to work a board and make records. I was inert. It was as much of a shock mentally as physically, learning how to function again."

The prospect of failure overwhelmed him when he went back into the studio. "The idea of being afraid to make music is probably the most alien idea I could think of," but shying from directly involving himself, he produced a record with a couple from Brooklyn providing the vocals. Alive and Kicking's "Tighter And Tighter" went top ten in 1972 and James gradually regained his confidence. "Draggin' The Line" and "Nothing To Hide" ("I'm satisfied/Gonna rest my soul on the other side . . .") bore witness to the strength of his newfound purpose.

"Sometimes it takes nine years to grow up," Tommy says. "My head is finally screwed on right. I'd like to do it all now, open a record label, the whole spectrum of music . . . concerts, publishing, recording, producing, writing . . . everything in between. I'd like to become an actor. Eventually I'd like to direct films. If the man upstairs is still smiling down. . . ." He casts his eyes heavenward.

# THE MONKEES

WITH A FIENDISH CYNICISM, EQUALED only by the machinations of the megalomanic villains that popped up weekly on their Monkees TV show, Bob Rafelson and Bert Schneider *created* the Monkees, and manufactured, manipulated and merchandised them like rock & roll robots. The mid-sixties was a period in rock particularly susceptible to images. Groups tended to look like the music they played. Can you imagine the Mamas and the Papas looking as they did and playing music like the Grateful Dead? It was inevitable that someone would come along, dream up an ideal group and then find the faces and the music to fit it.

The group image of course was the Beatles, and Rafelson and Schneider deliberately set about looking for four likely lads who could ape the antics of the Fab Four in *A Hard Day's Night*. With blatant bluntness they planted ads in the Hollywood trade papers, a plot in search of four characters. Among the 500 who auditioned was Steve Stills, who fortunately (for himself at least) was turned down. Rafelson and Schneider found the essential English accent in Davy Jones, who had been a teenage jockey in his hometown of Manchester, played the Artful

Dodger in *Oliver* on Broadway and had an unsuccessful try at solo singing with Colpix Records. A Ringo replica with doleful humor turned up in the person of Mickey Dolenz, a child actor in the TV series *Circus Boy*, who was also in a group called The Missing Links and had cut some records for Challenge. Peter Tork (Halsten Thorkensen), a folk freak who played with the likes of Mama Cass and John Sebastian on the Village coffeehouse circuit and a lanky, pensive, semi-professional comedian and singer from Texas, Mike Nesmith, completed the picture in this instamatic formula.

The show *The Monkees*, one of the most successful pieces of surrealist slapstick on TV, was first aired in September of 1966. It became an instant hit and their first record "Last Train To Clarksville," which came out the same month, made it to number one. Rafelson and Schneider had left their preteen audience little choice (and had left even less to chance) by calling in Don Kirshner to handle the music and promotion. He had succeeded with other rock species like the Animals, so why not the Monkees? Later he surpassed himself by creating a hit, "Sugar, Sugar" for a mythical rock group, the Archies, from a kids' Saturday

*(Globe Photos/Gene Trindl)*

morning TV show. Kirschner hired some of the best writers (Neil Diamond, Bobby Hart, Tommy Boyce, Carole King and Jeff Barry), got the Candy Store Prophets to play the instruments and soon the Monkees had a string of hits, "I'm A Believer," "A Little Bit Me, A Little Bit You," "Pleasant Valley Sunshine" and "Daydream Believer," on Colgems (even the flip sides became hits). In two years they won 24 gold records and 5 successive gold albums, an accomplishment at that time equaled only by the Beatles and Herb Alpert. The amazing success of such a calculated concoction only proved to some how mindless rock fans really were. Struggling rock groups were incensed to learn that the Monkees in the beginning weren't even playing their own instruments. The Byrds hadn't played on their first album either but the difference was that the Byrds created their own sound while the Monkees were merely inflated puppets of bandwagon capitalists. Their music was good, the TV shows original and the individual Monkees themselves were disarmingly candid about their canned image "if you think we're plastic wait till you find out how we do it." They brought Hendrix to the States on his first U.S. tour (he was soon removed by objections from irate moms). Monkees money helped finance *Easy Rider* and

even bought Three Dog Night their instruments. With the release of *Head*, a fantastic piece of lysergic lunacy, the tide of hip criticism had turned, and though not exactly heroes they became underground pets.

But the Monkee Machine was gradually grinding to a halt. Peter Tork was the first to leave to form his own "hippie type" group. Davy subsequently started another solo career as a cute mini-McCartney and then opened a boutique. Mike Nesmith returned to country music, wrote "A Different Drummer" for Linda Ronstadt and the Stone Ponies, and also produced an excellent instrumental album, *Wichita Train Whistle*. Mickey Dolenz faded from sight somewhat for awhile, reappearing irrepressibly on a Golden Oldies TV record package offer and in a film with none other than Linda Lovelace (of *Deep Throat* fame) titled *Linda Lovelace For President*.

The Monkees mined and primed a preteen audience of whom Mike Nesmith said "we speak for them in a way beyond semantics." They were the forerunners of pre-pube rockers like the Osmonds, David Cassidy, the Jackson Five. Their manufacture was inevitable but it was their own discerning honesty that overrode their plastic beginnings and left us little choice but to love them for what they were.

# THE MAMAS AND THE PAPAS

BETWEEN THE ARRIVAL OF THE BEATLES and the psychedelic apocalypse three years later, there was a brief era of innocent playfulness and boundless optimism in rock, and one of the mellowest sounds to come from this period was "good time music," a blend of folk, rock and pop that came together in the coffeehouses of New York's Greenwich Village. Out of groups like the Big Three (Mama Cass), the Mugwumps (Papa Doherty, Cass and Zal

Yanovsky), and the Journeymen (Papa John Phillips and Scott "flowers in your hair" McKenzie), two groups emerged that were the epitome of the sound and the times — the Lovin' Spoonful and the Mamas and the Papas.

Folk music, at first suspicious of rock's brash commercialism, by 1964 was slowly absorbing the harmonies and electricity brought over by the English groups. Pop folk trios like the Kingston Trio had been around since the

(Globe Photos/Irv Steinberg)

late fifties, but were still acoustic, collegiate and, like Peter, Paul and Mary, basically bubblegum. Nevertheless, their huge success inspired hordes of kids to pick up guitars and songbooks and head for Greenwich Village. John Phillips, kicked out of the U.S. Naval Academy after a fight over his guitar with his commandant, came to New York in the early sixties and got together a folk trio (the Journeymen) who recorded three not too successful albums for Capitol.

In the fall of 1964, he had written his winter reverie, "California Dreamin'" in a seedy hotel just off Washington Square. Early in 1965, unable to find a publisher who was interested, he decided to take off for the sun anyway, and left for the Caribbean island of St. Johns with little more than a credit card. John knew Denny Doherty from folk jams in the Village, and Denny knew Cass from solo gigs in Chicago and the two soon followed John and his wife Michelle to the islands. All four lived together through the spring and summer, and after running up a bill of some $7,000 on their American Express Card, they stayed on by scrounging for food, firewood and water.

In the shade of palms and backed by lapping waves, the four of them harmonized together perfectly. John's baritone blended with the lower register's of Denny's tenor and Cass' contralto (while she worked as a waitress a pipe had fallen on her head, increasing her range by three notes) gave weight to Michelle's delicate lyric soprano.

Neither their singing nor their exotic clothes were appreciated by the governor of the island, who suspected them of corrupting the natives, and banished them. All four flew to L.A. where they ran into an old friend from the New Christie Minstrels, Barry "Eve of Destruction" McGuire who was in the process of cutting an album with Lou Adler.

"Denny was wearing black leather; Cass

looked like the Mother of Mankind," recalls Lou Adler. "The whole group was not to be believed. I listened to five numbers, I couldn't believe anything that good had walked in off the street." He signed them to Dunhill for $1,500 and in October they put out their first single, "Go Where You Wanna Go"/"Somebody Groovy" (later a hit for the Fifth Dimension). "California Dreamin' " was first used as a cut on McGuire's album, but after Adler heard the back-up on the Mamas and the Papas vocals, he felt it shouldn't be buried on someone else's album, and withdrew it. It was cut by the Mamas and the Papas instead and three months later, in January of 1966 "California Dreamin' " was at the top of the charts. "Monday, Monday" was originally just an album cut but it received so much airplay it was re-cut as a single, selling 160,000 the first day it was released.

Lou Adler and John Phillips organized the Monterey Pop Festival in June 1967, and the Mamas and the Papas, with their clean-scrubbed scruffy look, were hailed as hippie heroes from Hollywood. But by the beginning of 1968 problems began to develop within the group, despite their popularity and a stream of hits like "I Saw Her Again" and "Words Of Love" in 1966, "Dedicated To The One I Love" and their autobiographical "Creeque Alley" in 1967. Tours were canceled, and the group spirit waned in what John Phillips calls their A.A. (after acid) period. By the middle of the year, Cass went solo, made one top-twenty single, "Dream A Little Dream Of Me." She was in England embarking on a comeback when her untimely death cut it short.

As closely knit as the group seemed (they originally wanted to call themselves "The Magic Circle") their lyrics even on the first album seemed to belie the good time spirit of the music. "Monday, Monday," for instance, was written after a quarrel.

The Mamas and the Papas created a cool California sound by extending the range of Beatle harmonies with the voices of Michelle and Cass, and matching them with Lou Adler's subliminal arrangements and subtle enveloping wall of sound production. The Mamas and the Papas were not simply folk singers who amplified their roots, they were rock singers who had abandoned the orthodoxy of folk. They admitted their city-ness, as did the Spoonful, and their sweet sad sound is a city dream, even as it harks back to the promised land.

# FRANK ZAPPA

*"There is no undertaking more challenging, no responsibility more awesome than being a Mother."*
RICHARD M. NIXON

"Thanks a lot, Dick," says Frank Zappa, middle finger on the rise. After ten years of guiding a seriocomic cabal known loosely as the Mothers of Invention through several dozen stages of personnel and repertoire, he more than appreciates the rigors of such a statement. Nor would he have it any other way. For Zappa, work is necessity (necessity, of course, being the mother of invention), and when he's not rehearsing, or touring, or eating/sleeping, he will spend up to eighteen hours a day in his basement studio, writing music, editing film, fitting new elements into the macrostructure that forms the conceptual continuity of his life's labor.

Zappa is not easy to pin down. Though he calls himself a rock musician, he is equally at home constructing precise symphonies, complex jazz measures or fifties doo-wop harmonies, usually to be played at one and the same time. He claims to be equally influenced by the Medallions as Edgar Varese, and sees no reason why the two shouldn't remain compatible. One of his early songs, "Trouble Every Day," painted a chillingly realistic portrait of the Watts riots;

one of his latest scales a man who dreams of raising dental floss on a ranch in "Montana." What, it may be asked, is going on here?

The cyborgic reply: "The basic blueprints were executed in 1962–63. Preliminary experimentation in early and mid-64. Construction of the PROJECT/OBJECT began late '64. Work is still in progress."

Francis Vincent Zappa was born of Sicilian-Greek parentage on December 21, 1940, in Baltimore. His family migrated to California when Frank was ten, and by 1956 they were settled in the Mojave Desert outpost of Lancaster. At Antelope Valley High School, he began dabbling in rhythm and blues with a group called the Blackouts, whose sound was grafted onto self-taught elementary music theory.

"I didn't start listening to music until I was about fifteen years old because my parents weren't too fond of it and we didn't have a radio or record player or anything. I think the first music I heard that I liked was Arab music . . . it was only by accident I ran into rhythm and blues.

"I didn't start writing songs, per se, until I was about twenty years old, twenty-one maybe, because all my compositions prior to that time had been orchestral or chamber music. I think the basic idea of being a composer is if you're going to be true to yourself and write what you like, you write what you like without worry whether it's going to make any mark in history or not. My basic drive for writing anything down is I want to hear it."

Zappa furthered the listening process by scoring a movie, *Run Home Slow*, purchasing a recording studio in Cucamonga, California, with the proceeds. He called it Studio Z, renting it out to local musicians and utilizing it as an audio laboratory, supporting it by forming a small band on the side known as the Muthers. This was strong stuff for San Bernardino County, and Frank soon found himself on the framed end of a lewd-filmmaking charge. In 1964, he left his provincial troubles behind to move to Los Angeles.

It was an L.A. in the dry heaves of social eruption. Clubs and restive youth dotted Sunset Strip, watched fitfully by the police, a sideshow soon to engender folk-rock, psychedelia and direct confrontation. Hanging out at Cantor's Delicatessen on North Fairfax, Zappa absorbed the twenty-four-hour ambience of emerging freakdom. He incorporated it into a newer organization of Mothers, added ex-gunrunner Herbie Cohen as manager, and picked up a recording contract when producer Tom Wilson (fresh from working with Bob Dylan) saw the band at the Whisky a' Go Go one night.

"Freaking out," Zappa defined on his initial album, "is a process whereby an individual casts off outmoded and restricting standards of thinking, dress, and social etiquette in order to express CREATIVELY his relationship to his immediate environment and the social structure as a whole." In translation, this became the United Mutations, crowned by Emperor Vito the dancer, stylized by Crown Prince Carl Franzoni, armed by a mongrel circle of anarchic soulmates. Over four sides of the first pop concept album, Frank delineated the paralogical borders of an expanding counterculture. Free-form pieces like "Help I'm A Rock" and "The Return Of The Son Of Monster Magnet" shaped and molded a random, accidental music of voices and odd instruments; he doffed his hat to the fifties in "Go Cry On Somebody Else's Shoulder," only to wheel and ask "Who Are The Brain Police?" He reserved the ultimate "what's got into you?" question for arch-heroine Suzy Creamcheese. *Freak Out* demonstrated that Zappa was certainly aware of many answers.

The album was completed in early 1966 and released later that year, taking the underground by storm. When Zappa brought his show to New York in 1967 for what eventually turned into a six-month stand at the Garrick Theater, the audio derangement spilled over into an ongoing theatrical disturbance. A long wire was stretched from the rear of the house to the stage, transporting a variety of appropriate props. In one memorable sequence, three marines were provoked to join the group on stage in a gory display of basic training, bayoneting doll babies and appending the traditional "Eat the apple, fuck the corps."

Zappa was basically working along two

The Mothers of Invention
in the late 1960s

**Frank Zappa**

lines, brandishing cynicism to pave a more accessible path for his music. He was a blunt-edged satirist, allowing little cant or hypocrisy to escape his pique. In *Absolutely Free*, his favorite targets were the vast quantities of "plastic people" that live in the shadow of mediocrity, and he dwelt endlessly and obviously on their many foibles. By the time of *We're Only In It For The Money*, a *Sergeant Pepper* parody (so much so that the album was delayed for eleven months while legal difficulties about the cover were resolved), his ire was extended to his own camp followers. Advising potential listeners to read Kafka's *In The Penal Colony*, he noted "Every town must have a place / Where phony hippies meet / Psychedelic dungeons / Popping up on every street . . . ."*

Interspersed with social commentary were long sections of musical bridgework, Frank very patiently explaining each of the intricate passages for any who cared to listen. The level of musicianship was generally high in the Mothers' organization, most of whose members had been culled from the ranks of studio players, and Zappa pushed them to their limits, mixing time signatures, keys and odd-ball phrasings from nearly every corner of compositional history. It was difficult work, and the Mothers' turnover in personnel was exceptionally high. Among regulars could be found "the Indian in the group," Jimmy Carl Black; drummer Billy Mundi (later Aynsley Dunbar); *lumpen* bassist Roy Estrada; woodwinders Bunk Gardner and Ian Underwood; and all-purpose Euclid James "Motorhead" Sherwood.

Even the breadth of the Mothers was not sufficient to contain Zappa's manifold interests,

and in late 1968 he disbanded the group to concentrate on solo projects. A pair of complementary record companies was set up, Bizarre and Straight, providing a haven for some of L.A.'s more outlandish performers. Frank's interest was usually more sociological than musical, and the antics of the G.T.O.'s (Girls Together Outrageously), Larry "Wild Man" Fischer, early Alice Cooper, and Captain Beefheart were nothing if not valuably intriguing. He began work on a movie-diary, *200 Motels* (after an original film, *Uncle Meat*, fell through except for a soundtrack), performed with the Los Angeles Philharmonic and turned out albums at a zippy pace: the solo and mostly instrumental *Hot Rats*, in which he displayed his considerable guitar prowess; *Burnt Weenie Sandwich, Weasels Ripped My Flesh* and other remnants of a proposed twelve-album set chronicling the life and times of the Mothers.

Zappa was turning away from his earlier social gadfly role to a more surreal, abstract idiom. The humor in his shows grew more blatant with the addition of ex-Turtles Mark Volman and Howard Kaylan (since become Flo and Eddie), and as his music purified, he even overcame his previous lack of "commercial potential." A paean to dog-sledding, "Don't Eat The Yellow Snow," was a near-hit single in 1974, while his later albums (*Just Another Band From L.A., Wakajawaka, Apostrophe, Grand Wazoo*) consistently achieved best-seller status.

For Zappa, it's all part of an overall blueprint, compressing the passage of time into one extended work, event to organism. "It incorporates any available visual medium," he once explained, "consciousness of all participants (including audience), all perceptual deficiencies, God (as energy), THE BIG NOTE (as universal basic building material), and other things. We make a special art in an environment hostile to dreamers."

# 14
# Outer Limits

## LOVE

MAYBE HE'S BACK. OR MAYBE NOT. ARTHUR Lee is transfigured by the spotlights of Nassau Coliseum, bathed in the glow of 18,000 who know that somewhere, somehow, his name speaks the familiars of mysterious legend, songs they've heard over late night FM, burned into their auditory systems with the effect of subliminal advertising. For most it will be their first glimpse of a band called Love, and if Arthur Lee has his way this time around, it certainly won't be the last.

"I'm planning on doing a lot better than I've ever done," he says quite evenly. "No matter what your hobby is, or what you do in your personal life, you gotta keep the business thing together. Enough so that you can at least come back and do the same thing again. But I don't want to stop there. I'm planning on selling more records, and playing more places, than anything I've ever been involved in. And I know I'm gonna do it. There ain't nothing that's going to stop me. That's the way I feel. It's work time, and I'm ready to work."

From other artists this might well be just an example of pretour enthusiasm, but within the checkered demon career of Arthur Lee and Love, it becomes a statement of near-crucial principle.

Since the time of Love's first incarnation as the premier Los Angeles folk-rock attraction, dark and laden with premonition, he has followed an erratic artistic trail that seemed virtually unconcerned with the day-to-day realities of the music business. His touring pace was always spotty, while the rare occasions that he did go out on the road were marked by personal idiosyncrasy and technical trials. Unable to be categorized by either his audience or the media, he developed a reputation for eccentricity, as slippery and unpredictable as quicksilver.

Yet as elusive as he came off personally, Arthur Lee has remained a man very much in control of himself and his music. His switches in direction (or, as he titled his third album, *Forever Changes*) might have proved abrupt or disconcerting, but they always worked, all somehow logical and extremely perceptive. By the time the hit single of his first record ("Little Red Book") had faded, he was already at work on a second album (*Da Capo*) that featured a long recitative expansion on a theme, not unlike the Rolling Stones' "Goin' Home" on *Aftermath*. *Forever Changes* expanded the contexts to include ironic orchestral arrangements and sly, multi-pronged lyrics, becoming one of the true classic works of mid-sixties progressive rock. *Four Sail* swept up the loose ends of their Elektra venture, returning to a band sound and approach that relied heavily on guitar dynamics.

Throughout, Lee never lost his edge, his eye for fleeting details and wry turns of phrase. When he and Love moved to Blue Thumb through Bob Krasnow, it might have appeared that they'd lowered their sights to the reality of a mediocre bar band, even to the point of flailing solos and inferior recapitulations of earlier hits ("Signed D.C."). It was not to be: the music on *Out Here* and *False Start* has shown a remarkable resiliency over the past years, pulsed by gut-ridden guitars whose importance wouldn't be felt until after the heavy metal giants of Grand Funk and Black Sabbath had bestridden the earth.

Obviously Krasnow felt the same. One morning before *False Start* was released, he told Arthur(ly) that if the album wasn't in the top twenty within six months, he'd voluntarily tear up his contracts. The album wasn't, and Arthur gathered in the bet, moving to A & M to begin work on *Vindicator*. Possibly his best effort since the early days of Love, it presented an ongoing tribute to Jimi Hendrix in the whirlpool of power trio basics, cut with short personal asides (McDonald's "golden tombstones") and a pair of priceless cover pictures showing Arthur in a janitor's uniform matched against the same figure in a blonde wig and marine fighter's robe.

"Come back?" he repeats the question. "I never stopped." He cut an album for Paul Rothschild's Buffalo label, unreleased because of a vinyl shortage, and then hooked up with RSO for *Reel to Real* and a firm rhythm and blues-based concentration. "An album a year, that's what I do, ever since 1965."

Before that, he'd been a small-time club musician in Los Angeles, having moved there from Memphis when he was five. As an organist, his first instinct was to emulate Booker T and the MG's; accordingly, his first band, the L.A.G.'s, recorded an instrumental with Capitol called "The Ninth Wave." It barely whispered, and he floated between groups like the American Four and the Grass Roots (not the later singles' combination). One night, he visited

Arthur Lee of Love

*(Collection Richard & Lisa Robinson)*

a Sunset Strip bistro called Ciro's where the Byrds were first testing their wings.

"The whole scene was great, man. I saw these guys . . . they kind of opened my head to the direction I went on my first album. There weren't too many long-haired musicians then, the Byrds were about the first I'd seen. In Hollywood, anyway. I flashed on myself when I saw them. When they split across the nation or Europe or somewhere, they had this huge following of people that were in Hollywood. The people didn't have anywhere to go. So we formed this group, and Bryan Maclean, who was the Byrds' road manager at the time, was pretty popular, a lot of people knew him, so I figured I'd get him in the group. We slipped right into the trip."

Along with Lee and Maclean, there was John Echols, Ken Forssi, and Alban "Snoopy" Pfisterer. Elektra president Jac Holzman saw them at Bido Litos one night and signed them to their first recording contract. The sound was reminiscent of the twelve-string Byrds, but even then Lee's barbed metaphors provided marked contrast to McGuinn-Crosby's ethical purity. By *Da Capo*, there was no comparison. Beginning the first of Love's many personnel shifts (only Arthur remains today from the original band), it rolled together influences like a lottery drum, harpsichord passages fitted to broad Spanish guitars to explosive sound effects. This was followed by the delicate instrumentation and Johnny Mathis vocals of *Forever Changes*. But any widely based success they might have had was diminished by the group's seeming inability to leave the west coast.

"We were always on the trip of wanting to do the right thing at the right time, making sure everything was the right time for us. And we passed up a lot of things. Here I'd been influenced by what people told me to do and I'd even written my songs according to this trip of trying to get air play and all this bullshit with the soft rock trip so that we could expand our group. And I went out to a place called The Brass Ring in the Valley in L.A. and here this four-piece group was. They were loud. They were out of sight. And like Jimi Hendrix had just come out, and it really tripped me out, here's a cat that came out three years after I had seen the Byrds and freaked out, and he comes along and plays this loud music that I always wanted to do in the studio." Following his heart, Arthur left Elektra for Blue Thumb.

Many lifetimes later, he runs a hand over his shaved head. Even off-stage his demeanor is double-bladed, riffing around sentences, meanings layered on top of meanings. "My music right now is for the United States," he says abstractly. "The United States is happening . . . always has been. I grew up here. I know when to jump out in the streets of L.A. and blow some dude's mind in front of a car, and when to hustle across the street in New York. I know the difference. I know to be cool in Detroit . . . hang loose in Cleveland [laughs] . . . and don't say nothin' in Alabama [laughs harder]. I mean, you go to Europe and it's all one thing, it's bland. Everybody's nice. But here . . . there's all these insane people here. They got people here who would kill you to

make a name for themselves. . . .

"The music I'm doing now is music I think appeals to this country. It's funny, and it's very much into the hearts of a lot of soul-minded people. It's kind of commercial, as far as commercials go, but after that it hits home. I never felt restrained doing anything. If I'm in a position where people are going to come out and see me. . . ." He shrugs. "To be able to do that in this day and age is a gift."

There is a new audience out there in the hinterlands, and Lee means to take full aim and measure of them. "How? By doing an appealing album. Working to get recognized all over again. A whole decade's gone by, ten years. People who are eighteen now were *nine* then . . . . I don't know about nobody nine years old. But they're getting out in the world now, and they're aware of me, they know me. That's a good thing. For me not to be jumping on the wagon, making some bread, singing some good songs and doing some good music . . . I'd have to be out of my mind. I've always believed in making an honest living."

Nor does he intend the burden of reputation to weigh him down. "I don't feel I have anything to live up to." A waiter wheels in a tray of cooked vegetables. "I feel like if somebody comes to see me and they know about me, that's great. If I'm turning some kid on to my music, that's great too. I live totally in the present . . ." — he waggles a finger in the air — ". . . totally gone."

There is more slapping of thighs, but beneath the anagrams Arthur is seriously pursuing a chain of thought. "I feel I've been treated as well as I treat myself, according to the rules and regulations of this business. If I become disgusted, or frustrated, it's solely with the way things go down if they don't go down the way I've lived my life. I'm always doing something for myself. I'm not going to be on any superman trip or nothing, but I've always got a song in my pocket; my back pocket. I got twenty in my front pockets, but one in my back. You do something for yourself, and if it's good to you, man, it's good for somebody else. Somebody somewhere. Keep the faith and it always comes back around."

# THE FUGS

SCATOLOGICAL AND IMPROBABLE, THE Fugs were an affront to reason that by all rights should never have existed. Poets, at least spiritually, they saw rock as a medium badly lacking in artistic grace, an awkward bit of "ephemeral nonsense" (Ed Sanders) that nonetheless might be utilized as a force for social change, "as much as art can be a force for social change" (Tuli Kupferberg). From this basic dichotomy they preceeded to slab together a music built on similar extremes, ranging from reworked verses of Willian Blake's *Songs of Experience,* to a Rabelaisian "I Couldn't Get High," to the olfactory tribute of "Dirty Old Man." Live, the porno-political mood of such songs as "Kill For Peace" and "Boobs A Lot"

would be heightened by vaudevillian props and theatrical flourishes. No sacred cow proved unmilkable; wit and obscenity mingled freely, even joyously.

Sanders and Kupferberg had gropingly come to terms with the group's broad ideas in December 1964, when each was a regular at poetry readings held at New York City's Le Metro cafe. Sanders had been raised in Kansas City, passing through the high school football team and class valedictory on his way to New York University and a major in classical languages. His first book, *Poem From Jail,* was written after illegally boarding a nuclear submarine in an early sixties' "ban the bomb" protest; he also gained a good deal of notoriety

*(© 1968 David Gahr)*

**The Fugs**

as editor of *Fuck You / a magazine of the Arts* and owner of the Lower East Side's Peace Eye Bookstore.

Sander's literary aspirations were complemented on a political level by Kupferberg, who often described himself as "the oldest rock and roll star in America," having high school memories that "went as far back as the Spanish Civil War." A proclaimed anarchist theorist and beat fellow traveler, he was immortalized in Allen Ginsberg's *Howl* when he "jumped off the Brooklyn Bridge," living to tell the tale. He picked the name of the group from Norman Mailer's euphemism in *The Naked and the Dead*, and though initially put off by rock & roll, quickly acknowledged the wisdom of using "the rhythm and the feel, the spirit of the music, only giving it a little more intelligence, or poetry, or what-have-you. . . ." Sanders did not have to be thus convinced: his Missouri roots easily encompassed Chuck Berry, Laverne Baker, Hank Williams.

Along with Ken Weaver, a nominal drummer-boxer from Galveston, Texas, undesirably discharged from the Air Force because of a marijuana violation, bassist John Anderson and guitarist Vinny Leary, the Fugs began appearing at various underground happenings. Their first performance took place at Izzy Young's Folklore Center, followed by a stand at the American Poets Theatre run by Diane Di Prima, finally reaching the Astor Place Theatre where the still-expanding group opened a lengthy run in mid-1965. It was at this juncture, assisted by Holy Modal Rounders Pete Stampfel and Steve Weber, that they recorded their first album for the small Broadside Records, coyly offering *The Village Fugs* in "Ballads of Contemporary Protest, Point of Views and General Dissatisfaction."

"If I put it in percentages," says Kupferberg today, "I'd say you get less than a third of what we did from the records. The whole spirit could hardly be represented on a one-dimensional disc." He is probably right. The Fugs' cross-breeding of high and low art had to be seen to be appreciated, especially after they took up capacity residence at the Players Theatre on MacDougal Street in Greenwich Village. Though

their debut album featured Ken Weaver's celebratory "Slum Goddess," the effect of seeing Weaver himself pawing the microphone stand could never be replaced; so too the spectre of Sanders, lost in the "tragic smutabilly" of "Coca Cola Douche" and "River of Shit," or Tuli's Vietnamese death-mask in "Kill For Peace."

"I think we opened, or at least hoped to open the music to everything. We were probably at our best at the Players Theatre. . . ."

The second album, on ESP-Disk, confirmed their steady evolution. *The Fugs* polarized a triumphal "Frenzy" with various group concerns (the teenage "Skin Flowers," Kupferberg's tranquil "Morning Morning"), and climaxed with "Virgin Forest," a multi-themed mythology that discoursed on primitive mating and Burroughsian time grids before swelling to a hymnal "Death Stay Thy Phantoms." Combining awarenesses deliberately and nonapologetically, the Fugs seemed on the verge of a major breakthrough; "the moods, modes and methodic complexities of poetry are one hundred years of music," claimed Sanders. The record, despite ESP's reputation as the world's leading Esperanto label, sold well. By 1967 the group was entertaining offers from the larger Reprise conglomerate and, as far as Sanders was concerned, preparing for commercial acceptance.

Kupferberg "bitterly opposed" the change in directions. "We should've stayed buffoons, as we'd started. The arranging, the music . . . it never happened anyway. It lost spontaneity and never gained any art." Sanders thought differently, feeling that here was an opportunity to broaden the group's "nonviolent shock" past the limitations of a jug-band format.

"I figured we could become a very complicated drug band," he recalled, "or we could turn our raunchiness into Rock music. As leader, I did what I could. If I had to do it over again, after about 1966, I suppose I would've gone further out . . . into animal voices, screaming of worms . . . experimentation. But I made a choice to go with the words, backed up by traditional instruments. Tuli may ultimately be right . . . I don't know. But I do know that I worked hard on those albums — fifteen, twenty hours a day sometimes, and I think in the long run a lot of it will continue to be listened to and remembered.''

Even without ideological conflict, the Fugs found the going rough. Pressing plants refused to manufacture records; distributors conveniently "forgot" orders. "People will never know the trouble we went through . . . picketed by right wing nurses, constantly on the verge of getting arrested. We went into it with a spirit of fun, but there was a certain amount of hideous work to it. Everytime we played some big hall, it could be guaranteed we would never go back. We were banned all over the country. It became a choice of continuing, or losing interest, or just getting out''

By the decade's end, Sanders felt the minuses far exceeded the pluses and did just that. Left behind were the brave attempts of their Reprise period — *Tenderness Junction, It Crawled Into My Hand, Honest,* and the live classic, *Golden Filth* — as well as such oddities as a successful exorcism of the Pentagon (October 21, 1967) and appearances at literally hundreds of benefits. For years, the Fugs were the only group with a national following that could be counted on to add their magic to the peace movement, ultimately raising many thousands of dollars in support of their chosen principles.

Returning to literature after a brief solo career, Sanders would go on to document the rise and fall of the Manson commune in *The*

*Family,* as well as a book about "life and times in pre-Fugs days" called *Tales of Beatnik Glory.* He is currently at work on a collection of his poetry and a study of police state activities in the Nixon years for which he is attempting to exhume his extensive CIA files.

Kupferberg wrote several humorous How-To books *(1001 Ways To Live Without Working),* collated photographs of famous people when young and is thinking of penning a comic novel on the history of the Fugs. Weaver returned to the Southwest to become, alternately, a zoo-keeper, a sawmill operator and a janitor.

Ed accepted the outcome philosophically. "With hindsight, I can fashion in my mind a fantastic career, rivaling that of Apollinaire, the Cubists and the Dadaists. However, historically, we were trapped in the foment of the sixties, a nightmare intertwined with a sort of paradise. Hacked off the set by the big ice-pick in the sky.''

# VELVET UNDERGROUND

OBVERSE, REVERSE, INVERSE, PERVERSE. A whiplash girl-child waits in the dark, splintered in blue fragments, pinpricks of white heat. The Velvet Underground cauterized their time, searing the bloodstream of hedonism and frustration. Theirs was a demimonde, offering salvation in place of morality, ends justified by means. To be real, they vowed, pitting the absurd against the vulgar. The black angel

would peal its death song, sufferance and understanding as final reward, while terror and certainty fused in scenes of rumbling destruction, buildings toppling, cities left smoldering in ruins.

They stood alone, regarded as a curiosity or a "bum trip," their darkling visions no match for the optimism engloving America. It was only later, when they'd at last broken under the

pressure of hindsight, that their truth would become known: beauty in evil, evil in beauty, taking the strange twists of the human soul and glorifying them in a play of passions, "All Tomorrow's Parties." Even their name, borrowed from a paperback expose of sexual fetishes, seemed to hint at unknown depravities better whispered in private. The Velvet Underground, as early as 1966, was the first band of the seventies, twisting violence and catharsis into a haze of articulate noise, prophetic and provoking. Their legacy — David Bowie, the New York Dolls, Roxy Music, Lou Reed himself — could only attest to the profound subterfuge of the original.

The Velvets were spawned by New York City, in a cold-water flat on Ludlow Street where Brooklyn-born Lou Reed, Welshman John Cale, a lanky guitarist named Sterling Morrison and drummer Angus MacLise spent a long winter in late 1965. Reed had met Cale, newly dropped out from a massive Leonard Bernstein Composition and Theory scholarship at Tanglewood, while working as a songwriter for Pickwick Records. He'd recorded a dance step, "The Ostrich," and needed a group to showcase it around local high schools and record hops. The Primitives — Cale and Reed — stayed together for about a week before descending into the Lower East Side and such interim titles as the Warlocks and the Falling Spikes.

They had little equipment, only a couple of songs that Lou had written with no hope of commercial sale ("Heroin," "I'm Waitin' For My Man"), and, or course, no jobs. Journalist Al Aronowitz, then managing a folk-rock group called the Myddle Class, helped them to their first actual work in the Summit, New Jersey, high school. When they finally gathered enough steam to guest at the Cafe Bizarre, in the heart of Greenwich Village, Angus had already left for India. They asked friend Maureen Tucker to loan her set of drums while they sought a replacement. By showtime, she was a formal member of the band.

The Velvet Underground at the Cafe Bizarre must have been quite a sight to behold. While other groups around the MacDougal Street area were dabbling in variations of the Byrds' harmonic twelve-strings and thinking how nice it was that the Lovin' Spoonful had *really* made it, the Velvets exposed a new wound of festering consciousness. Their style was set by drugs and urban dishevelment, Reed's monotoned impassivity nodding to Cale's grinding, pierced viola. It was while they were on display there that film-maker Barbara Rubin brought Andy Warhol, and by extension, the entire New York avant-garde, to view the electric carnage. Warhol had just been offered a large sum of money to put on a show at Murray the K's burgeoning World on Long Island, and had been looking for a rock band to help him with the multi-media project.

Warhol's effect on the group, though he was listed as producer on their first album, was more in the nature of environmental advisor than specific shaper, a mode he had familiarized through his pop art, his films, his recognition of fame's fifteen minutes. Most of the primary material had been written long before his arrival, the basic sound imprinted during the Bizarre tenure. "Andy had a good way of picking out situations for us to appear in," remembers John. "He would almost invent places for us to play." After the group was fired from the Bizarre, Warhol brought them to the Film-makers Cinematheque, gave them rehearsal space in the magic world of the Factory and helped them find jobs and equipment.

The Cinematheque opened the scope of what later became the Exploding Plastic Inevitable. Andy took a series of movies for the Velvets to accompany, experimenting with light projections as the group played free-form behind the movie screen. The *chanteuse* Nico joined them in this period, fresh from a bit part in *La Dolce Vita*, walking into the Cinematheque one night with Brian Jones to sing Dylan's "I'll Keep It With Mine." Her cool, languorous distance and European breeding marked her as Reed's counterbalance, and she stayed when the Inevitable moved to larger quarters in an old immigrant community hall on still-dormant St. Mark's Place, the Dom.

Reviewers who came drew parallels to Berlin in the thirties, but they were only partially right; this was New York in the sixties, removed from threatened decadence by the media prop of art. The atmosphere generated the Velvets' first album, simply titled *The Velvet Underground & Nico*, in which they outlined their subculture with diffracted accuracy, turning each song on the next to question and

subvert meaning, culminating in the broken glass and subterranean distortions of "European Son" (dedicated to poet Delmore Schwartz). Multi-phrenic, Reed wrote introspectively for Nico, melodic ballads that placed her as a mirror, a "Femme Fatale." With himself, he plummeted brain-first into debauchery, overpowering his senses from without, seeking escape and unassayed relief. "Venus In Furs," "Run Run Run," "Heroin" — each became a mannered recitation of sin, a confessional neither idealized nor exorcised by the pain of its telling.

It was not meant to be pretty. Returning from a cold-shouldered California in 1967, the Velvets found their lease voided on the Dom and the Inevitable waning. There were subsurface tensions within the group as well. The first to slip away was Nico, to appear as a solo performer at the small nightclub Dom downstairs. Her departure created a strain between Reed and Cale. "We were very distraught at the time," says John. "There was pressure building up — God knows from where — and we were all getting very frustrated." Part of the problem lay in establishing their independence from Warhol, who was getting further involved with his films and less concerned with the group.

*White Light / White Heat* was assembled at the height of this desperation, with formerly known and relied-upon landmarks crumbling around them. The music was harsh, blurred and indistinct, stamped with the black-on-black death's head of the cover. There was a feeling of hurriedness to it, an urgency which intensified each cut, an element of paranoia that began "I Heard Her Call My Name" abruptly, in mid-phrase, almost as if it were afraid the side would start without it. "The Gift," narrated unflinchingly by Cale, presented a claustrophobic fable of modern love; on "Lady Godiva's Operation," a subliminal voice hissed "you're a boy — you're a girl," tense, accusing. The album's masterpiece, "Sister Ray," mixed a throbbing single chord in a Genet-like altar of sailors and ding-dongs, cemented by a stolid, endlessly patient beat from Maureen. Reed spit his images into the wind of a drone played at

# Poor Richard's

## — PRESENTS —

# ANDY WARHOL AND HIS EXPLODING PLASTIC INEVITABLE (SHOW)

★ ★ ★ ★ ★ ★ FEATURING ★ ★ ★ ★ ★ ★ ★

## THE NEW SOUND OF THE VELVET UNDERGROUND

★ ★ ★ ★ ★ ★ ★ WITH ★ ★ ★ ★ ★ ★

★ NICO - Pop Girl of '66

★ ★ ★ ★ ★ ★ ★ ★ ★ ★ ★ ★ ★ ★ ★ ★ ★ ★ ★ ★ ★

# JUNE 21 thru JUNE 26

# POOR RICHARD'S

## 1363 NO. SEDGWICK ★
### (OLD TOWN)

Tele. 337-1497 After 3 P.M.

— SHOWS —
10:00 P.M.
12:00 P.M. & 2 A.M.

RESERVATIONS REQUIRED

top volume, words sharding into separate syllables and then individual letters, an aural nightmare of blind, naked stasis.

They had stepped over the edge; there was only return left. Cale quietly resigned after the album's release to produce and compose; his pivotal position became apparent when he assumed musical directorship of Nico. On her own, she had tinged her spare readings with hints of melancholy, resignation, songs of lost loves now remembered, perhaps an expiation of burden through the release of music. On *Chelsea Girl,* she could sing "Somewhere there's a feather falling slowly from the sky / You need not know the reason why." Under Cale's tutelage, in *The Marble Index,* she was transformed into a Circe of fury, shouting defiantly amidst the elements, bleak and wintry.

The turnabout was even-handed. When the Velvets returned to the studio with Reed in control, the result was almost ascetic in comparison. "Candy Says" genteelly mentioned that which "others so discreetly talk about" as Reed continued to pair himself against innocence, in this case new bassist Doug Yule.

Velvet Underground's religious symbolism and forebearance were made official in the following year's *Loaded,* where Reed stipulated just what he meant by the salvation of one's soul. Relinquishing Jack his corset and Jane her vest, he told the story of Ginny from Long Island, playing with the dials of a radio. "You know her life was saved by rock and roll. . . ."

But the Velvets, nurtured in torment, were not strong enough to withstand a new security. After a summer-long exhibition at New York's Max's Kansas City in 1970, on the verge of their greatest commercial acceptance, Reed suddenly disappeared, upset by managerial problems and his own sense of stress. It would be another year before he braved the waters of a solo career, the *Transformer* of "Walk On The Wild Side," *Berlin* and *Metal Machine Music.* Sterling Morrison became a college teacher in Texas; Maureen stayed with the Velvet Underground that Doug Yule attempted to keep going in Europe, with little success. Cale has continued to produce Nico ("Das Lied Der Deutschen") as well as his own eccentric career, and now lives in England. A real good time was had by all.

# THE MC5 / THE STOOGES

THE MOTOR CITY WAS BURNING, LICKED BY the flames of guerrilla strife and confrontation, linked by the twin symbols of guns and guitars. "Rock and roll music is the great liberating force of our time," midwestern father figure John Sinclair had proclaimed from the podium of the Grande Ballroom, and counterculture youth raised their fists in salute, exchanging beads for cartridge belts. Removed from entertainment, the music became a rallying cry, a "high energy," propaganda for a rainbow-colored army bent on establishing an alternative way of existence.

"The Detroit/Ann Arbor community is first and foremost a rock and roll culture," noted hometown *Creem Magazine.* "Whatever movement we have here grew out of rock and

roll. It was rock and roll music which first drew us out of our intellectual covens and suburban shells. It is around the music that the community has grown and it is the music which holds the community together."

There was, however, little choice. Given the factory climate of Detroit and much of the Midwest, rock won its battles almost by default, politicized as a natural response to repression. The outlaw stance was in itself attractive, and set in the context of an ongoing revolution, it both reacted against and partook of the city's assembly-line air. Where Detroit was bland, its rock was vibrant and exciting; where Detroit tried to smooth over interior violence, its rock was consciously and defiantly brutal; where

The MC5

Detroit emphasized middle-class virtues and restraint, its rock promoted running wild in the streets, drugs, any former taboo. What could not be turned about was simply subverted. Shying away from technical excellence, the music was raw, performed with intensity and total belief.

Sinclair, a poet, critic and musician, was the first to perceive the incipient power that rock & roll represented for the Detroit area. There had been previous glimmerings — Motown had established a musical base, while groups like Mitch Ryder and the Detroit Wheels, ? and the Mysterians, and the Rationals generated white interest — but Sinclair took the whole mixture a step further. With a struggling young band known as the MC5, he laid the foundations for what would eventually build into a bold new music scene of the late sixties.

He first began working with the Five late in the summer of 1967, at a time when they seemed at their lowest ebb of fortune. Formed several years earlier to service the bar and college fraternity circuit, they consisted of vocalist Rob Tyner, guitarists Wayne Kramer and Fred "Sonic" Smith, bassist Michael Davis and drummer Dennis Thompson. When they met Sinclair, they had just had their equipment repossessed because of a lack of jobs — they were considered unprofessional, and had to rely on borrowed amplifiers and transportation whenever they did get an occasional gig.

Sinclair, a proponent of free-form jazz, had been attracted by the group's volumetrics and ability to transcend defined sound; seeing that they were slowly dying, he became their manager, helping them secure new equipment, places to practice, steady work. In addition, he brought them into the life of his commune, Trans-Love Energies, and gave them his rhetoric of cultural overthrow.

The Five's physical assault was matched on a psychic level by the Stooges. Jim ("I was born in a trailer camp . . .") Osterberg had led a high-school group called the Iguanas, moving to Chicago to drum for a blues band before returning to Ann Arbor. There, with guitarist Ron Asheton, brother Scott Asheton on drums and bassist Dave Alexander, he switched his name to Iggy, premiering the Psychedelic Stooges on Halloween of 1967. While the group never benefited by Sinclair's direct influence, they easily fit into his new social construct, based on the principle that if one cannot make the audience come to them, then one must simply go to the audience. So they did, Iggy launching himself into the crowd at regular intervals, rolling amidst their bewilderment, scoring himself with a broken drumstick, cursing and spitting and inundating everyone with the sheer force of his personality. With guitars and drums howling in the background, he would prowl the stage, twisting his body into

The Stooges, 1973

*(Lee Black Childers)*

absurd positions, staring madly about and snapping his head.

Yet the Stooges were very different from the MC5's treble avalanche. Where the Five presented themselves as a blistering rock & roll band, with all implied magnificence, the Stooges seemed to reject such a role. They never set themselves up for dancing; watching them, seeing Iggy preen and strut only to turn and hit himself with the blunt end of the microphone, was akin to asylum therapy. Where the Five would try to take you somewhere beyond yourself, the Stooges bared their secrets to the blade of a knife, exulting in the "O-mind," the wrenching paw of terror and revolt. Their dominion was boredom, frustration, the curious mixture of self-hate and pride so much a part of growing up in the sixties, simply and surely projected in such a way that it could not be misinterpreted:

> *Oh last year I was twenty one*
> *Didn't have a lot of fun*
> *And now I'm gonna be twenty two*
> *Another year with nuthin' to do. . . . ** *

Detroit dug in for extended siege. Russ Gibb's Grande Ballroom, previously the only showcase for progressive rock, was increasingly driven into giving more space to local bands, allowing those very same bands — the Amboy Dukes, SRC, the Frost, as well as the Five and the Stooges — to wipe out the top acts on his bill. The Motor City audience sensed this upsurge, breaking ranks to add encouragement at a time when other cities' crowds were beginning to passively sit and nod. In true communal spirit, they felt the bands were of themselves, thrown up from their own number to serve notice of awakening. "We live and work in the highest state of consciousness we can attain," Sinclair noted in March 1968, "and we can't be brought down." When the MC5 traveled to the Democratic Convention to entertain the troops at the Battle of Chicago later that summer, the word blossomed nationwide. "It is all one message," Sinclair said in the founding "State-meant" of his White Panther party, "and the message is FREEDOM!"

But when, and where, and how much were questions not as easily answered. To convince America (and perhaps the world) of the Motor City philosophy required outside assistance, and

Sinclair's idealism met resistance as he opposed a harder-nosed business reality. At first it looked as if he might succeed. Danny Fields, then a perceptive "company freak" at Elektra Records ("schizophrenia is a very possible occupational hazard," he once said), had paid several early visits to Detroit as the scene emerged and convinced Elektra president Jac Holzman that here, indeed, was the wave of the future. Holzman, who had already proved amenable to the Doors and Love, agreed, and a massive signing ceremony was arranged. The Five opted for live recording of their initial album while the Stooges went into studio seclusion with ex-Velvet Undergrounder John Cale as producer.

Sinclair clarioned the call in his liner notes for *Kick Out The Jams:* "The MC5 is totally committed to the revolution, as the revolution is totally committed to driving people out of their separate shells and into each other's arms . . . *Separation is Doom.*" Nonetheless, the hoped-for unity with their record company began to deteriorate as distributors refused to stock the album, as newspapers declined to print incendiary ads, as the album itself met with unfavorable response outside of Detroit. The city may have excelled in live rock, but the Grande ambience only seemed like misdirected noise to outsiders not previously prepared. Prisoners of their own ideology, they set up a free concert to introduce the band to New York at the Fillmore East, but it foundered on dispute between political factions; others saw the Five's lack of musical training as a liability. Either way, the group backed off, chastened, somewhat shaken by the sudden spectre of derailment.

They needed direction, but there was no one able to help them. Sinclair, arrested for possession of marijuana, exhausted his appeals in 1969 and was sentenced to a ten-year term in federal prison, which effectively silenced his efforts on behalf of the band and the community. Writer-producer Jon Landau entered in an attempt to straighten out the Five's affairs, working rigorously to make sense out of their legal difficulties and recorded sound. With a new record label (Atlantic) willing to start afresh, *Back In The USA* crisply refined the group's basic rock attack and musicianship, yet

faltered on their own lack of confidence, neither brazen nor assertive enough to live up to the potential in such titles as "Teenage Lust" and "The Human Being Lawnmower." Its lack of success increased their debts as it withered their enthusiasm, and after a fare-thee-well *High Time* in 1971, they left for Europe and eventual dissolution.

The Stooges were luckier, avoiding reliance on Sinclair and the quicksand of Detroit politics to offer themselves alone to national consciousness. Unlike the Five, they were able to control their direction in the studio, bowing an introductory album that hypnotically attracted as it repelled, a negation-muting protest and rebellion in the name of prolonged,

Iggy

(Billy Maynard)

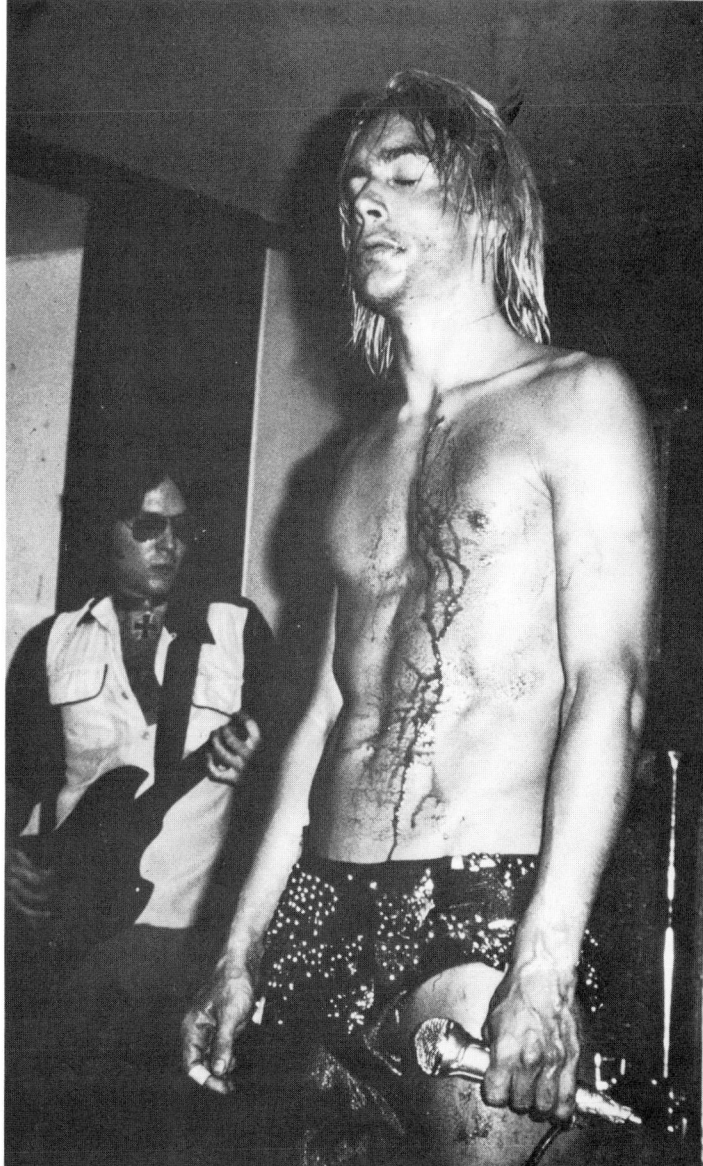

sinking resignation. Their live appearances provoked and entranced audiences, who were unable to believe the violations committed, Iggy lying panting on the floor to croon "The Shadow Of Your Smile" from cracked and bleeding lips.

A second album, *Funhouse,* compromised them even less, a wall of churning decibels that descended into the engulfing *malebolge* of "L.A. Blues." The toll was frightening. No longer able to separate their art from themselves, the group was seized by drugs and self-destruction. Iggy was often physically sick on stage, choking and throwing up, clawing toward the microphone to quote Renfield from *Dracula: "Flies . . . big juicy flies . . . and spiders. . . ."* Verging on tragedy, the band was revived by David Bowie in 1972 and taken to England, where *Raw Power* was recorded for Columbia with new guitarist James Williamson. They leaped joyously to the end of their rope, sustained by ricocheting newsreels of the Vietnamese war ("Search And Destroy") and the Stooges' own bespattered credo of "Gimme Danger." "Death Trip" provided the epitaph of a Hollywood exile.

The momentum was lost. Sinclair took the change in stride, musing from his prison cell shortly before his conviction was overturned in 1972. "This is the best I can do," he apologized in *Guitar Army,* a collection of his writings witnessing the passage of an era. "The only other thing I can suggest is that you get your hands on a copy of *Kick Out The Jams,* by the old MC5, put it on the record machine, turn up the volume, light up a joint, maybe take all your clothes off, roll around on the floor for a minute, and return with us now to those thrilling days of yesteryear . . . the spring of 1968, where this sequence begins. . . ." Praise the Lord and pass the ammunition.

# 15
# Psychedelia

## THE GRATEFUL DEAD

THE GRATEFUL DEAD ARE A LIVING HIPPIE
monument, lysergic storm troopers who have
carried "the Message" across continents and
psychic thresholds, oblivious of all laws and
boundaries, terrestrial or otherwise. The last
intact acid group from the great psychedelic age,
they have weathered earthquakes, chromosome
breaks, innumerable busts, endless additions
and subtractions from the band, hundreds of
thousands of mikes of Owsley acid, the death of
Haight Ashbury and the more tangible loss of
the irreplaceable Pigpen who "OD'ed on life" at
the age of twenty-seven. Through all these
cataclysmic events they remain faithful to their
original ideals, organizing their own tours,
dividing funds communally among members,
wives, girlfriends, and maintaining their stance
of extraterrestrial plain folks. The kosmic kids
have resisted the ultimate rock temptation — to
become stars, passed through regions where
reason totters and come through with their
sublime equilibrium intact. Major projects are
undertaken with alarming casualness — the
double *Live in Europe* album came about simply
because "some of the dudes in the band wanted
to check it (Europe) out."

As they describe their origins, it is as if
*something* were guiding them around the edges
of chaos. "One day we were all over at Phil's
house smoking DMT," Garcia says, recalling
how their weird name came to them like some
flash from the Bardo realm. "He had a big
Oxford dictionary, I opened it, and there was
GRATEFUL DEAD, those words juxtaposed. It was
one of those moments, y'know, like everything
on the page went blank, diffuse, just sorta oozed
away and there was GRATEFUL DEAD, big black
letters edged all around in gold, man, blasting
out at me."

Legend has it that the nucleus of the Dead,
Jerry Garcia, Bob "Ace" Weir, Pigpen (Ron
McKernan) gathered on New Year's Eve 1964 to
form an old-timey folk group called Mother
McCree's Uptown Jugband Champions. Jerry had
been in a band called the Zodiacs with Bill
Kreutzman and recruited him on drums. Phil
Lesh, a onetime child prodigy on the violin and
student of Darius Milhaud, and by then a
disenchanted electronics music freak, was
persuaded to take up the bass and join them.
When they started out they were little more than
suburban folkies, but under the deluge of Dylan,

## The Grateful Dead

soul music, *A Hard Day's Night* and the English invasion, they became one of the first groupie groups at the beginning of the west coast rock revival of the mid-sixties to play a mix of Beatles, Stones, Motown and Dylan with some old blues and a pinch of bluegrass.

By 1965 they were the Warlocks, and after a Palo Alto storeowner fronted them with equipment, they began playing bars and pizza joints. Their sound was becoming weirder and louder, developing into "living thunder" and then one day they met Ken Kesey. Kesey had been participating in LSD experiments at the State Hospital and he had transplanted these "experiences" to the more informal environment of his place in La Honda. These became the Acid Tests: 2,000 people helplessly stoned, going through insane changes, levitating, spiralling, vibrating, hyperventilating while bands played, tape loops manically repeated ominous sounds, liquid light shows sprinkled irridescent dust, participants discovered the fourth, fifth, . . . nth dimensions and paraded about in a space previously known only to Shamans, madmen, mystics and spirits.

It was the beginning of a new heaven and a new earth, and when the Dead moved into their house at 710 Ashbury in June 1966, they became the energy center for a culture that took the visions of rock literally. Millenial delusions were rampant. The trips festivals, the Free Store, the color clotted Oracle newspaper and Fillmore posters, the Mime Troup fantasies, the Diggers movement, the Family Dog dances, the Pranksters, the Summer Solstice celebrations, the Be-Ins, Love-Ins — all revolved around the San Francisco rock bands. The Dead were *the* band for flower children and freaks in search of the cosmic connection.

But, in spite of their wah-wah effects, cosmic chording, jazz jamming, electronic whines, frizzled feedback and alchemical mixes, the Dead are not the most psychedelic band. Their sound, somewhere between Sun Ra and rhythm and blues, with country and western and old blues seasonings, is basically hard rock slightly freaked. Their runs often resemble finger exercises or scales. They build their long crescendos around Jerry Garcia's pulsating airy

guitar in a lazy dialogue with Phil Lesh's bass and Weir's spooky vocals against Kreutzman's mathematical meters, spinning out their songs — "Alligator" can last up to two hours — into impossibly long sets.

*(Collection Richard & Lisa Robinson)*

Their most accessible albums are *Live Dead* and *Anthem to the Sun*, a tribute to Neil Cassidy (the first canonized crazy and hero of Kerouac's *On The Road*), but the Dead are a paradox among rock musicians, a great group whose essence has never been captured on vinyl. They are essentially a "live" band, the masters of the "vibe," the electrical flow between them and their audiences. The Dead, it has been said "play their audience," and their performances are studies in synergy and the dynamics of sound, massing tension in titanic jams like "Lovelight" or "St. Stephen" (with its cannon blast climax) until the ballroom seems ready to

THE GRATEFUL DEAD

CONCERT    DANCE

STEVE MILLER BLUES BAND
MOBY GRAPE
LIGHTS BY ROGER HILLYARD + BEN VAN METER
DEC 23 FRI 24 SAT 9 P.M.
SUTTER AT VANNESS · · · · · · SAN FRANCISCO
AVALON BALLROOM

FAMILY DOG PRESENTS

© 1966 FAMILY DOG

**TICKET OUTLETS:**

*SAUSALITO*: Tides Book Shop    *BERKELEY*: Moe's Books, Discount Records    *MENLO PARK*: Kepler's Book Store
*SAN FRANCISCO*: The Psychedelic Shop, City Lights Books, Bally Lo, Cedar Alley Coffee House, Sandal Maker (North Beach), Hut T-1 State College

The Bindweed Press, San Francisco

explode, and then cooling everything out at that breathtaking moment with a trickling steel guitar solo on a Merle Haggard shitkicker special.

Jerry Garcia's benign presence radiates through the Dead and binds them. He is their central sun and perhaps because of him there is something undauntedly optimistic about the Dead's intergalactic trips. Unlike more literal psychedelic groups, the Dead never attempt to duplicate the experience of acid. Their music serves as markers on lysergic trails to that still center of inner space, dead center, where their fanatic flock (called "Deadheads") expect to be led. The Dead with their tribal faith believe it can only be found together. "Only collective moral force can save the world," says Jerry, quoting the I Ching, and adding gracefully, "We are only incidental music to the celebration of life."

# JEFFERSON AIRPLANE

THE SUMMER OF LOVE HELD THE PROMISE. After one thousand, nine hundred and sixty-seven years the dark ages were about to end. A new Earth was in the making, reuniting the individual and the universe, harmonizing the shared blessings of humanity in a theosophy of brotherly-sisterly good. Eden was San Francisco, at the intersection of Haight and Ashbury Streets, where headshops acted as lay churches, the bible was the underground press, the gospel, as always, rested in music. Traditionally, the city played host to a joyous hodge-podge of styles, far removed from the beaten commercial path. Both jazz and folk had wide audiences, but except for the occasional breakthrough of a home-grown act (the Four Deuces, Vince Guaraldi, Bobby Freeman), San Francisco's only presence on the pop charts was to be found in Tony Bennett's heart-lost sentiments about riding cable-cars "halfway to the stars." Native rock & roll grew sparsely, and when it did surface, as in the Beau Brummels' 1965 hits of "Laugh Laugh" and "Just A Little," regional resemblance was only coincidental. It was still kid stuff as far as most were concerned, beneath serious notice.

The awakening wasted no time, carried by Dylan's shift to electricity, the respectability of the Beatles and the Rolling Stones, and more immediate pioneers like the Byrds and the Lovin' Spoonful. The Spoonful, especially, had a realizing effect on the city when they visited in the heat of "Do You Believe In Magic," and Marty Balin, a painter, designer and sometimes musician, might have watched and felt reassured, knowing that his band, Jefferson Airplane, was at least on the right runway.

He had begun thinking about forming an electric group earlier in 1965, adding members more by whim than conscious choice. Marty himself was the product of a short solo career on Challenge Records and a position in the local Town Criers, while Paul Kantner had been uprooted from The Drinking Gourd, a folk club where he played twelve-string guitar and banjo; Alexander Spence was a guitarist also, but Balin decided he looked too much like a drummer not to be one, and "Skip" picked up his first pair of sticks. Kantner supplied Jorma Kaukonen from the folk circuit, and Kaukonen in turn phoned an old friend from Washington, D.C., Jack Casady, to complete the rhythm section on bass. Signe Toly Andersen became, with Marty, the band's singer.

In the spring, Balin made sure Jefferson Airplane (after nonexistent blues singer Blind Thomas Jefferson Airplane) would always have a place to play by taking over a small music club named the Honeybucket, converting it into what would become the Matrix. The Airplane debuted there in August, and by the following fall had gathered enough enthusiasm to guarantee a

### Jefferson Airplane

following. Jorma was still finger-picking his guitar, Spence struggling along on drums, Casady with the mustache of a music instructor (which he'd been before Kaukonen's call), but the music was clean and modern, and San Francisco was starved for electricity.

They weren't the first band on the scene — that honor was reserved for the Charlatans, recently returned from the Red Dog Saloon in Nevada with a deliberate Western Edwardian air — yet they rapidly became its most typified spokesmen. Rising on the spell of sudden nirvana woven about San Francisco, their bumperstickers and buttons advertised "Jefferson Airplane Loves You." Ballroom dancing, rediscovered as a mixed-media experience by the Trips Festivals and molded into a structured event by Bill Graham (the

Fillmore) and the Family Dog (the Avalon), created a mind-over-matter environment in which anything could (and often did) happen. Freaking freely became a way of life, the blown mind of light shows and LSD, and as if they'd been specifically waiting, musicians of all persuasions heeded the siren call. By New Year's Eve of 1966, the primary rank of Bay Area bands was in motion, preforming regularly if not always consistently, with the early guiding improvisations of the Grateful Dead, Quicksilver Messenger Service, the Mystery Trend, Big Brother and the Holding Company.

The Airplane had the jump on most of these combinations through timing and accessibility, removed from the more formless, feedback-oriented groups because of their strength in songwriting. Donovan had paid them

*(Don Paulsen)*

tribute with his "Fat Angel," noting "Fly Trans-Love Airlines . . . gets you there on time." Actually, they were ahead of schedule. *Jefferson Airplane Takes Off* became the first album of the San Franciscan renaissance, released in mid-1966 to the not-inaccurate hype of "A Jet-Age Sound." Centered around soon-to-be anthem "Get Together" and Airplane originals like "Come Up The Years" and "It's No Secret," Balin's voice and songs predominated, with Kantner, Kaukonen and Casady making major instrumental contributions. Spence, never having fully adjusted to the drums, left the group shortly after the album's completion to play guitar for Moby Grape; Signe departed for the Pacific Northwest and family commitments, her folk voice lost in the Airplane's sweep of electronics. In their place, Spencer Dryden took over traps, and Grace Slick, late of Matrix-favorite the Great Society, entered as vocalist. She also brought two holdover songs from her previous group, "Somebody To Love" and "White Rabbit."

San Francisco was in full bloom, suspended in innocence before the world could direct its quizzical attention to the tremor beneath its nose. The Diggers supplied free food and materiel, the Victorian-turretted houses around Haight-Ashbury offered communal

accommodation, and the parks — the Panhandle and the Golden Gate — provided relaxing room and a choice of trees with which to hold spiritual conversation. It was meant to be shared, this revelatory way of being, and the hippies welcomed any chance to tell the world their fortune, not realizing that the world might take the message-bearer's position on the map for the good news itself. *Surrealistic Pillow,* the Airplane's second album, dangled "White Rabbit" 's dictum of "Feed your head" in the wake of "Somebody To Love". Like the dance hall posters of Wes Wilson, the first "Be-In" (January 1967), or a Monterey Pop Festival which drew national attention to San Francisco's representatives, the group was carrying the weight for an entire generation's hopes and dreams.

The surrogate's role wore heavily on them. Grace's presence, unlike Signe's, began to outflank Balin's leadership, and though they would often combine for duets of a soaring nature, her prominence increased after the hit singles, fraying the directional unity of the band. As Haight-Ashbury strained to contain a summer population explosion threatening to overturn its tenuous veneer of homogeneity, so the Airplane struggled to be all things to all of its members. "The death of hippie" was hastily declared by a wounded Bay Area populace in October, and two months later, *After Bathing At Baxter's* signaled that some remnants of glory might yet be salvaged. "The Ballad Of You & Me & Pooneil" took the mature Airplane to one of their most impressive statements, even as splitting seams began to weaken the superstructure.

Once started, there was no stopping. The real world, far from crumbling under the siege of love's minions, only stiffened its resistance, bearing down brutally in the form of addicting drugs, crime and the realization that man couldn't relinquish the burden of history overnight by pretending it didn't exist. For the Airplane, and the rest of the San Francisco groups, it would mean that no matter how they might feel internally, they would have to continue to deal with the venus flytrap of the music industry if they hoped to spread their music into the nation-at-large; though many held out for as long as possible, scheduling free concerts and aligning themselves with "the people," they soon discovered the solution was no more reliable or predictable than people themselves. Woodstock's "Three Days of Love, Peace and Music" could just as easily become Altamont's random scenes of horror. The Airplane knew; they had appeared at both.

It was not so much a break-up as a dismantle. The tracks of *Crown of Creation* and *Volunteers* were divided among various factions in the band, and even as the live *Bless Its Pointed Little Head* showed they could still outplay most of their competitors, solo careers were being considered. Hot Tuna featured Jack and Jorma in acoustic, and later electric, blues excursions; Grace combined her sulphuric wit and barbed politics with Paul's sci-fi ·ruminations to produce Jefferson Starship (sealed, in January 1971, by the birth of a daughter, China). Balin left the remnants of the group in spring of that year to start anew, seemingly unimpressed by a new Airplane-owned label formed to oversee all related product, Grunt Records. He has since rejoined the improved Starship, along with violinist Papa John Creach, ex-Quicksilver David Freiberg and assorted others: the code of the chromosomes, the spirit of '67.

# COUNTRY JOE & THE FISH

BY THE LATE SIXTIES COUNTRY JOE & THE Fish had become a symbol for acid-rock-revolution, and appropriately enough Joe McDonald *sang* his testimony (the "I-Feel-Like-I'm-Fixin'-To-Die-Rag") at the Chicago Seven conspiracy trial in 1970 before being silenced by a marshal. Then, the court, like some Kafkaesque straightman, attempted to ascertain his identity. COURT: You say some people call you Country. What is your real name?" WITNESS: "I'm afraid I don't know what *real* means." Country Joe & the Fish injected a Marx Brothers sense of the ridiculous into the self-congratulatory politics of the time. "The most revolutionary thing you can do in this country is to change your mind," Joe McDonald, the group's founding member, once said, but his subtlety of attitude made it hard on the group's image. They were caught in the crossfire between radicals, who accused them of revisionism, and straights, like the patrons of one Chicago club who demanded their money back because they did not appear with go-go girls. Meanwhile, Joe kept insisting, "I'm a musician who *plays* for the left wing."

Only the politically fermenting climate of Berkeley, however, could have produced a band like the Fish. They were the community's house band, resident musicians at the local Jaberwock coffeehouse. Joe and the Fish's future manager, Ed Denson, had put out a radical paper called Ragbaby since August 1965, and they decided to make the October issue, supporting the Oakland draft resistors, a musical one. Barely a month and a half old, the band recorded the "Fixin'-To-Die-Rag" and "Superbird" in the living room of Chris Strachwitz of Arhoolie Records, slipped the seven-inch discs into manila envelopes with a picture of a troop train on them, and shipped them out at 75 cents a copy. It wasn't until almost a year later that they began recording what was to be the basis for their first Vanguard album, *Electric Music For The Mind And Body*. It was comic-book cosmic. "High Flying Bird," their satire on L.B.J., brought in The Fantastic Four from Marvel comics, which reciprocated in a later issue by inserting Country Joe and a rock band playing at an assassination of one of the Fantastic Four. *Electric Music* was full of lyrical bottled Marin County afternoons as in the erotic chant "Happiness Is A Porpoise Mouth," and the tidal

(Vanguard Records)

tempo of "Bass Strings" (a Fish code phrase for grass) or the almost Koto-like mesmerizing effects in the tribute to Grace Slick. It contained an acid exposure of psychedelic fetishes in "Not So Sweet Martha Lorraine" and possibly the doomiest dirge to lost love ever written, "Death Sound."

Even the amateurishness of the first album seemed to contribute to its atmospheric Bay Area "looseness," but their second album with its tighter sound was no less amazing, this time including the original "Rag" with the soon to be infamous "F-I-S-H Cheer" beginning with the provocative "gimme an F . . . ." The four-letter FISH substitute became a legal matter when audiences in Worcester, Massachusetts, supplied the necessary vowels and consonants, and Joe McDonald in turn made it into a political issue in his classic letter to the court: " . . . kids are finding out that the real obscenities and immoral acts are committed by the Establishment . . . which chooses to manifest its hangups by

poisoning the rivers and the oceans . . . and by forcing their own children to go off into a foreign country and murder for them."*

As soon as the sessions on the second album were finished, the group split up for the first time in October 1967. Often what brings a band together in the first place is one of the prime causes for its disintegration, and in the case of the Fish it was their basic sense of anarchy that came out theatrically — the baseball games on stage that interrupted performances, the community of acid heads, the stepped-up political climate and tension between personalities that had originally been magnetised to each other. Joe, Barry Melton, David Cohen, Bruce Barthol and Chicken Hirsch reunited again in August 1969, pledging to stick it out for at least a year, only for the original members to go their own way in a Fish fillet in

*Quoted from Joe MacDonald's letter to the Court of Worcester, Massachusetts.

*(Collection Peter Kanze)*

1970 ("it happens every summer," said Barry casually), with Joe McDonald coming out with his first solo album the same year, *Thinking of Woody,* a collection of Woody Guthrie songs (his left-wing family had originally come from Oklahoma to California so it was a sort of tribute to his roots). Barry owned the copyright on the name the Fish and swam off with it and the other members. There's something of an irony in this since the name itself derives from a quotation of Chairman Mao's, "Every fish in the sea is a potential convert." Later Barry came out with his own solo or soul of Fish album, *Bright Sun Is Shining,* and although they came together again with different members, things still didn't pan out for the Fish, and Joe went his own way composing movie scores, performing as actor in his wife Robin Menken's troupe, the Pitschel Players.

"We played good sets and bad sets like every other band," Joe pondered in an interview with David Felton, in *Rolling Stone.* "We took dope just like every other band. We played far out music and we seemed to get ignored by people . . . the underground never defined to us what we were to them. They did it very well for other bands."* The problem was often that the political banner under which they emerged soon became a stigma they found hard to come to terms with. Neither Joe McDonald's haunting lyricism nor his irrepressible humor quite fitted the grim pigeonholes radical politics expected him to fit into, and with his sardonic attitude and folk voice he was never quite at home in rock. His sensibility is basically romantic and expansive. He began song-writing by setting to music Robert Service's sentimental ballads, like Jean Dupree, and was always more of a poet than a politician, picking out exquisite images through "the tiny door of his eye" — as in "Pat's Song" and "Porpoise Mouth," an audacious experimenter in "Colors For Susan," based on ideas from Eric Satie's "Les Sonneries De La Rose Croix," and always tempering his evocative moods with the irrepressible humor with which he began his first song, "I Seen A Rocket," about a man who runs his car off the road in the desert. A spaceship lands and spews out a thing who comes over to the petrified human and touches him, "Tag, you're it!"

*Copyright © Rolling Stone magazine, April, 1971

# PINK FLOYD

THE POSTER READ "GAMES FOR MAY. Space Age relaxation for the climax of Spring." On the 27th of May 1967, Pink Floyd performed at their most delirious peak in the staid Queen Elizabeth Hall of London's Festival Gardens. It was the day after the release of *Sergeant Pepper's Lonely Hearts Club Band.* Trendy London with its jaded need for astonishment, fetishism of fashion, dreams of past and future/present in Antique Market costumes, narcissistic poses, was almost *too ready* for Pink Floyd. Their hallucinated "music in colours" and enchantments in technology aimed at *disorganizing all the senses* through a mélange of multidimensional protoplasmic projections, flashing strobes, black light, ear splitting volume laced with echo, distortion and feedback all channeled through the first quadraphonic sound system.

At the center of this psychotropic maelstrom

**Pink Floyd**

was "the madcap" himself, Syd Barrett, fringed cape, hair matted with crushed Mandrax pills, a disquieting magnetic shadow against the melting images of the liquid light show. Three weeks after the Festival Gardens concert, his bizarre ballad "See Emily Play" made it to number three on the London Radio Survey and canonized him as the magus of London's loons. But Syd, suffering from extraterrestial terrors diagnosed as chronic paranoia, had by this time withdrawn to his parents' home in Cambridge. He continued to appear with the group over the next six months, but during that time few boundaries were acknowledged between "freak outs" and impinging insanity. In the space between, Syd had become slowly unhinged (R. D. Laing pronounced him incurable). He

appeared totally mute on Dick Clark's American Bandstand. A friend explained, "Syd wasn't moving his lips that day." As Syd slowly descended into the twilight of dementia, finally leaving the group for good in January, 1968, Pink Floyd gradually gained an international reputation.

Their first album, *Piper At The Gates of Dawn,* was number nine on the English charts soon after its release in September 1967. The sci-fi rock of the extended instrumental "Interstellar Overdrive," featuring Barrett's beep-beep satellite guitar, the cabalistic chants on "Astronomy Domine," its surrealistic tableaus, vertiginous phrasing effects and tortured texts put Pink Floyd in the forefront of electronic rock, equaled at the time only by Jimi

*(Dister)*

Hendrix and the Soft Machine. Barrett's acid guitar was influenced by the drone of the Byrds, the Stones (he wore out his first copy of *Between The Buttons*) and Love, from whom he borrowed the principle riff for "Interstellar Overdrive."

Pink Floyd began as the Abdabs (a.k.a. the T-Set) in 1964, in the hip elitist atmosphere of the English university town of Cambridge. They played the usual mix of blues and jazz at a local pub called The Mill with Richard Wright, Nick Mason, Roger Waters, jazz buff Bob Close and Roger Keith Barrett, affectionately known to his mates as Syd. Syd had three brooding interests at this time: religion, painting and music. When the visions of inner light of the Sant Saji faith were denied him on account of his age, he began seeking chemical enlightenment. Gradually he evolved his obsession with Soma paintings into the idea of painted sound, a principal theme of Pink Floyd's light shows devised by projectionist Jo Cannon, who was often considered the fifth member of the Floyd. About the time Bob Close fell out of the group, they came up with a name based on the names of two blues singers, Pink Anderson and Floyd Council. Their diet in these early years was mainly blues, rock and static, and the feedback effects became more frenetic as the primal croaks of West Coast crazies like the Mothers of Invention and the Byrds ("Eight Miles High") blew into London. They participated in the Films and Madness Festivals at The Roundhouse in Chalk Farm and ushered in the year of lysergic lunacy at a 1967 New Year's inauguration of London's hippest hang-out, The UFO.

Along with the somewhat more esoteric and jazzy Soft Machine, Pink Floyd were at the core of London's avant garde before they released their first single, "Arnold Layne," in March 1967. It was a typically bizarre Barrett effort and was soon banned by the usually sympathetic Radio London on the grounds that it promoted the use of drugs, thus enshrining Pink Floyd as the first media martyrs of psychedeliana Anglica. Syd's songs came across with an insane, abrupt immediacy, but as weird as they were, their images leapt with delirious clarity

out of the textures of the guitars and effects. "They appeared as if out of nowhere," the Floyd's manager, Andrew King, once said of Barrett's compositions, and they in turn seemed to have appeared to Syd out of the blue, as in his account of "See Emily Play," their second single: "I had fallen asleep in this wood after a gig up North, when I saw a young girl coming towards me through the trees crying and dancing. It was Emily."

Dave Gilmour, a childhood friend of Syd's, replaced him in the group early in 1968, and from then on the history of Pink Floyd is the history of a very different group. Where Syd felt he could embrace and reach the outer limits in one ecstatic short-circuited leap, the post-Syd Floyd realized that the actual treks into that infinity would be long, slow, often tedious voyages. Their music has consequently gravitated toward liturgies of space evoking cold, clear, remote interstellar regions on albums like *Atom Heart Mother* and *Dark Side of The Moon* which use a thickly layered texture similar to that used by the Moody Blues, a seamless wall of sound woven up from celestial choirs, swirling orchestral suites, sound effects and electronic muzak. The impression it leaves is almost subliminal, while their stage performance is an extravaganza of synthesized rock matched by *trompe l'oeil* explosions, mists and rings of fire. The refined, controlled sound that the Floyd have developed since Syd's departure seems designed to lay the spectre of Barrett to rest, though he still pops up in the lyrics, and it is in the lyrics that Floyd has suffered most since the madcap's departure.

Meanwhile Syd, who came out of his mad silence to cut two albums on his own, *The Madcap Laughs* and *Barrett*, attracted an international following of devotees including David Bowie and Blue Oyster Cult. The Syd Barrett Appreciation Society puts out a fanzine devoted to him called "Madcap," and for his descent into insanity (the ultimate dues paying) his admirers have enshrined him, as *The New Musical Express* put it, in "the realms of ye olde English whimsical loone, wherein dwelt the likes of Edward Lear and Kenneth Grahame."

(Don Paulsen)

# 16
# Supercool & Superbad

## JAMES BROWN

THERE WAS A TIME, IN THE MID-SIXTIES, when James Brown could outdance, outprance anything. His automatic body was perfectly in sync with the pulsating rhythm of his 30-piece band as he did his *Superglide* across the stage as if suspended on a layer of atoms. He could perform splits with stroboscopic speed, jerking, arching in the gymnastics of love and pain, could spin himself into a trance and then stop motion and seem to make time stand still. It was pure ego, defying the laws of gravity! Everything was so uptight, outasight and supercharged that Mr. Dynamite seemed in danger of exploding.

James Brown boasts that one night in the frenzy of his performance he will die onstage. He used to enact a sort of funky funeral nightly at the conclusion of his show, the most outrageous comic/pathetic piece of melodrama in show business. James Brown as defeated champion, dejected lover, king in exile and Black Christ swathed in fluorescent capes is dragged away sobbing from the microphone by the Famous Flames only to fling the cape off, stamp his feet in an infantile tantrum, fall to his knees convulsed in a rainbow of sweat and tears

and scream in the agony of ecstasy

> *Pleeeze, Pleeeze, Pleeeze!*
> *Ooohdahlinpleee-eeezedohngoh-oooowaaaah*
> *Aaahluhvyahsooo-ooo!*

It was with "Please, Please, Please" that James Brown and the Famous Flames had their first R & B hit in 1956. It was taped at a radio station Brown now owns, WDRW in Augusta, Georgia, where he used to shine shoes as a kid and dance for pennies from the soldiers from Fort Gordon Army Base. At sixteen he was sent to the work camp at Tacoa for armed robbery, from which he was paroled three years later — a lightweight boxing champion who had trained with Beau Jack and acted as sparring partner for Sugar Ray Robinson.

The nucleus of the group was formed when he met up with Bobby Byrd, who still performs with and is produced by Brown. They sang together in the Augusta Baptist Church, and their first efforts, with James on the piano and Byrd on guitar, were spirituals. The early Flames' things too, like "Please, Please, Please" and "I Love You, Yes I Do" (which preceded it and later in 1961 became an R & B hit for the

The Flames in action

group) mainly used gospel chords, a raw preaching style and minimum accompaniment.

The Flames — Don Terry, Syl Keels, Nash Knox, Floyd Scott, Byrd and Brown — were essentially a vocal group who played their own instruments. The highlight of their act was a musical baseball routine with Brown as the pitcher, Byrd the catcher, co-ordinated to the tune of "Good, Good Lovin'." Even with this grandstand gimmick and a record contract with King Records subsidiary Federal, work was scarce so they began impersonating more successful groups like the Five Royals and the Drifters, a common practice for little-known R & B groups then and now. "We would imitate them real good," remembers Bobby Byrd, "we sang like them, we dressed like them, we could even *look* like them. We had them *down*. I remember one night in Jackson, Mississippi, Hank Ballard and the Midnighters didn't show up, so we went on, and did their act. Then we did "Please, Please, Please" and it caused such an uproar it was like a new cloud had come into town so we just said 'We've got an announcement to make!' and started handing out pictures of ourselves. We were the Flames from there on in."

In 1958, and ten singles later, they had an R & B hit with another pleading ballad, "Try Me." After this effort, the Flames had a number of forgettable R & B singles on the King label.

James Brown always had an uncanny intuition about the "shape" of his songs. His best records are the ones he arranges and produces himself. Without that main ingredient, the James Brown sound with its supertight precision and quirky mix of instrumental patterns, his songs would be little more than repetitive riffs with jive jingles. He has an instinctive *feel* for when a song is "ripe." He usually tries songs out on the road and if people move to it, he'll get into the studio the same night and record it. Most of his hits have been recorded in one take to capture the raw edge of a sound, which gives his singles their spontaneity and direct voltage. He knows the sound he wants and has an uncanny intuition for assembling musicians who can get it, like his tenor sax player Maceo Parker and guitarist Jimmy Nolan.

At the beginning James Brown knew something was wrong with the way the Flames records were being made. He wanted to use his crack road band, the JBs, and produce them himself.

When King refused, Brown recorded "Mashed Potatoes" himself, calling the band Kendrick and the Swans. The result was a national hit in 1960 and after this they continued to top the R & B charts with "Think/You've Got The Power" (1960), "Lost Someone," "Night Train" in 1961 and "Prisoner Of Love" (1963).

## 221

### James Brown

Brown was still dissatisfied with the sound of the Flames on record, and moved over to Smash in 1964 where he was given a free hand in getting down the effect he wanted. He made his point. The result, "Out Of Sight," was a radical departure and the turning point for James Brown. Partly due to the interest given to soul music by English groups, the record became a big hit on both the pop and R & B charts and established him as a national figure in rock. Groups like The Who began recording his songs, Mick Jagger mimicked his dancing and his dance records — "I Got You," "Ain't That A Groove," "Ain't It Funky Now," "Hot Pants," "Papa Don't Take No Mess" — became disco staples into the seventies.

To pop audiences James Brown was a *freak* and related to his records as novelty dance songs. They were *so* black they sounded positively surreal to the unknowing white ear. Their trancelike repetition, mesmerizing tchakka-tchakka-tchakka-tchakka-tchakka rhythms and superjive street jargon — derived from hip black street rapping called "the dozens" where phrases are thrown back and forth like rhyming punches — were delivered by Mr. Dynamite as if he were smacking each syllable on the head with a drumstick. Many of his songs are so stream-of-consciousness — "Cold Sweat," "Sex Machine," "I Can't Stand Myself (When You Touch)," "Licking Stick," "Let A Man Come In And Do The Popcorn" — they would be the envy of a Dada poet.

"Out Of Sight" and "Papa's Got A Brand New Bag" (he was back on King with complete artistic control) were to have a revolutionary effect on soul music. JB's innovation was his radical shift of emphasis onto the rhythm section in R & B. While white rock experimented more and more with modulation and melodic sophistication, JB pared down the structure of his songs to complex contrasting rhythmic patterns that alternated and played off each other in a dynamic momentum, creating tension and excitement. "The rhythmic elements," as Bob Palmer pointed out in *Rolling Stone*, "became the song. There were few chord changes, or none at all, but there were plenty of tricky rhythmic interludes and suspensions. . . ."

The components of "Papa's Brand New Bag" were chunky, bass riffs borrowed from latin music, chicken scratch guitars and tight staccato horn bursts, typical of the Memphis Stax-Volt sound. Bob Palmer continues, "But James Brown put those elements together in a way that sounded perfectly natural, for all its newness, and furthur emphasized them by stripping away any elements in his music that might interfere with their impact."

It is ironic that JB's "elaborate counterpoint of pulses" has been condemned as monotonous black bubblegum, since this was the very ingredient used by Sly Stone to make his unprecedented bridge between white rock and funky soul in the late sixties. JB's approach has always been to get down to the basics. A lot of other black singers, notably Ray Charles, were experimenting with combinations of gospel and R & B at the time James Brown wrote "Please, Please, Please," but while Charles transposed gospel into jazz chording, Brown went back to the traditional three-finger chords to mine the mother lode of gospel and use its blocks to build his monolithic sound. His genius is his feel for the square root of funk; the fertility of sound that invests all his records with a physical intensity and sensual presence. On his "cry" ballads he seems so possessed by his passion and involvement that he actually *misses the note*, sliding passed it into a shriek in his frenzy, so that we are moved not only by his desolation but by the inarticulate expression to which it has driven him. This effect often comes close to self-parody, as on "It's A New Day" where he asks "Can I scream now?" and proceeds to do so for 30 seconds.

Beginning with "Money Won't Change You" in 1966, JB began to deliver a series of pocket sermons to his soul brothers — "Don't Be A Dropout," "Say It Loud (I'm Black And I'm Proud)," "I Don't Want Nobody To Give Me Nothin" — like slogans from the Red Book and hammered home with the same relentlessness as Chairman Mao.

Soul Brother Number One has so totally fused himself with black identity that his image on TV can stop a riot; in Africa his fanatic following approaches the reverence of a cargo cult, and in New Jersey his home is being converted into a shrine. An institution, he even talks about himself as his own caretaker: "I'm not JB, I'm me" he says modestly, "I don't want to wear JB because JB is the Main Man. If I could put it on the wall and come back and have a ball I'd wear it all the time. I have no personal life at all. I spend all my time keeping JB together."

His ego is so huge it transcends personal vanity. He is paradoxically selfless, so that even the 50 million records sold, the black Lear Jet "Sex Machine" he travels in, the seven pounds of sweat he loses at every performance, his 20 cars (not to mention the empire of quick food franchises, Black & Brown trading stamps, his network of radio stations) become symbols of black achievement and self-determination.

As direct and even blatant as he seems to be, JB is a mass of apparent contradictions — a multi-millionaire who professes "Money Won't Change You," a superjive conservative whose ambivalent language is epitomized by the word *"Superbad"* (it can also mean super *bad)* — but these inconsistencies all dissolve in the exultation and submission of his *act,* the ectoplasmic current that alternates between him and his audience. "He is not singing about black life, he *is* black life," Mel Watkins wrote in *Amistad,* ". . . which disdains abstract values and accepts the contradictions of reality (the immediate), it is an act without consequence in terms of personal evaluation. It simply is. If it works it is accepted; as JB would say, 'If it's all night, it's all right.' "

# ARETHA FRANKLIN

IN 1972 WHEN ARETHA FRANKLIN RECORD-ed *Amazing Grace,* her first gospel album in 14 years, at the New Missionary Baptist Church in Chicago, it was significant on two counts: it was a homecoming and reunion with the Reverend James Cleveland, who had taught Aretha how to play the chunky chords with their weird time signature that she uses so provocatively on her songs, and it was the fusion of gospel with its commercial child, soul. As far back as the early forties black musicians like Roy Brown had been mining their gospel roots for a commercial sound that gradually became *the* dominant black sound. Ray Charles, Little Richard, Sam Cooke, James Brown, all in different ways, used gospel chords and

harmonies to create the soul sound, substituting "baby" for "Lord," making the pentecostal "put your hands together" into the soul clap; but Aretha was *of* the church, and the first to be "sanctioned" as the messenger of the spirit, bringing the word to the people.

Even in Aretha's most earthy songs she doesn't so much secularize gospel as sanctify personal values, and unite the community of her audience with shared, mutual experiences. Even in her hymn to the bedroom, "Dr. Feelgood," Aretha is exalting love not debasing the music of the church, but "testifying" in the same way church and preacher in Baptist and sanctified churches pass the "soul" around until it gathers momentum from the collective energy. In the mid-sixties, when blacks were becoming aware of their identity and culture, the dynamics of gospel with its wordless moans, hums and shrieks — "the shorthand of the spirit" — became a powerful binding social force for a new attitude.

"If you want to know the truth," says the Reverend Cleveland, "Aretha never left the church," and Aretha adds, "The break (into commercial music) didn't matter because I carry the faith with me."

A second-generation gospel child, Aretha grew up amongst the giants of gospel — Mahalia Jackson, the greatest gospel singer of all time, who became her surrogate mother after Aretha's own mother left the family when she was six; Sam Cooke, when he was with the Soul Stirrers, Marion Williams and Alex Bradford were all friends of the family; and Clara Ward, whose singing of "Peace In The Valley" at a relative's funeral so moved the young Aretha that she said, "I'm gonna make a record and tell Jesus I cannot bear those burdens alone."

The robe of gospel fell naturally on Aretha. Her father, the Reverend C. L. Cleveland, was a star in his own right with some 70 albums of sermons on Chess. By the time she was eight, she was singing in his New Bethel Baptist Choir, and at fourteen she was a featured performer on his gospel caravan, driving hundreds of miles a day on "maypop" tires to often empty churches.

In her teens, she briefly formed a gospel duet with her older sister Erma (who wrote "Piece Of My Heart"), and when it dissolved made an album for Chess's Checker label, *The Gospel Sound of Aretha Franklin* at sixteen. A family friend and jazz bass player, Major "Mule" Holly, persuaded her to try to do what Sam Cooke had done with the gospel sound, and in 1960 on the basis of a demo she got a contract with Columbia records.

John Hammond, Sr., then head of A & R at Columbia, said he hadn't heard a voice like hers in twenty years, and at first guided her in the direction of the classic jazz/blues singers Bessie Smith and Billie Holiday. She had a minor success with "You Made Me Love You" and a lot of critical acclaim, but when her

records failed to sell, she was handed over to Mitch Miller and she found herself churning out torch ballads and standard Streisand/Sinatra "covers."

The early material on Columbia with the Ray Bryant Trio (reissued on *In The Beginning*) is not *bad*, but sounds ineffectual in comparison with what Atlantic's vice president Jerry Wexler did with her when he picked up her contract in 1967. "I took her to the church," Wexler says, "sat her down at the piano and let her be herself. There's only a few geniuses around, you know, like Ray Charles, who can come down to the studio and lay down a song and everything's implicit. The musicians just color it in." This is the way basically all the early Aretha albums were made on Atlantic. The lead vocal and rhythm would be laid down with Aretha on piano and a small group of studio musicians from the Stax/Volt rhythm section, later vocal backgrounds would be added and finally the horns and strings. Essentially, Wexler, using techniques he had evolved while working with Ray Charles, reconstituted the original gospel situation in the studio, playing off the roughness of Aretha's voice against King Curtis arrangements and backgrounds.

Wexler chose the legendary Ronnie Shannon tune "I Never Loved A Man The Way I Love You" as the first song for Aretha to record and took her down to the Fame recording studios in Muscle Shoals, Alabama. The effect of Aretha backed by a small driving combo (the equivalent of a holiness band) was devastating; her voice, here somewhat reminiscent of Mavis Staples, took on its full, booming range with its whining incomprehension of why things don't

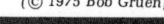

(© 1975 Bob Gruen)

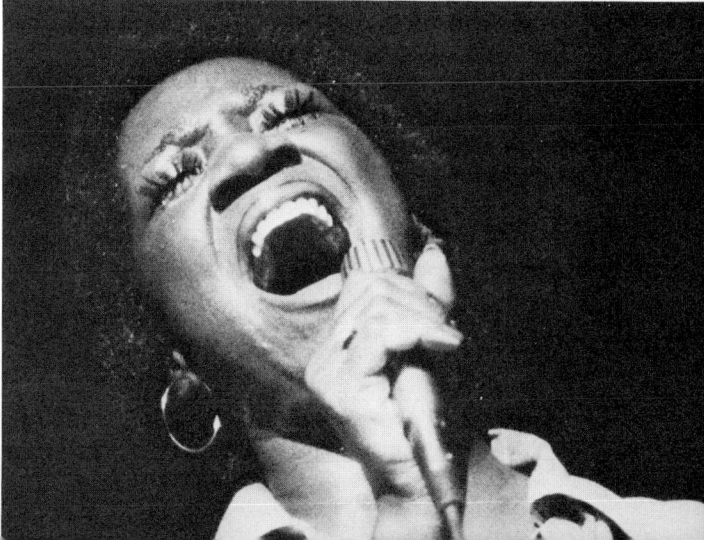

turn out better than they do, and made her an instant star. More million-selling singles followed including the classic, ''Respect.'' She got down with her sound even more on her second album using Wilson Pickett's back-up band on numbers like ''Satisfaction'' and ''Natural Woman.''

Lacking a consistent song-writing team and a permanent band on her album, the songs began to sound repetitious and she abandoned the Wexler formula for excursions into jazz, blues, big band, and MOR classics like ''Bridge Over Troubled Water.''

If Aretha became a symbol of black pride and womanhood to the black community, she *personified* soul to white audiences. Black women, less threatening to white audiences, have always been the first to introduce new black musical styles. With coifed hair and flowing gowns, Aretha was the dignified, majestic Queen of Soul, but what Lena Horne said, ''Inside every woman there's an Aretha Franklin screaming to get out,'' could be applied to Aretha herself. Under the weight of all these

symbols was still the shy, sensitive, somewhat immature and withdrawn girl who had made her nightclub debut at the Trade Winds Club in Chicago on the same bill as Buddy Hackett. Divorced from the anonymous choir of the gospel environment, she felt painfully exposed, ''I sang to the floor most of the time,'' she said.

After her huge success, she retired to a life of seclusion for several years then re-emerged in 1971 with an afro, a slinky new look and an album to match (*Brand New Me*), and began actively supporting black causes — putting up bail for Angela Davis, for one.

While vividly projecting personal pains and problems, Aretha's records have a certain surface anonymity (which derives in part from the gospel/community background) and often her moans and shrieks seem to conceal the singer as much as they release the listener. Each song is a message to the world, emotionally coded, and under the smouldering eroticism, layers of funk and shimmering harmonies is a restless, seeking spirit that pervades everything she sings.

# IKE AND TINA TURNER

IKE AND THE RHYTHM KINGS HAVE REVVED up the audiences as the Ikettes in micro-miniskirts charge across the stage, whipping their hair across their faces in sleek waves. They introduce tantalizing Tina Turner, sidesteppin', shakin', sparklin' and pouring pure sexuality on every movement of her lithe lean body barely clothed in sequined rags. She is the hallucinated superwoman of R & B and rock, the overamping vamp of the blues, the Devil with the Red Dress On, Brown Sugar, Honky Tonk Woman and Foxy Lady incarnate. From her first appearance on stage, gnawing at the air ''like a lioness in heat,'' this erotic extravaganza progressively accelerates until it reaches its climax in ''I've Been Loving You Too Long'' with Tina caressing the tip of the microphone with her two fingers, nibbling at it

explicitly and culminating in the by now voyeuristic conclusion — ''What you see is what you get.''

This amazing act got its first massive exposure during the Stones' 1969 tour, but the Ike and Tina Turner Revue had been one of the gutsiest, raunchiest and blusiest shows on the chitlin' circuit for almost ten years. Ike met Tina in the mid-fifties at a St. Louis nightclub where he was playing.

He was already a local celebrity with a vast history of playing and recording blues. He began professionally at the age of eleven as a piano player, backing Robert Nighthawk. While still in high school he formed his own band, the Rhythm Kings, and they had a minor hit with a version of ''Rocket 88.'' In the fifties he backed a number of blues giants like Howlin' Wolf and

### Ike and Tina Turner

John Lee Hooker on piano and worked as a scout for RPM and Kent, with B. B. King among the talent he discovered. Ike himself did some recording under the name J. Taub and wrote blues songs for Kent, including B. B. King's classic "Sweet Little Angel."

Tina's only experience till then had been singing at the Baptist Church in her hometown of Brownsville, Tennessee, but when Ike handed her the microphone one night, she jumped right into the act. They started recording together, and during 1957 they did "Do You Mean It" and "You Made My Blood Run Cold" for Federal. The next year they were married.

Their first hit happened accidentally in 1960 with "A Fool In Love." Ike had written the song for Art Lassiter and it was only when Art failed to show up for the recording session that Ike reluctantly let Tina try it. It sold over a million copies. They had a few more hits over the next couple of years — "I Idolize You" and a Mickey and Sylvia-ish "It's Gonna Work Out Fine," written and produced by Ike. In 1963 they began hopping from label to label (Atlantic, Pompeii, Warner Brothers, Loma) trying to establish themselves with another hit.

When the Revue formed, Ike switched from piano to guitar, becoming a polished and terse player, filling in the spaces between Tina's moans and shouts. In 1966 they cut what is considered by many to be the best rock record ever made, "River Deep, Mountain High."

Using the wall-of-sound production technique he had perfected with the Righteous Brothers, producer Phil Spector created a boggling density of massed orchestral effects, so infinitely complex in texture that it seems impossible for one piece of vinyl to contain it all. Yet it builds with dizzying momentum that matches Tina's abandoned vocals and the mutual crescendos soar with ethereal power. Though it made it to number two in England, "River Deep, Mountain High" did not become a hit in this country. A host of reasons have been advanced — that it was too pop for R & B stations and too soulful for pop radio. Others suggest that deejays resented Spector's sonic megalomania, which his postscript to this Wagnerian epic seems to confirm: "I was just

(A & M Records)

Tina Turner

(© 1976 Bob Gruen)

saying goodbye and I wanted to go crazy for four minutes on wax."

Since the Stones' tour they have had a number of big hits on the Liberty label with funky versions of X-rated rock songs, like "Honky Tonk Woman," "Proud Mary" and "Come Together," but coping with the problem of how to project their dynamic act and Tina's sex-charged presence onto vinyl has been Ike's principle project since the Revue was formed. Even their live albums fail to capture the raw excitement of their stage act. Where Tina prowls and growls on stage, she only purrs on records.

On stage Tina seems like the ringmaster of the Ike and Tina Turner Revue with the get-it-on soul grease sass ("If you can't stand the heat get out of the kitchen"), but it's Ike who runs the show. There is something of a gorgeous Frankenstein creation about her thrashing, convulsive contortions as if driven by Ike's electric guitar, but even her beautifully awkward crablike dance step is, in fact, imitated from Ike (who is actually bow-legged). Her name was chosen for her by Ike (her maiden name was Annie Mae Bullock). Perhaps the reason she so successfully fills the fantasies of her audience is because she is Ike's fantasy woman materialized on stage; as she says, "My whole thing is the fact that I am like to Ike — I'm going to use the word 'doll' — that you sort of mold. In other words he put me through a lot of changes; my whole thing is Ike's ideas."

# WILSON PICKETT

FLASHING ACROSS THE STAGE IN A PURPLE Edwardian jacket lined in Sunkist orange, ultrawide collars to the shoulders, lilac frills and ruffles bursting out of his sweat-soaked body-suit like satin flames, the Wicket Pickett, "Mr. Magic Man" of the Midnight Hour, spreads his sex and soul sauce around like a voodoo pimp and minister of macho. Aggressive, assertive, superconfident and with enough jive to keep the "man and a half" alive, Wilson Pickett, with his relentless synchronized rhythm and super-sex-machine arrogance, is the epitome of the hard driving, signifying soul singer.

Wilson Pickett came up with Sam and Dave, Arthur Conley, Otis Redding and Aretha Franklin in the mid-sixties as soul and R & B began to be absorbed into pop music. He was born in Prattville, Alabama, in 1941, the same year as Otis Redding, but developed a harsher city soul sound closer in delivery to James Brown and less bluesy than Otis.

He began singing gospel in his teens with a Detroit group called the Violinaires. Willie Scorefield, a member of one of motor city's more popular R & B vocal groups, was impressed with his dramatic gospel "cry" style, molded after the Reverend Julius Cheeks of the Sensational Nightingales, and asked Pickett to join his group as lead singer in 1959. His frantic, pleading vocals were especially effective in the context of the mellow, low-keyed harmonizing of the Falcons and got the group its first hit written by Pickett, "I Found A Love," in 1962. A year later he was recording as a solo artist on Lloyd Price's LL label. "If You Need Me," which he also wrote, was successfully covered by Solomon Burke, and brought him to the attention of Jerry Wexler, a producer for Atlantic Records, Burke's label. At the time Atlantic was one of the leading soul companies, distributing artists like Otis Redding, Joe Tex and Sam and Dave, and in 1964 Pickett signed with them and began the most successful period of his career. After a couple of moderately successful soul hits, "For Better Or Worse" and "I'm Gonna Cry," Jerry Wexler suggested recording with a rhythm section who had backed Otis and Sam and Dave and other Stax-Volt artists.

Out of this session came his monster hit, "In The Midnight Hour." This was one of the

first marriages in soul music between people from different parts of the country. Pickett was a New York based soul singer who'd developed his style in Detroit, and his collaborator and arranger, Steve Cropper, was the lead guitarist with Booker T and the MG's who were from Memphis. Wilson came to the session with a basic choppy bass riff, typical of urban R & B and a gospel refrain, "Yeah, wait for the midnight hour!" which he used in his shows at the Apollo. On this Cropper overlaid the basic Stax afterbeat rhythm, more "country" in flavor, and they came up with a delayed 2/4 beat. When the producer Wexler suggested synchronizing the whole thing to "the jerk," a current dance craze, they hit upon the distinctive sound that characterized most of Pickett's great hits, "Land Of A Thousand Dances," "Funky Broadway," "Mustang Sally," "634 5789" and "Don't Fight It."

Part of the reason for the mass pop acceptance of soul music in the mid-sixties came from an interest in singers who had inspired English invasion groups — the Stones had recorded Pickett's "If You Need Me" on their second album, *12 x 5* — but as rock

gravitated more towards psychedelic sounds in the late sixties, interest in R & B waned, and soul, which derived its excitement from the spontaneity of gospel, further diluted its impact by relying more and more on formula arrangements and "covers" of white rock hits and became as contrived as any other form of pop music. Pickett's cover versions of "Hey Jude" and the bubblegum "Sugar Sugar," however, managed to transcend this banal situation by their sheer emotional force and the relentless interplay between his drums, sax and his raucous vocals. Though close in attitude and sound, Pickett has always been smoother, cooler and more laid back than his only contender for the soul heavyweight title, James Brown, and in 1970 he began to work with Philadelphia's Gamble and Huff on a more sophisticated, orchestrated sound that would mesh with his own particular blend of hard-driving yet supercool sound and attitude, producing two great singles, "Don't Let The Green Grass Fool You" and "Get Me Back On Engine Number 9," with its incredible psychedelic guitar solo. Since his move to RCA in 1973 his career, like those of a number of other "tuff soul" singers, has leveled off, due to lack of great material and arrangements and a prevailing taste for creamy vocal groups.

The essence of Pickett's style, as in most gospel singing, is the contrast between Pickett shrieking his "message" against the sympathetic environment of background singers or its equivalent, the horn section. Most of his songs are structured around simple repeated phrases that rarely develop beyond the title. "I Found A Love" has a total of three different phrases, while "Funky Broadway" describes everything — dances, crowds, women, nightclubs as funky, broadway or both. It is the directness, the unrefined funk of his songs that communicate the "feel" of his music and its essential sexuality. Wilson Pickett's commitment to an attitude and unrelenting style gives him the power to deliver his "up" songs with such power and conviction. Arrogance is an essential part of his persona, as he says, "The reason I'm still big today is that like Mohammed Ali, there's nobody out there in my class."

# CURTIS MAYFIELD

THE MESSAGE SONG, INSPIRATIONAL AND secular, has long been an important facet of black music. Gently chiding, thoughtful and understanding, there is no better spokesman of its virtues than Curtis Mayfield, a slight, bespectacled figure who sings his parables of optimistic hope in a whispered falsetto, advising rather than calling to task. Rejecting anger and bitterness, he offers the possibilities of pride and self-fulfillment within the everyday currents of life, a potential grasped by belief in one's own capabilities, protest divided by the hallelujah chorus of "Keep On Pushin'."

He calls them songs of faith. "I used to write church songs, too. I used to write gospel and sing in a gospel group, and actually the only difference later was that instead of putting the word 'God' in it, I would just leave that open for the individual. It makes me feel that there is truly something to contribute, other than just being a singer. That's the way I write — through things I observe, through people around me. I'm not singing against anything, I'm only singing happenings, the actual reality of what's going on around us."

In 1956, the reality for fourteen-year-old Curtis was Chicago's north side. He'd known the more mature Jerry Butler from a small gospel combination, the Modern Jubilaires, while he himself sang with a group called the Alphatones further over on the west side. Butler had begun working with the stricter R & B Roosters, however, whose three-man nucleus (the Brooks brothers, Arthur and Richard, and Sam Gooden) had been transplanted from Chattanooga, Tennessee. When Curtis found the commutation between north and west too difficult, he joined the Roosters as their fifth member.

The Roosters became the Impressions, and after "rehearsals, back and forth, auditioning with record companies, sitting in their lobbies all day," it was ironic that their first hit record split the quintet apart, at least temporarily. The 1958 "For Your Precious Love" remains one of the most beautiful delineations of love and fealty extant, Butler's robust voice positioned

against the enshrined harmonies of the Impressions in a spare, gliding arrangement. Unfortunately, their record company (Vee-Jay) credited the song to Jerry Butler and the Impressions, which Curtis says "created hard feelings among fellas that were all striving equally and trying to make it." Butler gravitated to a solo career, and the Impressions returned to Chicago.

Curtis went to work as Butler's guitar player, co-writing "He Will Break Your Heart" as part of a two-year payment of dues. When he'd saved enough money to rejuvenate the Impressions, he brought a fourth Rooster, Fred Cash, from Chattanooga, and recorded "Gypsy Woman" in 1961. It set the tone for much of Mayfield's early work, described by Johnny Copasetic as ". . . allegory . . . the appearance of archetypal figures, acting out a small, story-like episode." The dual themes of the wisdom of age coupled with loss of innocence became increasingly prominent as Curtis developed a lyrical and emotional stance toward his music.

The Brooks brothers were gone by 1963, and

*(Collection Richard and Lisa Robinson)*

the Impressions prospered as a trio. Their blend of R & B and gospel was enhanced through such hits as "Amen," "People Get Ready," "I'm So Proud" and the later, more socially relevant, "Mighty Mighty" and "Choice Of Colors." "I don't take credit for everything I write," Curtis would say. "I only look upon my writings as interpretations of how people — how the majority around me — feel. I only take credit for being able to put what they think into lyric form."

It was in the same spirit that he amicably broke away from the Impressions in 1970, forming his own Curtom Record Company (with manager Eddie Thomas) and embarking on a solo career. "This is just another way of being able to open our scope and take in others who are just as creative and give them a guideline as to where they can go. I think this is very important for black people simply because it tends to help to make you independent, an individual, and it is such a great inspiring thing. You can show people, well look, I can do it too."

He did it, too. With the movie score from *Superfly*, issued in 1972, Curtis was able to fully amplify the beauty, the anguish, the desperate courage of the ghetto experience. "Freddie's Dead" cut away the gloss of drug addiction to provide a powerful human warning; the title track pinpointed the sagging romanticism of black exploitation. "You have to understand that half of every big city is the ghetto. I make good money after fifteen years, and the place where we live in Chicago is very nice, but it's still the only place we can live, so it's still the ghetto."

For Curtis Mayfield, as for the millions his words have touched, there is no thought of relinquishing the struggle. "We're A Winner," he wrote in one of his best known songs,

*. . . and never let anybody say*
*Boy you can't make it cause*
*a feeble mind is in your way*
*No more tears do we cry*
*And we have finally*
*dried our eyes*
*And we're movin' on up*

*Lord have mercy*
*we're movin' on up. . . .*\*

\*Copyright © by Curtom Records.

# JERRY BUTLER

AS MUCH AN INDUSTRY AS AN ART, ROCK music is dependent on a host of intermediaries between the artist and his audience in the making of a hit record: managers, deejays, producers, record company A & R men, distributors and publicists who take the three minutes of inspiration and package, promote and air it. Without any one of these links a hit is almost impossible. Jerry Butler who has had some four separate careers, describes this symbiotic relationship in his typical down-to-earth fashion: "I look at it this way, a man and a woman are in love but they still have to get the other things together that make their life *work*. To me, my life is a love, the other parts are the business of keeping it alive." Butler admits that in this kind of liaison a little prostitution creeps in here and there (like his 1962 hit "Moon River") but the most successful phase of his career came about as a result of a collaboration between different elements of the music business which produced a string of hits with "Lost," "Never Gonna Give You Up," "Only The Strong Survive" and "Moody Woman" which won him number one position in *Billboard's* poll of male vocalists in 1969.

When Jerry Butler began working with producers Kenny Gamble and Leon Huff, who pioneered the "Philadelphia Sound" in the late sixties, he was a fading soul singer, playing in sleezy clubs on Philadelphia's Southside. Gamble and Huff were the creative catalysts for

the resurrection of Jerry Butler (he had already gone through two careers). Their incomparable technical control gave Jerry's voice something to work against and their microscopically detailed productions could contain his versatile singing style, but without the heavy exposure over WDAS-AM from two Philadelphia deejays, Jimmy Bishop and Joe "Butterball" Tamboura, who had a corner on Philly's soul music, the new Jerry Butler might never have been heard. They helped popularize this new cool sound in soul, while Gamble and Huff had found a new context for Jerry Butler's voice.

Jerry began singing with the Northern Jubilee Gospel Singers at the age of twelve touring with their Travelling Soul Spirit Church. Three years later he turned to gospel singing professionally to support his family, when his father died. After a brief attempt to become a chef, he was drawn back to music in his late teens, forming his first R & B group, The T Quails. Subsequently he formed another R & B group, the Roosters, and when Curtis Mayfield (whose grandmother was the pastor of the Travelling Church) split from *his* group, the Alphatones, they formed the Impressions.

The smooth creamy quality of the Philadelphia sound, "not as bluesy as Stax, not as pop as Motown," had its roots in Chicago with singers like the Impressions, Gene Chandler and Billy Stewart. Jerry Butler's career with the Impressions, for whom he wrote and sang lead on their first hit, in 1957, "For Your Precious Love," belongs to the history of the R & B vocal groups of the late fifties. But it was the restrained harmonies of those R & B groups, muted instrumentation and emotionally controlled vocals, that eventually became the basis for Gamble's and Huff's cool productions.

When Jerry left the Impressions in 1958, he remained with VeeJay records as a solo, and after the Impressions broke up, he and Mayfield began writing together, producing his first hit on his own, "He Will Break Your Heart," in 1960. With Mayfield, Butler formed Curtom, the only black publishing company outside of Sam Cooke's, and continued to have minor hits up till 1962. In 1964 he teamed up with Betty Everett for a couple of successful duos ("Let It Be Me" and "Smile") where she said her thing, he said his thing, but by 1966 VeeJay had gone into bankruptcy and as a result, Jerry began to slip into the obscurity from which he was rescued by Gamble and Huff.

One of Jerry's early occupations had been as ice sculptor and this possibly suggested the supercool persona of *The Iceman* which he developed while working with Gamble and Huff; his laid back, no sweat sublety and cold control drove his audiences into a frenzy. But Jerry's style of singing has always had this relaxed quality which borders on a sort of conversational gospel, and it was the tension of

Gamble and Huff's tight productions that created the ideal context for his loose style. When he left Gamble and Huff in 1970, he began working on a looser, more community type of sound, using the collective talents of his Chicago workshop, but his sound lost definition, and his subsequent albums seem so crammed with musical ideas that they lacked the necessary consistency.

Jerry Butler's image has never been quite as focused as other soul singers of his stature, and perhaps because of that he has always wanted to remain in the gospel context as part of a group. His music is an acquired taste, and his range of material, from the funky "Power Of Love" to Vegasy, Latin Casino type material like "Moon River" to the gentle insistence of his mankind-get-it-together songs like "Stop Steppin' On My Dreams," makes it hard to identify him with any specific sound. His

interpretations transcend even the most banal MOR standards, and he comes off best on his own songs — he is a sensitive songwriter whose lyrics are always direct (he co-authored "I've Been Loving You Too Long" with Otis Redding).

A principal innovation in the Gamble and Huff productions was the spectacular use of stereo effects on soul records, creating an enveloping mood that still maintained great clarity. By combining the lush texture of orchestral effects with R & B they created a "rainbow effect" out of which the emotional sincerity of Jerry's voice projected vividly. Because of his distinct vocal personality, the backgrounds set his voice in relief, but unlike groups using similar techniques (The Dells, for example) his plaintively sweet vocals, urging you on like some cool pentecostal preacher, never melted into the arrangements.

# SLY AND THE FAMILY STONE

JIMI HENDRIX WAS THE FIRST BLACK TO PLAY acid rock, but he remained a black musician playing to white audiences; he did not get played on soul stations. When Sly and the Family Stone's first album *A Whole New Thing* appeared in 1967 it was such a radically new sound that initially neither soul nor white rock audiences knew quite how to react to it.

Sly's sound was the first workable fusion of soul music and psychedelic rock that didn't sacrifice any of the flash or funk of a soul band. His *new thing* was a music that in its very structure seemed to express change. The songs came in a series of flashing sound images with fast shifts in range from soprano to Larry Graham's basso voice (a relic from groups like the Dominoes). The melody was split up between the vocals and a spectrum of instrumental sounds, and in turn Sly's electric piano, wah-wah guitar and Cynthia Robinson's hot-lips trumpet traded off riffs. The lead vocal

was often passed between three different members of the group, and the dynamics — building tension and breaking off abruptly — came in staggered thrusts that seemed all the more dramatic because of the fast dance tempo. All these transitions were solidly held together by Larry Graham's funky fender bass.

"I was a radio announcer in California for a couple of years. I was into everyone's records, I'd play Dylan, Hendrix, James Brown back to back, so I didn't get stuck in any one groove," says Sly, suggesting how he came up with his eclectic sound. His sureness in combining these disparate musical fragments comes from a lifetime of intimate involvement with music, starting at the age of four when he recorded "On The Battlefield For My Lord" with the family gospel group, the Stewart Four (his given name is Sylvester Stewart). In his senior year in high school at Vallejo, California, Sly had a local hit, "Yellow River," with a group called the

Viscanes. After studying music composition at Vallejo Junior College, he worked as a producer for now defunct Autumn Records, wrote "The Swim" and "Mojo Man," and arranged for local groups like Bobby Freeman and the Beau Brummels.

Sly felt producing was too anonymous and after three months at radio announcing school he landed a job at KSOL, later moving to KDIA. Although he became a very popular west coast deejay, he *wanted to do his thing*," and he put together a group called the Stoners with an old high-school friend, Cynthia Robinson. As Sly became more ambitious and demanding about the music he wanted to put out, he and Cynthia started looking around for a "family" that they could build around his sound. Two of the members, Freddie and Rosie, were actually from Sly's own family, Larry Graham was Cynthia's cousin and the two other members, Greg Errico and Jerry Martini, were also related.

Sly's music was the ideal ingredient for newly established FM rock radio, and beginning with "Dance To The Music" from the second album, *Life*, Sly and the Family Stone's singles like "I Want To Take You Higher," "Sing A Simple Song," "Everyday People," "Everybody Is A Star" and "Stand" became standards. *Life* was easily the most radical soul album ever to be released. Not only did it have a revolutionary effect on music, its chants of communion came at a time of despair and racial friction. Many of his songs, like "Stand," "Everybody is a Star," "You Can Make It If You Try" and "Everyday People," contained gospel type messages of self-awareness, togetherness and tolerance underlined by a joyful and harmonic music that pulsed back and forth between audience and group in a continuum of sound and synergy. These anthems, as in his classic closing number, "Higher," built up momentum in staggering surges, using the simplicity of repeated phrases as musical steps to raise up the audience through solid mesmerizing progressions.

The image of Sly's integrated band also had a unifying visual effect on his audiences. Sly's fantastic outfits and huge cavalier hats sparkled with glitter, his glinty eyes flashing, his hair like an electric symmetrical shrub of a halo, and the whole group, moving on stage not in mechanical Motown but swaying, dancing with their own choreography, looked like a strutting sequined street theatre.

The high point of this visual magnetism is the indelible image of Sly at Woodstock in 1969, arms dripping in fringes raised in victory sign. If Sly had become a symbol musically and personally for everything that had been coming together in the sixties, his own feelings about becoming a culture hero led to a severe crisis of identity. In the following year only one single was released, significantly enough called "Thank You (faletinme bemice elf)." For almost two years nothing was heard from Sly. He developed a chronic habit of turning up two to three hours late for concerts, often he did not appear at all. At a concert in Chicago a riot broke out, aggravated by his failure to appear. At the Apollo, where he had promised a free concert (canceled because of the Chicago riot), he failed to turn up at a couple of shows and at those where he did get it together he appeared so stoned he couldn't remember the number he just played. "Say man, didn't we just play that tune before?" His record company, Epic, began to issue a greatest hits album in place of any new material. At his concerts he stuck mainly with his "oldies" — "That's what people ask us for so we play them," he explained lamely.

In the winter of 1971–72, Sly put out a successful new album *There's a Riot Goin' On*, pushed by the hit single "Family Affair," which cracked open the door to his personal life. The tone of the album is tortured, it is almost a reversal of the optimistic interracial interpersonal uptempo anthems of the late sixties. It seemed as if he wanted to untangle himself from the simple-minded cliche choruses of his earlier songs. The wrenching and pulling away appeared an almost deliberate attempt to alienate his white audience, and justify himself to his "brothers" in songs like "The Skin I'm In."

Sly's history is almost a classic case history of how to blow a career, whether from involvement with drugs, a shrinking away from his own monumental success or racial undercurrents. Despite his conspicuous absence and mediocre output over the last few years, Sly remains the most influential force in rock of the late sixties and early seventies, and he is still the most widely imitated musician in either rock or soul. The elements that Sly successfully synthesized and integrated into the mainstream of pop music — Miles Davis type jazz, the funky percussive bass rhythm of James Brown, Hendrix's cosmic guitar, Lambert, Hendrix and Ross, scat, western movie soundtrack sound, Latin and gospel elements — will take some time to fully absorb. If Sly could not maintain *his* high, he took us there, and like he says, "The nicer the nice, the higher the price."

# AL GREEN

FINDING AN UNDISCOVERED TONE ON THE soul scale in the early seventies was almost like inventing a new color, but Al Green scanned the high gospel spectrum's upper octaves, found that sliver of sound no one else had heard before and slipped into it.

Al Green had been brought up on the ozone of high spiritual sound. At nine he was in a gospel group, the Green Brothers, in which his father sang bass. "I was the terrible little kid who broke up the good old-fashioned family group," says Green about the traumatic split with the Brothers, genetic and soul. At sixteen, he'd decided to go it alone as Al Green and the Creations, belting out Sam Cooke, James Brown and Otis Redding in the El Grotto Club in his home town of Battle Creek, Michigan. In 1967 he got himself a minor hit with "Back Up Train," written by two members of the Creations, and a B side, "I've Got To Stop And Check Myself." It came out on the *Hot Line Music Journal* label distributed by Amy-Mala-Bell. But he had no

*(Globe Photos)*

backup and, as he says, "Everybody hates a one-record act. I was doing the chitlin' circuit, walking tables in a club in Midland, Texas, when Willie Mitchell spotted me." Mitchell was a bandleader and trumpet player from Memphis who had recently been given a free hand as a producer at Hi records after his success with Isaac Hayes. Mitchell suggested Green come to Memphis and "get the feel of the land." After an unfortunate Beatle cover, "I Want To Hold Your Hand," for Hi in 1969, he found his groove on the Temptations' "I Can't Get Next To You." Green's vocal style in fact resembles the falsetto voice in a soul/gospel group, and his main influence has been on groups like the Spinners. He got his first million seller with a song he wrote himself, his "bachelor song," "Tired Of Being Alone." "I began to hear music in my head, I'd never heard music like that before, I *had* to have that record but I realized it was inside me, I'd just have to make it up."

Memphis had a great deal to do with slowing down Al Green's tempo and temperament. When they first met, Mitchell had told Green he'd make him a star in 18 months. "I told him I can't wait that long — and I didn't crack a smile." By the time he'd made 1972 *his* year, he'd given up his slick processed "do," electric blue suits with ruffles and crude nightclub routine for a cool stage delivery that matched his voice. He approaches his songs as he does his audience — obliquely; sort of sidling up to them just as he insinuates himself into a lyric, handling it with delicious care that combines the coolness of Jerry Butler with Otis Redding's vulnerability. "I feel they feel me," he says elliptically about his audiences, and it is this intimacy rather than aggressive soul flash that has caused him to be called Otis' inheritor. While his soft, whispering vocals seem to take off from Redding's last and only hit single "Dock Of The Bay," Green sees their connection only in the sensitivity of the way they both treat slow songs. "To me," Green says, "Otis was like GATTA-GATTA-GATTA, you know, very choppy, which was very effective but a little rougher than me. I'm usually tinkling with the high notes and floating between the chords. . . trying to create some, uh, color."

The people who were early influences were almost all gospel singers, and he especially liked the beautiful pure highs of Claude Jeter of the Swan Silvertones. "The feel of my music is from a gospel taste," he says, "those highs in spirituals are sung to the *Real Man*. It's the highs that create the weightlessness in a song, you're trying to feel for the center, for the soul of a song. In other words we start from *here*, and elevate. . . ." At the end of his songs Green's voice almost disappears. His high sensuous vocals don't so much bend notes as squeeze them gently with a tantalizing slowness, spinning the syllables into as fine a thread as possible until they virtually atomize, trailing off at the edge into nothingness. He compares his voice to "taste," "color," "feel." "I like to *touch* a song, to reach into it and pull out the emotion that is lying just under the surface."

Green and his producer, Willie Mitchell, have refined the Al Green sound with a subtlety and precision that melts one song into another. The tracks, introduced by Charles Hodges caressing organ chords or Green's own acoustic guitar, blend into a single tonal flux: Al Green suites. In the light of his evocative voice everything turns Green, and this is exactly what Al and Willie Mitchell want: for Green's Greenness to permeate every song. It is more of an emblem than, as some have interpreted it, a caricature of his own style. It is the Green Book of Love. "See," he says, "I think of my albums like a book, you open it at the first track and that'll be the opening theme of my album, like on *Love and Happiness* it begins with "I'm Still In Love With You," therefore I hope we can appreciate "Love And Happiness" and dig "What A Wonderful Thing Love Is.""

Green's message is love, and his background in gospel gives him a special ability to transform the songs into personal messages whispered into the inner ear. "Once after a performance," he says happily, "this couple walks up to me, about forty-seven years old, and they're holding hands, smiling and they say, 'You know, we're newlyweds and the reason for us getting married was that song you done, "Let's Stay Together." ' Now, that's what I call getting through!"

# 17

# Highway 61 Revisited

## CREEDENCE CLEARWATER REVIVAL

PSYCHEDELIC MUSIC WAS PEAKING AND rock was undergoing a period of exhaustion in 1968 when Creedence Clearwater Revival arrived out of nowhere with their "lean, clean and bluesy" sound. The most innovative thing about them was that the music they were putting out was over ten years old, but there were no overtones of oldies nostalgia in Creedence's first two singles, Dale Hawkins's "Susie Q" and Screamin' Jay Hawkin's "I Put A Spell On You." With their *revival* sound, they brought the original energy of rock & roll back into rock. Although their sound was derived from early rock & roll, as if it had been scooped out of some time loop, Creedence sound was more a re-creation than mindless reproduction. Like the early Stones, they came across unornamented, stripped down to the essentials and buzzing with vitality. As John Fogerty told a reporter, "I'm not a seventies press agent for the fifties . . . all we did was to sort of clean it up and make it not more traditional, just not so darned irritating."

The sound was so refreshing that Creedence sounded like a newly hatched band, but they had been together as professional musicians for ten years, ever since thirteen-year-old John Fogerty had hand-picked the members from his high school friends in El Cerrito, a suburb of San Francisco. Although the group was first named for John's older brother (Tom Fogerty and the Blue Velvets), John did most of the singing. They were imitating the Ventures and Johnny and the Hurricanes, in matching dinner jackets, continental ties and greased ducktail hairdos. They put out four records on the local Kristy and Orchestra labels, but as Tom said, "The reason we weren't making it was because we were terrible, the ultra white, Mickey Mouse musicians."

Between the Blue Velvets and late 1967, when they became Creedence Clearwater Revival, they had logged some 2,000 hours in the studio, backed a number of local talents (James Powell on "Beverly Angel") and developed their trademark sound, a thick throbbing soul rhythm under Fogerty's simple rockabilly riffs, combined with tough gritty vocals, and lyrics as tasty as Louisiana gumbo.

In March 1964, they approached a San Francisco label, Fantasy (known for its jazz classics, Lenny Bruce recordings and

(Globe Photos/M. Randolf)

unbreakable vinylite discs), with some instrumental demos. Fantasy told them to put some words to them, and changed their name to the Golliwogs. Over the next three years they released a series of singles exploring every music trend around from the first Beatley "Don't Tell Me No Lies" through a series of surf, Anglophilic records, to Sam Cooke-ish numbers. The flip side of the last Golliwogs' single, "Walking On The Water," suggested, with its mystical Bayou punch, the shape of things to come. In 1967 Fantasy was sold to an ardent Golliwog fan, Saul Zentz, and with a new name expressing their intentions, Creedence Clearwater Revival set about to fulfill the Whole Earth Catalog promise of its title. The first break came during the KMPX radio strike in early 1968, when the whole staff moved over to form KSAN. As a result of Creedence support at benefit concerts, the new station began playing the unreleased tape of their first album. Creedence fever caught on quick in the Bay area, and by some stroke of luck, one of the singles, "Susie Q," got picked up on the notorious and powerful Bill Drake top forty radio format. After that the hits just kept on coming: "Proud Mary," "Bad Moon," "Green River," "Down On the Corner," "Fortunate Son," "Travellin' Band," "Up Around The Bend" and "Lookin' Out My Backdoor."

With the release of their fifth album, *Cosmo's Factory*, in the summer of 1970, they summed up all the people who had influenced their sound: Little Richard shrieks, Marvin Gaye soul and Bo Diddley on one side; their own extensions of these sounds on four great originals, "Run Through The Jungle" and "Bad Moon Rising" with their brooding, doomy superstition, the wistful "Who'll Stop The Rain" and the ecstatic "Long As I Can See The Light."

Creedence perfected the singles format at a time when most other "serious" rock groups were issuing only albums. Their successful revival of the single was to have a huge impact on the attitude towards 45's in the seventies, but after three years of turning out great singles and tasty albums built around them, the rigid hand of Fogerty in the studio — *Cosmo's Factory* was so named by Tom in reference to the relentless production line of Creedence's rehearsal schedule — began to tell on their records; they had become over-precise, and their last few singles (with the exception of the whimsical "Looking Out My Back Door") lacked humor and were close to sterility. Fogerty gave the others in the band more say in writing and production, but their sound and the band's unity deteriorated further and in 1972, following a sold out world wide tour and their seventh gold album, *Mardis Gras*, they announced their official breakup. Fogerty went solo with *The Blue Ridge Rangers* (1973), a collection of his C & W favorites on which he played all the instruments.

In the best of the Creedence repertoire, Fogerty seemed to turn out the songs effortlessly, though the lyrics themselves were anything but facile. Beneath an insistent deliciously primitive rhythm and the machine-tooled "rockabilly shud and shimmer" were nightmarish suggestions, ancient, newly unearthed images of the ruminating southern landscape Fogerty loved to fantasize and project.

It was a pure feel for the mother lode of American music that made "Proud Mary" a rock standard, but it was the musical mythical space which he created, picked out of the fabric of hillbilly and rhythm and blues, that produced such melancholy vision as the "rain" songs or the triggering images of "Up Around The Bend."

# LEON RUSSELL

AT HIS XANADU OF FUNK IN DISNEY, Oklahoma, home of Shelter Records, Sheltervision TV, and site of the Rock equivalent of the Sistine Chapel — Jim Franklin's armadillo-decorated swimming pool — Leon Russell holds court like some pope of pop, to an entourage of freaks, supersession musicians, resident Okies and bevies of worshipful maidens. Occasionally he scoots into Tulsa (where he's the second largest taxpayer in town) to soak up some Lone Star beer with the rednecks, or tear apart the ancient Bliss Hotel. All this is captured on film for his celluloid biography, *A Poem Is A Naked Person,* which he commissioned Les Blank to shoot. Yet, in spite of this constant exposure and his flagrant exhibitionism as the ringmaster of rock's most raucous traveling circus, the self-styled master of space and time, remains a remote presence, his eyes perpetually concealed behind shades and his face curtained by streaked hair.

His slow, calculated climb up the rungs of rock could be said to have begun more than thirty years ago when, at the age of three, he began toying with his dad's piano. At fourteen

he ran away from his hometown of Lawton, Oklahoma, to play in Tulsa's tawdry nightspots. Three years later he headed west, and by the time he was in his twenties he was playing on sessions for Sinatra, Jan and Dean, Glen Campbell and the Byrds, and appeared on many of Phil Spector's legendary productions with the Ronnettes and the Righteous Brothers. Despite the nude ads for his *Look Inside The Asylum Choir* with Marc Benno, this embryonic first album for Smash did not make much of an impression. He began to emerge from the anonymity of the studio in 1969 when he was featured on Delaney & Bonnie's first album and Joe Cocker's second. Leon, in fact, master-minded the carnival atmosphere of Cocker's Mad Dogs and Englishmen show where, as Janis aptly put it, he brought "all life onto the stage." For his television debut on NET he duplicated this commune ambiance with a 30-piece band, which included the ravishing Claudia Lennear and Kathi McDonald, mothers nursing babies and a large earth mama baking a pie.

Meanwhile he had recorded his first album

## 238
**Leon Russell**

for Shelter Records (of which he is half owner), a blast of gospel funk and blues on which he was backed by a Who's Who of Rock aristocracy: Eric Clapton, Stevie Winwood, the Stones' own rhythm section Bill Wyman and Charlie Watts, and two Beatles (George and Ringo), to name but a few. To his credit *Leon Russell* does not come off *sounding* like a supersession album, dominated as it is by Leon's idiosyncratic dozing-off style of singing and vamping boogie piano. On songs like "Delta Lady," "Dixie

*(Collection Richard & Lisa Robinson)*

Lullaby" and "Song For You" he used a vein of southern music that had almost disappeared since the fifties, restored the piano as a rock instrument and revived the horn section as integral parts of rock's syntax. His sound is a mix of Ray Charles, Texas funk, R & B, hard rock and ballads with a touch of Dylan (he later played on and produced Dylan's single "Watching The River Flow"). What might seem like creative chaos — every available musical space stuffed with sound and spiced with gumbo gimmicks — had the refreshing effect of a casual late-night goodtime jam. But in spite of the deceptively amateurish production and laid-back atmosphere of his sound, behind it is the meticulous ear of a seasoned L.A. session man.

On stage, this multiphrenic, multi-talented musician (he plays some dozen instruments on his albums) gives the appearance of a carnival barker with his Uncle Sam hat, hooded eyes, and his voice, tinged with religiosity, whipping up instant charisma. On his "tour de funk" rockers like "Youngblood" and "Jumping Jack Flash," he often seems to parody a holy roller, and the ease and mellow arrogance with which he controls his audiences during his extended two-hour sets have led some to compare his stage strategy to that of professional evangelists like Oral Roberts.

Leon Russell's chameleon-like personality seems to come from a desire to be all things to all people: gospel singer, rocker, crooner, country singer *(Hank Wilson's Back)*, jazz interpreter *(Stop All That Jazz)*, and music mogul. His sly albums with their weird visions of Americana in the border zones occasionally reveal the fiercely shy spirit hiding behind this tent-show facade. This comes across poignantly on his most intimate and profound album, *Carney*, where in a series of grotesque and beautiful self-portraits he reveals a deep-rooted ambivalence about his role as a rock star. In "Tight Rope" he is suspended in a tense hope/hate, love/fear relationship with his audience, stranded like a vaudeville vampire between shows on "Manhattan Island Serenade" or on "Magic Mirror" reflecting bitterly on the paradox he presents to a world which only sees him as a distortion of itself.

# THE ALLMAN BROTHERS

THE ALLMAN BROTHERS ROLL THROUGH the night of American music, foot pressed to the floor, following the call of two-lane blacktop as revealed in the glare of their headlights. They slow, perhaps, the road passing no judgment on tragedy and ill fate, but the motion is constant, drawn together by family and ancestral heritage.

In their years as a brother (and sister)hood, the Allman Brothers have suffered more than their share of setbacks. Two of their finest spokesmen, Duane Allman and Berry Oakley, died just as the band was verging on its greatest success, bitterly ironic climaxes to lives spent struggling up each step of the music business

ladder. Yet the Allmans carry on, as they always have, closing ranks and willing themselves to become stronger, filling the void with their own steely determination. Blood remains thicker than water.

The original Brothers, Duane and the younger Gregg, had grown up in Nashville and Daytona, Florida, starting at the very bottom when they formed a youth club band, the Y-Teens. As the Allman Joys, they recorded briefly for Dial Records, and then were discovered in a St. Louis nightclub by William E. McEuen, who took over personal management and their "national fan club." Named the

*(Collection Richard & Lisa Robinson)*

Duane Allman

*(Collection Richard & Lisa Robinson)*

Hourglass, with Paul Hornsby, Mabron McKinney (later Jesse Willard Carr) and drummer Johnny Sandlin, Duane and Gregg were quickly whisked off to Los Angeles and the big time.

Whatever illusions they may have had were rudely shattered not long after arrival. "It wasn't how good you were musically," frowned Sandlin at the memory. "You had to make the scene in the right way."

Gregg minced less words. "They handed us a boxful of demos and said pick out your album."

At that, they didn't do badly. Writers on the first Hourglass release include Goffin-King, Del Shannon, *Riot On Sunset Strip* propagandist Ed Cobb, Deon Jackson, Curtis Mayfield and Jackson Browne. The idea might have been to break in the group in the tradition of Mitch Ryder and the Detroit Wheels, shouting rhythm and blues over a rock rhythm and instrumental backing; unfortunately, the band was never

## The Allman Brothers

given a chance to work out such music for themselves. Gregg's vocals were lost in a swimming lack of artistic control, with Duane reduced to playing choppy fills. Performing seldom, and then only in conspicuous "name" bookings, they had no opportunity to develop stage presence, a condition not helped by the record company's decision to feature Gregg excluding the band.

The Hourglass dissolved after their second album met with as little success as the first, and the Allman brothers returned to the South with Sandlin. "It had gotten to the point where we were beginning to doubt ourselves. We knew we could play, but you couldn't tell that from the recordings." In April of 1968 they cut a few trial demos at Muscle Shoals, Alabama, where Atlantic Records was beginning to build a producing base. Studio owner Rick Hall was impressed with Duane's prowess and invited him to become a regular salaried guitar player. Nicknamed "Skydog" by Wilson Pickett, he stayed to participate in the work of such artists as Aretha Franklin, King Curtis, Pickett himself, and many others. In addition, he made the acquaintance of two members of a local Florida group, bassist Berry Oakley and guitarist Dickie Betts, who led him to the combined drummers' arsenal of Butch Trucks and Jai Johnny Johnson, also Floridians.

In early 1969, the six came together as the Allman Brothers Band. Sandlin continued at Muscle Shoals as a session musician and producer, while the group, with Gregg on keyboards, began recording their first album for Phil Walden's Capricorn label. They were careful to learn from their previous mistakes. Walden was no stranger, having managed Otis Redding, and he was willing to allow the group as much room as they wanted.

They trod gingerly at first, as if unable to believe their good fortune. The Allmans' first album holds its own as a good indication of things to come, blues with a feeling, Duane's slide guitar wrapping itself around Betts' crisp punctuations, flushed by Gregg's sweeping organ and vocals, propelled by a wall-hugging rhythm section that seemed tireless. Their second, *Idlewild South*, was equally proficient,

but it was soon apparent that the Allmans were outdistancing themselves in live performance, cracking the studio shells of their recordings to unfold long interplays of melody and beat, daring each to go the other one better.

It drove audiences crazy. At any moment, the Allmans might take off from a song, solos improvised as a unit rather than individually, the truest test of a working band. Cream had foundered on the possibilities of improvisation; the Grateful Dead had raised it to a high art form where the silences meant as much as any given note. The Allmans simply plowed straight ahead, unrelenting, not content to stop until both themselves and the audience were dizzy from exhaustion.

Recognizing they could never capture this excitement in the confines of a studio, the Allman Brothers recorded a live album at New York City's Fillmore East in early 1971. Warming up with "Statesboro Blues" and "Stormy Monday," they took "You Don't Love Me," "In Memory Of Elizabeth Reed" and twenty-two minutes of "Whipping Post" to prove they were the best live band in the country. When the Fillmore East closed later that year (in June), they measured their appreciation by playing for over seven hours, until dawn, on the next-to-final night. The last evening was reserved for an industry party, they said, and they wanted to salute their fans.

For Duane, it was to be a last hurrah. On October 29, he swerved on his motorcycle to avoid a truck and was trapped in the resultant skid. He died four hours later in the Macon, Georgia, Medical Center. One of the world's great guitarists, he had been the focal point of the Allmans, a musician's musician, able to draw the best out of those with whom he played. Eric Clapton, especially, seemed to find in Duane an equal, and their collaboration for Derek and the Dominos' *Layla* stands as the finest moment for each. The band — in the midst of recording *Eat A Peach* — took time off to mourn the loss, and then decided Duane's memory would be better served by remaining together. There was no thought of replacing him.

Betts shouldered the load gracefully as they went back on the road. *Eat A Peach* was a triumph combining live (with Duane) and newer studio tracks, and the public exhibited loyalty and faith in the new combination. Chuck Leavall was brought in on piano, and the Allmans began looking upward again. Throughout the South, their example was being taken as gospel, a boogie-blitzed swarm of bands leaping out of the roadhouse and bar circuit in a distinct style of breeding aimed at shaking believers off their money-makers and into the aisles. Wet Willie, Lynyrd Skynyrd, Black Oak Arkansas — all owed a debt of gratitude to the Allmans. On a Saturday afternoon in November 1972, Berry Oakley drove his bike into the back of a Macon city bus. It was a virtual replay of Duane's accident, but he left the scene claiming he felt all right. Two hours later, another heart had been cut from the Allman Brothers.

You play because it's all you can do. In July 1973, the Allman Brothers, with Lamar Williams on bass and with the able assistance of the Grateful Dead and the Band, bore witness to over half a million people at Watkins Glen's grand prix raceway. *Brothers and Sisters* and its hit single, "Ramblin' Man," brought Betts' talents to the fore even as it substantiated Gregg's assured role as bearer of the family name. There have been solo albums from each, without the duress usually encountered in such flights. Having sustained their losses, the Allmans know full well the strength of endurance.

# VAN MORRISON

ON THE WALL OF HIS NORTHERN CALIFORNIA home, a note announces to friends and visitors that "Van Morrison the person only sometimes has anything to do with Van Morrison the name." To which it might be added that the art he has so painfully bled from the Cyprus Avenues of his life has similar slight regard for attachments of celebrity. A Belfast visionary with the guiding motto of "It's too late to stop now!" Morrison admits to no master but his own fiery instincts, the erratics of brilliance and ecstasy combined into one of the most psychically arresting performers of our time.

"I'm not someone who just plugs in and gets it on," he says, and to be sure, the stage has never come easy for Van. Struggling against the mobile weight of his emotions, he can often seem unnerved and high-strung, at the mercy of a volatile moodiness. In previous years, a faulty sound system or an out-of-tune musician would be enough to jar his delicate balance, rendering him unable to come to grips with his deep commitment. Inconsistent, refusing to compromise, he let his frustration overflow into a roar of primal stalemate, knuckles gripped whitely around the microphone stand, a tense and nerve-wracking spectacle to a bewildered audience, and a darting, hastily contrived exit.

Today, such scenes are rare within the pastoral world of Van Morrison. Continual winnowing of his songs and their settings has brought him a measure of peace and satisfaction; left to his own devices, he has experimented broadly in the hope of exorcising his past. What remains is the perceptual reliability of insight, the breadth and expressiveness of his voice, the almost formal elegance he grants both his listeners and his music.

Born in Belfast, Ireland, on August 31, 1945, Van had wanted to be a cowboy — "I loved those Lash LaRue movies and Hopalong Cassidy" — but by the time he was twelve his father's interest in Leadbelly turned his maverick nature toward blues, from John Lee Hooker and Slim Harpo to Hank Williams. It inextricably colored his vocal mannerisms: while he still speaks with a thick Irish accent, his singing is as American as his influences. By the age of sixteen he was playing in Germany with an R & B band called the Monarchs, then

returned to Belfast and a regular engagement at the Maritime Hotel to join Them. The latter were a raw, brutally efficient quintet whose stock in trade was taking traditional blues (Harpo's "Don't Start Crying," Joe Williams' "Baby Please Don't Go") and flogging them mercilessly, like the Animals and the Rolling Stones.

It brought them success in 1965 in England. but their American prominence was based on a Bert Berns' ballad, "Here Comes The Night," Though Van later regarded it as "a producer's trip — he did the arrangement and said, 'sing this way here and that way here' " — it did give

him a base to start writing. Few were prepared to cope with the angry roughhewn sexuality of early Morrison. "Mystic Eyes" talk-songed its way through an eerie tale of graveyard madness and shivering harmonica, spread-eagled by the back-door woman so decisively spelled out in "Gloria."

Van described it as "the good times, the sad times" in "The History Of Them," a single not released until long after the original band had broken up. Management had never been kind to the group, their producers at continual odds with Morrison's need for freedom of expression, and personnel shifted rapidly. In May 1966, Them toured America for the first time. Van's growing mistrust of his handlers and consequent faith in himself prompted a move to his spiritual homeland, and the next year, when Bert Berns asked Van to record for his Bang label, Morrison headed for Boston. "Brown-Eyed Girl" showed that he could make it on his own, a soulful slice of top forty celebrating the pleasures of love but the album that followed, *Blowin' My Mind,* only foretold how far he had yet to go. "T.B. Sheets" blurted lyrics in a seven-minute stream of images, Joycean and splattered, numbing in overall impact.

It was the producer who did it," Morrison told *Rolling Stone's* Greil Marcus without bitterness, "and that record company. They had to cover it with the big electric guitar and the rest. It all came out wrong and they released it without my consent." Berns died in 1968 at about the same time Van's dissatisfaction was becoming manifest, and Morrison signed with Warner Brothers, hoping for an end to internal and external restrictions. *Astral Weeks* gave him that and more, a song cycle in which he once and finally confronted "that mansion on the hill," the repose of dreams and phantasms, a mystery swayed and lightened by jazz-based voicings, smoothing and fulfilling the grainy texture of his voice and lyrics.

Once freed, Morrison could return to the punchy commerciality of a sure musical style. No longer trapped between conception and finished product, *Moondance* combined a mature, confident Van with the simplicity of a finger's snap, the all-out release of "And It Stoned Me," "Crazy Love," "These Dreams Of You." As if to make up for his previous emotional sprawl, *Moondance* tightened him like a drum; again assuaged, the follow-up, *His Band the Street Choir,* eased his touch, spontaneous and playful, the redolent jive of "Domino" set beside "Blue Money."

Each new Van Morrison album has continued to explore his individual terrain, at times improvisatory and scatting, at others restrained and direct. *Tupelo Honey* found him Woodstock-domesticated, "Starting A New Life"; *St. Dominic's Preview* and more recent work have come full-circle, once more within the realm of the mythic ("Jackie Wilson Said") and the poetically untouchable. Live, his stage insecurities completely at rest, Morrison will never do a song the same way twice, whether appearing with a large group (including strings and horns, as on *It's Too Late To Stop Now*) or a more intimate backing quartet. A shake of his head leads to a study in total absorption, man and art as one, speaking the unknown tongue. Into the mystic.

# THE BAND

THE BAND WAS ONCE DESCRIBED AS THE only group who could warm up the crowd for Abraham Lincoln. When they first appeared late in 1968, they were both a musical oddity and a curiosity in the history of rock & roll.

They seemed to stand for the conservative, law-abiding traditional American values of the rural heartland; biblical morality, family life (they had themselves photographed on the inside cover of their first album surrounded by their relatives!), contentment and maturity,

everything in fact that rock in its violent, dissenting, urban teenage fantasy had been trying to escape from in the fifteen years since it began.

Their name, a reaction to the prevailing gimmickry, suggested the organic, unpretentious quality of the music they made; harmonious, countrified in its rich tumbling river textures, egoless to the point where it was difficult to tell who was singing lead, and devoid of the exhibitionism and flashy feedback solos that

*(© David Gahr)*

and had a minor hit with Bo Diddley's "Who Do You Love?" backing Ronnie Hawkins in 1963. They provided Dylan with the best rock backing he ever had, both as a touring band and as a recording group on *Blonde on Blonde* and the *Basement Tapes*. Their fundamental style and repertoire of country songs had an influence on Dylan, especially on his Nashville ventures, while the Band in turn absorbed Dylan's lyrical ambiguity and parabolic imagery.

Following Dylan's motorbike accident in 1966, the Band retired with him to the bucolic atmosphere of Woodstock to write their masterpiece, *Music From Big Pink*, their first album. It was loosely described as "country rock" and the group tried their best to look like good old boys (they had considered calling themselves Crackers, another name for rednecks) but in reality only its themes were country. The music itself drew on a vast storehouse of American folk music rarely touched on by rock — Baptist hymns, Appalachian ballads, cajun tunes, Scott Joplin rags — fitted together with expert craftsmanship and built around a pared-down R & B rhythm core at the heart of which was Levon Helm's funky pumping backbeat. An acute sensibility about the character and timbre of their instruments allowed them to be able to give expert shading to any particular song. The vocals were sung in a plaintive whine reminiscent of Chester in *Gunsmoke*, which gave their sound an authentic hokiness, while Garth Hudson's ethereal organ, floating between Bach flourishes, Messiaen tonalities and Disneyland doodles, added a whimsical inventive element.

As simple and down home as it sounded, the Band was a complex musical entity and depended on teamwork and craftsmanship that took years to develop. They had been together in one form or another since 1959, when Frankie Avalon's "Venus" was at the top of the charts. Each member had had his own group in high school (Richard Manuel & the Revols, Levon and the Jungle Bush Beaters) and had been rigidly disciplined by the wildman of Canadian music, Ronnie Hawkins, who had recruited all of them in their teens. As Ronnie Hawkins and the Hawks they got a rigorous and rough musical

characterized the frenetic climate of the late sixties.

Dylan had set the tone for this sober development, and it was Dylan who had summoned Levon and the Hawks, as they were then known, from relative obscurity to be the back-up band for his Hollywood Bowl concert in the summer of 1965. The Hawks consisted of four Canadians — Robbie Robertson, Richard Manuel, Rick Danko and Garth Hudson — and one Arkansas boy, Levon Helm, from West Helena, hometown of the legendary Sonny Boy Williamson. They played a funky mixture of blues, country and western and old rock & roll, education playing to gun-toting, brawling hillbillies in Zinc, Arkansas, heckling rednecks in Molasses, Texas, and loud-mouthed lumberjacks on the timberline.

This itinerary through the mythic underbelly of America they later incorporated into the fabric of their songs, creating a poetic vision of the classic American landscape and its history, the Frontier West, the apocalyptic South of Faulkner and a Brady daguerrotype of Old Glory.

On their second album, *The Band*, they crystallized this evocation of Americana in songs like "The Night They Drove Old Dixie Down" and "King Harvest Must Surely Come." Their imagery and the music that fit the vision blended so perfectly that they could sing about the Civil War and make it sound *believable.* But it would have been impossible for them to excavate this vein of legend and history indefinitely.

The rural simplicity that the Band affected was a stance as artificial as any other in rock — they were no more "good old boys" or despairing Confederate veterans than David Bowie — and when they began to re-enter the reality of the city on *Stage Fright* and *Cahoots*, specters of alienation, paranoia and despair began to emerge: police, violence, garish sideshows, the extinction of their sacred emblems (the railway, the eagle and the buffalo) and the more personal aggravations of ruthless booking agents, rampant rumors and stagefright

itself. The huddled congregation on the bank of the river in "River Hymn" on *Cahoots* seems in desperate retreat, as they, along with the Band, mourn the loss of ancient values as the river runs its eternal course. The restlessness and anxiety they had unearthed was the voice of the city which had given rise to rock & roll and could not be sedated by bucolic fantasies or a retreat into history.

As if an antidote, their following albums, the "live" *Rock of Ages* and the oldies collection *Moondog Matinee*, seemed to imply a refusal to fall victim to the vicious circle of innovation that has made the lifespan of most rock groups so brief. In a form which is in constant flux, the "timelessness" of the Band is their special paradox. The attitude and their music rests on a delicate balance between the enduring values they had both resurrected and fantasied and the inevitable smugness of their vintage morality.

There is a basic honesty in the Band's use of white musical idioms, but the term they use to describe their sound, "mountain music," refers more to an Appalachian ideal of economy, restraint, tradition and community than any specific music they play. It's a group in which each member takes his turn — there are four lead singers and no stars, and the group itself is the featured instrument. What they have tried to create, as the title of their album *Rock of Ages* implies, is a form of rock which will endure, a *tradition*, like that shared by country music and the blues.

# 18
# Comp. Lit.

## SIMON & GARFUNKEL

LIKE A BRIDGE OVER TROUBLED WATER, the folk-based pop of Paul Simon and Art Garfunkel brooked no obstacles as it crossed boundaries of age and sophistication to become America's most appreciated, listened-to music in the later sixties and early seventies. Collegiate, almost scholarly perfectionists, the pair blended Simon's developed flair for songwriting and supple eclecticism with the crystal clarity of Garfunkel's voice to picture a society in flux — alienated, lonely, detached from its own comforting cultural symbols and humanity.

Simon and Garfunkel clung stoically to a breath of hope in the midst of this rootlessness and self-despair, the possibility of solution within the anguished cry of "Oh my Grace, I got no hiding place." As they grew as artists and performers, the suicidal escapes of "Richard Cory" and "A Most Peculiar Man" transformed into "the fighter still remains" of "The Boxer," they seemed to find in themselves the contained strength to carry on, their eventual solo careers offering no apologies, as each followed his self-stream of being to its logical artistic extension. That they would separate in the effort perhaps attested to the commitment, and to the maturity no less deserved or hard-won because of their lush commercial success.

The team of Simon and Garfunkel had existed as a working partnership long before "The Sounds Of Silence" stunned a waiting America at the end of 1965. Both were born in 1941 and attended P.S. 164 in Queens, where they began working together while serving after-school detention. "Paul always had a weird sense of humor," Art admitted. "One particularly nasty joke he cracked [about the fattest girl in class] got us both sent to detention. Each day after that during music period we had to go to a little room in the tower to serve our time. Paul brought his guitar and we would sing."

This soon grew into occasional side-trips to Manhattan, touring record companies and publishers with minor encouragement. After the usual frustrations, they were cutting a demo of one of Paul's songs, "Hey Schoolgirl," at the tiny Sanders Recording Studio on Seventh Avenue when Sid Prosen of Big Records happened by. It resulted in a medium-sized hit for the newly named Tom and Jerry in late 1957, *Bandstand* prominence, and the stymied ambitions of one-hit wonders.

Still, they were hooked. Even today, Simon's pseudonymous names can be found attached to scores of unknown and unusual

(Don Paulsen)

Paul Simon

(Don Paulsen)

Art Garfunkel

records from the period: Tico and the Triumphs' "Motorcycle," "The Lone Teen Ranger" (as Jerry Landis), as well as a writing-producing relationship with Amy Records (Dottie Daniels, the Fashions, Richie Cordell). He sang on numerous demos, and his earliest work on his own appeared to be strongly influenced by Buddy Holly. Garfunkel similarly recorded under the name of Arty Garr, though again, there were no tangible results.

By the early sixties, Simon's style was changing. Attending Queens College, working as a song-plugger for publishers E. B. Marks, he was taken with the newer wave of folk artists, especially Bob Dylan. As Paul Kane he recorded "He Was My Brother" (about friend Andrew Goodman, one of three slain civil rights workers) for Tribute Records, and then, with

Garfunkel — at the time studying architecture at Columbia University — talked himself into an audition with Tom Wilson of Columbia Records. It provided the acoustic basis for their first album, *Wednesday Morning 3 A.M.*, containing six original Simon tunes and a scattering of Dylan and spiritual songs.

Paul left for England shortly thereafter, where his poetic sensibilities and furrowed awareness fit easily into the growing folk movement. "I start with the knowledge that everything I write will turn and laugh at me," he deprecatingly wrote on the liner notes for the *Paul Simon Songbook*, but he nonetheless gained a strong underground following. Garfunkel came over to join him during semester vacations. In their absence, Wilson decided to take advantage of the folk-rock boom to add electric guitars and drums to one of the more requested cuts from the *Wednesday Morning* album, "The Sounds Of Silence." When Simon and Garfunkel returned to America, it was the number one record in the country.

The song was steeped in existential solitude, caught at its most literal in Guy Peelleart's *Rock Dreams* portrait of Simon and Garfunkel broodingly riding a subway car, the faces about them lost within private reverie, each man an island. Paul both accepted its premise — he had written the song, after all — and recognized its total non-applicability to himself. The years he'd spent on Tin Pan Alley had effectively disbarred him from a messianic role.

" 'The Sounds Of Silence' was written about a year before it was recorded on *Wednesday Morning*," he told Jon Landau in a July 1972 *Rolling Stone* interview. "So that puts it in '62, '63, I guess — two years before it came out as a hit single . . . a lot of these songs are written in the past, and they come out as if this is what we're up to. Then, a kid comes back from England with a big hit record, and everybody says, 'You seem to write a lot about alienation.' 'Right,' I said. 'Alienation seems to be your big theme.' 'That's my theme,' I said. And I proceeded to write more about alienation. Actually, Dylan was writing protest, and whatever it was, everybody had a tag. They put a tag on the alienation. And it was a self-fulfilling prophecy, so I wrote alienation songs. Of course we all had a feeling of alienation. . . ."*

The elaborations were offered through "I Am A Rock," and "Somewhere They Can't Find Me," and "Blessed," lifting an angry cry of "Oh Lord, why have you forsaken me?" Thrust up as voices of a New Generation, they might have pursued this spartan fatalism had not the somber kaleidoscope beauty of *Parsley, Sage, Rosemary and Thyme* shifted their emphasis into realms less tied to the psyche. From himself, Simon turned to others, taking his cue not so much from archetype as from individuals. He broadened the base of his images, and in such outings as "The 59th Street Bridge Song

(Feeling Groovy)" and "A Simple Desultory Phillipic" toyed with his own leanings toward serious statement, sacrificing none of the songs' emotional intent. He seemed cheerier, even as "Homeward Bound" drew on the privations of a tired musician, and "A Dangling Conversation" juxtaposed Robert Frost against Emily Dickinson in the manner of "7 O'Clock News / Silent Night."

They were a natural choice to score *The Graduate*, a 1967 movie by Mike Nichols whose lead character, played by Dustin Hoffman, might have been transported intact from one of Simon's songs. The song he penned for it, "Mrs. Robinson," showed marked subtlety, the American dream of Joe DiMaggio held against the two-dimensional reality of back-room affairs and "candidate's debates." He could neither put down nor moralize over his heroine.

The movie's popularity and "Mrs. Robinson" 's arrival as their second number one hit insured that Simon and Garfunkel would soon become unwieldy household words. In *Bookends*, they swelled their compassion to "Old Friends," prologued by Garfunkel's tender experiment in recording the oral histories of the aged. Along with some of their more frivolous singles ("At The Zoo," "Fakin' It"), the album also contained "America," seen from the eye of a Greyhound bus. "Leaves That Are Green" from *The Sounds of Silence* had found him only able to foresee a single cycle, finished when crumbling brown was touched by a (hazy) shade of winter. Now the seasons would return again with the spring, and die, and return again. The feeling was of emptiness, as if washed of ongoing emotion, effortless and peaceful.

It was the perfect setting for "Bridge Over Troubled Water." The album itself was built in an ever-widening rift between Simon and Garfunkel, with engineer Roy Halee holding a tenuous balance between the two. Art was in Mexico for much of the recording, pursuing his acting aspirations in *Catch-22*, while Simon delved into his music toward quirky, personal songs that unraveled life's secrets with a note of wry humor and forgiving perspective, often arranged around simple, exotic folk melodies. But it took "Bridge Over Troubled Water" to

*Copyright © Rolling Stone magazine, July, 1972

close their books with finality, a spiritual of trust and sacrifice that allowed each to go his own way. The gesture took precedence over the strained reality; as a team, they were at the end of their energies.

With the pressures of Simon and Garfunkel left behind, their recent solo careers have found each in his element, unwilling or uninterested in becoming active competitors. Art has won acclaim as an actor (*Carnal Knowledge*) and released a symphonic *Angel Clare* album that allows his vocal purity to fully luxuriate between the satin sheets of billowy orchestration. Paul, on the other hand, has followed a more journeyman path, solo albums encompassing reggae and New Orleans gospel, producing old Peruvian friends Urubamba

(formerly Los Incas), writing with the same faultless Kodachrome ability that makes him one of the most intelligent, accessible, and astutely pop craftsmen in the field of music today.

Old friends, like bookends. At the seventeenth annual presentations of the Grammy awards, Paul Simon and John Lennon stood at the podium, announcing Record of the Year. The winner was Olivia Newton-John's "I Honestly Love You," and in her absence, Art Garfunkel strolled up the stairs to accept the award. "Still writing, Paul?" he needled, grinning. "Still acting, Art?" replied Simon with the same wary pleasure. Lennon, who knows about these things, leaned over and inquired in his best *A Hard Day's Night* voice, "Are you guys ever going to get back together?"

# CAROLE KING

THE BRILL BUILDING STANDS SILENT ON Broadway these days, no longer awash with the sound of tinkling pianos and june-moon rhymes. Here, in what was once considered the headquarters of a publishing industry that set America's musical standards for several generations, older songwriters and publishers had resisted rock & roll for as long as they dared. By the late fifties they admitted the winds of change, opening pop music's door to a host of talented young newcomers. For the next several years, locked in tiny cubicles, these tunesmiths would determine the fancies of pop and, at least in the case of Carole King, use the building's legacy as a stepping-stone to their own dreams of performance and artistry.

Four-year-old Carol Klein started taking piano lessons from her mother in their Brooklyn home. Mrs. Klein had hoped to direct her daughter into acting, but Carole had other ideas. In high school, she formed a singing group with three other girls called the Co-Sines (they all were studying geometry), entertaining at local and school affairs. Advancing to Queens College

with the intention of becoming an elementary teacher, she met Gerry Goffin, a junior majoring in chemistry, and Paul Simon, both of whom were attempting to break into the music business.

Her first actual forays into the world of recording were as a singer. In late 1958, she became "The Right Girl" on ABC-Paramount; RCA saw her as "Queen Of The Beach." None of the records caused a stir, but when she answered Neil Sedaka's "Oh Carol" (written to and for her) with "Oh Neil" on a small label named Alpine, she came in contact with publisher Don Kirshner. "She did the session for me," he recalls. "When I heard her feel for the piano it was over . . . . I knew she was a giant."

But she needed a writing partner. "Until I met Gerry," Carole said at the time, "I was just a musician who wrote bad lyrics. Now we do everything together, and it's impossible to tell where his work begins and mine leaves off." There was more than professional truth to the statement; their partnership had been sealed by marriage shortly after graduation.

# 251
## Carole King

(Dimension Records)

As staff writers of Aldon Music (Al Nevins and Don Kirshner), the prolific team of Goffin-King became a familiar sight on the charts of the early sixties. The Shirelles' "Will You Still Love Me Tomorrow" was their first major hit, and they followed it with successes for Bobby Vee ("Take Good Care Of My Baby"), Tony Orlando ("Halfway To Paradise"), Gene McDaniels, Steve Lawrence, Teddy Randazzo, Gene Pitney and the Everly Brothers. For a time they virtually monopolized the output of the Drifters, contributing such gems as "Up On The Roof," "At The Club" and "Some Kind Of Wonderful."

They weren't seeking to expand pop boundaries, but rather to work creatively and safely within its limitations. The songs were sentimental, rich and personal without becoming mawkish, their best compositions caught with a spare tinge of incomplete yearning. It was boy meets girl, but Gerry and Carole never left it at that; like the other great songwriting combinations of their time — Jeff Barry and Ellie Greenwich, Burt Bacharach and Hal David, Barry Mann and Cynthia Weil, they spoke in the first person, one to one, and the situations they described were timeworn and familiar.

Kirshner formed Dimension Records expressly for the purpose of expanding on Goffin-King's success. Though Carole had initially no intention of returning to recording, she and Gerry had worked up many demos of their songs, learning production (Goffin) and conducting/arranging (King). Dimension allowed them to bring all their skills into play, justified when the label's first record, Little Eva's "The Locomotion," took their seventeen-year-old babysitter into the top ten. The Cookies ("Chains," "Don't Say Nothin' Bad About My Baby"), Big Dee Irwin and even Carole herself fell under the Dimension touch. She released a total of three records on the label, the biggest of which — "It Might As Well Rain Until September" — reached number 22 in September 1962.

The rise of self-contained artists in the mid-sixties, writing and playing their own material, was bound to hurt the songwriting profession as a whole, but Goffin-King were left relatively untouched. Their style proved adaptable to nearly every mode, and they moved easily between the Animals ("Don't Bring Me Down"), the Monkees ("Pleasant Valley Sunday"), the Byrds ("Goin' Back," "Wasn't Born To Follow") and Aretha Franklin ("Natural Woman"). Indeed, the breakdown of barriers between performer and writer could work both ways, and as selling songs became increasingly troublesome, Carole began appearing in 1968 with a group called the City, comprised of session musicians Danny Kortchmar, Ralph Shuckett, Joel O'Brien and bassist Charles Larkey. The enterprise was a failure, but she wed Larkey when her marriage with Goffin broke up.

Lou Adler had known Carole since 1963, when he headed the west coast office of Aldon, and he encouraged her to try a solo career. *Writer*, released in 1970, was an attempt to find the best framework for her voice and piano, but it wasn't until *Tapestry* that both performer and medium found each other. It became one of the

top-selling albums in musical history, winning a 1971 Grammy for Album of the Year, while her own rendition of "It's Too Late" became Record of the Year; James Taylor picked "You've Got A Friend" from the collection and earned Song of the Year.

Tapestry's effect was unprecedented, even in an era that seemed to long for the subtle art of the singer-songwriter over the high-volume tensions of the later sixties. Her style was clean and unaffected; released from the strictures of AM radio, she loosened her phrasing and progressions, opening her music outwards, leaving turmoil behind in the search for security and friendship. The touchstone was honesty, revealed in lines that seemed to hint rather than enclose, like Japanese brush strokes.

That she herself is able to win the peace she desires is evidenced by her further work and personal life. In Carole King Music, the more jazzy Fantasy, and Wrap Around Joy, trial and triumph become part of an ongoing cycle, the "Sweet Seasons." She resists the trappings of stardom, preferring to live in an unassuming Mediterranean-style home in the Hollywood hills with her family, touring infrequently and never giving interviews. Carole King allows her songs to speak for themselves.

# JONI MITCHELL

I was born in Fort Macleod, Alberta, in the foothills of the Canadian Rockies — an area of extreme temperatures and mirages. When I was two feet off the ground I collected broken glass and cats. When I was three feet off the ground I made drawings of animals and forest fires. When I was four feet off the ground I discovered boys and bicycles. When I was five feet off the ground I began to dance to rock & roll and sing the Top Ten and bawdy service songs around campfires, and someone turned me on to Lambert, Hendricks & Ross and Miles Davis and later Bob Dylan. Through these vertical spurts there was, briefly, the church choir, grade one piano, bowling, art college, the Twist, marriage, runs in the nylons and always romance — extremes in temperatures and mirages.*

(Warner Brothers Publicity)

This is Joni Mitchell's own account of her life, from a Warner Brothers bio, and like her songs which are often so autobiographical that they come close to exploiting her love affairs, it is a deceptively simple story laced with subtle, disturbing psychological undertones, loaded with nuance by unexpected juxtaposition of images — "broken glass and cats" — and what

*From Warner Brothers publicity biography.

otherwise would be a matter-of-fact description of climatic conditions — "extremes in temperature and mirages" — become ominous signs of impending inner turbulence.

Joni Mitchell has specified an emotional geography uncharted by anyone else. Her songs are constructed like cerebral maps of an anxious inner landscape whose contours are generated from suggestive outlines.

Bringing with her her initial roots in folk

and mountain music she began singing in coffee houses in Toronto and New York, developing a lyrical intensity in songs like "Michael From Mountains" and "Chelsea Morning." Her early songs were heard mainly through the interpretations of other singers like Judy Collins, Dave Van Ronk and Buffy Sainte-Marie — there are over a hundred cover versions of "Both Sides Now" from her second album, *Clouds*, produced by David Crosby. It was "Woodstock," from the following album, *Ladies Of The Canyon*, and a hit single for Crosby, Stills & Nash that marked the turning point for her commercially, and propelled her acceptance into the mainstream of pop music. With her fourth album, *Blue*, in 1971, the personal authority of her songs established her as a major artist and a distinct persona in rock rather than as a mere folk songsmith.

She began to chart the slipstreams of urban life with increasing precision and insight on *For The Roses* on which she was accompanied by James Taylor. By *Court And Spark*, she had developed her art from that of a naïve and sensitive lyricist into a wry observer of L. A. ladies and cowboys aiding and abetting each others' illusions.

But like Neil Young's early songs, Joni's sound remains on the borderline between folk and rock.

"I think that there is a lot of prairie in my music and in Neil Young's music as well. I think both of us have a striding quality to our music which is like long steps across flat land."

Her first two albums were basically vocal and acoustic guitar. From there she developed a style of production that subliminally matched her voice. On *Court And Spark*, she went back to the early influence of jazz, adopting a full rhythm section by using Tom Scott's L. A.

Express to provide a jazz/rock accompaniment that offset her vocals. If her singing style is essentially folk derived, her sensibility is electric, stringing telegraphic disjointed images on the high tension wire of her almost neurasthenic whine.

She is essentially a poet, but unlike her folk sisters, Judy Collins and Joan Baez, neither of whom are particularly distinguished as songwriters, she avoids condescension through her own moral ambiguity and genuine compassion. In her pursuit of romantic love as a religious quest, she always has had the courage to risk the ridiculous in pursuit of the sublime. Joni Mitchell is in a sense a voyeur of her own life, but her fiercely personal and ruthlessly honest vision avoids bathos and cloying self-pity by passing skillfully from one emotional condition to another.

She oscillates between loneliness and ecstasy under the painful scrutiny of her introspection and seismic sensitivity — the scapegoat of her own fantasies, a willing victim in her own tales, a wild but inevitably compromised spirit — pathologically reopening her own wounds in order to find their cure.

# JAMES TAYLOR

"I USED TO BE REALLY HUNG UP ON AMbivalence and dichotomies," James Taylor confessed to *Rolling Stone*, "about something going into your mind and striking all the resonant frequencies and half of them can be positive and half of them negative. I felt I was being torn apart by dichotomies." This is the voice of Existential Man, driven mad by a world itself so insane it can only be comprehended by a schizoid, reflective intelligence, like James Taylor.

Even with Dylan's oblique lyrics, this language in its analytical explicitness is alien to rock, unknown in pop; yet James Taylor along with his brothers, Livingston and Alex, and his sister Kate, was heralded at the opening of the seventies as "The First Family Of Rock." This is not the only contradiction in "Baby James" — a dreamer in his visionary solitude who intones his tales to millions over AM radio, a shy introvert who fills stadiums with soft ballads more suited to coffeehouses, a hyper-sensitive neurasthenic who ruthlessly operates on himself to glean "remedial and comforting" messages from his psychic incisions, a private personality who protests hype and thereby generates it, and an artist, as Ben Gerson put it, "whose career gives the lie to his art."

The supreme irony was that when he appeared on the cover of *Time* magazine, hailed as the "bittersweet and low" figurehead of a new and mellower sound which epitomized "the cooling of America," he was savagely attacked by those who did not want to let go of the fantasies of the sixties. They saw in him only the whiny soliloquizing singer of wimp rock ballads that ushered in an era of lassitude and narcissism. Whatever the times brought, it was a phenomenon that James Taylor had not created. The rise of the songwriter singer (as opposed to a performer who writes his own material), in the persons of Neil Young, Joni Mitchell and Carole King, was an inevitable stage in the "maturing of the counter culture." Using songs of a smaller scale, James Taylor, with his scholarly gentility was able to reveal startling intimacies of his own psychic weather. His attempts at rock often come off sounding merely patronizing, like the "Suite For 20 G," and his attitude to most rock musicians is that their stance is only another form of blackface.

James Taylor was the first folk singer since Bob Dylan to enter the mainstream of pop, and

**James Taylor**

(Globe Photos)

he sees folk music as the natural inheritance of white Americans. "People like to talk about roots, but I find it difficult. I am the product of a haphazard musical environment, which, I suppose makes me a folk artist." He grew up listening to his father's sea chanteys, sitting in on "kitchen concerts," played hillbilly jug band music at hootenannies with his brother Livingston, regaled students at Boston's Unicorn Coffee House with his friend Kootch (Danny Kortchmar, lead guitarist for Jo Mama) and with brother Alex and three friends assembled a sort of R & B band, the Fabulous Corsayers, to play at proms and fraternity gigs.

"In the fall of 1965," James recalls, "I entered a period of intense adolescence and spent nine months in the McLean Psychiatric Hospital in Massachusetts." His stay is graphically described in "Knockin' Round The Zoo." Eight months after he got out of the hospital, he made a getaway to New York where, at eighteen, he formed the Flying Machine, wrote some of his most morbid ballads — "The Blues Is Just A Bad Dream," "Rainy Day Man" — and played at the legendary folkie hangout, The Nightowl.

While on vacation in London, he wrote songs for Tom Rush's *Circle Game* album, and cut a demo for Peter Asher at Apple Records, who signed him and eventually became his manager. The album *James Taylor* includes "Carolina On My Mind," with which he would later be associated, but the album was a flop nevertheless. After a record label change and the American release of his second album, *Sweet Baby James*, he became an overnight success. The U.S. album had been relieved of the heavy string arrangements, and several singles from it, like "Fire And Rain," were perfectly in tune with the religious tone of the times.

Early in 1974, with two other albums off his chest (*Mudslide Slim* and *One Man Dog*), James Taylor announced that he didn't want to make any more "James Taylor Albums," married Carly Simon in the first superstar merger in rock, and settled down to a domestic life on Martha's Vineyard. It seemed as if there was no more to say. All the dichotomies had been paired off, all the anxieties answered back in their own sullen voice, all the roads traveled and tales told. Later the same year, however, he decided to say goodbye to an old friend, and in an album of radiant self-acceptance, *Walking Man*, says "so long" to his fiendish doppelganger, that darker side of himself who had dominated his earlier albums. With this demon gone, James, too, seems to gradually grow fainter, if happier, as he sings,

> *"Well it's really not so bad to be fading away*
> *Come along with me and we'll go fading*
> *away"*

\*"Fading Away" by James Taylor. Copyright © Country Roads Music. All rights reserved.

# 19
# White Noise

## BLACK SABBATH

SPORTING LITTLE AIR PLAY, A VIRTUAL vacuum of critical approval, and only the smallest sense of "star" personality to help along the cause, the Sherman tank of Heavy Metal rolled inexorably over the world's music charts at the turn of the seventies. The term had originally been coined by William Burroughs in his book *The Soft Machine*, and was later picked up as apt description for a breed of band both Heavy (i.e., a thing not to be lightly reckoned) and Metal (as in loud, searing, the cutting edge of a jet engine's scream). The model for most of these groups was the early English edition of Cream — bass, drums and guitar forming an improvisatory power trio — combined with a taste of American renegade Blue Cheer. The sound of armageddon, it was left to Britain's Black Sabbath to set the psychic parameters of the style.

They had come from Aston, a dead-end downtown section of Birmingham, the sons of a dustman, a factory worker, a packer and a toolmaker: John "Ozzy" Osbourne on vocals, lead guitarist Tony Iommi, Terry "Geezer" Butler on bass and drummer Bill Ward. Of the four, only Geezer was making an attempt to

break out of the bottom of his life's lot, studying to be an accountant. Bill Ward alternated between truck driving and laboring in a rubber mill, Iommi fixed typewriters and Ozzy worked in a slaughterhouse.

Black Sabbath, then called Earth, was the first band for all of them, formed in January 1969. Though none of the group knew much about black magic, they chose their new name from a Boris Karloff horror film and fleshed it out with a few appropriate symbols. "You have to understand the fact that we were just four ordinary losers," Ozzy confided to the British press three years later. "We just bummed around in an old Transit van, doing it anywhere, playing at Irish workingmen's clubs, anything just to get a gig, just to play to people. Then this cigar came walking in the room one day and said 'sing here.' And we signed there and it all happened."

Their rise was pitiless, the effect on audiences uncanny and impenitent, as if they'd indeed made a pact with the devil. They had no stage trappings to speak of, words and music usually slabbed together in a thick molasses-like stumble. Yet they moved through the ranks of

## 258
### Black Sabbath

their constant tours with an inexorable swath, headliners before their debut album, *Black Sabbath*, had cleared reorders, a phenomenon even more misunderstood than their closest American equivalent, Grand Funk. At least the latter could claim massive promotion and singular guidance; Black Sabbath seemed to be succeeding on nothing more than belief alone.

*Paranoid*, the second album, discarded the group's black mass image in place of an even darker vision. With the title cut as altar-piece, colored by the dull, glutinous throb of their music, they unveiled a philosophy of good and evil mingled together in constant struggle. While most were singing about the beneficial hopes of the counterculture, the Sabs lifted the underside to reveal decay and destruction, a world in the shadow of atomic doom. "War Pigs" cinematized a coven of huddling generals; "Iron Man" cast the plight of an unloved robot arrayed against the forces of society. Such blunt imagery earned for them the title of "downer rock," but Black Sabbath remained unshaken. "We don't plan things," responded Ozzy. "We just play music."

If there was any hope along the group's

*(Collection Richard & Lisa Robinson)*

sight lines, it lay in the possibilities of escape. On their third album, *Master of Reality* (recorded in four days), "Into the Void" urged "Freedom fighters sent out to the sun / Escape brainwashed minds and pollution, / Make a home where love is there to stay, / Peace and happiness in ev'ry way."* "Children of the Grave" put the division even more succinctly: "Listen to what I say. / If you want a better place to live, / then spread the word today / Show the world that love is still alive, / You must be brave, / Or you children of today are children of the grave."*

Straight-faced, their point made, they couldn't help but pick up speed. In rapid succession, such blast-oriented fodder as Mountain, Uriah Heep, Dust, Budgie and Sir Lord Baltimore climbed to the fore. Sabbath stayed on the road, making seven separate tours to America before the end of 1972. It was a crippling schedule, with large arenas and brutal crowds. Ozzy appeared perpetually plagued by laryngitis, Iommi fell ill, the band verged on

*© Copyright 1971 and 1974 Essex Music International Ltd., London, England. TRO–Essex Music International, Inc., New York, controls all publication rights for the U.S.A. and Canada. Used by permission.

total exhaustion. In desperation, they called a temporary respite from touring, confiding their intent to slow their pace in *Volume 4*, a work which alternated the familiar cored Sabbath monotony with definite nods in the direction of musical enhancement. *Sabbath, Bloody Sabbath* further broke away from their druidesque archetypes, programing the instrumental interlude of "Fluff" between the pistol machismo of "A National Acrobat" and the equally scarred "Sabra Cadabra."

Ozzy will still flash a V-sign to the crowd when he runs out to take his place on stage, but there's no longer desperation implicit in the signal. "We're all just simple, ordinary people who became . . . *this*. I think it's just starting to affect us, what's actually happened to us. Once the whole band was a giggle . . . . I still enjoy it, don't get me wrong. I love it. I wouldn't change it for the world. But we've covered a lot of ground, been a lot of places and met a lot of people. When the day comes that Black Sabbath is no more, if it's kept up as good as it's kept up to now, I can't complain. If it ends tomorrow or five years . . . ten years from now, I can just turn around and say that I've had a good time and enjoyed it. It's been one hell of an experience for me." Pass the claret, Barrett.

# GRAND FUNK RAILROAD

"INSIDE LOOKING OUT" HAS JUST LUNGED to a close, the high beams of Shea Stadium turned on full to pick out the strength of this extraordinary crowd, 55,000 rippling along like so many seas, a huge mirror reflecting the suddenly small three people gathered on stage near second base. Mark Farner stumbles back to the microphone, adjusting his armband, dazed and out of breath. "Y'know," he begins, the audience rumbling in cadence. "We've just come back from Europe . . . we're going to Tokyo, Japan, to play the Olympic Stadium there . . . I know I said this at Madison Square

Garden . . . I've said this before, but when it's the truth you can't help but say it again." He stops for a second, and then: *"You're The Best Fuckin' Audience In The World!"*

They answer him with a sustained roar, recognizing their own justification in the Grand Funk mythology. While the radio pointedly ignored gold album after gold album, while the critics and older guards of the music business joined together in a concerted effort to destroy the group's credibility, a power trio from Flint, Michigan, and their single-minded manager, Terry Knight, had risen to become the most

*(Collection Alan Betrock)*

stunningly successful attraction in rock & roll. Bypassing all previously accepted middle channels, the Railroad had taken their case to the people, and the people had proved them indelibly right.

Terry Knight, slouching behind the sound board, permits himself a satisfied smile. He had become a disc jockey in the Detroit area at the age of twenty, maneuvering it into a musical career as Terry Knight and the Pack, attracting a modest amount of national attention through such almost-hits as "I (Who Have Nothing)" late in 1966. Don Brewer was his drummer, and Mark Farner often substituted as bass player. By February 1969, the Fabulous Pack, minus Terry, adding Mel Schacher on bass with Mark switching to guitar, found themselves stranded in the midst of a New England winter, verging on selling their instruments to get home. Knight offered to take over their management if they agreed, unconditionally, to follow his complete instructions. With no other prospects, the soon-to-become Grand Funk Railroad affixed their signatures.

Knight had his operation in full swing by the following summer. He opened the group at the Atlanta Pop Festival on July 4, playing them free for the exposure, sure he was on the right track when they were received with a standing ovation. He realized that his targeted audience cared little for subtlety and precise virtuosic displays; they were interested in volume and instantly alerting stage-grabbers. The band's first album, *On Time*, propounded a simplistic blues-based velocity of drive, emphasis on guitar and drums. It was promptly written off by knowledgeable sources as "one-dimensional"; but Terry, with tenacious marketing acumen, realized the last thing that would matter about Grand Funk Railroad would be their music.

Instead, he concentrated on building their image, setting them up as a direct response to contemporary pop trends. In a year of post-flower Woodstock, Grand Funk rejected cloudy lyrics, attempts at compositional sophistication or bonded eclecticism, reveling in their allegiance to transliteral basics. Farner, bare-chested and proud, would drop to his knees to wrench another ounce of noise from his guitar, straddling the Schacher-Brewer rhythm section like an erotic jockey, an instantly recognizable imprint. There could be no distance between those on stage and those in the audience. As Grand Funk embarked on a lengthy series of tours, the fact was increasingly and unmistakably hammered home. The ferocity of reaction in the pop press only served to accentuate this crude identification, arraying Grand Funk and their fans against the rock establishment, the latter unaware that most

## 261

### Grand Funk Railroad

verbal barbs echoed word-for-word the criticisms that had once greeted an earlier generation's Elvis Presley or Little Richard.

Knight harped on this theme of confrontation until the very presence of Grand Funk was enough to start heated controversy. "Grand Funk is here if you want it," he'd shrug, making sure that the choice was nowhere near as casual or avoidable as he made it sound. Everything about the group was gauged to be colossal and inescapable, from the Times Square billboard that he rented to show the world their glory to the unending stream of press releases diabolically recounting album sales and concert attendance. By the time the group was large enough to play Shea Stadium in July of 1971, Knight had accomplished all he'd dreamed and more.

For both Terry and the group, Shea was to become a watershed. Throughout, Knight never lost his touch. Two weeks before the event, full-page ads ran in most of the New York entertainment sections, announcements of the impending occasion with big *Sold Out's* plastered gleefully on top. Within five minutes of each new development, it was known that all seats had gone within 72 hours (the Beatles had taken six weeks to sell out Shea); that kids had camped before the box-office days before their scheduled openings; that the ticket sellers had "never seen anything like it" in all their years of working the stadium. The coup de grace was a press conference called by Terry in late May to announce the historic date, to which only six media representatives came. Though Knight neglected to say that most of the invitations had never been mailed, he was still able to bemoan to (of all places) the *Wall Street Journal* that "it's the grossest case of nonrecognition in the history of the business!"

Yet where do you go after you've done it all? The answer was a blow to Knight's foresight and schemes of empire, the honeymoon over by March 1972. Tired of seeing themselves put down as nonmusical puppets, aware of the trust and loyalty of their fans, Grand Funk decided to strike out on their own, without Knight's restrictions. It became a crucial choice, as Grand Funk readied to prove they were pointedly

Mark Farner

*(Collection Alan Betrock)*

aware of the role that had brought them prominence. Always moralistic, avoiding abstracts for the ecological "right" of every situation (as in their anti-hard drug commercials — "We love ya just the way ya are!"), they shared the intuitive knowledge that they owed a great debt to their audience, a debt that could only be repaid by their best efforts, on record and in concert. Through a blizzard of Knight-inspired lawsuits, unending equipment confiscations and injunctions on every phase of their operation, they attempted to demonstrate their new-found dedication.

At first it was rough going. Their initial album without Knight, *Phoenix*, was a haphazard affair, easing in new organist Craig Frost and testing the boundaries of their independence. Todd Rundgren was engaged as producer for their next release, and when *We're An American Band* (in album and single form) rocketed to the top of the charts, a lot of unregenerate scoffers were forced to revise previously inviolable opinion. Backed by a large bulb-lit American flag, their tours took on new life and honesty, the specter of exploitation laid to rest in the healthy give of footstompin' gratitude. As one of their more recent efforts put it, *Shinin' On.*

# LED ZEPPELIN

ON MAY 5, 1973, A CAPACITY CROWD OF 56,800 paid $309,000 to watch Led Zeppelin perform for nearly three hours in a Tampa, Florida, football stadium. The largest paid concert attendance for a single musical act in the history of the United States, it topped the Beatles' previous high of 55,000 and a mere $301,000 at Shea Stadium. Records are made to be broken, but if there's any shattering to be done at this point, Led Zeppelin will probably be the ones to crack the mark again. Like their namesake, they defy gravity to ride a core of flaming vapor, the acknowledged heavyweight band champions of the world.

When Jimmy Page brought his New Yardbirds back from Scandinavia in 1968, he could only guess at the implicit power contained within the group. As the original Yardbirds' final lead guitarist, he had inherited their experimental mantle after a farewell at the Luton College of Technology in July, hoping to augment the loss of Keith Relf and Jim McCarty with singer-guitarist Terry Reid and drummer Paul Francis. Reid had signed a solo contract with producer Mickie Most, however, and suggested a young vocalist named Robert Plant in his place.

"I went up to see him sing," Jimmy reminisced to England's *Zig Zag*, "he was in a group called Obstweedle or Hobbstweedle, something like that [actually, Obbstweedle], who were playing at a teachers training college outside of Birmingham — to an audience of about twelve people . . . you know, a typical student set up, where drinking is the prime consideration and the group is only of secondary importance."* He didn't care for the band's San Francisco outlook, "but Robert was fantastic, and having heard him that night, and having listened to a demo he had given me [of songs recorded with his previous group, Band of Joy], I realized that without a doubt his voice had an exceptional and very distinctive quality."*

Plant was indeed a find, a multi-octave spread built on a freewheeling vocal attitude that would often discard words for rococo improvising, spiraling upwards in tandem with Page. Robert recommended another ex-Band of Joy member, drummer John "Bonzo" Bonham, and when Chris Dreja decided to pursue a career in photography, John Paul Jones was added on bass, an acquaintance from Jimmy's session days who had arranged, among other things, Donovan's "Mellow Yellow." They dropped the name of the New Yardbirds — "We felt it was working under false pretenses"** — and, courtesy of Keith Moon, became Led Zeppelin.

In a small rehearsal space in London, they put the pieces together. "We played for a while, and then we started laughing at each other. Maybe it was from relief or maybe from the knowledge that we knew we could groove together. But that was it. The statement of our first two weeks together is our first album. Between us we wrote seven of the tracks and it only took us thirty hours to cut it. I suppose it was the fact that we were confident and perpared which made things flow so smoothly in the studio. We recorded them almost exactly as we'd been doing them live."**

And live, Led Zeppelin had quickly established themselves as a powerhouse of stage charisma and pyrotechnics. Coming across the ocean in an uproar of guitar and vocal mayhem, their earliest and most apparent roots were blues, Willie Dixon songs ("You Shook Me," "I Can't Quit You Baby") mingled in sexual metaphor and electronic extension, pinioned by the folk-ish calm of "Black Mountain Side" and "Communication Breakdown" 's amphetamine acceleration. Page, frustrated in his attempts to imbue the Yardbirds with his personality, had taken calculated vengeance here, showcasing a mastery of his instrument that instantly rearranged the pop hierarchy of Clapton, Hendrix and Beck. Led Zeppelin had their antecedents — Beck himself had scored heavily with his own Yardbirds' spin-off, featuring

*Reprinted by permission of Zig Zag, The Rock Magazine, 10, Kennet Street, Reading, England.

**Reprinted by permission of Hit Parader magazine.

(Atlantic Records)

(Neal Preston-Andy Kent)

vocalist Rod Stewart — but the vacuum created by the demise of Cream called for nothing less than the colossal. With the short-lived fad of the supergroup (Blind Faith) seemingly shaky, Led Zeppelin demonstrated they could not only be the biggest, but the best.

Primeval, not primitive, the march of the dinosaurs that characterized their first release broke open the flattened planes of Zeppelin's appeal. They seemed to bask in the glory of stardom, swashbuckling and daring rock and rollers. For American audiences, much of England's lure had always been its slightly decayed air of kinky glamor, and as Robert Plant sang of having his lemon squeezed, strange stories circulated of dead sharks being found in deserted Zeppelin hotel rooms. The promise of lifestyle drew as many adherents as their music drew critics. "Who said that white men couldn't sing blues?" queried critic John Mendelsohn in a devastating *Rolling Stone* parody of *Led Zeppelin II*. "I mean, like, *who?*"

"That's the sort of thing we used to get," Page noted. "The public was always 100 percent behind us, but we had few allies in the press."* The last is an understatement. As the beachhead of what would become a full-blown metallic invasion (Deep Purple, Humble Pie, as well as Black Sabbath and Grand Funk Railroad), Led Zeppelin were unmercifully called to task, victims of their own abrupt rise and decibel attack. Much of the criticism was unfounded; they might have been blatant, but there was conscientious effort behind each of the tracks on their albums, especially after Plant began writing lyrics. His strain of Celtic mysticism surfaced in *Led Zeppelin III*, whose material grew to life in "a small derelict cottage in South Snowdonia," Bron-Y-Aur, a bucolic setting of gallows poles and highwaymen.

By late 1971, even the critics had to reconsider. Were Zeppelin as crass as portrayed, the expectation might have been a hurried succession of albums and tours, exploiting their formula to indifference. Instead, there was no formula, and Zeppelin showed a distinct willingness to remove themselves totally from the public eye when it came time to work. "You can compare it to a successful author," Plant told *Hit Parader*'s Lisa Robinson. "If he writes a book and it's a fantastic success — then he's not expected to follow it up immediately with something else, because that makes him a slave to the wrong thing . . . it has to be presented to the people when it's ready. It's the same with us."*

Their wait was rewarded with "Stairway To Heaven," on a fourth album which bore no name but a series of runic symbols, one for each member. The song was written in stages, beginning at the Bron-Y-Aur cottage, moving from acoustic soft to slashing electric in deliberate movements, its verses reminiscent of *The Faerie Queene*, opening to a miles-long depth and resolve. On the same album, "Rock and Roll" let their fans know that megatonnage could never be forgotten.

It is this ability to be in all places at once that has allowed Led Zeppelin to outlast their many imitators. Future albums (*Houses of the Holy, Physical Graffiti*) have shown an even greater leaning to the unexpected, an absorption of structures from Moroccan to Jamaican to James Brown rhythm and blues that transforms each into the stylized energy emphasis of Zeppelin's own. Arguably the world's most popular group (in the sense that there are only unreliable measuring sticks), they travel in style: a private jet, one of the world's largest sound systems, their own record company (Swan Song), and a manager, Peter Grant, whose burly ex-wrestler's figure befits their image. Along with platinum albums, even misfortunes take on grander scales: while performing the final concerts of their 1973 tour in New York, their hotel safe-deposit box was milked of $180,000 in cash.

And yet they've never talked of solo careers — "Once you've done a 'Stairway,' and you've listened to it after you've recorded it," says Robert, "you've reached a point where you can't play with anybody else"*  — or given any less than their utmost.

"It's a bit awe-inspiring," admits Page. "You drive up and see all those people and it hits you that *you're* the people they've all come to see. To coin a phrase, it's your arses that are on the line. But then I suppose that's one of the reasons people always come to see us and always came to see us in the past, is that we try our hardest. We've never ever gone out there and chewed gum and sort of messed about, we've always played our bullocks off. Whether you like it or not is another issue altogether. When you've done all you can do, then you're happy with what you're doing and you're not compromising."*  Beset by a broken left finger before a recent tour, he promptly developed a three-finger style to compensate, seemingly unaffected.

*Reprinted by permission of Hit Parader magazine.

# 20
# Mirror, Mirror...

## SANTANA

DRUMS. THE STEAM OF RHYTHM, THE
pulse of life. "It's music to make love by —
raw and basic," Carlos Santana once said, and
though his spiritual definition of the phrase has
changed over the years, moving from lust to
light, the band that bears his name continues its
inner connection with the beat of the heart.

"I think there's a new awakening all over
the world; everybody's becoming aware that
when a musician just plays for people he only
reaches so many people, but when he plays for
the Supreme, he embraces everybody."

Carlos speaks from the lotus position,
dressed in white. The road to enlightenment has
not been an easy one for Santana, who has
survived the hedonism and casual cruelties that
take their toll on working musicians. Growing
up in San Francisco's Mission district, he had
emigrated when he was thirteen from the small
town of Autlan, Mexico, where his father was a
Mariachi violinist. Carlos followed in his
footsteps until his father bought him an electric
guitar and amplifier. "He stopped playing
violin," Jose Santana shrugs today.

After graduation from high school, Carlos
disappeared from home. He went to Tijuana
where he worked in bars, playing a combination
of Mexican and pop music, scraping together an

essential education. "I wanted to join this band
that was really happening at the time, this cat
who was influenced a lot by Ray Charles and
Little Richard and B. B. King. His name was
Xavier. He inspired me to get into my
instrument. He didn't really teach me as much
as people say. He was sort of stingy. He used to
play, and if I was looking where he was playing,
he turned the other way, so I wouldn't see the
chords. But it was cool, because when you want
to, you achieve."

He came back to a San Francisco awash in
1966 flower power. One night at the Fillmore he
was invited to a sprawling jam session with
members of the Butterfield Blues Band. With the
slight recognition provided, he gathered the
seeds of the Santana Blues Band in January
1967, among whom were organist Gregg Rolie
and percussionist Mike Carabello. "We were
playing songs like 'Misty' and 'Taste Of Honey,'
only with Latin percussion. To me, it wasn't
music. It was just a process of learning."

The inevitable reshuffles took place, conga
player Marcus Malone's temporary presence
giving them a firm, Afro-Cuban direction, most
apparent in Olatunji's "Jingo." Recognizing the
repetition of much blues improvising, they
found themselves relying more and more on

# 266

**Santana**

their rhythmic diversity. Bill Graham, an avowed "cowbell nut" and Latin music aficionado, shepherded them in their early months, hiring Santana for his ballroom shows and finding them rehearsal space. More percussion was added — Mike Shrieve on drums, Jose Chepito Areas on timbales — and David Brown filled out on bass. Dropping the "Blues" from their name, they became one of the most popular bands in San Francisco, an anomaly among light shows and "do your thing" feedback exhibitions, Rolie's organ and Carlos' melodic fluidity texturing their solid backdrop of pulsation.

Santana's debut album was heralded with an appearance at the Woodstock festival, one of the few unknown bands present at that historic occasion. It sold well, and the group expanded its "Evil Ways" appeal through magnetic live performances. *Abraxas* followed, integrating their triple percussion with the sensual sway of Tito Puente's "Oye Como Va" and Fleetwood Mac's "Black Magic Woman." A third album saw them bowing increasingly toward jazz, Carlos' tonal brilliance silvered by Neil Schon's aggressive second guitar. But by the spring of 1971, the group was in no position to take

advantage of their good fortune, dazed and divided from financial, management and drug problems. The trouble had begun when Chepito became ill and was replaced by Coke Escovedo, opening a conflict between Carlos and Carabello. More important, from a band that had once considered themselves equals, the split turned on Carlos' growing leadership awareness of his need for change and duty.

"I became disillusioned because I was losing my friends," he explained. "You see, they thought I was actually something that I wasn't, just because I'd earned a lot of gold albums and received a lot of public attention. That was just one aspect. Also I was watching the band decay on the wrong energy flow. I myself would be seeking God and the next moment I was in bed ballin' this chick and that chick and feeling that I wasn't being what I really wanted to be. I realized that I was grabbing and experiencing every temptation that came to me, and it wasn't doing me no good, man. I just wanted more. I realized that human pleasure is endless and would only lead to the destruction of a man. What I really was seeking was illumination, not satisfaction."

The opened door was provided by

*(Columbia Records)*

(Collection Richard & Lisa Robinson/Michael Putland)

Carlos Santana

Ceylonese guru Sri Chinmoy. "After I met Sri Chinmoy I had no doubt that I needed him more than any other thing. In his eyes I see my spiritual father. I see the Father, the Son and the Holy Ghost. I see Christ. Everything I need to live. Regardless of all the talent that God gives you, your life is useless unless you have a divine direction."

As Deva Dip, "the lamp, light and eye of God," he has pursued his philosophy, reflecting his faith in such albums as *Caravanserei* and *Welcome*, the Elysian free jazz of John Coltrane and Pharoah Sanders supplanting Latin polyrhythms. There have been collaborations with Mahavishnu John McLaughlin, another student of Sri Chinmoy (*Love, Devotion and Surrender*), Buddy Miles and Alice Coltrane. His new group includes holdovers Shrieve (now known as Maitreya) and Chepito, Doug Rauch on bass, Richard Kermode on keyboards, and yodeling vocalist Leon Thomas, best known for his work on Sanders' "The Creator Has A Master Plan." There is a restaurant called Dipti Nivas in the Mission district and a moment of prayer before each set.

"I think Mahavishnu said it and I agree with him, that we are the strings, the Guru's the instrument and God Himself is the musician." Talk about hit singles. . . .

# ROD STEWART

ROD THE MOD, A STAR IN HIS OWN RIGHT, preferred to be thought of as just one of the Faces, an ultimate goodtime band of high rolling rockers who share their energies with the audience and get that old synergy pulsing through their audiences. The Faces are a people's band, working-class blokes who've made good and share a built-in sense of community with their audiences. But for all his modesty it's Rod Stewart who sells the songs. He pitches them in that rusty raspy voice like a cocky costermonger — Mr. Fantastic, the Faces' front face.

Oddly enough this epitome of the English rock star began as a folk singer playing and singing Woody Guthrie and Ramblin' Jack Elliott songs at the Aldermaston "Ban the Bomb" marches. Leading the life of a vagabond minstrel in Spain, he played soccer with the lowly Brentford team (along with Dave Davies of the Kinks), resided on a barge (prematurely sunk by the coppers), worked as a gravedigger and, not being too adept at any of these, took to playing the harmonica with a Birmingham group, Jimmy Powell and the Dimensions. This was about 1964, when Rod recorded his first soul effort,

## Rod Stewart

"Good Morning Little School Girl," for English
Decca. By the time he joined the Jeff Beck Group
in 1967 he had already been in two
semi-supergroups, Steampacket with Brian
Auger and Julie Driscoll (which evolved out of
Long John Baldry's Hootchie Cootchie Men) and
Shotgun Express. He'd also been in and out of a
dozen blues, folk and soul groups including one
of his own, Rod Stewart and the Soul Agents.
He recorded singles for Columbia and Andrew
Oldham's Immediate label and developed that
gravelly sandpaper voice from belting and
boozing around London clubs, his own vocal
equivalent for electrical distortion.

The Jeff Beck Group with bassist Ron Wood
(who'd come out of the Birds and, later, Creation
which did Who type parodies "Biff, Bang, Pow"
and "Painter Man") and drummer Mickey
Waller, was the best group Beck had had since
he left the Yardbirds. But Beck's superblues and
Stewart's rasp were often wasted on songs like
"Hi Ho Silver Lining" and "Love Is Blue," what
Rod refers to as "the kind of soppy stuff you're
forced to listen to during the ice cream break in
suburban cinemas." In 1969 Beck fired both
Waller and Wood and shortly after Rod packed
it in with the group, too.

In 1965 while Rod was going through his
many metamorphoses in search of his Golden
Catarrh, a gaggle of East End lads had got their
gnomelike selves together: Steve Marriott,
Kenny Jones, Ian McLagen and Ronnie "Plonk"
Laine. Each was five-foot, five-inches with
button faces and they called themselves the
Small Faces after a mod expression meaning one of
the lads. Along with other teenybopper groups
like Davy, Dee, Dozy, Beaky, Mick and Tich,
they produced dozens of hits with Marriott's
aggressive singles like "Whatcha Gonna Do
About It" and "All Or Nothing." With the
mellowing of English rock in 1967 the Small
Faces had turned their Cockney craftiness to
psychedelic humor in their single "Itchykoo
Park." Their "Happydays Toytown"
prankishness in a fantasy "opera," *Ogden's Nut
Gone Flake*, told about Happiness Stan and a
passing fly finding the dark side of the moon
with the help of Mad John, and was whimsically
narrated by Stan Unwin in his Boorogrovian

(Collection Richard & Lisa Robinson)

dialect. This was all contained in the world's first round album cover. Pinnacle of their career that it was, it put the lid, so to speak, on Small Faces, and a year and an album later (*Autumn Stone*) their lead singer/guitarist/songwriter Steve Marriott stalked off to form Humble Pie. After the crisis of losing Steve Marriott in 1968, the Small Faces Kenn, Ronnie and Ian tried to stick together as a band, without any real success. While they were struggling, Ron Wood joined to try and strengthen the struggling trio. Sometimes, Rod Stewart would sit in on rehearsals and eventually Kenny Jones invited Rod to join the Faces.

"Rod was just what the group needed," Kenny explains, "he loved the group and the personalities and we were knocked out to be with him. We had a great laugh. It was just like old pals. The big thing started out from there."

A slight problem remained, however, in that the Faces were signed to Warner Brothers while Rod remained on Mercury as a solo artist, but what first seemed like an obstacle, turned out to be a double serving of two quite different types of albums.

The Faces are the epitome of the British hard rock band of the seventies: loud, electric, eclectic yet playing with care. There's Ian McLagen's tasteful, understated organ, Ron Wood's stinging slide guitar, Kenny Jones, one of the best drummers in rock and the inimitable Ronnie Lane, replaced in May 1973

by Free's bassist, Tetsu Yamauch. It took a couple of albums, the initial *First Step* and *Long Player*, before Rod could successfully subsume himself within the group, but with the Faces' successful single "Stay With Me" off their great third album *A Nod Is As Good As A Wink*, the synthesis had been resolved. On vinyl, the Faces come off a great deal less philosophical than Rod Stewart on his own, projecting the revelry, humor and mild cynicism of their ribald life on the road, parodies of the lovelorn, locker room jokes, a touch of the old nostalgia 'ere and there, but always infused with the bubbly perennial party they serve up on stage.

Rod Stewart, left to his own devices, is a horse of another color. From the first track of *The Rod Stewart Album*, it was obvious that a very subtle and original musical personality was being revealed to us beneath the trendy trappings of Rod the Mod. On his second solo album, *Gasoline Alley*, he had evolved an uncanny sound filtered through the rich texture of acoustic instruments (mandolins, fiddles, acoustic guitars) and backed with pulsing hard rock rhythm and drums that gave a mournful drone and punch to his sorrowful picaresque ballads of lost and remembered loves and places — "Lady Day," and "Jo's Lament" next to an evocative version of "Country Comfort" and the stomping "You're My Girl" and "Cut Across Shorty." This album is such a classic that even its great sequel *Every Picture Tells A Story* with

(Globe Photos/Richard Fitzgerald)

Rod with the Faces

"Maggie May" and "Mandolin Wind" seemed to fall under its shadow.

When the group embarked on their successful 1973 tour, Rod made it clear he wanted to be thought of as just another Face, but the conflicting demands of their parallel careers were putting a visible strain on the collective Face. Rod had a few disparaging words to say about the latest Faces album, *Ooh La La* (1973), and by 1975 with the release of his solo album, *Atlantic Crossing*, recorded in Muscle Shoals, using none of the Faces, it was the beginning of the end.

Despite his successful if insipid single "Sailing" from *Atlantic Crossing*, and another solo *Night On The Town* a year later, it was obvious that if the Faces sorely missed their most prominent feature, Rod's departure also meant cutting off his own nose to spite his Face. There was something symbiotic about the relationship that enabled them, jointly, to succeed.

If Rod on his own albums and the Faces on theirs projected two quite different kinds of music, on stage both worked together magnificently at bringing their joint effervescence to every performance. English groups have always had a touch of the East End music hall in them — it's what made them great entertainers as well as great musicians. In the Faces with Rod Stewart it was like a florid rock pantomime lifted directly from a Christmas show at the London Palladium: artificial palm trees and a real bar, streamers, giant pinups of Al Jolson and Mick Jagger, tinsel stars twinkling over an atmosphere of genial loonery, Laurel and Hardy pratfalls, mock Punch and Judy fisticuffs, all led by the pied piper of rock, Mr. Fantastic, hoisting the mike stand with the ease of a weightlifter. Rod the Mod in his boas, leopard skin suits and negligees, his hair like an unkempt blonde lawn. He was the leader of these knockabout barrow boys of Rhythm and Booze, the Mad Hatter's Tea Party thrown by a group of animated Tenniel cartoons from Alice in Wonderland.

# ALICE COOPER

*LA GUILLOTINE* HAS DONE ITS DIRTY WORK, the severed head ghoulishly kicked around by various mambers of the band, memories of boa constrictors and switchblades carefully tucked in their respective cages for tomorrow's show. The stage is littered with feathers, the remnants of a giant toothbrush, dismembered baby dolls, an unbuckled straitjacket. "God Bless America" booms through the loudspeakers.

"That's what I like about you," chuckles the newly resurrected Alice Cooper, dressed in white tails and top hat, shaking a walking stick at the audience. "You're even sicker than we are!"

It was a remark that would take on added significance some months later when he stood unprotected in Toledo, Ohio, dodging fireworks and the venom of a crowd more than ready for anything the Cooper machine was prepared to give. Alice had ridden well on his triple bill of Sex, Death and Money ("though not necessarily in any order"), but now he was wondering how long it might take before unwilling sacrifice was made to the Frankenstein monster of his stardom. After all, it was only entertainment. . .wasn't it?

"We're the ultimate American band," he liked to say, "merely the end product of an affluent society." For Vincent Furnier, Detroit-born February 4, 1948, there could be no higher aspiration. The son of a missile engineer and minister in the Church of Jesus Christ, he had moved with his family several times before they decided on the suburbs of Phoenix, Arizona. He did moderately well in school, starring on the track team and gaining a reputation as class clown, but what fired his imagination was television, where situation

**Alice Cooper**

comedies mingled with incessant reruns of horror movies, *77 Sunset Strip* balanced against *Peter Gunn.*

The sensibility this brought to his music was one of melodrama, an approach that saw rock through the eye of a camera, visual and theatrical. He was not a musician, and indeed, seldom claimed to be. Yet he took to the music as a way of life, modeling himself after the newer, more irreverant breed of English pop star, poised against the predictability of day to day Phoenix living. "We had the idea . . . everybody had the idea of going into rebellious rock music," he recalled to writer Steve

(© 1976 Bob Gruen)

Demorest. "My parents *hated* the Rolling Stones, my parents *hated* the Beatles, and so we really enjoyed that, immediately enjoyed the fact that they hated them."

The generation gap notwithstanding, it wasn't surprising that the beginnings of Alice Cooper centered on the creation of an image. First as the Earwigs, and later the Spiders, the group concentrated on mod clothes and soundalikes of English records. Furnier was helped in these endeavors by Dennis Dunaway

and Glen Buxton, alumni of the track team, and later Mike Bruce, who joined after a band named the Trolls conveniently broke up. By the end of 1965, they'd even scored an area hit, the self-produced "Don't Blow Your Mind."

There was a brief fling at art school for most of the members, and then the Spiders—now called the Nazz — decided their growth might better be served by moving to Los Angeles. They had already become fairly tired of their Carnaby Street look, gradually changing it over into a personality calculated to shock and bewilder any crowd. Drummer Neal Smith was added to the line-up; when they discovered a Philadelphia group (led by Todd Rundgren) known as the Nass, they took the final step with the help of an ouija board to become Alice Cooper, collectively, and for the former Furnier, individually.

It was in their first horror-show period, when they would come out on stage in dresses and violently disorient audiences, that Frank Zappa—a man who knows a good image when he sees one—first became interested in them. The group had been scheduled to play a celebration at the Los Angeles Cheetah for the late Lenny Bruce, but the opening notes of their performance had been met with a sudden mass migration to the exits. Zappa was intrigued, along with another onlooker who felt mesmerized by their "negative energy," Shep Gordon, soon to become the band's satyric manager.

Zappa worked with Alice through most of the first album, *Pretties For You*, but it was as if he and the group had only partly touched similar ground. "I think he wanted to produce us in more of a humorous vein," but the results were disjointed and inconsistent. A second album, *Easy Action*, faltered on the same problem; the music was filled with ideas, often abruptly changing direction several times within a song, but there was little integration. By then, however, their reputation was on the move. As the band began to consciously grasp the meaning and importance of their emerging musical stance, a growing economic frustration pushed them closer to the edge of their fantasies. The attack escalated considerably. They would drive on stage in wheelchairs and proceed to fight among themselves with boxes of laundry detergent; Alice would toss dead chickens to the audience; with Miss Christine of G.T.O.'s (Girls Together Outrageously) directing, he dressed in sexual ambiguity, chains, leather and make-up converting him into a dark, esoteric caricature of the archetypal lead singer.

As California was becoming increasingly hostile to their stage demeanor, the Cooper group decided to move to Detroit. "Midwest audiences are a lot more energetic," Alice said at the time, but they were also better prepared for controversial performers, having already given rise to such combinations as the Stooges, the MC5 and even Grand Funk Railroad. The group began referring to their music as "Third Generation" rock, an anthem to provide foundation for the seventies, bringing along producer Bob Azrin to give their recorded sound the cohesion previously so lacking. When "I'm Eighteen" became a surprise hit single, Alice Cooper was ready for America. And vice-versa.

The execution was perfect. Cooper had captured the twilight zone of adolescence with uncanny accuracy, holding it as tantalizing bait for the elaborations of his stage show. The theme was insanity, exaggerations and subtle mugging, fraught with tension in the comic relief. As they took to the road with headline precision, the props grew more elaborate, the depravities more exotic, the punishments more breathtaking. Their music lapsed away from songs into soundtrack, serving a variety of scenarios: "The Ballad Of Dwight Frye" led the creator of *Dracula*'s flies to his doom in the electric chair; the axe murderer of *Killer* was hanged on a monstrous gallows; the baby demolisher of *Billion Dollar Babies* lost his head in the French fashion.

There seemed to be no limit or end to the variations, but then Cooper had all of American culture to borrow and scandalize. They lifted the Jets' theme from *West Side Story* and used it to choreograph a classic street rumble. They threw real money to the audience, delighting in the expected stampede. "School's Out" extended the annual vacation to *forever*; Alice even ran for President of the United States with "Elected."

Yet for all his leering and sly, sinister smiles, Alice never really became the malevolent, bisexual grotesque he attempted to portray. He would move to pull off his silver lamé suit, awkwardly, like a stripper lost in the haunt of amateur night, pale and scrawny body outlined in a black Danskin. Offstage he was pleasant, drank innumerable cans of Budweiser and talked about his favorite television shows.

Vincent Furnier of Phoenix, Arizona, wearing Beatleboots and shaggy hair, was merely playing out his fantasies on another level.

In the end, they had tantalized their audiences to the breaking point. Short of actual bloodletting on stage, there was little they could do to top the massive *Billion Dollar Babies* tour that spun around the country in the spring and summer of 1973 (61 cities, a total audience of nearly one million). After the *Muscle of Love* album, in which the group took a half-hearted stab at massage parlor sex, and a Christmas 1973 mini-circuit in which they were unable to satisfy the passions of the crowd, they realized they'd gone about as far as they could go in their present structure. Individual members made plans to follow solo careers, though the break-up was never made official. Michael Bruce placed a solo album on the boards; Dennis and Neal promptly got married. Alice worked on a solo album and show, *Welcome To My Nightmare*, put together a movie of the Cooper's rise to fame, and spent his time — you guessed it — on television talk and quiz shows, including *The Hollywood Squares*. His golf handicap has gone down to eighteen.

# ELTON JOHN

ELTON JOHN, WITH ALL HIS PREDICTABLE put-on ("people expect me to come out looking like the Eiffel Tower") — his bulby booties, 60-foot parachute, wooden trousers with 60 colored snakes leaping into the audience, driving the masses mental with his giant bunny hops at the piano in purple panty hose — is possibly the first performing Professor of Rock. He is a scholar of rock & roll, a vinyl junkie who mines his mammoth collection of LPs, singles, tapes and cassettes for obscure jewels of fifties and early sixties pop funk — Neil Sedaka whom he successfully produced in 1974 is one of his idols. He refines them into re-creations of the innocence and exuberance of an earlier era in songs like "Crocodile Rock" (his first gold single) or recreations of current black disco music or "Benny And The Jets." The range of his excavations is vast if not deep. The first rock superstar of the seventies, the 8-million-dollar man, under his boas and 90 pairs of custom-made glasses is a plump, balding, undistinguished looking asexual introvert, almost a total contradiction of what a rock idol should look like.

A master manipulator of fashion and fad, Elton John's constant innovations come from his adaption of every trend. He borrowed glitter and outerspace from David Bowie, and he and his lyricist Bernie Taupin tapped the ruminating landscape of the Band and Creedence Clearwater's mythic American South for their countrified second album, *Tumbleweed Connection*. His songs are tableaus, vividly recollected and projected. In the tradition of Jim Morrison and Van Dyke Parks, his albums are imagistic and evocative rather than rock realities, heavily scored in Gus Dudgeon's lush cinematic productions. His obsession with Hollywood's faded glamor becomes crystallized in his artistic high point, *Honky Chateau,* and the two albums which followed it, *Don't Shoot Me I'm Only The Piano Player* and *Goodbye Yellow Brick Road*. Here his tinted vignettes become lavishly induced nostalgia sequences where he slithers over his fantasies like a chromatic chameleon.

"Dancing With Mr. D.," the Rolling Stones song, is widely known to be about John, born Reginald Kenneth Dwight in Middlesex,

(Kate Simon)

(Collection Richard & Lisa Robinson)

England, of middle-class parents whose respectability and smugness drove him to eke out this remarkable creature. Little Reggie began playing piano at four, and was fed on a steady diet of Kay Starr and Tennessee Ernie Ford until one day his mum brought home some discs by Jerry Lee Lewis and Little Richard. Something stirred in Reg's head and he soon began vamping the hit records of the day. After a brief stay at the Royal Academy of Music, he joined Bluesology at eighteen ("We played in scout huts and youth club dances with a 10-watt amplifier"), who eventually got to back the likes of Patti La Belle, the Drifters and the Inkspots, doing the "ooohs" and "whoop doop doops."

Reg Dwight had to go, and while playing with *Elton* Dean (from Bluesology) in Long *John* Baldry's blues group, he found a name for his new identity. The real beginning of the Elton John Story though, starts with Bernie Taupin's mum, who fished a letter he'd written in answer to an ad for a lyricist placed by Liberty records out of a wastepaper basket and posted it. From this correspondence came Elton's and Bernie's first collaboration, "Lady Samantha," later recorded by Three Dog Night. Elton continued to receive words in the mail, put them to music and make them into demos long before ever meeting his future partner.

This basic principle of writing independently has continued to this day. They fit the songs together like components, and between them they have created a two-man music industry, producing, with their ingenious grasp of the nature of pop, the perfect product, the perfectly timed and disposable song. Elton John had only one album out in England, *Empty Sky* on the DJM label, when MCA released *Elton John* in America, the first of eight gold albums in a row.

The second phase of this relentless musical monster, Elton himself, was set in motion when he was unveiled at the Troubador Club. The phenomenon of Elton John is the malleable product of the L. A. publicity machine — "It's all hype and luck," he concurs modestly. He is a consummate performer, the most flamboyant since Liberace, who has skillfully accommodated himself to the media — supplying a constant stream of sensation while being careful never to overstep the boundaries of outrage.

Despite his flashy act, packed with midgets and chorus girls, Elton is essentially a creature of the studio. There he manufactures the fantasy factory of his others — gunfighter, astronaut, teenage suicide, lonesome country boy — Bernie's lucid lyrics and his own sultry semi-operatic voice straining at the top of its range in a strange blend of soul, folk and pop. "We are just a blatant rock band," Elton confesses, and when Bernie proudly admits that he has "never written a song that means more than it says," we are listening to the pure voice of pop.

The "catchiness" of the songs depends on what Robert Christgau calls "the man's gift for the hook — made up whole or assembled from outside sources — [it] is so universal that there is little small statistical likelihood that one of them hasn't stuck in your pleasure centre. Or your craw. Or both." (*Village Voice*, November 24, 1975.) Elton John's appeal, reaching both transistorized teenyboppers and MOR moms, is the broadest of all rock singers, comparable in its universal attraction to that enjoyed by the old stars of the movies. Appropriately he was awarded his Sidewalk Star in the Hollywood Walk of Fame (alongside Ricky Nelson and Helen Reddy) outside Grauman's Chinese Theater in November 1975. He is the reality of hype. Once free of Reg Dwight, he found an infinity of selves to try on. It's too late to stop now, as Mr. John says, zipping into his latest creation. "There are too many fantasies to act out to just settle for one."

# DAVID BOWIE

HE IS, AS HE HAD PLANNED, MAGNIFICENT. The stage appears impeccably struck, lights arranged to catch the finer angles of his face, making him seem at times wonderfully apelike and primitive, at others supremely regal, capable of the grand gesture. The band stands behind him in a shock of silver reflections, just a stride or two to hint the presence, precise, punctuating, emphatic. There is never any question of whether they will make a mistake, lose their footing, leave a stone unturned. David Bowie has waited a long time for his time, and now that it's here, five years stuck on his eyes, he's not about to let it pass him by.

Bowie is the seventies' superstar, manipulating his image as often as many vary clothes, impossible to define or categorize. "I'm searching all the time for an identity," he has commented. "I constantly change . . . it stems, actually, from being unsure about what one self is oneself. It's usually visual changes, to give other people the identity more than myself; it doesn't seem to help me much. I mean, I've been changing every since I was thirteen, and I've never helped myself. I'm my own worst enemy. . . ."

The self-effacing charm is evident, but David's abrupt transitions have often seemed whimsical and capricious. "I find that I slip into my skins very easily," he says. "I'm not looking for a specific reaction. I'm content to portray my songs my way; all I require, as an artist, is an audience. I certainly don't have any preconceptions about where I'm heading."

The actor removes his mask, only to reveal another underneath. David Robert Jones was born January 8, 1947, on Stanfield Road in the shadow of London's Brixton prison. His family situation was unstable, and he formed a close attachment to his older brother, Terry, who introduced him to jazz and the beat movement in the late fifties. At the age of twelve he was intrigued enough by King Curtis to begin studying the saxophone, leading a group called George and the Dragons while attending Bromley Technical School. In 1963, he neatly progressed to R & B as David Jones and the Kingbees, releasing one single, "Liza Jane."

This group soon evolved into David Jones and the Lower Third (later the Buzz), retaining its R & B roots but heavily influenced by the power pop stance of the Who (then called the High Numbers). David shared the bill with them on many occasions during 1965, and when he was signed to Parlophone the next year, the Who's producer, Shel Talmy, worked with him as well. Despite a regular Sunday afternoon residency at the Marquee Club, he soon grew disenchanted. He changed his name because of the Monkees' Davy Jones, putting out a solo album, *Love You Till Tuesday*, seemingly ambivalent about his career:

"Oh, that thing . . . that was on a very semi-professional basis. I was still working as a commercial artist then, and I made that kind of in my spare time, taking days off work and all that. I never followed it up, did any stage work of anything. I just did an album, 'cause I'd been writing, y'know, sent my tape into Decca and they said they'd make an album. Thought it was original."

It did have considerable merit, early Bowie's picturesque observations on a character-laden English window; still, it was almost too predictable, and David longed for the extraordinary. In casting about for a more meaningful vehicle, he developed an interest in Buddhism, at one point seriously considering joining a monastery. He fell in love with a ballet dancer, Hermione Farthingale, and performed with her in an arts' trio named Feathers. He did bit acting in commercials and television, became entranced with Anthony Newley, and probably most relevantly, pursued an interest in mime.

"I went to see a one-man show in London," he recalled, "by a guy named Lindsay Kemp. I'd never seen mime before, and the power of it smothered me completely. I knew that there was nothing else that I wanted to be involved in than what that man was doing, the kind of magic he was projecting. I would write music for him and he would teach me mime. That's the only way we could work because we both were very broke."

Throughout David's metamorphoses, his

*(Mercury Records)*

manager, Kenneth Pitt, remained patient. "David was always coming under different influences at that time. I used to rib him about it." Pitt was finally rewarded when David returned to recording in 1969, charting his first hit, "Space Oddity." It was the year that mankind touched the moon, yet David's *2001*-scope was not limited to mere timeliness. The drama of an astronaut caught in the raptures of space, bidding farewell to his wife and earth, was imaginative and touching, but David again shied in the face of its success.

"It was very hard. It was 1969, and I went on in front of those gum-chewing skinheads. As soon as I appeared, looking a bit like Bob Dylan, with this curly hair and denims, I was whistled and booed. At one point I had cigarettes thrown at me. It turned me off the business. I was totally paranoid and I cut out."

The experience was not without its value. At odds with the audience even before he sang a note, Bowie must have painfully come to realize the domineering sway that a performer's looks

## David Bowie

and approach hold over his presentation. He had already rejected the standard stylistic modes as hopelessly common; the only conceivable direction left would be the other extreme, the theatre of shock, anticipating and manipulating trends. Part calculation, part impressionable instinct, David was hastened in these leanings by his new manager, Tony DeFries, a lawyer who intended to play Colonel Tom Parker to Bowie's ascending Elvis.

The keynote was struck in 1971, when *The Man Who Sold The World* was released with a cover portrait of a sulky, feminine form in a long dress, draped over a chaise longue with wisps of Lauren Bacall hair caressing his/her shoulders. The music of this new David Bowie stood in direct contrast to his past, bordering on heavy metal, the "turn around/go back" of "The Width Of The Circle." Suitably vague on whether he was hetero-, homo-, bi-, or even tri-sexual ("I'll try anything!"), he reserved opening of the closet door for January 22, 1972, when he announced to the British press that "I'm gay and always have been, even when I was David Jones. . . ."

Whether he was or not was beside the point, and the issue (if there is one) has yet to be clarified. For one, he was married (in March 1970, to the lovely Angela), and had a son, Zowie, which only added to the confusion. However, it was a confusion common to traditional male and female roles following the free-love sixties, and Bowie's pronouncement only made things official. This time he was prepared to go all the way, presenting an album, *Hunky Dory,* with all proper cultural references — Andy Warhol, Velvet Underground, Bob Dylan — as well as some breathtaking examples of his own excellent voice and songs, the stuttering "Changes" (funny that . . .) and the hope-after-death "Life On Mars?"

*Hunky Dory* won him critical acclaim, but Bowie and DeFries knew that was only a partial step. Even before the album was out, David was hard at work on another personality. Repeating a page from Kubrick, he regaled himself in *Clockwork Orange,* cropping his hair and wearing virtual space-suits. Once again, the

contrivance of his image was believably reinforced by its soundtrack. *The Rise And Fall Of Ziggy Stardust And the Spiders From Mars* was an ambitious, multi-leveled concept album, flying in the face of the seventies while most were still concerned with tying the loose ends of the sixties. Garnished by the actual Spiders (Mick Ronson, Trevor Bolder, Woody Woodmansey), it related the saga of a "moonage" rock band, growing their leader from the social bewilderment of "A girl my age went off her head . . ." to a "leper messiah" to eventual and tragic "Rock 'n' Roll Suicide." Time takes a cigarette. "I've adopted Ziggy for the next couple of months," said David. "By the time people start realizing about Ziggy, I may be Tom Blogs or someone."

The stage show was an equal revelation. Mick Ronson stood toward the middle of the mise-en-scene, legs spread. David stalked him, Mick appearing to move away, then back again, as if to welcome the invasion. In a flash David was under him, hands clasped around the guitarist's buttocks, gnawing at his crotch, his Gibson, metaphorically draining him to assorted plaints and moans from the back amplifiers. He swept England, and in the fall of 1972 came to America. Glitter rock, glam rock, rock and rouge; whatever it was called, Bowie was at dead center of the "hot tramps" he later commemorated in "Rebel Rebel."

His musical combine was extended to Lou Reed, Iggy Pop, Mott the Hoople. He produced the first two, and wrote the latter's most evocative anthem, "All The Young Dudes." As the poesies of *Hunky Dory* had given way to *Ziggy, Alladin Sane*'s metallic cracked thespian drove Bowie across America, brittle, with a painted streak of lightning splashed across his face. On July 3, 1973, he stunned his British fans at the Hammersmith Odeon by declaring his intention to retire from the stage, though by the following October he was hosting his own television show on the *Midnight Special,* singing a duet with Marianne Faithful. He took the Trans-Siberian Express to Japan (Bowie is a notorious nonflyer), and returned to England to do an oldies album of his favorites from the beat-group sixties, with loving dabs at the

David and Angela Bowie

*(Mainman, Ltd.)*

Mojos, the Merseys and the Easybeats.

For the Burroughsian *Diamond Dogs* in 1974, he returned to the concert trail in the guise of theatre. A surreal cityscape was built, a high catwalk run between two towering sheets of buildings, an atmosphere of decay and malice. He wore a simple off-white suit, yellow socks, red Mary-Jane ballet slippers, was attentively choreographed, surrounded by herculean props (a huge mirrored pleasure dome to encompass 1984's "Big Brother," an incorporeal cherry-picker for "Space Oddity" 's simulated interstellar flight). He seemed oblivious to his audience; the art of distance, the cool, poised uninvolvement of the professional model.

Most performers tend not to progress at all, falling into a trap of endless repetition. David, unable to be pinned for more than a fraction, has been successful in taking his followers through a bewildering montage of style and sentiment, be it the black discotheque sound of Philadelphia (*Young Americans* and its hit single, "Fame"), a starring title role in Nicholas Roeg's *The Man Who Fell To Earth,* or the neon technology of his latest stage set, as witnessed in *Station To Station.* Tomorrow. . . .

# Index

# 280

## Index